AF655611

Hindustani Music in Colonial Bombay

Hindustani Music in Colonial Bombay

Aneesh Pradhan

Three Essays
COLLECTIVE

First Edition November 2014
Reprinted 2024
copyright©Aneesh Pradhan 2014
All rights reserved

No part of this book may be reproduced or utilised in any form or by any means, electronic or mechanical, including photocopying, recording or by any information storage or retrieval system, without the prior written permission of the publisher.

ISBN 978-81-88789-96-2

Three Essays
COLLECTIVE

B-957 Palam Vihar, GURGAON (Haryana) 122 017 India
Phone: +91 98681 26587, +91 98683 44843
info@threeessays.com Website: www.threeessays.com
Printed and bound at Replika Press Private limited, India

Dedicated to
Dr. Ashok Da. Ranade

Contents

List of plates

PREFACE

I was privileged to have received instruction in the traditional *guru-shishya parampara* after a short period of institutionalized training, in the forty odd years that I spent studying North Indian art or classical music, more popularly known as Hindustani music. In a professional performance career spanning almost twenty-five years, not a long span by any stretch of imagination when one considers 'time' in the context of Indian tradition, I was fortunate to have had a personal experience of what it means to be a student, performer and teacher, of Hindustani music in the late twentieth and early twenty-first centuries. I have been witness to radical transformations that took place in performance, pedagogy, and patronage, in an age when music is not just mechanically reproduced and amplified, but is also digitized and engineered often to a point beyond recognition. These changes have caused immense worry to senior musicians and die-hard connoisseurs whose notions of authenticity, purity and tradition seem threatened by these vicissitudes.

A liberal middle-class family background in Bombay, now officially known as Mumbai, provided me with an intellectual environment that encouraged curiosity and inquiry. The multiplicity of cultures in the city inexorably enveloped me, much in the way as it has impacted so many musicians since the past hundred and fifty years or so. What intrigued me was the manner in which musicians in those times had responded to challenges that they were faced with. I was, therefore, almost naturally drawn to revisiting the city's past to understand ways in which musicians had negotiated the very questions that seem to affect students, performers and teachers, such as myself in the present global economy – questions related to larger issues like tradition, modernity, national culture, along with those more specific to music.

My proximity to hereditary and non-hereditary performers, teachers and scholars, gave me an opportunity to engage with them on these subjects and to closely observe their circumstances. The conversations, filled with a mix of factual information, keen observation, nostalgia and myth, eventually steered me towards their concerns and perspectives. In the absence of any significant articulation on their part in the public domain, one might hastily conclude that theirs is a 'spiritual' existence far removed from the hustle and bustle of everyday life. Indeed, this is what they often choose to portray too. But behind this veil is a world that is as real and as arduous as it is for others in society. It was so for their predecessors as well.

The present book is based on my doctoral dissertation, which focused on trends in Hindustani music in nineteenth century and early twentieth century Bombay and their impact on practitioners. This study would not have been possible without the experiences of many musicians who chose Bombay as their temporary or permanent home, and whose lives and work have provided precious insights into the period. They will continue to inspire students of music and history such as myself.

I would like to record my gratitude to those who encouraged me during the course of my inquiry.

I am deeply indebted to J.V. Naik for guiding my research and for putting me through the rigours of research methodology. Ashok Da. Ranade was a source of inspiration and wisdom in my endeavor and I will remain eternally grateful to him and Hemangini Ranade for making me a part of their home. Long years of music training under my *guru* Nikhil Ghosh prepared me to comprehend and appreciate performance-related aspects. I am also extremely grateful to Adrian McNeil for significant inputs and direction in anchoring my thoughts during this study.

Aban Mistry was generous in sharing with me the Report of the Parsi Gayan Uttejak Mandali, which was so vital to this study, and Dina Mistry patiently helped translate relevant portions of the Report. Sharad Mehta, Batuk Diwanji, Shalini Narvekar, Kaushalya Manjeshwar, Dinker Manjeshwar, Arvind Mulgaonkar, Abdul Halim Jaffer Khan and Purushottam Walawalkar, very kindly shared their invaluable thoughts and life experiences during long interview sessions and I thank them for giving me this privilege. Kishore Udipi and Mohini Mundkur were helpful in providing information that threw fresh light on the study. Rohit Desai, Girish Gogate, Arvind Mulgaonkar, Gert M. Wegner, Vajahat Hussain Khan, Kausalya and Dinker Manjeshwar, permitted me to reproduce photographs from their collection.

I would also like to acknowledge the comments and suggestions I received at various stages from Jim Masselos, Aroon Tikekar, Vasanti Damle, Miriam Dossal, Arvind Ganachari, S.D. Pillai, S.N. Nadkarni, Suresh Chandwankar, Naresh Fernandes and Sudhir Nayak. Sohail Hashmi very kindly agreed to translate some of Urdu lyrics. Sudev Sheth prepared the maps that are included in this book. His inputs at the final stages of this publication were particularly beneficial. Manolete Mora, Kalpesh Kamath, Raghav Pasricha, Dhaval Mudgal and Sushan Mhatre also helped in bringing this work to fruition.

My gratitude is equally due to the staff of the University of Bombay and the Asiatic Society of Bombay libraries, and of the Government of Maharashtra archives.

Three Essays Collective have been most responsive as publishers. In particular, Asad Zaidi and Nalini Taneja were very encouraging since my first interaction with them. I cannot thank them enough for having agreed to publish the book.

I am deeply indebted to my parents Kisan and Vasant Pradhan for their continued support to my music and research. My sisters Nishita Mhatre and Deepti Pradhan have also been sources of abiding hope. My wife Shubha Mudgal patiently read and critiqued drafts of the manuscript and translated some of the Hindi lyrics. Being a performer and researcher herself, I cherish the fact that she has always been there for constant dialogue and for jointly exploring the magical world of music and musicians.

INTRODUCTION

The dynamics of cultural nationalism in nineteenth century India were reflected in the modernization of Hindustani music. Projecting the Hindustani musical system as a symbol of an ancient national culture, nationalist Indian middle-class intellectuals sought to classicize the tradition and link it to a Hindu/Sanskritic past to combat the highly prejudiced account of Indian history provided by British colonial-administrator historians like James Mill and other writers of his ilk.[1] Influenced as they were by Western norms of education, they chose to put to use these in the Indian context. They held that there was a disconnect between contemporary performance practice and music theory enshrined in Sanskrit treatises. Placing the blame for this perceived anomaly squarely on the shoulders of Muslim rulers and 'illiterate' practitioners, they portrayed themselves as reformists systematizing

1 Mill gave a despairing account of the Indian civilization and Hindu character. Writing about the Hindu character, Mill observed: "In truth the Hindu like the Eunuch excels in the qualities of a slave". "People of Europe", he wrote, "even during the feudal ages, were greatly superior to the Hindus". He further adds, "In the still more important qualities, which constitute what we call the moral character, the Hindu ranks very low". See James Mill, *The History of British India, (first pub. in 1818), Vols.I & II*, Notes by Horace Hayman Wilson, "Introduction" by J.K. Galbraith, Chelsea House Publishers, New York, 1968, Vol.II, p.365. Cited by, J.V. Naik, "An Early Appraisal of the British Colonial Policy", *Journal of the University of Bombay, Arts No. Vol.XLIV & XLV No.80-81*, 1975-76, pp.243-270.

Hindustani music and sanitizing it of its association with professional women performers, their male associates, and erotic song-texts.

Music educationists in various parts of the country aligned themselves with this perspective and went on to institutionalise this conceptual framework. Conventional writing on the history of Hindustani music pertaining to the colonial period has restricted itself to hagiographies of music educationist and scholar Vishnu Narayan Bhatkhande (hereinafter Bhatkhande) (1860-1936) and music educationist and vocalist Vishnu Digambar Paluskar (hereinafter Paluskar) (1872-1931), with minimal reference to previous efforts in this direction. Recent writings by ethnomusicologists and historians have, however, assessed the impact of colonial perspectives, and nationalism, on Hindustani music. In the process, they have also examined the endeavours of individuals and organizations that predate Bhatkhande and Paluskar, in Hindustani music as we now know it. Works by Ashok Da. Ranade, Daniel Neuman, Gerry Farrell, Allyn Miner, Adrian McNeil, Charles Capwell, Ian Woodfield, Michael Rosse, Eriko Kobayashi, and Janaki Bakhle, are noteworthy in this context.[2] In particular, Rosse, Kobayashi and Bakhle have brought to light significant data related to reform movements in Hindustani music. But despite these efforts at under-

2 See Ashok Da. Ranade, *Indology and Ethnomusicology: Contours of the Indo-British Relationship*, Promilla & Co., Publishers, New Delhi, 1992; Ashok D. Ranade, *Maharashtra: Art Music*, Maharashtra Information Centre, Government of Maharashtra, New Delhi, 1989; Daniel M. Neuman, *The Life of Music in North India: The Organisation of an Artistic Tradition*, Manohar Publications, New Delhi, 1980; Charles Capwell, "Sourindro Mohun Tagore and the National Anthem Project", in *Ethnomusicology*, Fall 1987; Gerry Farrell, *Indian Music and the West*, Clarendon Press, Oxford, 1997; Allyn Miner, *Sitar and Sarod in the Eighteenth and Nineteenth Centuries*, Motilal Banarsidass, Performing Arts Series 7, Reprint, New Delhi, 1997; Adrian McNeil, *Inventing the Sarod: The Marketing of a Musical Tradition*, Seagull Publications, Calcutta, 2004; Ian Woodfield, *Music of the Raj: A Social and Economic History of Music in Late Eighteenth Century Anglo-Indian Society*, Oxford University Press, Oxford, 2000; Michael David Rosse, *The Movement for the Revitalization of "Hindu" Music in Northern India, 1860-1930: The Role of Associations and Institutions*, PhD Dissertation, University of Pennsylvania, Philadelphia, 1995; Eriko Kobayashi, *Hindustani Classical Music Reform Movement and the Writing of History, 1900s to 1940s*, PhD dissertation, The University of Texas at Austin, Austin, 2003; Janaki Bakhle, *Two Men and Music: Nationalism in the Making of an Indian Classical Tradition*, Oxford University Press, Oxford, 2005.

standing the process of classicization of the tradition, practitioners continue to be on the periphery of historical research. That they were in fact at the centre of this radical transformation, that they were directly affected by it, and that they greatly influenced it, does not reflect fully in current discourse.[3] The lack of sufficient contemporary textual evidence that explicitly demonstrates the active participation of hereditary and non-hereditary musicians in giving shape to modern Hindustani music format compounds this lacuna, as it implies their non-involvement in extant developments.

Neuman refers to the changing social organization of musicians in the face of modernity. Miner and McNeil address specific issues related to the evolution of particular instruments, the music that was made on them, practitioners related to those instruments and their upward mobility, both aesthetically and socially, in a hierarchy that was dominated by vocalists.

Bakhle too refers to practitioners, but not as much to demonstrate their proactive role in a challenging situation as to argue that modernizing activities were deliberate attempts at dispossessing hereditary Muslim musicians of their traditional preserve. Her contention is valid to the extent that middle-class intellectuals and many music educationists even used the nomenclature 'Hindu music' to describe Hindustani music. But it does not take into account certain historical realities. For one, in the absence of any concrete demographic study concerning this period, it would be hasty to surmise that Hindustani music was primarily practiced by Muslim musicians. Indeed, many well-known musicians were Muslims, but Bakhle's position negates the role of Hindu hereditary and non-hereditary musicians and several Muslim and

3 Protest, dissent and the potential for modern progressive development existed in the Indian intellectual tradition before British colonial intervention. But westernisation and modernisation in the Indian context have been generally regarded as synonymous, as both processes were set into motion by forces that came in the wake of the British rule. They were, therefore, not indigenous movements, and modernisation was not a phenomenon started entirely from within Indian society.

Similarly several changes had been witnessed in the context of Hindustani music in pre-colonial times, but the modernisation of this system of music manifested due to the dynamics of Indian cultural nationalism at work in the late nineteenth and early twentieth centuries.

Hindu women performers, who made vital contributions to Hindustani music. Kobayashi counters Bakhale's perspective by pointing out multiple factors like region, caste, lineage, and musicianship, other than the more obvious communal element, which affected the modernizing process.[4] Additionally, any evaluation of this period needs to recognize that musicians, hereditary or non-hereditary, Hindu or Muslim, were not monolithic communal fraternities that were unaware of the larger socio-political canvas. Performance practices and aesthetic choices of musicians reveal ingenuity, resilience and an uncanny ability to negotiate changing times. Ranade makes a departure by examining artistic choices made by individual musicians belonging to this period, which shaped their performance practice. Although his comments do not deal directly with the discussion on the socio-cultural context in the colonial times vis-à-vis Hindustani music, he alludes to larger forces that stimulated them to adopt a particular aesthetic. His observations, though pertaining to vocalists, make it amply clear that musicians were making subtle and overt changes in the performance arena, which were by no means of lesser significance to the work of educationists, as they went a long way in establishing what we now consider as conventional performance practice.[5]

The contribution of performers and teachers in modernizing Hindustani music was best experienced in Calcutta and Bombay. This book concentrates on the crucial part played by Bombay since the last quarter of the nineteenth century up until the mid twentieth century, in supporting musicians bring to fruition new trends in performance practice and pedagogy, which in turn moulded the musical ethos of this period. Colonial rule gave rise to socio-economic and political conditions that necessitated the influx of musicians to Bombay from various parts of the country. A decline in Indian princely power as an aftermath to the establishment of British suzerainty in India, led to a gradual withdrawal of royal patronage to Hindustani music. The colonial government was

4 Eriko Kobayashi, *ibid*, p.x.

5 See Ashok D. Ranade, *On Music and Musicians of Hindoostan*, Promilla and Co., Publishers, New Delhi, 1984; Ashok Da. Ranade, *Some Hindustani Musicians: They Lit The Way!*, Promilla and Co., Publishers, in association with Bibliophile South Asia, New Delhi, 2011.

disinclined to patronizing any activity in India that did not directly or indirectly serve its purpose of exploiting India economically and politically. Traditional arts such as music were prime casualties in these circumstances and musicians had to perforce find new patrons. They identified the Indian commercial, industrial and intellectual elite present in colonial cities as prospective patrons and began migrating towards these areas. Enjoying a pride of place in colonial India, Bombay attracted scores of musicians, who wished to take advantage of these potential benefactors.

Urban historiography in India has largely dwelled on Bombay's political and economic past and its spatial and demographic growth, with little being written on the city's role in the realm of Hindustani music. While not attempting to provide a chronological history of Hindustani music in Bombay, the present book hopes to record a significant part of the city's musical culture. It also briefly touches upon modernizing trends in other parts of Western India and in Calcutta.[6]

Musicians in nineteenth century Bombay came up against adverse living and working conditions that were at variance from those they had been accustomed to under princely patronage. The average attitude of the British population in India towards Hindustani music ranged from complete antipathy to indifference. This sentiment probably stemmed from the colonial policy of maintaining a separate and distinct identity from that of the subordinate and the ruled. The British maintained a distance from the Indians by segregating physical spaces in the city for their own habitation and limiting social interaction with them, with the exception of those Indians who had close links with them in business, administration or such other activity. Clubs like the Princess Mary Ladies' Gymkhana and the Orient Club permitted Indian members too, but these instances were few and far between.[7] A. D. King notes, "They provided a culturally familiar and recognizable environment which-like

6 For a detailed discussion on culture in nineteenth century Calcutta, see Sumanta Banerjee, *The Parlour and the Streets: Elite and Popular Culture in Nineteenth Century Calcutta*, Seagull Books, Calcutta, 1989.

7 S. M. Edwardes, *The Gazetteer of Bombay City and Island (Facsimile Reproduction), Volume III*, Gazetteer Department, Govt. of Maharashtra, Bombay, 1978, pp.296, 316.

dressing for dinner-was a formal, visible symbol providing psychological and emotional security in a world of uncertain events."[8] There were exceptions when members of the colonial administration attended musical soirees organized by the Indian elite, or when some British and other European residents in India took an interest in observing and documenting existing musical forms in India. While the latter are of immense historical relevance, there was virtually no patronage for Hindustani music from the colonial government. The introduction of radio broadcasts of Indian music would be an exception in this context.

The social status of musicians within Indian society was ridden with paradoxes that they had no control over. While affluent Indians in Bombay hosted music and dance concerts featuring women performers to entertain their business associates and other friends, these performers were condemned as a debauched lot by some sections of the Indian elite influenced by a Victorian sense of morality. Chapter I of this book describes early migration of male and female musicians to the city, amidst these circumstances. Chapter II discusses private patronage for Hindustani music in the city and the musical culture that developed as a result.

The urban space also placed musicians in an environment surcharged by nascent national consciousness, which regarded Hindustani music as a symbol of national cultural identity. The intellectual elite desired to establish this system of music on par with other subjects of learning and sought to achieve this goal by drawing parallels with Western notions of musical excellence. Inspired by music clubs in the West, they made efforts to set up similar institutions to further their objectives. Chapter III discusses ways in which newly formed music clubs encouraged members of upper and middle class families to learn music in a classroom situation and become amateur performers, in turn objectively bolstering the erratic support that the musicians received from the urban elite and the vestiges of princely rule. Music clubs were instances of early institutionalized music education in the city, as they

---

8 A.D. King, "Colonialism and the Development of the Modern South Asian City: Some theoretical considerations", in Kenneth Ballhatchet and John Harrison (ed.), *The City in South Asia: Pre-modern and Modern*, Curzon Press, London, 1980, p.15.

made traditional knowledge available to the general public – knowledge that had until then been the preserve of hereditary courtesan and musician families. Concomitant efforts at introducing music in school curriculum and at establishing special music schools are examined in Chapter IV.

Chapter V looks closely at music conferences, which brought musicologists and performers on a single platform. Public patronage for performances was firmly established by music circles run on subscription. This has been discussed in detail in Chapter VI.

The new performance space and context placed demands on the musicians' conventional pedagogy and performance format. Chapter VII discusses adaptive strategies adopted by musicians in pedagogy. More individuals outside families of performers began learning music and the 'tuition' ethos took shape with students engaging the services of professional musicians as teachers on a fixed salary. Individual musical styles practiced by particular families of musicians were defined for a largely uninitiated urban audience. Chapter VIII looks at strategies employed to negotiate requirements for a new performance format.

Alongside Hindustani music performance and teaching, musicians also found other methods of supplementing income. Theatre had been a source of employment for some musicians, and technological advancement ushered in recording and broadcasting techniques. The jobs created by these networks in conjunction with those that were thrown up by studios producing feature films, provided further avenues of pecuniary gain. Chapter IX discusses new performance networks that emerged as a result of techniques in mechanical reproduction, and the manner in which these impacted music. The epilogue examines the period immediately after independence, when many policies that had been influenced by the colonial experience were put into practice with or without government support. The shifting environment encouraged the study and performance of music among amateurs, and gradually helped give a respectable status to professional musicians and Hindustani music in an unfavorable colonial situation.

This study has relied on primary sources like reminiscences of musicians and musicologists, reports and compilations, periodicals of the time, in addition to secondary sources pertaining to the subject. The sources examined are in English, Marathi, Gujarati and Hindi.

Edited transcripts of interviews with senior musicians and connoisseurs have been arranged thematically in order to maintain a narrative flow. Interviews conducted in Hindi, Urdu and Marathi, have been translated.

Honorific titles such as Pandit or Ustad have been omitted, but in certain cases suffixes like bai and rao have been included. Indian terms have been spelt either according the phonetic method or as per convention.

THE CITY BECKONS

Patronage to Hindustani music in pre-colonial India came primarily from the Indian royalty. This continued until the early nineteenth century only to be curtailed when British political and administrative policies crippled Indian princely power. Lord Wellesley's subsidiary alliance treaties and Lord Dalhousie's pursuance of the doctrine of lapse led to the annexation of numerous princely states to the British East India Company's dominions.[1] After the suppression of the Revolt of 1857, the Queen's Proclamation in 1858 declared the British Crown as the paramount power in India. The royal courts of Rampur, Gwalior, Baroda, and smaller principalities, continued to patronise Hindustani music, but princely power was debilitated and the movement of musicians and courtesans towards new urban centres suggests that there was a general decline of royal patronage to music and musicians.

1 The subsidiary alliance treaty signed between the British East India Company and several princely states, required the states to accept the British army within their dominion and pay for its maintenance, accept the presence of a British Resident, agree to not enter into alliances with any other powers, accept overall British supremacy, agree to abide by the Company's decisions in case of disputes with other powers, and forego territory in case of non-payment of dues for maintaining British forces. According to Dalhousie's doctrine of lapse, Indian princely states could be automatically annexed if the ruler was considered incompetent or if a Hindu ruler died without a direct heir. See Percival Spear, *A History of India – Volume Two*, Penguin Books, London, 1990, pp.103, 141.

Bombay in 1893

The losses suffered by Hindustani music were compounded by the fact that the colonial government did not support the art.[2] Rare instances of British patronage occurred in Bengal and Western India when Indians propagating Hindustani music took opportunity of their close association with British authorities and convinced them to extend financial aid to such activity. For instance, the Government of Bengal provided a grant-in-aid to The Bengal Music School in Calcutta established in 1871 by Sourindro Mohun Tagore (1840-1914), a prominent musicologist and patron of music of the Pathuriaghata Raj family. Similarly, the Marquess of Dufferin and Ava as the Viceroy of India in 1881, was the High Protector of Tagore's Bengal Academy of Music, an institution set up in 1881, to encourage the practice of music by awarding titles and insignia to distinguished musicians.[3] In Western India, Sir James Fergusson's Government in the Bombay Presidency supported the Poona Gayan Samaj, a music club, in securing the patronage of the Prince of Wales and the Duke of Edinburgh.[4] But this occasional British support to Hindustani music was not part of a long-term official policy and did not indicate a larger vision to support indigenous music.

---

2 V.N. Bhatkhande, *A Short Historical Survey of the Music of Upper India*, "B.S. Sukthankar", Bombay, 1934, p.34.

3 Raja Sir Sourindro Mohun Tagore, *Universal History of Music: Compiled from diverse sources together with various original notes on Hindu music, The Chowkhambha Sanskrit Studies, Vol.XXXI*, The Chowkhambha Sanskrit Series Office, Varanasi, 2nd ed., 1963, pp.87-88. For a biographical sketch of S.M. Tagore, see Surendra Mohan Tagore, *Public Opinion and Official Communications about the Bengal Music School and its President*, pub. by Panchanun Mookherjee, 1876, pp.225-234. Also see, Allyn Miner, "The *sitar*: An Overview of Change", in *the world of music, le monde de la musique, die welt der musik India*, Journal of the International Institute for Comparative Music Studies and Documentation (Berlin), Vol.XXXII, No.2-1990, p.44; Laxminarayan Garg, *Hamaare sangeet ratna*, (*pratham bhaag*), (Hindi), Sangit Karyalaya, Hathras, 1957, pp.67-71. For an analysis of patronage to music in Bengal and the work of S.M. Tagore, see Michael David Rosse, *The Movement for the Revitalization of "Hindu" Music in Northern India, 1860-1930: The Role of Associations and Institutions*, *op.cit.*, pp.12-63; Adrian McNeil, *The Dynamics of Social and Musical Status in Hindustani Music: Sarodiyas, Seniyas and the Margi-Desi Paradigm*, PhD dissertation, Department of Music, Monash University, Melbourne, 1992, pp.115-125.

4 Balwant Triumback Sahasrabuddhe, *Hindu Music and the Gayan Samaj*, The Madras Jubilee Gayan Samaj, Madras, 1887, p.43.

The lack of colonial support was reflected in the attitude of most British travelers to India in the late eighteenth and nineteenth centuries, whose musical universe was restricted to European music. Their observations about Hindustani music performances, on the rare occasions that they attended these, demonstrate a mix of indifference, ignorance, mild curiosity, antipathy, and oblique praise.

Describing the setting for a performance, eighteenth-century traveller Mrs. Kindersley states:

> A large room is lighted up; at one end sit the great people who are to be entertained; at the other are the dancers and their attendants; one of the girls who are to dance comes forward, for there is seldom more than one of them dance at a time; the performance consists chiefly in a continual removing the shawl, first over the head, then off again; extending first one hand, then the other; the feet are likewise moved, though a yard of ground would be sufficient for the whole performance. But it is their languishing glances, wanton smiles, and attitudes not quite consistent with decency, which are so much admired; and whoever excels most in these is the finest dancer.[5]

Mrs. Kindersley's reference to the supposed lack of propriety on the part of the dancers represents the colonial tendency to stigmatize Indian performers. She goes on to describe the musical instruments and the music, both of which had obviously not found consonance with her aesthetic sensibilities:

> The girl sings, while she is dancing, some Persian or Hindostan song; some of them are really pleasing the ear, but are almost entirely drowned by the accompaniment: several black fellows stand behind, who likewise sing with all the strength of voice they are masters of, making, at the same time, the most ridiculous grimaces; some of them playing upon a sitar, which is something like a guitar, but greatly inferior even to that trifling instrument; others on a sort of drum, or tamborin, usually called tomtom; but all this, loud as it is, is drowned by those who play with two pieces of bell-metal which they work between their fingers, and make the same noise as braziers at work upon a large copper.[6]

---

5 Excerpt from Mrs. Kindersley, *Letters from the Island of Teneriffe, Brazil, the Cape of Good Hope, and the East Indies, 1777, pp.231-2*, reproduced in Ketaki Kushari Dyson, *A Various Universe: A Study of the Journals and Memoirs of British Men and Women in the Indian Subcontinent, 1765-1856*, Oxford University Press, Delhi, 1978, p.336.

6 *Ibid.*

British accounts often recorded the visual impact of Indian performances, as is apparent in this description provided by The Marquess of Hastings:

> The nautch girls then sang only two at a time, but without any attempt at a duet after our fashion. It is very remarkable that, when it must be a great object to every one of these girls to show herself off to advantage, female tact has never instructed them to adopt a dress which might display gracefulness of form, or to attempt a dance which might exhibit accuracy of ear and lightness of step. On the contrary, they wear cumbrous trousers which entirely cover the feet; they have a profusion of petticoats with broad fringes, which they seem to be under the continual necessity of hitching up . . .[7]

As with Mrs. Kindersley, The Marquess of Hastings also does not seem to find the performance engaging:

> . . . the only movement is the shuffling forward three or four paces, and then retiring in the same way, sometimes extending a stiff arm with the fingers spread, sometimes bending the arm on the head; and their highest elegance in wiling airs appears to be the slipping off and putting up again the part of the mantle or veil which is thrown over the head. There is a perpetual repetition of this last gentility. The natives will sit for hours enjoying this exhibition. To us nothing can be more tiresomely monotonous.[8]

Many other colonial writers found Indian performances unintelligible, monotonous and noisy. Mrs. Sherwood residing in India from 1805 and 1815 summarily dismisses what she had heard:

> In the chamber above, but dimly distinguished, was a part of the Nawab's band, every instrument being in full exercise. It is impossible to give any idea of this music. It appeared to me as if every instrument of which it was composed was tuned and screwed up to the highest pitch of which it was capable, without the smallest reference to the agreement of one instrument with another. Never before had we heard such fearful screeching and skirling as proceeded from this *nobut khanna*.[9]

Obviously, the inability to fathom and appreciate the aesthetic subtleties of Indian music and dance was a result of colonial prejudice and the absence of a sustained exposure to these arts. Captain Augustus N.

7 Excerpt from *The Marquess of Hastings, The Private Journal of the Marquess of Hastings, 1858, I, 145-6*, reproduced in Ketaki Kushari Dyson, *op.cit.*, p.338.

8 *Ibid.*

9 Excerpt from *The Life and Times of Mrs. Sherwood*, reproduced in Ketaki Kushari Dyson, *op.cit.*, p.337.

Willard, an Army Officer commanding the Services of The Nawab of Banda, and one of the few Englishmen keenly interested in Indian music, candidly admitted:

> It is perhaps owing to this general want of acquaintance with it, that Oriental music is not so much esteemed as perhaps its merit deserves. Although I have met with some European ladies who eagerly desire to possess a copy of an India song, or air, yet it seemed to me that they esteemed it more as a relic of curiosity, perhaps to be sent home than for its intrinsic worth in their eyes.[10]

Admittedly, there had been instances of British engagement with Indian music. British amateur musicians and music enthusiasts stationed in various parts of India engaged with Indian musicians. Their experiences found expression not only in travelogues, but also in their performance repertoire. As early as 1784, Francis Fowkes published an article on the *veena* at Banaras in the *Asiatick Researches*. Similarly, in 1789, transcriptions of Indian songs were included in a publication entitled *The Oriental Miscellany: being a collection of the most favourite Airs of Hindoostan, compiled and adapted for the harpsichord. &c.*[11] But prominent orientalist Sir William Jones (1746-1794), published a book entitled *On the Musical Modes of the Hindoos* in 1792, which became a landmark academic work for many discussions related to Indian music that engaged European and Indian music theorists.[12] European curiosity in Indian music continued well into the nineteenth century. For instance, *The North India Tune-Book, containing Bhajans and Ghazals with Native Tunes, as usually sung*, compiled by Mrs. J.D. Bate, is yet another example of the urge to document Indian music and make it accessible to Europeans.[13] These were exceptional cases of individuals, who

10 Augustus N. Willard, *Music of India*, Sushil Gupta (India) Private Ltd., 2nd revised ed., Calcutta, 1962, p.14. This is a revised edition of Willard's original work published in 1834 called *A Treatise on the Music of India*. See note in Augustus N. Willard, *ibid*, p.80.

11 Raymond Head, "Corelli in Calcutta: Colonial music-making in India during the 17th and 18th centuries", in *Early Music, 13(4)*, Oxford University Press, November 1985, pp.551-552.

12 Gerry Farrell, *op.cit.*, pp.23-26.

13 Mrs. J.D. Bate (compiled by), *The North India Tune-Book, containing Bhajans and Ghazals with Native Tunes, as usually sung*, North India Tract and Book Society's

tried to inform themselves about Indian music and wrote on the subject, though they saw it as a representation of the exotic and ancient orient. While acknowledging their contribution, V.N. Bhatkhande pointed out the limitations in their inquiry. He noted, "I am aware, several Oriental scholars like Sir William Jones, Dr. Griffiths and others made some attempts to study the subject, but the records they have left go to show that their interest in it was not more than academic or antiquarian."[14] Shortcomings in their methodologies and approaches, notwithstanding, the contribution of writers like Sir William Jones, Captain Augustus Willard and others, provides essential source material for research pertaining to this period.[15]

But the overwhelming and lasting impression of nineteenth century colonial writing on the subject is one that is indisputably prejudiced. Coloured by prevalent Victorian social mores of chastity, temperance and morality, colonial authors described women performers as 'dancing girls', equating them with prostitutes and condemning them and their colleagues as a depraved lot.[16] The Reverend M.A. Sherring in his work on tribes and castes in India commented, "In India all professional singing and dancing, when performed by women, with very few exceptions, is performed by prostitutes. Indeed, a prostitute and a professional dancer or singer are, in common speech of the people, correlative terms."[17]

Thus, musicians had little to fall back upon in terms of patronage from Indian princes, colonial government and British residents in India. Circumstances deteriorated when many Indian princes lost an in-

---

Depot, Allahabad, and Alexander and Shepheard, London, 1886.

14 V.N. Bhatkhande, *A Short Historical Survey of the Music of Upper India*, *op.cit.*, p.34.

15 Ashok Da. Ranade, *Indology and Ethnomusicology: Contours of the Indo-British Relationship*, *op.cit.*, pp.31-45. For a detailed discussion on Western engagement with Indian music from the eighteenth century to the twentieth century, see Gerry Farrell, *op.cit.*

16 Joep Bor, *The Voice of the Sarangi: An Illustrated history of bowing in India*, National Centre for the Performing Arts, Quarterly Journal, Vol.XV, 324; Vol.XVI, 1, Sept., Dec.'86 and March '87, pp.81-82.

17 Rev. M.A. Sherring, *Hindu Tribes and Castes, Vol.I*, Thacker, Spink, and Co., Calcutta, n.d., p.274.

terest in Indian music. Music educationist and scholar Vishnu Narayan Bhatkhande commented, ". . . the native princes who in olden times showed a great deal of favour and sympathy towards it, under the new system of education they received, began to be entirely indifferent to it. The result was that the older race of musicians died away without leaving their best art to their descendants and representatives."[18] For instance, Maharaja Ram Singh II (1835-1880), had been a major patron of music, but his successors were more keen to support leisure and sport activities.[19]

Contrasting European and Indian patterns of patronage, Margaret Cousins, British educationist, suffragist, and Theosophist, contrasting European and Indian patterns of patronage said:

> Europe very quickly gave the musician an honoured place in its social and educational spheres. India at one time also must have done so, as tradition has made each of the gods of the Indian pantheon an exponent of some aspect of music, but during the last two hundred years at least the standing of musicians has fallen deplorably low. The payment offered to them either as soloist entertainers or as teachers is incredibly low, and the lack of honour shown socially to first-class virtuosos used to make me blush with shame and indignation when I first came to the East . . . Patronage, appreciation, honour are essentials in the environment of artists. These are given freely in the West; but withheld or given grudgingly generally in Asia.[20]

Evidently, while empathising with Indian performers, Cousins' appraisal of the British government ignored the fact that colonial rule had created unfavourable conditions for Indian music and any widespread support to music was impossible without a proactive government.

In this adverse situation, musicians and courtesans were compelled to explore alternative avenues of patronage. They moved from northern and central Indian princely courts to colonial cities, seeking patronage

---

18 V.N. Bhatkhande, *A Short Historical Survey of the Music of Upper India, op.cit,*, p.34. For a brief overview of patronage to music and dance in eighteenth century Northern India, see Muhammad Umar, *Urban Culture in Northern India during the eighteenth century*, Munshiram Manoharlal Publishers Pvt. Ltd., Delhi, 2001, pp.300-308.

19 Joan L. Erdman, *Patrons and Performers in Rajasthan: The Subtle Tradition*, Chanakya Publications, Delhi, 1985, pp.77-78.

20 Margaret E. Cousins, *The Music of Orient and Occident: Essays towards mutual understanding*, B.G. Paul and Co., Publishers, Madras, 1935, pp.104-05.

in these centres of rising urban economic prosperity and cosmopolitan culture.

By this time, Bombay had prospered after the East India Company's Charter Act of 1813 permitted private trade and abolished the monopoly of the Company in Eastern trade. In 1817, the city acquired greater importance, when the British overthrew the Peshwa regime and shifted the region's political and administrative centre from Poona to Bombay. Private trade flourished even more after the Company's Charter Act of 1833 provided for the discontinuation and abstinence of the Company from all commercial business and appointed the Company only as administrator and ruler in India. Soon, Bombay became the hub of commercial activity and a major modernizer in the political-administrative and socio-cultural realms. Expectedly, there was an exponential rise in the total population of the town and island of Bombay from 16,000 in the year 1716 to 2,21,550 in 1814 and to 2,34,032, in 1833-1834.[21] The introduction of The Great Indian Peninsula Railway, the East Indian Railway, the Madras Railway, and the Bombay, Baroda and Central Indian Railway, provided a further impetus to the city, as these rail networks made Bombay more accessible than ever before.[22] In 1896, the population of the city had reached 8,20,000, and the population was always on the rise, except for the large exodus during the bubonic plague of 1896-1898.[23]

Predictably, the city became a veritable melting pot of diverse cultures. Many resident communities celebrated festivals with specific music and dance forms. For instance, *The Gazetteer of Bombay City and Island* mentions the Siddis from Madanpura dancing to the accompaniment of drums. Similarly, Gujarati Hindu women sang *garba* songs to

---

21 *Census of the Town and Island of Bombay, taken on the 9th February, 1906, with the sanction of Government and of the Municipal Corporation for the city of Bombay accorded under Section 454 of the Bombay Municipal Act III of 1888, by the Municipal Commissioner*, n.p., n.d., p.20.

22 For more details on the Indian railways during the colonial period, see Michael Satow and Ray Desmond, *Railways of the Raj*, Scolar Press, London, 1980.

23 Ian Catanach, "'Who are your leaders?' Plague, the Raj and the 'communities' in Bombay, 1896-1901" in Peter Robb (ed.) in collaboration with K.N. Chaudhuri and Avril Powell, *Society and Ideology: Essays in South Asian History*, Oxford University Press, Second Impression, Delhi, 1994, pp.198, 201.

invoke the Goddess during the Navratri or the nine nights preceding the Dassera festival.[24]

A variety of entertainers and alms-seekers also made their way to the city to procure the support of various social groups residing here. It is difficult to ascertain the exact number of male and female performers at any given moment or the musical genres they were involved in, as their roles were not explicitly documented. This lacuna is clearly noticeable in the Census of 1906, which categorizes all performers as 'Players, actors, dancers, etc.' under the section entitled 'Art'. According to this Census estimate, the entire group in the Town and Island comprised of 972 males and 268 females, all of who were described as actual workers, and 592 dependents including both sexes. The distribution of these individuals across the city is detailed in the Census.[25]

Itinerant folk performers like *pangul*, *pauda*, and *vasudev*, sang and played musical instruments as they sought alms, and *tamasgir*s from present-day Karnatak, Sangli, Rajapur, Goa, Gujarat, Poona and other areas, went from door to door in Bombay performing *dashaavtaari*, *dafvaalaa*, *saagadbaahuli* and *khamsutra* dances. Wandering mendicants like *bairagi*s, *bairagin*s, and Muslim *fakir*s from Delhi, Mecca, Sind, Kabul, Kandahar, Hyderabad, Punjab and other regions, roamed the streets reciting Kabir *doha*s and gathering alms.[26] But it was Bombay's early association with practitioners of Hindustani music from northern and central India, and from Goa and neighbouring areas, that in many ways defined the trajectory of this form of music in later years.

Social organization

Caste affiliations among practitioners of Hindustani music were mentioned in sources dating back several centuries, but their nomenclature and hierarchical organization were constantly redefined with the pas-

---

24 S.M. Edwardes, *The Gazetteer of Bombay City and Island (Facsimile Reproduction), Vol.I*, Gazetteer Department, Govt. of Maharashtra, Bombay, 1977, p.191, 172-173.

25 *Census of the Town and Island of Bombay, op.cit.*, pp.144-147, 154-155.

26 Govind Narayan Madgavkar (hereinafter G.N. Madgavkar), *Mumbaiche varnan*, (Marathi), Itihas Sanshodhan Mandal, Mumbai Marathi Granth Sangrahalaya, Mumbai, 1961, pp.298-299, 307-314.

sage of time.[27] Some of these affiliations may have continued among migrant musicians in Bombay, but they gradually lost their relevance in the new urban environment.

Historically, women performers received marginal acknowledgement for their contribution to music and they were often socially ostracized. But it is a well-known fact that they played an integral role in the music-making process.[28] Women performers from hereditary courtesan families belonging to northern and central India were more commonly addressed as *baiji* or *tawaif*.[29] Muslim women performers were addressed variously as *kasbi*, *randi*, *deredar* and *tawaif*, depending on their professional roles. They mainly came from Punjab, Gwalior, Sindh, Hyderabad, and Gujarat. Conventionally, girls were taught to sing and dance from an early age. Their puberty was marked by ceremonies called *sarfaraz hona* (to become exalted) or *misi lagana* (apply vitriol or hydrous sulphate of a metal to the teeth), after which they were available for entertaining their patrons and entering into alliances with them.[30]

Women performers also came from Goa and neighbouring areas. They belonged to the *devadasi* tradition existing in various parts of the country, which married off women from this community to a particular temple deity. Thus, they became permanent temple attendants and were

---

27 Daniel M. Neuman, *op.cit.*, pp.86-87. See also, M.V. Dhond, *The Evolution of Khyal*, Sangeet Natak Akademi, New Delhi, (n.d.), p.37; Ashok Da Ranade, *Music Contexts: A Concise Dictionary of Hindustani Music*, Promilla & Co., Publishers in association with Bibliophile South Asia, New Delhi, 2006, pp.45-56.

28 Jennifer Post Quinn, *Marathi and Konkani speaking women in Hindustani music, 1880-1940*, PhD dissertation, University of Minnesota, UMI Dissertation Information Service, University Microfilms International, Ann Arbor, Michigan, June 1982, pp.12-13.

29 Daniel M. Neuman, *op.cit.*, p.100. Also see Jennifer Post Quinn, *op.cit.*, p.13; Joep Bor, *op.cit.*, p.95.

30 K. Raghunathji, "Bombay Dancing Girls", Jas. Burgess, *The Indian Antiquary: A Journal of Oriental Research, Vol.XIII-1884*, reprinted by Swati Publications, Delhi, 1984, p. 171. *Nath utaarnaa*, also known as *nath utaraai* or *nathi*, was another rite of passage associated with *tawaifs*, which readied them for intimate contact with a patron. See Amelia Maciszewski, "Nayika ki Yadgar: North Indian Women Musicians and Their Words" in Amlan Das Gupta, *Music and Modernity: North Indian Classical Music in an Age of Mechanical Reproduction*, Thema, Kolkata, 2007, p.164.

assigned specific duties in the temple precinct.[31] The Goan *devadasis* were divided into an eight-tiered hierarchy reflecting the roles they had to fulfill. The *devadasis* involved in singing and dancing before the deity were called *naikins*, *kalavatis*, *kalavantins*, *kalavantinis*, *kulambinis*, or *kalavants*.[32] The temple duties of the *devadasis* were laid down by convention, but their sexual exploitation by wealthy patrons was as much a reality. The *Gazetteer of the Union Territory: Goa, Daman and Diu*, mentions:

> . . . even before they attained puberty, the ceremony known as *shes* in the case of Kalavant, had to be undergone. The *shes* ceremony included a prototype of marriage in which the girl garlanded a knife held by another girl dressed in male attire, after which she was free to be a mistress. However, if a Kalavant became somebody's mistress without undergoing the ceremony of *shes*, she was looked upon with contempt. Once this ceremony was over and after the girl had attained puberty, *hatlavni* used to take place, when a rich youth would pay a sum of several hundred rupees to possess the girl for the first night and keep her as his mistress for one year, paying a huge sum of money to her mother. During that year, she assumed the status of a second wife and even considered his family her own. After the first year, if he so desired he could continue to keep her as his mistress sometimes even until his death, after which she lived a widowed life. However, if her benefactor left her before his death, she was free to seek another partner. It may be mentioned here, that she always remained faithful to her benefactor. Even after becoming somebody's mistress, the girl continued her services in the temple.[33]

31 For more information on the association of the *devadasi* system with fertility cults, see Devangana Desai, *Erotic Sculpture of India: A Socio-Cultural Study*, Tata McGraw-Hill Publishing Co., New Delhi, 1975, pp.106-107. Also see, B.D. Satoskar, *Gomaantak: prakriti aani sanskriti, Vol 1–Samaaj rachanaa va samaaj jeevan*, (Marathi), Shubhada-Saraswat, Pune, 1979, pp.64, 67-69. For information about the *devadasi* tradition in the erstwhile Madras Presidency, see Anandhi S., "Representing Devadasis: 'Dasigal Mosavalai' as a Radical Text" in *Economic and Political Weekly*, Vol.XXVI Nos.11 and 12, Annual Number 1991, Sameeksha Trust, Bombay, 1991, pp.739-746.

32 See V.G. Gune (ed.), *Gazetteer of the Union Territory: Goa, Daman and Diu, District Gazetteer Part 1: Goa*, Gazetteer Department, Government of the Union Territory of Goa, Daman and Diu, 1979, pp.249-250; B.D. Satoskar, *op.cit.*, pp.261-263; Prabhakar Angle, "Indian Music", in Mário Cabral E Sá, *Wind of Fire: The Music and Musicians of Goa*, Promilla & Co., Publishers, New Delhi, 1997; Anant Ramkrishna Sinai Dhume, *The cultural history of Goa from 10000 B.C.-1352 A.D.*, the University of Michigan: Ramesh Anant S. Dhume, 1986, pp.73-75, 130; Jennifer Post Quinn, *op.cit.*, pp.62-63, 75.

33 V.G Gune (ed), *op.cit,*, p.250.

Even Hindu women performers practised the *misi* ceremony, as is evident from the contemporary account presented by Arthur Steele:

> In the Caste or profession of dancing girls, girls of beauty and accomplishments are made Naikins by the ceremony of applying Misee (a powder made of vitriol) to their teeth – cardamums are distributed to the guests, turmeric is put on the girl's person, after which a religious ceremony is performed in honor of the Gods, or Peers. The Caste are feasted, the Misee is applied by several Naikins, one of whom, of hereditary office and repute in the Caste, takes the girl on her lap and presents her with a Saree.[34]

According to nineteenth century commentator K. Raghunathji, the *devadasis* migrated to Bombay to escape Portuguese persecution in Goa and to seek patronage from the urban commercial and industrial elite.[35] The *devadasis* followed a specific living and working pattern in Bombay, as described by Raghunathji:

> The ceremony of *seja* is compulsory before a woman can style herself a Naikin. She places herself generally under the protection of some individual, as an ordinary married woman, and passes the greater portion of her time in dancing and singing. The money she earns is her own property, and her protector has no claim to it. But the money she earns by singing and dancing on Mondays, in the month of Sravan (July-August) and on holidays is considered as charity money, to be applied towards charitable purposes, such as giving dinners to her caste fellows, or feeding Brahmans, and in case this latter is not attended to, excommunication follows. This is not made known to the party excommunicated till the heads of the caste, when invited for any ceremony, refuse to go to her house, and when asked the reason tell her what her offence was, and fine her from Rs.150 to Rs.200. On the fine being paid, the whole caste is invited to the feast, and she, coming before the dining table, with her hands joined, makes a bow and begs forgiveness. This is granted, and then she dines with them, observing the caste of her master for the time being.[36]

The *devadasis* adopted and maintained religious and caste exclusivity practised by the patron's community. Raghunathji describes this phenomenon thus:

---

34 Arthur Steele, *Summary of the Law and Custom of Hindoo Castes*, "Honorable The Governor in Council", Bombay, 1827, p.171.

35 K. Raghunathji, *op.cit.*, p.167.

36 *Ibid*, p.165.

> A Naikin in the keeping of a Musalman will not dine in the same line with one in the keeping of a Parsi or a Banya, and so on. And in this way there may be seen a number of rows of these women at their feasts. Their castes are not fixed, but change with their masters. One may be a Musalman to-day, but to-morrow a Prabhu or a Brahman, and again on a later date a Parsi or a Musalman again.[37]

A social hierarchy existed among male performers before their migration to the city. The Reverend M.A. Sherring mentions specific groups involved in the professional pursuit of music and dance. Each of these played a definite occupational role and had its set of rules, which determined its status within the musician community.[38] Sherring describes the *dharhi*s as, "A class of Mahomedan players. Both men and women perform on musical instruments, or sing, or dance, wherever they can obtain employment. When they have no engagements they wonder about the country, visiting villages and towns, or performing in private houses, and in this manner earn a livelihood".[39] The *kalavant*s were also Muslim performers, but were ". . . much higher in rank than the Dharhis; are regarded, indeed, as persons of reputation and respectability".[40] These *kalavant*s are not to be confused with the Goan *devadasi*s bearing the same nomenclature. The *mirasi*s were Muslim performers who taught girls singing and dancing. Sherring states that *mirasi* women ". . . not only sing and dance, but are also employed as jesters in the presence of native ladies, in zenanas, or female apartments, of large houses. The men are said to be highly respected by Mahomedans, though, for what reason I have been unable to learn".[41] The *kathak*s were Hindu musicians who sang and danced and taught these arts to women performers.[42] The *ramjana*s or *ramjani*s were another Hindu

---

37 *Ibid.*

38 Rev. M.A. Sherring, *Hindu Tribes and Castes, Vol.I, op.cit.*, pp.271-276.

39 *Ibid*, p.275.

40 *Ibid.*

41 *Ibid.*

42 *Ibid*, pp.273-274.

caste of performers, who taught singing and dancing.[43] The *gaunharins* were yet another caste of performers.[44]

Correspondingly, Sherring's sketch of musicians in Bombay and the neighbouring areas, suggests that the *kalawant, kawaltapi, ganihari, utak* or *kathain* and *basphor* castes may have been practitioners of art music. The *kalawants*, *kawaltapi* and *ganihari* have been described as castes of dancers and singers. The *kalawants* were further divided into five interrelated branches known as *patra, ramjani, ghikari, ranganli* and *kanchan.*[45] The *utak* or *kathain* were teachers to 'dancing girls'.[46] Further, Sherring describes the *basphor* thus: "Musicians who attend dancing girls. They beat the *pakwaj*, and play, on the *saringi*. They also prepare the skin for the *pakwaj*, a kind of drum. They come from Northern India, where they are regarded as a very low caste."[47]

Nineteenth century lexicographer J.T. Molesworth mentions *dhadi* as, "a class or an individual of it, of Muhammadan singers", and describes *kalawant* as "singers and musicians and more especially *pakhawaj* and *sarangi* players accompanying songstresses-dancing girls". Molesworth also mentions *kalavantin* as a "dancing girl".[48] Males from the *devadasi* families also migrated to the city and provided musical accompaniment to women performers.

There is scant information to suggest that such caste categories were as clearly demarcated in late nineteenth century Bombay, but evidently female and male performers organized themselves separately. Women performers had a broad system of organising themselves, similar to the one that was followed in their hometowns. They were part of a *jamaat* or community of such performers headed by a senior member

43 *Ibid*, p.274.

44 *Ibid*, p.275-276.

45 Rev. M.A. Sherring, *Hindu Tribes and Castes*, Vol.II, Thacker, Spink, and Co., Calcutta, n.d., pp.192, 200, 201.

46 *Ibid*, p.200.

47 *Ibid*, p.201.

48 J.T. Molesworth, (comp.), *A Dictionary, Marathi and English*, Asian Educational Services, 2nd ed. (reprint), New Delhi, 1989, pp.359, 142.

holding the post of *chaudharaain* or chief of the group.[49] While caste lines were blurred to an extent, differentiation on the basis of place of origin, religion and professional role perhaps continued as is evident from their choice of locality to set up permanent residence. Notably, groups sharing such commonalities often stayed in the same vicinity, and a similar decision of performers in this regard was therefore not an isolated example. *The Gazetteer of Bombay City and Island*, indicating the tendency of migrants in the 1880s to reside in "certain definite areas according to traditional belief, social instincts or tribal affinities", states, "the dancing-girls drifted to Khetwadi and Byculla, 'the scarlet woman' to Kamathipura."[50] Goan women performers and others of the Marwadi, Bene-Israel and Muslim communities lived in the neighbourhood of Kalbadevi Road and Grant Road.[51]

Women performers seem to have been flexible in matters concerning religion, but this could as well have been their way of coping with the challenges posed by the urban situation. As described by *The Gazetteer of Bombay City and Island*:

> Excluding the pure Naikins of Goa and Kanara there is a tendency among Hindu and Bene-Israel dancing-girls to style themselves Musalmans and even embrace the Musalman faith, in consequence possibly of the fact that a Muhammadan, no matter his or her caste or class, is always assured of decent burial after death and can count upon other Muhammadans in the same *mohallaa* or street to arrange that the death ceremonies are properly performed.[52]

Laws and customs concerning inheritance and acceptance into the profession governed Hindu women performers elsewhere in the country, but it is unclear whether they also prevailed in Bombay.[53]

---

49 S.M. Edwardes, *The Gazetteer of Bombay City and Island (Facsimile Reproduction), Vol.I, op.cit.*, p.190. Also from interview with Abdul Halim Jaffer Khan held on 6 May 1997.

50 S.M. Edwardes, *The Gazetteer of Bombay City and Island (Facsimile Reproduction), Vol.II*, (originally printed in 1909), Gazetteer Department, Govt. of Maharashtra, Bombay, 1978, pp.189-190.

51 S.M. Edwardes, *The Gazetteer of Bombay City and Island (Facsimile Reproduction), Vol.I, op.cit.*, p.190.

52 *Ibid*, p.191.

53 Arthur Steele, *op.cit.*, pp.201-202, 215-216.

Male musicians migrating to Bombay as accompanists and teachers to women performers resided in the same geographical area as the latter. In the absence of documented information, it is difficult to draw conclusions about the social organisation among male performers, though there are anecdotal references to similarities between the organisation of male and female performers. Some sources believe that this organisation was restricted to Muslim performers providing musical accompaniment to soloists, who are believed to have been part of the Qureshi *jamaat* that had a *panchaayat* (an assembly of arbitrators, usually five) with a *chaudhari* (the chief of a trade or caste group).[54] The post of the *chaudhari* was not hereditary.[55] Popular vote in the *jamaat* elevated a musician to this status and this was symbolically declared when elders or respected members in the *jamaat* tied the *pagadi* to the newly appointed *chaudhari* in the *pagadbandh* ceremony. The *chaudhari* was allotted the task of resolving disputes within the musician fraternity, in consultation with the *panchaayat*, thus avoiding the need to seek intervention from the court of law. An offender, who did not mend his ways even after the issuance of three warnings, was ostracised from the *jamaat* throughout the country and this order was strictly adhered to. The *jamaat* collected a nominal amount from its members and helped them to get established in the city.[56] Evidently, other caste-like groups in nineteenth century Bombay involved in different occupations were similarly organized.[57]

Social organization, convention, performance practice and financial transaction, indicate the existence of a hierarchy among musicians in the nineteenth century. Vocalists enjoyed the highest place in the musician fraternity at a time when instrumental solos had not gained popularity. Vocalists were identified by musical styles and family lineages, and were accorded respect as per their chosen musical genres.

54 The position of the *chaudhari* was prevalent among Muslim musicians since a few centuries. See M. Mujeeb, *The Indian Muslims*, George Allen & Unwin Ltd., London, Second Impression, 1969, p.211.

55 The situation seems to have been different in North India, where the position of the *chaudhari* was hereditary. See Daniel M. Neuman, *op.cit.*, pp.126-132.

56 Interview with Arvind Mulgaonkar held on 4 January 1993.

57 Ian Catanach, *op.cit.*, p.200.

Next in order came instrumentalists who were not only accompanists, but had established themselves as soloists. The main performer enjoyed prime position in an ensemble, and as per the musical logic prevalent in Hindustani music, soloists had the prerogative to take decisions concerning repertoire and presentation in a musical performance and accompanists had to follow suit. Accompanists were relegated to the lowest rung. Their subordinate position is obvious from the general lack of information pertaining to them in nineteenth century music-related literature. This was so, despite the fact that accompanists played a vital musical role in any performance.[58]

58 This information is based largely on diverse oral sources and on communication during training sessions with Nikhil Ghosh.

PRIVATE PATRONAGE

Colonial rule was largely looked upon as a divine dispensation by the Indian intellectual elite in nineteenth century India. Not surprisingly, therefore, British victory in the Revolt of 1857 was celebrated by offering prayers through popular song-forms and poetic meters like *abhang*, *pad*, *aaryaa*, *saki* and *dindi*.[1] Similar celebratory prayers were offered in the city earlier in 1855 when the British won the Anglo-Russian War.[2] However, this perception of benevolence was misplaced, as the colonial government continued to pursue exploitative policies that met with criticism from some sections of the Bombay intellectuals.[3]

The harsh reality of the colonial situation was similarly experienced in the case of Hindustani music in Bombay. For British residents in mid-nineteenth century Bombay, it was Western music and not Hindustani music that provided them with recreation, as was the case with their compatriots elsewhere in India.[4] Though Western music concerts were not held at regular intervals, Richard Bentley notes:

---

1 G.N. Madgavkar, *op.cit.*, pp.133-134.

2 *Ibid*, p.145.

3 J.V. Naik, "The Seed Period of Bombay's Intellectual Life, 1822-1857" in Sujata Patel and Alice Thorner (ed.), *Bombay: Mosaic of Modern Culture*, Oxford University Press, Bombay, paperback edition, 1996, p.64.

4 For a discussion on Western music in India and its performance space and context pertaining to an earlier period, see Raymond Head, "Corelli in Calcutta: Colonial music-making in India during the 17th and 18th centuries" in *Early Music, 13(4)*, *op.cit.*, pp.548-552.

> As the season advances, every description of gaiety thickens fast around us; and those who enter with zest into such scenes, are scarcely ever disengaged for a single night.
>
> A series of subscription balls, or reunions, is the only successfully established public amusement in Bombay, and this is carried on with tolerable spirit and liberality throughout the season . . .[5]

British residents in Bombay met socially at clubs like the Bombay Club, the Byculla Club, the Bombay Gymkhana, The Ladies' Gymkhana, the Commercial Gymkhana, and the Royal Bombay Yacht Club. Later, theatrical productions and the occasional music concert provided them with added sources of entertainment and opportunities for informal gatherings. Music was included in functions held at the Town Hall, the Byculla Club, or at private homes at Malabar Hill.[6] The Governor's band also presented Western music thrice a week, at the bandstand situated a little way from the Apollo Bunder for an audience consisting of British families.[7] In 1869, a Philharmonic Society was founded specifically for Western music.[8] Interestingly, this Society received a gift of sixty pounds from Cowasjee Jehangirji Readymoney, a well-known Parsi trader, for the purchase of musical instruments.[9] Even American minstrelsy shows received patronage in Bombay since the mid-nineteenth century, drawing European and Indian audiences.[10]

Various services catering to Western music were set up in the city. The section entitled 'Miscellaneous Professions' in *The "Bombay Times"*

---

5 Richard Bentley, *Life in Bombay, and the Neighbouring Outstations With Illustrations*, "author", London, 1851, pp.56-57.

6 M.D. David, *Aik Mumbai tujhee kahaanee*, (Marathi-trans. Purshottam Dhakras), Priyank Prakashan, Thane, 1993, p.162. Also see, S. M. Edwardes, *The Gazetteer of Bombay City and Island (Facsimile Reproduction), Volume III*, Gazetteer Department, Govt. of Maharashtra, Bombay, 1978, pp.223, 239-240, 294, 296, 334-335.

7 G.N. Madgavkar, *op.cit.*, pp.293-294.

8 Pestanjee Firozeshah Kapadia (hereinafter P.F. Kapadia), *Gayan Uttejak Mandali: tenee ponee sadinee tawaareekhno ahewaal*, "Mrs. Freni M. Cama", Mumbai, 1946, p.16.

9 Cited from the *Times of India*, Bombay, 20/11/1871, in Bomanjee Byramjee Patell, *Parsi Prakaash, Vol.II*, "Dinbai Byramjee Patell", Bombay, 1910, p.382.

10 Naresh Fernandes, *Taj Mahal Foxtrot: The Story of Bombay's Jazz Age*, Roli Books, New Delhi, 2012, pp.45-53.

Calendar and Almanac for 1851 lists four 'music masters' residing in different parts of the city. The *Almanac* also mentions two sellers and repairers of Western instruments.[11] Similarly, *The Bombay Calendar and Almanac for 1853* lists a pianist, Mrs. Bromley, who lived in Nesbit Lane in the Fort area of the city and conducted a school for young women. The section entitled 'Miscellaneous Professions and Traders' in the same source also refers to two repairers of musical instruments and three 'music masters', and also mentions two instrument makers and repairers in the list of inhabitants on the Island and other parts of the Presidency.[12] A circulating library for literature related to music was also said to have existed in the 1830s in the fort area.[13] More stores selling Western instruments were seen in the city in the second half of the nineteenth century and in the early twentieth century. For instance, James & Co. established in 1865 on Hornby Road, Fort, sold and hired out German pianos, violins, mandolins, French Paquet metronomes, gramophones, radiograms and records in all languages. The store also overhauled old pianos.[14] There were other stores that sold music-related merchandise in addition to other products. One of these was Marcks & Co., established in 1863 on Esplanade Road, Fort. It sold musical boxes, though it mainly stocked jewelry, and other gold, silver and electroplated articles, and also undertook repair of watches, clocks, and chronometers.[15]

On occasions when influential individuals from both sides of the colonial divide engaged informally, they included Western and Indian music as part of the entertainment. As stated by James Douglas, "The

---

11 See "Miscellaneous Professions" in *The "Bombay Times" Calendar and Almanac for 1851*, Bombay, 1851, p.63.

12 *The Bombay Calendar and Almanac for 1853*, Bombay, 1853, pp.300,313,317.

13 Meera Kosambi, *Bombay and Poona: A Socio-Ecological Study of Two Indian Cities 1650-1900*, "author", Stockholm, 1980, p.86.

14 H.D. Darukhanawala, *Parsi Lustre on Indian Soil:-Lives and Portraits of Professionals, Historians, Scholars, Educationists, Parsi Religionists, Philanthropists, Politicians, Officials, Reformers, Pioneers, Industrialists, Merchants and others of The Past and Present, Vol.II*, (n.p.), 1963, p.xiii.

15 H.D. Darukhanawala, *Parsi Lustre on Indian Soil–Vol.I*, G. Claridge & Co., Ltd., Bombay, 1939, p.764.

greatest native entertainers were the Parsis. Hormusjee gave a masque ball in 1810, and Limjee Cawasjee's ball in 1826 was a great affair."[16] British businessmen and government officials hosted *nautch* parties for their British and Indian guests, and similar parties were hosted by the shetias to honor British dignitaries. The *nautch* parties held to honor Danby Seymour, Member of the British Parliament, are but instances of this convention.[17] Similarly, Indian art music was included as part of the entertainment at a People's Fair organized during the visit of Prince Albert Victor, son of Queen Victoria, to Bombay in 1890.[18]

Apart from such instances, however, the absence of any significant inter-cultural musical dialogue indicates that British residents in Bombay perhaps did not respond favourably to Hindustani music much in the same manner that many of their compatriots did elsewhere in India. Performers, therefore, looked upon Indian merchants in Bombay as potential patrons. Commonly known as *shetia*s or merchant princes, these private traders included Dasa Oswal Jains, Parsis, Banias, Bhatias, groups of Muslim traders like Khojas, Memons, Bohras, Arabs and Moghuls, and some families from Marathi castes like Sonars. They made considerable profits in the city and many acquired properties in and around Bombay by the middle of the nineteenth century. The Bhatia and Banias acquired most of the properties on Kalbadevi Road and in its vicinity.[19] In his critique of the Vallabhacharya sect, contemporary educationist and journalist Karsandas Mulji cites a newspaper report from the Times of India dated February 1, 1862, which referred to the wealth of Bhatia, Marwadi, Lohana and other devotees, and to the tax

16 James Douglas, *Bombay and Western India, Vol. I*, Sampson Low, Marston & Company, Limited, London, 1893, p.177.

17 G.N. Madgavkar, *op.cit.*, p.301.

18 Jim Masselos, "Spare Time and Recreation: Changing Behaviour Patterns in Bombay at the turn of the nineteenth century" in *South Asia: Journal of South Asian Studies, New Series Vol.VII, No.1*, June 1984, p.46.

19 S.M. Edwardes, *The Gazetteer of Bombay City and Island (Facsimile Reproduction), Vol.I, op.cit.*, pp.166-199. See also, F.B. Tyabji, "Social Life in 1804 and 1929 amongst Muslims in Bombay" in *Journal of the Bombay Branch of the Royal Asiatic Society*, New Series, Vol.VI, London, 1930, p.293, and Eckehard Kulke, *The Parsees in India: Minority as Agent of Social Change*, Vikas Publishing House Pvt. Ltd., Delhi, 1974, p.153.

imposed by their religious heads on every commodity that they traded in. According to the report, the main Vallabhacharya temple in Bombay at the time collected a total annual income of Rs.50,000/- in the form of this tax, which in turn amply demonstrates the wealth of the devotees.[20]

Indian merchants managed cotton and opium trade to the east, and later, cotton traders also began investing in the indigenous textile industry.[21] During the 1850s, there was a phenomenal rise in Indian entrepreneurial effort. C.N Davar, a Parsi banker and trader, started the first cotton textile mill in 1854, and other Parsi and Gujarati traders in Bombay and Ahmedabad followed his example. The Parsis and Gujaratis became the wealthiest Indian business communities and became Bombay's early Indian stockbrokers. Influential members of these communities contributed generously to activities related to education, publishing, civic development and more.[22]

The period between 1861 and 1865 was particularly prosperous for Bombay, as Indian merchants involved in the Kaapad Baazaar or cloth market amassed huge fortunes. Bombay became a focal point for cotton trade after the American Civil War jeopardized the supply of raw cotton from United States of America to the Manchester mills. England looked towards India for replacing this supply. In the huge cotton trade that ensued, Bombay's cotton exchange experienced an unprecedented boom. The Petit family, for instance, made huge profits during the American Civil War, thus becoming Bombay's leading textile family.[23] Many merchants lost fortunes as soon as the Civil War came to an end and the original supply of cotton from America resumed, but Bombay's temporary prosperity attracted more people to the city. The total population of the town and island of Bombay (Bombay) in 1864 rose to 8,16,562, of

---

20 Karsondas Mulji, *History of the Sect of Maharajas or Vallabhacharyas in Western India*, Trubner & Co., London, 1865, pp.145-148.

21 Helen B. Lamb "The Indian Business Communities and the Evolution of an Industrialist Class" in *Pacific Affairs, Vol.XXVIII, No.2*, June 1955, Institute of Pacific Relations, New York, pp.102-103. For a exhaustive account of opium trade conducted by traders in Bombay, see Amar Farooqui, *Opium City: The Making of Early Victorian Bombay*, Three Essays Collective, Gurgaon, 2006.

22 Helen B. Lamb, *ibid*, p.104.

23 *Ibid*, p.105.

which the city population numbered 7,83,980 and the harbour population was 32,582.[24]

Not only did the *shetia*s amass huge wealth in the city, but they also played an integral role in public life. Regarded as leaders of the entire Indian community, they occupied important official positions as Justices of Peace and as members of the Board of Conservancy and the Board of Education. Foremost among the *shetia*s, Sir Jamshetjee Jeejeebhai was regarded as spokesman for all Indians in Bombay until his death. Born in 1783, he made huge profits in the opium trade with China. He was the first Indian to be awarded the Baronet and Freedom of the City of London. He donated heavily for the J.J. Hospital and Grant Medical College. J.J. College of Arts was established due to his support. He brought his wife and daughters-in-law out of *purdah* and took them to public gatherings and feasts. He hosted parties in honour of the Governor and princely rulers at his palatial houses – Fort House, Mazgaon Castle, and Mahalaxmi Mahal. For example, he hosted a grand party at Mazgaon Castle in 1849 to honour of Governor Lord and Lady Falkland.[25] After the death of Jamshetjee Jeejeebhai, Jagannath Sunkersett came to be regarded as the spokesman for all Indians in the city.[26] Born in 1803, Nana or Jagannath Sunkersett was competent in English and Sanskrit and encouraged education. He took a lead in establishing the Bombay Native Education Society. It was through this Society that the Elphinstone School and College were started. He even established a girls' school and aided the girls' school started by some Elphinstone College students in 1842. He established the Bombay Association in 1852 with the help of Dadabhai Naoroji, to inform the British Government of the obstacles and troubles encountered by Indians. He was the main inspiration for starting the Grant Medical College. The Victoria

24 Cited in the *Census of the Town and Island of Bombay, op.cit.*, p.20, and in S.M. Edwardes, *The Gazetteer of Bombay City and Island, Vol.I, op.cit.*, p.163.

25 M.D. David, *op.cit.*, pp.147,149.

26 J.C. Masselos, *Towards Nationalism Nationalism: Group affiliations and the politics of public association in nineteenth century Western India*, Popular Prakashan, Bombay, 1974, p.18.

Garden, the zoo, and the Bhau Daji Lad Museum, were also started due to the efforts of Sunkersett.[27]

The public status occupied by Jeejeebhai and Sunkersett was incomparable, but there were other *shetias* too whose wealth and public engagement brought them attention. They provided migrant musicians with the much-needed patronage.

The *nautch*

Documented evidence seems to suggest that women performers were featured more frequently than male soloists in mid-nineteenth century concerts. Women from the patron's household were not part of the audience, as this was a period when women from 'respectable' families were not permitted to openly interact with the public. This societal norm was even noted by Sir George Arthur, Governor of Bombay, when he spoke at a large party hosted by Sir Jamsetjee Jeejeebhoy in 1843.[28]

The *shetias* organized *nautch* parties to celebrate festivals and familial occasions like weddings and thread ceremonies. Describing the festivities held eight days prior to Ram Navami, *The "Bombay Times" Calendar and Almanac for 1851* states:

> From the first day the temples of Rama are whitewashed and illuminated in the evening, and the image of Rama is adorned with costly ornaments. In the evening the *Ramayan*, or the legendary History of Rama, is read in the temples, and in the night *Kirtun* is preached by the *Hurridass*, who describes the morality and heroic actions of Rama. Nautches are also not omitted during the nights.[29]

Even wealthy Muslims patronized women performers. *The "Bombay Times" Calendar and Almanac for 1851* states:

> The conclusion of the month Rumzaun is celebrated as an *Eed* or festival, and is hailed with great rejoicing and merriment, as a sort of reward for their severe abstinence. In every house the same dainties are provided, every amusement that can be thought of is indulged in, the Nautch-women in the

27 M.D. David, *op.cit.*, p.142.

28 *The Bombay Calendar and Almanac for 1853*, Bombay, 1853, p.377.

29 *The "Bombay Times" Calendar and Almanac for 1851*, Bombay, 1851, p.30. See also, K. Raghunathji, *op.cit.*, p.166.

> apartments of the gentlemen, and the domenee in those of the ladies, are in great request; the Zenanahs ring with festive songs . . .[30]

The Gazetteer of Bombay City and Island describes Muslims feasting, attending theatrical performances and visiting the lodgings of women performers on Bas-Id, the day after Id-i-Ramzan:

> Urdu plays like *Dil-Farosh* draw enormous audiences, and the *divankhanas* of Foras road and the neighbourhood are swept, garnished and brightly lighted for the benefit of the Memons, Arabs, Konkanis, and others of the Faith, who come to while away an hour or two amid the strains of the *sarangi* and the muffled bourdon of the tom-tom.[31]

K. Raghunathji mentions that the task of engaging women performers for a recital was assigned to an individual who frequented their lodgings. He often received a commission from them for any professional engagements that he facilitated. The performer was offered earnest money of a rupee wrapped in a *vida* or betel leaf if the terms of engagement were found acceptable.[32]

Performance practice followed by women performers in the nineteenth and the early years of the twentieth centuries would appear incongruous to the cognoscenti today. For several decades now, Hindustani music performers, female or male, have usually seated themselves on the floor or on a specially erected platform for performances, and have specialised in music or dance as separate arts. However, Raghunathji describes radically different performance practices followed by women performers. For instance, *nach* referred to a combined performance of singing and dancing, *baithak* was a vocal recital by a seated singer, and *jalsa* saw the singer alternating between singing and sitting. These three types of performances were held at the patron's residence or sometimes at the lodgings of the women performers. The *pachamba* is described as a vocal recital of a woman performer held at the house

30 *The "Bombay Times" Calendar and Almanac for 1851, op.cit.*, p.35.

31 S.M. Edwardes, *The Gazetteer of Bombay City and Island (Facsimile Reproduction), Vol.I, op.cit.*, pp.183-184.

32 K. Raghunathji, *op.cit.*, p.170.

of a leading member of her community, where the singer was seated through the performance.[33]

When engaged to perform at a thread ceremony or a marriage ceremony, the performer visited the patron's house for a few hours on the eve of the ceremony and sang in a seated position to compliment the family on the auspicious occasion. This performance was called the *mujra*. On the day of the ceremony, she danced and sang for an audience consisting of the host and his male guests. Women of the household witnessed this performance through windows in the walls. Women performers did not perform at such functions when they were going through their menstrual cycle, as prevalent social norms regarded them 'ceremonially unclean' during this period. They did not return the earnest money due to this change in the agreement, but the patron had to engage the services of another performer.[34]

On days that their services were not exclusively retained by a single patron, women performers would entertain patrons at their personal quarters through the night. Such performances attracted a larger audience on Saturday nights. Each person in the audience paid between one and twenty rupees or more per night.[35] Raghunathji mentions, "One Saturday nights their houses are full of visitors. This night is called by pleasure-loving people the *golden night*, and Sunday the silver day, but Monday is called by them the *black* or the *iron day*, as on Monday they have to attend to business."[36]

Women performers were trained in singing and dancing from an early age, and incorporated both arts in their performances. They retained the services of teachers, but they often learnt singing from their *sarangi* accompanists.[37] Lessons in vocal music and dance were given for an hour each before daybreak and continued in the evening for two hours. The women were believed to have acquired competence in both arts within a period of approximately three years of such training. They

33 *Ibid*, pp.166, 170.

34 *Ibid*, p.170.

35 *Ibid*.

36 *Ibid*.

37 *Ibid*, p.168. Also see, Jennifer Post Quinn, *op.cit.*, p.91.

were ready to perform by the age of fifteen or so and pursue their careers till the age of forty or fifty.[38]

The *kalavantin*s or *naikin*s engaged *vastadji*s as dance teachers. The *vastadji*s were sons or brothers of other Hindu or Muslim women performers. They were paid between fifty and five hundred rupees and were offered other gifts depending on their calibre. A contract was drawn up between the teachers and the *kalavantin*s to this effect. This was probably the earliest marker of a new urban environment that introduced a financial and contractual arrangement in the traditional *guru-shishya parampara* or master-disciple system of music education.[39]

Women performers originally from northern and central India focused more on genres like *thumri* and *dadra*, as the representational nature of the song-text in these forms lent easily to a combined song and dance interpretation. The *sarangi* and *tabla* provided melodic and rhythmic accompaniment, respectively. The *tabla* would play a rhythmic section known as *laggi*, *laggi-chanti* or *laggi-nada*, which was a dialogue with the singer-dancer's footwork. At times, other vocalists accompanying the main performer would provide a vocal refrain during the interplay between the footwork and the *tabla*. A *manjira* player also maintained a constant rhythm alongside. This performance practice formed part of what became popular as the *nautch*.[40] Women performers from Goa and neighbouring areas were relatively secluded from Hindustani musical influences, and therefore, probably focused more on religious and folk songs. It was only when they migrated to other areas like Bombay, that they had an opportunity to learn Hindustani music from leading stalwarts.[41]

The proportional distribution of fees among the members of the ensemble illustrates the position enjoyed by each of them. The main performer occupied the highest status in the ensemble, as she received

---

38 K. Raghunathji, *ibid.*

39 *Ibid.*

40 Information procured during training sessions with *tabla* player Nikhil Ghosh. See also, Aneesh Pradhan, *Tabla: A Performer's Perspective*, "author", Mumbai, 2011, pp.11-12.

41 Jennifer Post Quinn, *op.cit.*, pp.82-84, 89-90.

the entire fee, retained the largest share and distributed the balance among the rest. She received between thirty and sixty rupees for a single performance held at the house of the patron. As per convention, she paid two *anna*s and three *anna*s in a rupee to the *sarangi* and the *tabla* players, respectively. At times two *sarangi*s were used in performance. On days that their services were not exclusively retained by a single patron, they would perform at their lodgings through the night and every member of the audience paid between Re.1/- and Rs.20/- or more per night. Such performances held on Saturday nights were better attended.[42] Women performers also provided the accompanying musicians with lodging and boarding facilities, in addition to a fixed percentage of the earnings. In lieu of this, the musicians carried out minor tasks for the women.[43] Clearly, women performers enjoyed a better financial standing in the fraternity.

At special concerts, patrons also gave awards to women performers in addition to the performance fee. For instance, Govardhandas Goculdas Tejpal, the adopted son of Goculdas Tejpal, who continued his father's charities and established several public service institutions, hosted a concert that featured vocalist Anjani Malpekar among others. Anjanibai's concert continued through the night and ended in the morning at 9.30 am. She was declared the best singer and won an award, which she gifted to Tejpal's temple.[44]

Thus, it is obvious that this period saw women performers receiving large patronage from Bombay's elite. A song presented in July 1907 by the inimitable Gauhar Jan at the Darbar Hall of the city Town Hall, eulogised the philanthropy of specific *shetia*s and showered praise on Bombay's generosity, respect and patronage to her. Through the song, the performer prayed for the residents of the city, and for the long life of King Edward, the British monarch at the time. A source provides a transcription that gives an indication of the import of the song:

---

42 K. Raghunathji, *op.cit.*, p.170.

43 S.M. Edwardes, *The Gazetteer of Bombay City and Island, Vol.I, op.cit.*, p.191.

44 Anjanibai Malpekar, "*Hum gaayakon kaa bhaagya khul gayaa*", (Hindi), in *Bhatkhande smriti granth, op.cit.*, p.324. See also, M.D. David, *op.cit.*, pp.152-153.

Chali gulzaar aalam mein havaaein fazl rahmaanee
Phalaa phulaa khadaa hai kyaa ise har nakhl-bostaanee

Garza Hindu Musalmaan sab ke sab hain khandaaeen peshaanee
Hain to yeh asahaaq ab haath gar dastayon bhee man

Zaheeye majlis hoon jin ke sadar ser meedor ko maheenaa
Vah barq andaaz gokul das jee iqbaal hon baanee

Rahe aabaad ya rab bambai or bambai vale
Kahaan main ek musaafir aur kahaan yeh qasar sultaanee

Mujhe izzat jo baqshee aur jo qadar kee meree
Rahengee yaad mujhko bambai vaalon kee mahmaanee

Jooheen school ke maalik ratansee seth jee saahab
Kareen bacchon kee khidmat or karen un kee nigahbaanee

Khudaayaa shah Edward ko tu rakh zindaa qayaamat tak
Rahe qaayam hakoomat aur hove fazle rabbanee[45]

The first three couplets are incoherent, but the third mentions Goculdas, probably referring to Goculdas Tejpal. The following couplets can be translated as:

I, an insignificant visitor to this magnificent edifice
Pray that Bombay and its citizens may forever prosper

I was treated with great honour and respect
And (I) will forever remember the hospitality of the people of Bombay

The owner of schools, Ratansee Sethjee saahab,
Serves children and is a guardian to them

May God keep King Edward alive till the Day of Judgement
May his regime last and be showered with divine blessings[46]

45 This song was released on a 78 rpm disc entitled Dhun Kalyan, ending with an announcement, "My name is Gauhar Jan. *Yeh gaanaa Town Hall mein gaayaa*, Pherozeshah Mehta *ki taareef mein*" (trans. This song was sung at the Town Hall, in honour of Pherozeshah Mehta). See Mister S.P. Jaini (compiled by), *Hindi gramophone record sangeet-Pratham bhaag*, "author", Calcutta, n.d., pp.94-95; *The Record News*, Society of Indian Record Collectors', Volume: Annual, TRN 2010, Mumbai, 2010, pp.59-60.

46 I am grateful to Sohail Hashmi for translating these couplets.

Male musicians

Male musicians primarily earned their livelihood in the city by teaching and performing with women performers. By the second half of the nineteenth century, affluent women performers in the city engaged teachers from leading hereditary musician families on a monthly salary. This was probably a decision driven by artistic compulsions and their desire to climb the social ladder within the fraternity, as such tutelage enriched their repertoire and provided authenticity and respectability in a competitive market.

Sher Khan (1805-1862), nephew and disciple of Ghagge Khudabaksh of the Agra lineage, was one of the earliest prominent musicians to have travelled to Bombay and to have taught many disciples here.[47] Similarly, Haider Khan, believed to be the first of the Sahaswan-Badayun-Gwalior lineage of vocalists to have come to the city, taught Bayabai Wadkar, among other women performers. On his departure from Bombay to the princely states, he passed on his teaching assignments to other musicians, one of who was Mohamed Khan (1870-1922), son of Natthan Khan of the Agra lineage.[48] Mohamed Khan taught women performers like Champabai Kapileshwari, Bakabai Bandodkar and Shrimatibai alias Bai Narvekar (c.1906-1989).[49] Likewise, Murarba Govekar and Ali Hussein of the Qawwal Bachche lineage taught vocal music to Tarabai Velingkar.[50]

Though not widely acknowledged, women performers also acted as patrons, as they not only engaged male musicians as teachers and

---

47 The dates of his arrival and stay in Bombay vary in different sources. See Laxminarayan Garg, *op.cit.*, p.195; N. Jayavanth Rao, *Sajan Piya: A biography of Ustad Khadim Husain Khan*, Sajan Milap, Bombay, 1981, p.21.

48 Bayabai Wadkar was the mother of vocalist Indira Wadkar and grandmother of theatre and film actor Hansa Wadkar. Interview with Sharad R. Mehta held on 29 April 1992.

49 Jennifer Post Quinn, *op.cit.*, p.127.

50 Another source refers to Tarabai Velingkar and her sister as having been disciples of Balkrishnabuwa Ichalkaranjikar and Hyder Khan. See Prabhakar Angle, "Indian Music", in Mário Cabral E Sá, *op.cit.*, p. 158.

accompanists, but also featured them in soirees that they hosted. Visiting musicians sought to establish their credibility in the fraternity by performing at such soirees or *daavat*s. Performances continued into the early hours of the next morning featuring several performers in a single session. A successful concert in such a setting attended by important musicians, enhanced the prestige and popularity of the performers and often increased their chances of acquiring sustained patronage.[51] The informality in this competitive atmosphere inspired performers to maintain and acknowledge quality, knowledge and discipline.

In his memoirs, Govindrao Tembe (1889-1946), harmonium virtuoso, composer, theatre personality, brings alive the informal but charged ambience at a *daavat* held at the Kalbadevi Road residence of well-known Goan performer Tarabai Velingkar alias Tarabapu alias Baputara (1857-1918). Tarabai Velingkar and her sister Saraswatibai, had learnt music and dance in their hometown, Veling village in Goa, before they came to Bombay. They were believed to have been supported in Bombay by Premchand Raichand and by Lala Dunichand alias Babu Dulichand, both wealthy *shetia*s based in Bombay and Calcutta, respectively.[52] Of the noteworthy performers on this occasion was Bablibai Salgaonkar alias Chandrabai alias Chandraprabha (1860-1925), a reputed Goan performer and disciple of Natthan Khan Agrewale, who sang for about an hour and a half. Such was the impact of Bablibai's performance that no one was expected to sing thereafter. But after finishing her performance at 5 a.m., Bablibai requested Alladiya Khan (1855-1946), disciple of his father Khwaja Ahmed Khan and his paternal uncle Jehangir Khan, and innovator of the vocal style that later came to be known as the Jaipur-Atrauli *gayaki*, to perform after her. She publicly acknowl-

---

51 Jennifer Post Quinn, *op.cit.*, pp.102-104.

52 See note prepared by S.V. Gokhale in Govindrao Tembe, *Maazhaa sangeet vyaasang*, (Marathi), Maharashtra Rajya Sahitya Sanskriti Mandal, Bombay, 2nd ed., 1984, pp.112-113. The Velingkar sisters are also referred to as Bapu and Tara in Prabhakar Angle, "Indian Music", in Mário Cabral E Sá, *op.cit.*, p. 158. Another version of the Velingkar family tree is given by Jennifer Post Quinn, *op.cit.*, p.131. For biographical sketch of Premchand Raichand see M.D. David, *op.cit.*, pp.149,150.

edged his command over the art during his performance.[53] Tembe also recounts a similar session held at the same venue where eminent vocalists Mohammad Khan, Bhaskarbuwa Bakhale (1869-1922), disciple of Faiz Muhammad Khan, Natthan Khan and Alladiya Khan, and Miajan (c.1880-1919), disciple of Ali Bakhsh of Patiala and Mia Kalu Khan, *sitar* player Barkatullah Khan (c.1850/60-1928), disciple of Imratsen (c.1814-1894), and *been* player Majid Khan, were present in the audience. The session continued until 5 a.m. and concluded with a *thumri* rendition by Moujuddin Khan (c.1870-1921), who had been trained by his family elders, and eminent musicians-composers Sadiq Ali (1800-1910), Mehboob Khan 'Daras', and Lalanpiya.[54]

After establishing their credentials in the city, male musicians received support from the urban elite, albeit not as often and as commonly as the patronage enjoyed by women performers. Faced with new living and working conditions and the social stigma that they had to ride under due to their association with women performers, the lives of male musicians in the city were fraught with insecurity.

Towards the end of the nineteenth century, traders, businessmen and industrialists gradually began featuring male performers in private home concerts attended by their business associates and friends. Held to mark important occasions in the patron's family or to entertain their guests, these concerts typically had a small audience of fifty-odd listeners. Sometimes, more than one ensemble was featured in a single concert that began at night and continued well into the early hours of the next morning. There is no information about the fees that were paid to the soloists or whether there was a fixed ratio between soloists and accompanists as was the case with women performers and their accompa-

53 Govindrao Tembe, *Gaayanmaharshee Alladiyakhan yaanche charitra*, (ed. Deshpande Vamanrao and Joshi Baburao), (Marathi), Maharashtra Rajya Sahitya Sanskriti Mandal, 2nd ed., Bombay, 1984, p.52.

54 Govindrao Tembe, *Maazhaa sangeet vyaasang*, *op.cit.*, pp.101,103. See also, Suresh Chandwankar, "*Thumriche Badshah: Moujuddin Khan*", (Marathi), in *Sangeet Kala Vihar*, Akhil Bharatiya Gandharva Mahavidyalaya Mandal, Miraj, March 1994, pp.9-10. According to Suresh Chandwankar, Moujuddin Khan was born in 1874/75 or 1882/89 and he died in 1922/26. Chandwankar writes that Moujuddin Khan was trained for a while by Bhaiyya Ganpatrao in Calcutta, but his ability to learn by listening to other musicians helped him greatly.

nying musicians. Tembe recounts Daulat Khan's *dhrupad* recital at Govardhandas Goculdas Tejpal's bungalow, where his nephews Alladiya Khan and Hyder Khan provided vocal support.[55] On another occasion, Mammu Sheth, a notable patron, hosted a performance by Daulat Khan at his bungalow, where prominent artistes and music lovers from the city were present. But Daulat Khan could not perform on this occasion, and his nephew Alladiya Khan volunteered to perform instead. He sang *dhrupad-dhamaar* for nearly three to four hours and was accompanied on *pakhawaj* by Makkhanbhaiyya and Parvatsingh.[56]

Some patrons would have a retinue waiting upon them, much like their feudal counterparts. Lala Dunichand alias Babu Dulichand (c.1850-1921), a wealthy businessman from Calcutta, is noteworthy in this context. Babu Dulichand came from a family of rich Marwaris, who were based in Calcutta for three generations. He was involved in a variety of businesses, which included money lending, transactions in bullion, and forward trading in jute, tea and cotton. A connoisseur of music and dance, he had studied music and employed several musicians. Babu Dulichand visited Bombay for almost two months in around 1906, with an entourage that included his family, musicians and their disciples, and domestic help. He followed a daily routine during his stay by hosting concerts that would begin at 11 p.m. and would continue until 4 or 5 a.m. or even 6 a.m. Different male and female performers of Bombay would be called to perform daily. He would retire at 9 a.m. and wake up at 4 or 5 p.m. At 6 or 7 p.m. he would meet his friends and return home by 9 or 10 p.m.[57] Babu Dulichand visited Bombay yet again in 1918 and there was music for three consecutive days, with Tarabai Shirodkar (1889-1949), disciple of vocalists Ramkrishnabuwa Vaze (1871-1945), Bhaskarbuwa Bakhale and Muhammad Khan, singing every night.[58]

---

55 Govindrao Tembe, *Maazhaa sangeet vyaasang, op.cit.*, pp.162-163.

56 *Ibid*, p.85. Alladiya Khan's account of the same incident mentions five *pakhawaj* players. See Amlan Das Gupta and Urmila Bhirdikar (trans. with introd.), *Sangeet Samrat Khansaheb Alladiya Khan: My Life*, Thema, Calcutta, 2000, p.82.

57 See note prepared by S.V. Gokhale in Govindrao Tembe, *Maazhaa sangeet vyaasang, op.cit.*, p.112. Also see, *ibid*, p.101, 104; Jotin Bhattacharya, *Ustad Allauddin Khan And His Music*, B.S. Shah Prakashan, Ahmedabad, 1979, p.24.

58 B.R. Deodhar, *Thor sangeetkaar*, Akhil Bharatiya Gandharva Mahavidyalaya Mandal, Bombay, 1973, pp.197-198. See also, Laxminarayan Garg, *op.cit.*, pp.185-186.

The patrons' likes and dislikes determined the choice of musicians at private concerts, as was exemplified several years later by Seth Gopaldas, a businessman, who organised monthly concerts of vocalist Kesarbai Kerkar (1892-1977) at his residence. Her *guru* (master) Alladiya Khan would remain present and Abdul Majid Khan and Vishnu Shirodkar would provide the *sarangi* and *tabla* accompaniment, respectively.[59]

Given the opportunities that Bombay thus provided, the city became a prime location for musicians to seek their fortunes. Vocalists and instrumentalists from Delhi, Lucknow, Agra, Jaipur, Gwalior, Patiala, Baroda, Hyderabad, and other parts of the country, made brief visits to Bombay during the late nineteenth century and many even migrated to the city.

Noteworthy vocalists in the city were: Mahadeobuwa Gokhale (1813-1901), disciple of Zainulabdeen Khan of Hyderabad; Muhammad Khan alias Chhote Muhammad Khan (d.1874), son and disciple of Haddu Khan of Gwalior; Natthan Khan of Agra (1840-1901), disciple of his paternal uncle Ghulam Abbas Khan (c.1815/1820-1932) and other elders of his family; Rehamat Khan (d.1922), son and disciple of Haddu Khan of Gwalior; Balkrishnabuwa Ichalkaranjikar (1849-1926), disciple of Ramkrishna alias Devjibuwa Paranjpe, Vasudeobuwa Joshi and Muhammad Khan of Gwalior; Miya Qutub Baksh (d.1890) more popularly known as Tanras Khan of Delhi, disciple of his father Qadir Baksh and Miya Achpal; Ali Hussein alias Ali Baksh and Fateh Ali, disciples of Tanras Khan; Hyder Khan; Muhammad Khan (son of Natthan Khan); Banne Khan. Among the instrumentalists were: Ali Hussein (*been* player); Pannalal Vajpeyi (d.1885) (*sitar* player); Barkatullah Khan (c.1850/60-1928) (*sitar* player), disciple of Imratsen.[60]

This is not a comprehensive list, but it illustrates the wide variety of musical styles pursued by these musicians. Once in the city, they also

---

59 B.R. Deodhar, *ibid*, p.31.

60 For biographical information on some of these artistes see Vilayat Hussein Khan, *Sangeetagyon ke sansmaran*, Sangeet Natak Akademi, New Delhi, 1959; Laxminarayan Garg, *op.cit.*; B.R. Deodhar, *Thor Sangeetkar, op.cit.* See also, S.N. Ratanjankar, "*Jeevan charitra*", in *Bhatkhande smriti granth*, (Hindi), Indira Kala Sangeet Vishwavidyalaya, Khairagarh, M.P., 1966, p.10; Govindrao Tembe, *Maazhaa sangeet vyaasang, op.cit.*, pp.84-88, 89, 94.

found patronage from the Western-educated intellectual elite. For instance, one of Alladiya Khan's early concerts in Bombay was held at eminent jurist Justice K.T. Telang's residence.[61] Musicians made the city their temporary home taking up teaching assignments during their stay here, while others made visits for a few concerts. The need to retain contact with the last vestiges of princely patronage while consolidating their links with the urban elite, led some musicians to seek periodic patronage in Maharashtrian principalities like Satara, Jat, Kolhapur, Sangli, Ichalkaranji, Kurundwad, Bawade, Aundh, and Jamkhindi.[62] But they accepted the challenges of modern urban life, and shaped their music to suit the needs of changing times and contexts.

---

61 Govindrao Tembe, *Maazhaa sangeet vyaasang, op.cit.*, p.157. See also, B.R. Deodhar, *Thor Sangeetkar, op.cit.*, pp.21, 68-69.

62 Ashok D. Ranade, *Maharashtra: Art Music, op.cit.*, pp.54-55.

MUSIC CLUBS

Divergent colonial ideologies created a Western-educated intellectual class in India. To begin with, the orientalists studied various aspects of Indian society and sought to link them to an ancient exotic civilization. In the process, they supported Indian languages, and published literature to acquaint Indians with Western rationalism and scientific temper. The Evangilicals set up missionary schools to further the cause of Christianity among Indians. But above all, it was the Anglicist viewpoint so vociferously put forth by Lord Macaulay in his famous Minute of 1835 that made English education inevitable in the Indian context.[1] In Bombay, the influence of Western education was widely experienced after Mountstuart Elphinstone, as Governor of Bombay Presidency from 1819 to 1827, laid a firm base for modern learning in the region.[2] Bombay saw the birth of several institutions that gave an impetus to the

1 For a detailed account of the impact of orientalist work, see David Kopf, *British Orientalism and the Bengal Renaissance: The Dynamics of Indian Modernization 1773-1835*, University of California Press, Berkeley, 1969. See also, Clive Whitehead, "The Historiography of British Imperial education policy, Part I: India" in *History of Education, May, 2005, Vol.34, No.3, Journal of the History of Education Society*, pp.315-329, tandfonline, October 30, 2013.

2 J.V. Naik, "Early Anti-Caste Movement in Western India: The Paramhansa Sabha" in V.M. Kulkarni (ed.), *Journal of the Asiatic Society of Bombay*, Asiatic Society of Bombay, Bombay, 1979, pp.137-138.

city's intellectual life. Among these, the Students Literary and Scientific Society established in 1848 and its vernacular branches known as the Marathi and Gujrati Upayukta Jnyan Prasarak Sabhas (1849) are of particular relevance here.[3] Members of the intellectual elite played a prominent role in these organizations and challenged the position of the *shetias*, who had until then been the leaders of the Indian community and had supported the spread of education by donating generously to such organizations, but had often been sectarian in serving the interests of their individual castes and communities.[4] Western ideas of liberty and equality inspired intellectuals to question British administrative, political and economic policies. Spurred on by a nationalistic sentiment, they endeavoured to prove that Indian civilization was in no way inferior to the West and that India was a repository of ancient culture.

The rise of national consciousness, a growing urge for social and political change, and the search for a national cultural identity, thus compelled English educated Indians to explore and project facets of indigenous culture that challenged racial and cultural superiority flaunted by the colonial masters. The revivalists among them contradicted Western influences and Christian missionary propaganda by reviving memories of India's 'golden past' and by taking pride in this cultural inheritance.[5] As part of these attempts to promote Indian culture and influenced by the orientalists, some intellectuals promoted Hindustani music as an ancient legacy and a symbol of India's 'glorious heritage'. They sought to establish links between this system of music and a Hindu/Sanskritic past, ignoring Islamic influences or the patronage that had been provided by Muslim rulers and also condemning the lat-

3 J.C. Masselos, *Towards Nationalism*, *op.cit.*, pp.22, 29-30, 163. See also J.V. Naik, "The Seed Period of Bombay's Intellectual Life, 1822-1857" in Sujata Patel and Alice Thorner (ed.), *Bombay: Mosaic of Modern Culture*, *op.cit.*, pp.61-62.

4 J.C. Masselos, *Towards Nationalism*, *op.cit.*, pp.29-30, 17, 21. Also see, Eckehard Kulke, *op.cit.*, p.154.

5 In defence of ancient Indian culture, see Vishnu Bhikaji Gokhale, alias Vishnubawa Brahmachari (1825-71), "The First Great Revivalist" in Matthew Lederle, *Philosophical Trends in Maharashtra*, Popular Prakashan, Bombay, 1976, pp.191-203; see also Frank F. Conlon, "Vishnubawa Brahmachari-A Champion of Hinduism in Nineteenth Century Maharashtra" in A.R. Kulkarni and N.K. Wagle (ed.), *Region, Nationality and Religion*, Popular Prakashan, Bombay, 1999, pp.157-184.

ter for having destroyed a rich and ancient tradition.[6] Thus, patronage from the intellectual elite was not motivated merely by their interest in Hindustani music, but was part of the larger discourse that sought to contend with colonial notions of Indian culture.

Sections of the Indian intellectual elite, who wished to embrace all that Western civilization had to offer and reform Indian society of its evils, were also influenced by colonial writing that reflected Victorian social mores and stigmatised Indian musicians. They considered music and dance performances featuring women performers a social evil and sought to stop them by leading an Anti-Nautch Movement in Madras and Calcutta in the 1890s.[7] In Madras, Venkata Ratnam Naidu led the campaign against *nautch*. Issues relating to social purity and temperance were discussed at the National Social Conference, which met after annual sessions of the Indian National Congress.[8] The Anti-Nautch Movement may not have found widespread support in Bombay, but reformists seeking to rid Indian society of 'immoral' activities assumed a leading role in the social and political life of the city.[9] For instance, Sir Narayan Chandavarkar (1855-1923), one of the leading reformist voices in the city, clarified his stance regarding *nautch* parties before he agreed to become Chief Minister at the court of Maharaja Tukoji Holkar of Indore. He informed the Maharaja:

> I have all along been on principle opposed to 'Nautch' parties. I have refused invitations to them and have both publicly and privately condemned them. At Durbars and other functions in Native States, such parties are customary. If that is the case in Your Highness's State and if Your Highness is of opinion

6 Balwant Triumback Sahasrabuddhe, *op.cit.*, pp.82-83.

7 G. N. Madgavkar, *op.cit.*, p.301.

8 Kenneth Ballhatchet, *Race, Sex and Class under the Raj: Imperial Attitudes and Policies and their Critics, 1793-1905*, Vikas Publishing House Pvt. Ltd., New Delhi, 1979, pp.157-159. Also see Jennifer Post Quinn, *op.cit.*, p.52. For an analysis of the reformist and revivalist trends that impacted the *devadasis* in South India, see Shankar Jogan, *Devadasi Cult: A Sociological Analysis*, Ashish Publishing House, New Delhi, 1990, pp.14-15. For an analysis of the movement to classicize the Carnatic music tradition and to proscribe *devadasis*, see Lakshmi Subramanian, *From the Tanjore Court to the Madras Music Academy: A Social History of Music in South India*, Oxford University Press, New Delhi, 2006.

9 Kenneth Ballhatchet, *op.cit.*, p.125.

> that a long established usage cannot be abolished at once, I should have the liberty to stay away from such parties.[10]

In his address on social reform delivered at the Fourth Anniversary of the Madras Hindu Social Reform Association on November 28, 1896, Chandavarkar stated:

> Men now may make light of and ridicule your attempt to denounce and put down what are called nautch parties; they may laugh at you and take you for visionaries; but be sure enthusiasm in the cause of morality has unrivalled charm and power which does not fail sooner or later to assert itself.[11]

Thus, the English-educated Indian intellectual elite found itself in a complex situation. Some were influenced by the liberal and rational phase of the Indian Renaissance, there were those who advocated a revivalist path, and there were still others who were influenced by Victorian morality.[12] As pointed out by Justice M.G. Ranade, ". . . caught as we are in the midst of two civilizations we live a divided and conflicting life".[13]

But the growing interest in Hindustani music, the objective of bringing respectability to the art, and a nationalistic spirit, motivated Bombay's intellectual elite to form music clubs that promoted education and performance among amateurs. Until then, music education had followed the traditional *guru-shishya parampara* with oral transmission as its primary pedagogic tool. Music was taught mainly to those from hereditary families of professional male and female performers and to some disciples outside these families. The *guru* occupied an exalted

---

10 Ganesh L. Chandavarkar, *A Wrestling Soul: Story of the life of Sir Narayan Chandavarkar*, Popular Book Depot, Bombay, 1955, p.128.

11 Cited in L.V. Kaikini (ed.), *The Speeches and Writings of Sir Narayen G. Chandavarkar Kt.*, Manoranjak Grantha Prasarak Mandali, Bombay, 1911, pp.47, 76.

12 For a comparative study of individuals leading these trends, see J.V. Naik, "Raja Rammohun Roy, Swami Dayananda Saraswati and Indian Renaissance" in Nirmal Kanti Bhattacharjee (ed.), *Granthana: Indian Journal of Library Studies*, Quarterly Vol.1, Number 2, January-March 2005, p.30.

13 Cited in L.V. Kaikini (ed.), *op.cit.*, p.29; see also J.V. Naik, "Intellectual basis and Ideological Premises of Maharashtrian Response to British Colonial Rule" in *Changing Identities: The transformation of Asian and African societies under colonialism*, ed. by Joachim Heidrich, Verlag Das Arabische Buch, Berlin, 1994, pp.241-254.

position and was regarded as an omnipotent figure. The system made it obligatory for the *shishyas* to prove their worthiness to the *guru* before the training could begin. Once accepted, the *shishya* seldom made cash offerings to the guru for the training, but performed various menial tasks for the *guru*. Those wishing to train as professionals but were not from the *guru*'s family, were expected to serve the *guru* and win his confidence for him to agree to impart knowledge that was otherwise a closely guarded secret, as was seen in the case of Bhaskarbuwa Bakhale during his studentship with his *guru* Faiz Mohammad Khan's residence. Teaching sessions would take place as per the whims of the *guru*. Disciples from the *guru*'s family were given more importance over outsiders. Thus, Bhaskarbuwa would be sent on some errands while his *guru* would teach his nephew on a regular basis.[14] However, at times, even those from the *guru*'s family were expected to serve the *guru*. For instance, Khadim Hussein Khan (c.1904/05-1993) of the Agra lineage and his brother Anwar Hussein Khan, who learnt from their great granduncle Kallan Khan in Jaipur, were expected to serve him at all times during their years of training.[15]

Usually, traditional training did not encourage inquiry and discussion during teaching sessions. Disciples were expected to obediently learn what the *guru* chose to teach. Noting song-texts was forbidden, compositions were seldom notated and solfège was used only to learn basic exercises. Everything had to be committed to memory, with the result that the disciples often enunciated words according to what they had comprehended of the *guru*'s singing and had reproduced innumerable times. Any questions from disciples were met with reprimand, to the extent that they would be asked to leave.[16]

In addition to musical knowledge, the *guru* also went on to introduce the disciples to extra-musical aspects and etiquette that became the basis for social interaction in the specific milieu of hereditary per-

14 B.R. Deodhar, *Thor sangeetkaar*, *op.cit.*, p.85.

15 N. Jayavanth Rao, *op.cit.*, pp.44-46.

16 B.R. Deodhar, *Gaayanaachaarya P. Vishnu Digambar*, Akhil Bharatiya Gandharva Mahavidyalaya Mandal, Mumbai, 1971, pp.20-21.

formers.[17] The *guru*'s pivotal role as a knowledge-giver and interpreter in an essentially oral tradition was emphasized through various rituals. The *guru* tied a *ganda* or ceremonial thread to the wrist of the *shishya* during the *ganda-bandhan* ceremony symbolizing the disciple's initiation and signifying an everlasting bond between the *guru* and *shishya*.

Such rituals and the traditional training pattern continued in the urban environment, although teaching in the city had become a commercial transaction. Thus, Bablibai Salgaonkar became a *ganda-bandh shishya* of Natthan Khan Agrewale.[18] Similarly in 1891, Anjanibai Malpekar became a *ganda-bandh shishya* of Nazir Khan Bhendibazarwale (d.1920), a reputed *sarangi* player originally from Muradabad.[19] As was the case in the traditional pattern, only those from hereditary performers' families could undergo training. In rare cases, *shishya*s from outside these families were taught for some special consideration. Learning and performance of music was not encouraged among non-hereditary musician families, primarily because of the social stigma that plagued the musician fraternity and adversely affected the art.

It was in this atmosphere that enlightened intellectuals decided to bring the art into public domain, by establishing music clubs. Like many other choices that the Western educated Indian intelligentsia made, the idea of starting clubs was also borrowed from the West.[20]

Music clubs

In favour of setting up music clubs in various parts of the country to propagate music education, V.N. Bhatkhande prescribed a multi-pronged role for them. He believed clubs should compile, print, publish and translate all available ancient Sanskrit treatises on music, organize

---

17 For an extended discussion on the *guru-shishya parampara* in Hindustani music, see Ashok D. Ranade, *On Music and Musicians of Hindoostan*, *op.cit.*, pp.6-7, 31-35, 39, 42.

18 Govindrao Tembe, *Maazhaa sangeet vyasang*, *op.cit.*, pp.166-167. Also see Jennifer Post Quinn, *op.cit.*, pp.134-135.

19 Govindrao Tembe, *ibid*, pp.64-65. Also see Jennifer Post Quinn, *ibid*, p.137.

20 See Percy A. Scholes, *The Oxford Companion To Music*, Oxford University Press, London, 10th ed., 1970, pp.197,199,39-40,227-232, for entries on "Clubs for Music-making", "Annotated Programmes" and "Concert" in the Western context.

regular music conferences and invite scholars to discuss issues related to music theory and practice, document the current state of Hindustani music, codify the *raag* rules and publish this codification, consider the opinions of leading musicians regarding the structure of controversial *raag*s and standardize these, seek the help of musicians under the patronage of various principalities, procure the histories of musicians through the documents available with the princely patrons, organize periodic programmes featuring famous vocalists to create an opportunity for the general public to listen to presentations of uncommon *raag*s, employ good musicians to impart regular music lessons as per a syllabus, acquaint musicians with *raag* rules and notation, and maintain records of the clubs' proceedings or publish them in monthly magazines.[21] This was an ambitious proposition for music clubs, but many of them took steps in this general direction.

Music clubs, like several public organizations established in this period, had definite community linkages. Notably, Hindu clubs and societies included the Dnyan Prasarak Mandali for promoting educational activity, Hindu Burning and Burial Grounds Committee, Hindu Mahajan Committee for managing temples and charitable institutions, and the Hindu Union Club established in 1875 by Justice K.T. Telang.[22] Gymkhanas for sport like the Paramanadas Jivandas Hindu Gymkhana, Parsi Gymkhana, and the Islam Gymkhana were also organized along communal lines.[23] Likewise, the Pathare Prabhu Social Club was set up in 1886.[24] It was, therefore, not uncommon for even music clubs at

21 As mentioned in P.N. Chinchore, "*Sangeetoddhaarak P. Bhatkhande meri drishti mein*", (Hindi), in *Bhatkhande smriti granth*, Indira Kala Sangeet Vishwavidyalaya, Khairagarh, MP, 1966, p.56.

22 S.M. Edwardes, *The Gazetteer of Bombay City and Island (Facsimile Reproduction), Vol.I, op.cit.*, p.172.

23 S.M. Edwardes, *The Gazetteer of Bombay City and Island (Facsimile Reproduction), Volume III, op.cit.*, pp.295-296.

24 M.D. David, *op.cit.*, pp.63-64. For a discussion on the evolution of community-based organisations in Bombay and the hinterland, see Rosalind O'Hanlon, "Historical approaches to communalism: perspectives from Western India" in Peter Robb (ed.) in collaboration with K.N. Chaudhuri and Avril Powell, *Society and Ideology: Essays in South Asian History*, Oxford University Press, Second Impression, Delhi, 1994.

the time to be run along similar lines, as is borne out by the fact that a Hindu music club functioned in the Kalbadevi area in 1868, and a subscription-based Muslim music club organised gala nights featuring women performers, who entertained members and their friends.[25] But these clubs were of an informal nature and the ambience at their concerts was similar to the relaxed atmosphere at concerts held at the private homes of wealthy patrons. It was only with the establishment of the Parsi Gayan Uttejak Mandali that the concept of a formal music club took seed in the city.

Parsi Gayan Uttejak Mandali[26]

Kaikhushro Navrojee Kabrajee (1842-1904) (hereinafter Kabrajee), a novelist, playwright and journalist, took the lead in establishing the Parsi Gayan Uttejak Mandali (hereinafter Mandali) at New Foras Road on October 1, 1870. Kabrajee had been the Editor of the *Parsi Mitra* before he went on to occupy the same position with the *Rast Goftar*. Through the columns of the *Rast Goftar* and as founder of the Mandali, Kabrajee sought to propagate music education and performance among Parsi families. An intellectual who represented the catholic approach that many of his contemporaries shared, Kabrajee was Member of the Bombay Municipal Corporation, Member of the British Institute of Journalists and a Fellow of the Bombay University (1882). He was associated with the Victoria Theatre Mandali until 1875, and later, started his theatre troupe called Natak Uttejak Mandali. He staged Ranchodbhai Udayram's play *Harishchandra*, which gained considerable popularity to the extent that 1100 shows were staged in that period.[27] He was also Secretary of the Guzrati Dnyan Prasarak Mandali, a branch of the

25 P.F. Kapadia, *op.cit.*, p. 15. See also S.M. Edwardes, *The Gazetteer of Bombay City and Island (Facsimile Reproduction), Vol.I, op.cit.*, p.189.

26 Unless otherwise mentioned, this section is based on information provided in P.F. Kapadia, *op.cit.*, and in Aneesh Pradhan, "Cultural Interaction and Social Change: The Contribution of the Parsi Gayan Uttejak Mandali to North Indian art music in Bombay" in Miriam Dossal and Ruby Maloni (ed.), *State Intervention and Popular Response*, Popular Prakashan, Bombay, 1998.

27 H.D. Darukhanawala, *Parsi Lustre on Indian Soil–Vol.I*, *op.cit.*, p.303. Also see, M.D. David, *op.cit.*, p.165.

Students' Literary and Scientific Society, for the years 1872 to 1873 and 1873 to 1874.[28]

The first Working Committee included Khurshetjee Nasherwanjee Cama (Chairman-1870-1885), Jeejeebhai Jehangeerjee Lam (Treasurer-1870-1872), Kaikhushro Navrojee Kabrajee (Honorary Secretary-1870-1881), Mancherjee Maherwanjee Narielwala, Mancherjee Sohrabjee, Baheramjee Faramjee Madraswala, Maneckshah Dhanjeeshah Doctor and Dadabhai Maneckjee Shethna. Jamshetjee Khurshetjee Cama was nominated to the post of Vice-Chairman in 1887 and continued in this capacity until 1894.[29]

The formation of the Mandali came at a time when reform in education was a major point on the agenda of the educated elite in the city. Hence, the Mandali found among its benefactors, eminent individuals from this section like Sohrabjee Shapurjee Bengallee (1831-1893) and Dadabhai Naoroji (1825-1917). A leading journalist, author, social reformer, Bengallee held several important public positions. A member of the 'Young Bombay' group, Bengallee was a staunch advocate of social reform. He started a monthly magazine *Jagat Mitra* in 1850, which was devoted to critical discussions on various social issues. In 1851, he started a monthly magazine called *Jagat Premi*, aimed at Parsi readership. He edited the *Sanj Samachar* and the *Rast Goftar* and went on to become one of the proprietors of the latter. His advocacy for social reform and progress probably encouraged Kabrajee to approach him for help in forming an organisation dedicated to the popularisation of Hindustani music in Bombay. Bengallee responded by becoming one of the donors of the Mandali.[30] Prominent nationalist and educationist, Dadabhai Naoroji had lectured as Professor at Elphinstone College, Bombay, and at the University College, London. He was Dewan of Baroda (1874-1875), Member of the Bombay Municipal Corporation (1875 and 1883), Justice of Peace (1883), Member of the Bombay Leg-

28 *Report of the Students' Literary and Scientific Society for the Session of 1874-75*, Bombay, 1876, p.13.

29 There is unfortunately no detailed biographical information available on these individuals.

30 For biographical details on Bengallee, see Nowrozjee Sorabji Bengallee, *The Life of Sorabjee Shapoorjee Bengallee, C.I.E.*, "author", (n.d.), pp.7-9, 14-15.

islative Council (1885), and Member of the Liberal Party in the House of Commons (1902). Playing a major role in the founding of the Indian National Congress, Naoroji presided over Congress sessions (1886, 1893 and 1906). He started a newspaper called the *Voice of India* (1883) and contributed frequently to other journals and magazines. His assessment of the impact of colonial political and economic policy on India's national income was known as the 'Drain Theory'.[31] Dadabhai Naoroji frequently advised the Mandali between the years 1870 and 1883 and was made Honorary member on October 11, 1884. He was President of the Mandali for a period of five years from 1885. Members of the mercantile and industrial elite like Sir Dinshah Maneckjee Petit, First Baronet, were among the patrons of the Mandali. A successful businessman, Petit started the Maneckjee Petit Mills in 1860 and was President of the Millowners' Association from 1879-1892.[32] In fact, the Mandali was supported by three generations of Petits namely Dinshah Maneckjee Petit, his son, Bomanjee Dinshahjee Petit and his grandson, Jehangir Petit. Limjibhoy Batliboi, a trader, broker, and Justice of Peace, also supported the Mandali. His portrait was unveiled at the Mandali premises in appreciation of his support and services.[33] Other affluent Parsis also donated to the Mandali in cash and kind.

The Mandali charged a monthly membership fee of three rupees in 1870, a handsome sum in those days.[34] By 1878, the Mandali had ninety members. Public response to the Mandali was encouraging during the first two decades of its establishment. Like other contemporary Parsi organizations, the Mandali also reflected the exclusivist nature by primarily exposing Parsi families to traditional musical knowledge and performance.[35] It was only after 1876 that Hindu guests were allowed to

31 See V.K.R.V. Rao, "Dadabhai Naoroji" in Rafiq Zakaria (ed.), *100 Glorious Years*, Reception Committee of the Congress Centenary Session, Bombay, 1985, p.187.

32 M.D. David, *op.cit.*, p.121.

33 H.D. Darukhanawala, *Parsi Lustre on Indian Soil–Vol.I*, *op.cit.*, pp.528-529.

34 For details on Dinshah Maneckjee Petit, see Eckehard Kulke, *op.cit.*, p.153; M.D. David, *op.cit.*, p.121.

35 For more information on other exclusive institutions, see J. C. Masselos, *Towards Nationalism*, *op.cit.*, pp.39-40.

attend some concerts. Sir Mangaldas Nathubhai, Nanabhai Haridas and other well-known non-Parsis were part of the audience.

Professional musicians like Imdad Khan (d.1880), Raojibuwa Belbaugkar (d.1895), Ali Hussein and his maternal uncle Vilayat Hussein, were engaged as teachers on a monthly salary. Among these, Imdad Khan, nephew and disciple of Muhammad Khan, was an exponent of the Gwalior *gayaki*. Raojibuwa Belbaugkar, a disciple of his father and Zainulabdeen Khan of Hyderabad, was a *dhrupad* exponent.[36] In later years, the Mandali appointed on its teaching staff other musicians like P.R. Lisbo, Haji Mia Sarangiwala, Purshottam Bhikaji Tabalchi, Bhai Pherozeshah Master, Nazir Khan, Ganesh Vishwanath Manerickar, Vazir Khan and Rahim Khan.

In an unfavorable social climate, the Mandali took the radical step of featuring amateurs along with professional musicians in its periodical concerts called *jalsas*.[37] After an initial reluctance to sing in public, the students gradually began performing under the auspices of the Mandali. Some of the early amateur singers were Cawas Hormusjee Gandhibhai, Mancherjee Maherwanjee Narielwala, Maneckjee Hormusjee Barbhaiya, Mancherjee Sorabjee, Kaikhushro Navrojee Kabrajee, Maneckshah Dhanjeeshah Doctor and Dadabhai Pestanjee Workingboxwala.[38]

Formal private and public *jalsas* were organised on Fridays and Saturdays. Some of these marked Parsi festive occasions. The first public *jalsa* was held on August 1, 1874, followed by two others on January 23, 1875, and March 11, 1876. Another public concert was organised at the Novelty Natak Shala on November 24, 1895, to mark the Silver Jubilee Year of the Mandali. Reportedly, the theatre was packed to capacity on this occasion.[39]

---

36 S.N. Ratanjankar, *Pandit Bhatkhande*, National Book Trust, India, New Delhi, 1967, pp.8-9.

37 These *jalsas* are not to be confused with those featuring women performers described in the earlier chapter.

38 There is unfortunately no biographical information available about these individuals.

39 *Gayan Uttejak Mandali: Taa. 28 mee April 1871 thee taa 18 mee December 1886 sudhee jalsaaomaa gawaaelaa gaayanono sangraha*, (hereinafter *Gayan Uttejak*

In 1887, the Mandali published a compilation entitled *Gayan Uttejak Mandali: Taa. 28 mee April 1871 thee taa 18 mee December 1886 sudhee jalsaaomaa gawaaelaa gaayanono sangraha*. The compilation contains song-texts of 1100 vocal compositions that had been performed at the Mandali *jalsa*s between 1871 and 1886.[40] Despite the absence of any musical notation, these compositions provide clues about the musical sensibilities of the members, the manner of presentation, the content that was taught, the selection of concert repertoire, the teaching methodology, and the performance capabilities of the amateurs.

As is apparent from this compilation, each of the *jalsa*s organised between the years 1871 and 1886 included between thirteen and forty-eight compositions. Each of the public *jalsa*s included as many as many as nine compositions.[41] Unfortunately, this source does not mention the persons involved in selecting concert repertoire or the factors that may have inspired their decisions. Detailed improvisation and elaboration of so many compositions in a single concert would not have been possible, but the decision to introduce such variety may have been driven by the need to reach out and cater to diverse audience preferences. The Mandali or its teachers may have also wanted to focus on students acquiring diverse compositions, rather than consciously focusing on musical elaboration that was the mainstay of Hindustani music. It was a convention for professional musicians to incorporate several hundred compositions from established forms of Hindustani music like *dhrupad*, *khayal*, *tarana* and *thumri*, but the Mandali seems to have extended that practice to include compositions that did not belong to such genres. Though a majority of compositions in each *jalsa* were based on a particular *raag*, the desire to present different forms of art, folk and religious music in a single evening indicates an open and non-hierarchical approach towards musical forms. Indeed, it is equally possible that the students were not competent enough to elaborate each piece. Whatever the reasons, the obvious deviation from the traditional format of presenting Hindustani music may have encouraged amateurs to take to

Mandali), Gayan Uttejak Mandali, Bombay, 1887, pp.145-146, 157-159, 178-183.

40 *Gayan Uttejak Mandali, op.cit.*

41 *Ibid*, pp.178-183.

performing without being bogged down by technicalities and subtleties that a conventional performance would have otherwise demanded. But the Mandali's policies concerning repertoire and presentation does not seem to have had any direct impact on performance practice followed by professionals.

A closer examination of the repertoire presented at the first *jalsa* held on April 28, 1871, illustrates the diversity of musical forms. Thirty items were performed on this occasion.[42]

RAAG	FORMS
Yaman Kalyan	1 *dhrupad*, 1 *chatarang*, 1 *khayal*
Jhinjhoti Pahadi	1 *tappa*
Kalyan	1 *ghazal* (Persian?), 1 *khayal*
Jhinjhoti	1 *thumri*
Kalyan	1 *ghazal* (Khurshand), 1 dadra
Jhinjhoti	2 *horis*
Kalyan	1 *lavni* (with *jhul*) (Hindi-Marathi mix), 1 *pad* (Kabir)
Janglo	1 *garba* (Narmad)
Ingraji gayan	"Just before the battle mother"
Khamach	1 *khayal*
Ingraji gayan	"Beautiful star in heaven so bright"
Jhinjhoti	1 *tappa*, 1 *hori*
Bhopali	1 *ghazal* (Persian – Khakani)
Todi	1 *tillano* (words, mnemonic syllables from *pakhawaj*, dance, and *sargam* – this *tillano*, surprisingly, has no *tarana* syllables, which are the mainstay of such compositions)
Kalingdo	1 *ghazal* (Wali)
Kahanaro	1 *khayal*
Asavari	1 *ghazal*
Bhairavi	1 *pad* (Surdas)

42 *Gayan Uttejak Mandali*, *op.cit.*, pp.1-15.

Desh	1 *ghazal* (Zafar)
Pilu	1 *tappa*, 1 *dadra*
Jhinjhoti	1 *ghazal*

A report on the Mandali activities entitled *Gayan Uttejak Mandali: Teni Poni Sadini Tawarikhno Ahewal* (hereinafter Report) published in 1946 provides a list that is at variance to the one given in the compilation of 1887. The Report states that the concert was divided into three sections and included thirty-six compositions. The first section consisted of thirteen song-forms based on *raag* Kalyan. The following section entitled 'instrumental *gat*', contained a *tillana* in *raag* Khamaj played by an instrumental ensemble. This section indicates that the Mandali presented ensembles that included Indian and Western instruments. The ensemble in this case included pianoforte, harmonium, violin, mini-flute, *sarangi*, and was accompanied by *tabla*. The second section also contained eleven other songs sung in *saki* style, an English song and readings from Dickens and a Gujarati text. The concluding section consisted of repertoire selected by members.

Notwithstanding the differences in the description of repertoire in the two sources, it is clear that the *jalsa* included a variety of forms. The Report also demonstrates that the Mandali was influenced by Western music and encouraged the inclusion of Indian and Western instruments in a single ensemble, something that is commonly seen today but is considered to be a recent occurrence. In the same way, it would be unimaginable for most to consider *sargam* or *swar maalikaa* compositions as part of concert repertoire today. These compositions did not use poetic text and instead employed the abbreviated name of each *swar* to represent the structure of the *raag* and as an introduction to the concept of *taal* and musical form. Indeed, such compositions were not known to have been performed by professionals, and were probably considered pedagogic tools. But the Mandali seems to have given importance to *sargam* or *swar maalikaa* compositions and included these in its *jalsas*. *Suravartana*, a term synonymous with *sargam* or *swar maalikaa*, has been mentioned elsewhere as a genre included in existing concert repertoire. These compositions may have been used as tools to equip students with the intricacies of *raags*. Or else, beginners found these compositions easier to handle, rather than the more complex pieces.[43]

Interestingly, although *swar maalikaa* compositions were added to Mandali concerts, the compendium of 1887 and most other compilations published in this period only included poetic texts without any notation. This probably reflected the lack of importance given to notation in printed works. But in 1909, the Mandali seems to have changed its course, when it published Bhatkhande's *Swar Maalikaa*, a collection of *swar maalikaa* compositions notated in the system he had devised.[44] Later, the Mandali also published the Gujarati translation of Bhatkhande's *Hindustani Sangit Paddhati*. This change needs to be seen in the context of the predilections that influenced the founders of the Mandali and other like-minded individuals. The assertion of a national cultural identity was accompanied with a strong need to prove India's ability to be on par with Western culture. This desire was also reflected in efforts to disseminate music, as was seen in the case of the Mandali, which held that the traditional oral transmission method was inadequate and that there was a need to introduce a system of notation in the classes. The idea of introducing notation in its classes may perhaps have been prompted by the inclination of the English-educated Mandali members to incorporate aspects of Western music, a system belonging to the colonial rulers whose connection with India was seen as divinely ordained. But on another level, the growing national consciousness may have prompted these members to prove that Indian music could be notated just like Western music.[45] The impact of the West was also seen when Kabrajee proposed the introduction of Western harmony and rhythm in Indian music. He believed this would rectify defects that he thought existed in Indian music and would thus make it acceptable

43 Balwant Triumback Sahasrabuddhe, *op.cit.*, p.9.

44 Mr. Vishnu Narayan Bhatkhande, *Swar maalikaa*, (Gujarati), Bombay Gayan Uttejak Mandali, Bombay, 1909.

45 See preface of Mr. Vishnu Narayan Bhatkhande, *Swar maalikaa*, *op.cit.* For a brief discussion about the prevalent views on the merits and demerits of using an indigenous system of notation and the Western system, see Charles Capwell, "Musical Life in Nineteenth-Century Calcutta as a Component in the History of a Secondary Urban Center", in *Asian Music*, Vol. 18, No. 1 (Autumn - Winter, 1986), University of Texas Press, Austin, 1986, pp. 139-163.

to European ears. Such was the attitude, despite the fact that the Mandali had been established to propagate traditional Indian music. This admiration for the Western system led the Mandali to start a class for Western music in 1875.

The inclination to emulate the West was not surprising, since nascent national consciousness during that period among most intellectuals including social reformers, with a few exceptions, was tempered by an overriding belief that colonial rule was 'Divine Providence'.[46] This belief was amply reflected in the Mandali through special items that were presented to express the members' loyalty to the British Crown. In 1882, a National Anthem Committee was set up to establish "God Save the Queen" as the National Anthem in India. This was to be accomplished by engaging specific Indians to translate the Anthem in various local languages. Kabrajee was assigned the task of translating the Anthem into Gujarati. His Gujarati version was sung at a function held at the Framji Cawasjee Institute in the presence of Sir James Fergusson, the Governor of Bombay. It was later sung on other occasions and in the Mandali *jalsa*s.[47] Later, at a *jalsa* held on February 23, 1884, a eulogy to Lord Ripon, the Viceroy of India, composed by Kavi Firoze Batliwala, a member of the Mandali, was presented as a *hori* set to *raag* Kafi. Notably, the Indian community regarded Lord Ripon's stint as a successful and benevolent Viceroyalty, as was represented by Justice K.T. Telang in his speech at the meeting convened by the Sheriff in the Town Hall on November 29, 1884, to honour Lord Ripon on his retirement:

> Whether we look to the popularity which his Lordship has won among the people over whom he has borne sway for he last four years, or whether we consider the various measures of his administration, the conclusion is forced upon all unbiased minds that Lord Ripon's Government has been most successful . . . Whether we look at the repeal of the Vernacular Press Act or the resolution for making public the aims and scope of Government measures, or the practice of inviting people's opinions on contemplated projects, or

46 For a detailed analysis of this belief, see J.V. Naik, "Perceptions of the British Rule in Maharashtra: A Selective Study", in A.J. Quaisar and S.P. Verma (ed.), *Art and Culture: Endeavours in Interpretation*, Abhinav Publication, New Delhi, 1996, pp.107-118.

47 Charles Capwell, "Sourindro Mohun Tagore and the National Anthem Project", *op.cit.*, pp.407-430.

whether we look to the great scheme of local self-government . . . we see clearly the liberal policy of Lord Ripon's Government.[48]

Kavi Batliwala's *hori* echo these sentiments and is reproduced below with a translation:

Satya nemkee hori rachaee,
Dhanya laayee Ripon chaturaayee.
Bhale pita aap bhaye Hindke – diye bhaagyako jagaayee,
Prem preetse sabko udhare – rai rank ek thaayee;
rahye teri nazare samaayee.

Jaati bhedko bed na jaano – rakhalee sabson sagaaee,
Satya nyayako gulaal udaake – jash pichkaaree chalaaee;
rangmein hindko bhigaaee.

Kheteemein khedut jash gave – ghar ghar baaje badhaaee,
Kahaten koee so karat nahee hai – tumne kahee nahee kaaee;
gup chup karke bataaee.

Kaarkhaanemein hunnar naache – udhyam phagvaa gaaee,
Pardesho jo loot lagaa dhan – lejaatethe bhaaee;
rakhee sab hyaanhee kamaaee.

Svet chaamko daam ek kar – rakhee nahee sarsaaee,
Kaalese ab nahee vo aale – dhoon garvakee udaaee;
apakshapaat raajya chalaaee.

Raaj kaaj phir diyo hindko – angrejee baadshaaee,
Sakal lok prabhuson yun kahave – de aayushya badhaaee;
binatee Firoze sunaaee."[49]

Truth and order tint the colours of this Holi!
Praise be to the sagacity of Ripon, benevolent father figure to Hind,
The land whose destiny you have rewritten,
And for whose people, prince and pauper alike, you are a loving saviour.

Caring nought for barriers of caste
On each you shower your affection,
Showering truth and justice like the colours of gulaal
You drench the land of Hind with your eminence.

---

48 K.T. Telang, *Selected Writings & Speeches*, Gaud Saraswat Brahmin Mitra Mandal of Bombay, Bombay, 1916, pp. 202-208.

49 *Gayan Uttejak Mandali*, *op.cit.*, p.374-375.

The farmer sings your praise
As he toils in the fields,
And there is merry making and festivity in every home.
Unlike others who boast of their achievement where there are none
You say nothing but silently let your actions speak for themselves.

Our mills and factories yield gold in plenty
Yet our wealth is robbed and sent to alien shores.
But now, you have ordained that we keep that which we reap.

You govern without discriminating
Treating the fair skinned and the dark as equals.

You bring prosperity to Hind
Under British sovereignty,
There is a prayer on every lip
Asking for you the boon of a long and healthy life,
Says Firoze with humility.[50]

Furthermore, the Mandali even organised a programme on February 15, 1887, to celebrate the Golden Jubilee of Queen Victoria's ascension to the throne of England.

On the issue related to music education for women from non-hereditary musician families, the Mandali's efforts were path-breaking though not very successful. Through his editorials in the *Rast Goftar*, Kabrajee urged Parsi families to permit their womenfolk to study music, stating that music education for girls at the schools' level should not be restricted only to *garba* songs, but must also include *raag*s with *taan*s and *aalaap* in vocal and instrumental forms. His advocacy of music education for women came at a time when Parsi women were not permitted to sing even in the presence of their family members.[51] This was not easily achievable as conservative sections opined that Parsi women once trained in music would lead an immoral life. But Kabrajee provided a chauvinistic explanation for his support to music education for women. He believed, a girl with a trained voice would serve her parents and husband well and would prevent men from visiting prostitutes,

50 I am grateful to Shubha Mudgal for this translation.

51 For social taboo on public performances by women not belonging to families of hereditary women performers, see Rev. M.A. Sherring, *Hindu Tribes and Castes, Vol.I*, *op.cit.*, p.274.

as they would now be entertained at home. Not only did his statement reflect the social restrictions imposed on women, but it also highlighted yet again the fact that professional women performers were stigmatized as prostitutes. However, even with his prejudiced view, Kabrajee could not convince the Mandali to start classes for women. The Mandali, thus, remained a male preserve, and only allowed the public appearance of Parsi women in the audience. A special programme held on the occasion of the Parsi *papeti* festival featured female singers. It immediately drew criticism from a gentleman by the name of Mansukh, who later claimed claimed that older girls were made to sing songs that contained objectionable lyrics. Kabrajee denied this and clarified that girls between the ages of five and ten sang devotional and *garbi* songs. While it is not clear from available information whether Kabrajee's stance was a statement of fact or was defensive, it prompted him to file a defamation suit against Mansukh. Pherozeshah Mehta, the eminent lawyer, represented Kabrajee and won the case. The Mandali also met with criticism from newspapers like *Jame jamshed* and *Mumbai Samachar.*

Clearly, social taboo along with the Mandali's administrative lapses delayed the implementation of the original agenda, and it was only in 1912 that the Mandali decided to give an opportunity to Parsi women, boys and girls, to learn and perform music. In fact, classes for them were advertised as late as in 1924. The Mandali was slow in reacting to the changing conditions of women in the country. Curiously, the taboos associated with women performers, did not prevent the Mandali from including song-texts and forms that were decidedly erotic.[52] To illustrate the point, here are a few lines in Hindi from a bi-lingual (Hindi-Marathi) *lavni* in *raag* Kalyan that was performed in the first *jalsa*:

Mere piyaa kaa navrang baag chali main khelan ko
Phool rahee phulwaaree champa kalee aayee bahaaranko
Gaflat kar bichavene kaataa aag bhayee tan ko[53]

A literal translation would read as follows:

52 For complete song-texts of pieces presented at Mandali *jalsas*, see *Gayan Uttejak Mandali, op.cit.*

53 *Ibid*, pp.5-6.

> In the nine-coloured garden owned by my beloved, do I go to frolic
> The flowers bloom and the budding *champa* indicates that it is spring
> But as I remained inattentive and careless, the scorpion's sting burns
> my body as if on fire[54]

Obviously, the scorpion's sting, like Cupid's arrow, suggests a heightened state of love, desire or arousal.[55]

Contrary to the taboo that existed against public performance of Hindustani music by 'respectable' Parsi women, there were some instances of Parsi women involved in Western music as students, performers, and teachers, during the same period and more so in the early twentieth century. Thus, a concert held in November 1872 to honour the then Viceroy, Lord Northbrook, featured a vocal music recital by a Parsi woman. The main performer on this occasion was Senor Maras, a musician of European origin. Similarly, Bhikhaiji L. Palamkote (1867-?) was a notable Parsi lady to be actively involved in Western music. A pianist from 1885 and Professor of Music from 1890 to 1935, she was Life Academic Member of Trinity College of Music, London. She trained several students, 218 of who were successful in the examinations held by the Trinity College of Music, London, between the years 1901 and 1935. A Life Member of the Parsi Writers' Association, her efforts at popularizing the study of Western music among Parsis are evident from the fact that she presented Rs.25,000/- to the Trinity College of Music, London, to provide prizes and gold medals for Parsi Zoroastrian candidates securing highest marks in the Diploma Examinations held by the College in India. She also organized sixteen concerts between the years 1912 and 1935 and gave in charity Rs.41,662/- raised from these concerts.[56]

54 I am grateful to Shubha Mudgal for translating these lines.

55 Jürgen Wasim Frembgen, "The Scorpion in Muslim Folklore" in *Asian Folklore Studies, Volume 63, 2004*, pp.95–123, http://nirc.nanzan-u.ac.jp/nfile/631, October 31, 2013.

56 H.D. Darukhanawala, *Parsi Lustre on Indian Soil:-Lives and Portraits of Professionals, Historians, Scholars, Educationists, Parsi Religionists, Philanthropists, Politicians, Officials, Reformers, Pioneers, Industrialists, Merchants and others of The Past and Present, Vol.II, op.cit.*, p.231.

Other Parsi women and men also showed keen interest in Western music. Mary M. Kanga, a Licentiate and Fellow of the Trinity College of Music, London, in piano playing, Ardeshir Muncherji Khodaiji (1864-1916), Professor of Music, Jehangir Ardeshir Khodaiji, Director of Music, and Jal Jehangir Khodaiji, Conductor for Khodaiji's band. The three Khodaijis were certified by the Trinity College of Music, London. Cursetji Jamshetji Ardeshir Wadia, was a well known composer with several pieces to his credit. After his early training under German musician Stuckel, he continued his studies under Bombay-based Italian pianist Giovanni Scrinzi. The British Broadcasting Corporation's Symphony Orchestra and the Jerusalem Symphony Orchestra performed Wadia's compositions. All India Radio also broadcast some of his works.[57]

The reasons for the involvement of Parsis in Western music would need to be examined separately elsewhere, but this engagement is not altogether surprising, as many Parsis sought to maintain close business and social links with the British, and perhaps chose to adopt Western conventions.[58] It was, therefore, logical that a more liberal approach was adopted by the community with regard to the association of Parsi women with Western music. Ashok Ranade draws a class distinction between those patronizing Western and Indian music when he states, ". . . the Parsi-support to Indian culture seems to have followed a pattern: the higher middle class went for 'Indian' entities while the higher aristocracy looked to the west."[59] But as has been mentioned earlier, wealthy Parsis also supported the Mandali.

The Mandali changed its premises several times. It moved to the Queen's Road (1876), later to Zoroastrian Building at Chikalwadi, to Khetwadi, to Adi Mansion at Gowalia Tank, and then to Zaiphalwadi on Motlibai Street, Tardeo. The Mandali continued its activities well into the twentieth century, but the public response to the Mandali's activities was not as encouraging as the period between the 1870s and

---

57 *Ibid*, pp.157, 233, 150,152.

58 Zenobia E. Shroff, *Contribution of the Parsis to the Development of Education and Social Change in Bombay City (1820-1920)*, PhD thesis, Dept. of History, Wilson College, Bombay, 1987, pp.267-268.

59 Ashok D. Ranade, *Maharashtra: Art Music*, *op.cit.*, p.74.

1890s. The Mandali could not muster as much support for itself as it was essentially a Parsi organisation. The twentieth century also saw an increasing westernisation among affluent Parsis leading to the lack of their support to the Mandali. In 1911-12, the Mandali decided to start free music classes for needy but interested Parsis from outside Bombay and began *dilruba* classes in 1928. These projects could not however withstand the decline that had crept into the activities of the Mandali. Games and feasts overshadowed musical activities. This, in addition to the rising popularity of other music organizations, led to the loss of the Mandali's pre-eminent position in this sphere. The decreasing support and the rising costs of maintaining the organisation, forced the Mandali to move its premises on a number of occasions.

The year 1924 proved to be a critical juncture in the very existence of the Mandali. By this time, the Mandali had relieved most of the teachers from service. Addressing a meeting held on February 24, 1924, Kaikobad Adenwala, the President of the Mandali, predicted that the membership would further decrease in future. As per his proposal, the Mandali was closed down and all its assets were formed into a trust for promoting music.

Bombay Branch of the Poona Gayan Samaj

Like Bombay, other parts of western India also fostered institutions of intellectual pursuit. The case of Poona is of particular relevance here. According to historian J.C. Masselos, "By the mid-1870s Poona's professional, administrative and educated men had noticeably begun to make an impact upon its pattern of life. They were responsible for the establishment of a variety of institutions and for their subsequent growth. The Native General Library, previously inadequate and struggling, was invigorated while the Prarthana Samaj, founded in 1870, and the elocution association, in 1868, likewise gained strength . . ."[60] Thus, in 1874, Mahadeo Moreshwar Kunte founded the Poona Gayan Samaj in Poona with the help of Balwant Traimbak Sahasrabuddhe, Anna Gharpure and Balwantrao Ketkar. Unlike other music clubs where musicians did not really enjoy any decision-making status, the Samaj saw

60 J.C. Masselos, *Towards Nationalism*, *op.cit.*, p.173.

Balkoba Natekar (1855-1910), disciple of his father and Wazir Khan (son of the Hapud Nizam) play an integral role in its activities. Natekar gave several concerts and delivered speeches under the auspices of the Samaj. The Poona Gayan Samaj started a music school for boys on January 1, 1879. Branches of the Samaj were formed in Bombay, Madras, Baroda, Wadwan, Bhavnagar and Kolhapur, with patronage from British officials, Indian royalty, and commercial, industrial and intellectual elite. The Bombay branch was called the Bombay Branch of the Poona Gayan Samaj, and the Madras branch was called the Madras Jubilee Gayan Samaj.[61]

The chief objectives of the parent organization included the setting up of a platform for music performances in order to provide musicians with financial support and to give them a respectable place in society. On the social level, the Samaj sought to bring about a closer interaction among its members and entertain them with performances. Driven by national consciousness the founders of the Samaj stressed the indigenous identity of the music they were propagating and the need to continue its existing character.[62]

The parent organisation was inextricably linked to Bombay in matters of patronage. Its main patrons included *shetia*s of Bombay in addition to princely patrons like the Maharajas of Baroda and Travancore and a few Europeans. The Nabob of Janjeera and Jamshedjee Nusserwanjee Petit of Bombay paid an annual subscription of Rs.100/- each. The members included graduates from the Bombay University and reputed citizens of Poona.[63]

The Bombay branch was established in 1883 under the patronage of Sir Mangaldas Nathoobhoy, Knight, C.S.I., Rao Bahadur Lokhitạ-

61 Balwant Triumback Sahasrabuddhe, *op.cit.*, pp.44-50. Also see Vamanrao Deshpande, *Between Two Tanpuras*, Popular Prakashan, Bombay, 1989 (trans. By Ram Deshmukh and B.R. Dhekney from Marathi original *Aalaapini*, with addition of piece on Bhimsen Joshi), p.158, Govindrao Tembe, *Maazhaa sangeet vyaasang*, *op.cit.*, p.24, and note prepared by S.V. Gokhale in the last mentioned source.

62 Balwant Triumback Sahasrabuddhe, *ibid*, p.34.

63 *Ibid*, p.43, 40.

wadi Gopalrao Hari Deshmukh, among other Indians and Europeans. This branch arranged to regularly teach over thirty boys in Bombay.[64]

The formation of the Indian National Congress followed soon after in 1885, and the growing awareness of nationhood seems to have been experienced to some degree in the musical sphere. The presentation of music from South and North India on the same platform at a function held in 1886 by the Bombay Branch of the Poona Gayan Samaj perhaps reflected the gradual evolution of a pan-Indian consciousness. This function included a lecture on Indian music followed by Carnatic music recital on the *veena* by M. Venkatesh Shastri of Madras as well as a vocal rendition by a Hindustani music practitioner, at the Jagannath Sankarshet House, situated on Girgaum Road in Bombay. There seems to have been an informal collaboration between the Parsi Gayan Uttejak Mandali and the Samaj, as Kabrajee moved the vote of thanks to Shastri. Kabrajee's remarks on the occasion, favouring the incorporation of harmony in Indian music and utilizing aid from European music without losing national identity, once again demonstrated his fascination for European music, his desire to make indigenous music suitable for European listeners, and his belief in a common Indian national music. Sir William Wedderburn, known for his candid pro-Indian stance despite his association with British bureaucracy, was invited to chair the session. His efforts to develop friendly ties between Britain and India found voice in his comments on Indian music at this occasion. He stated that his interest in Indian music had increased after listening to several performances held under the aegis of the Samaj and other institutions, and that he felt assistance from 'scientific' European musicians would reveal the common basis of the European and Indian systems of music, thus strengthening ties between the two.[65] Reporting his speech, the Bombay Gazette mentions, "He believed that for music, as for other matters, India had a well-defined national genius, and if, as has been observed, the object was to develop that genius and not to weaken it, it must be strengthened by outside influences."[66]

64 *Ibid*, p.50. Also see J.C. Masselos, *Towards Nationalism*, *op.cit.*, p.173.

65 Balwant Triumback Sahasrabuddhe, *op.cit.*, pp.66-73.

66 Reproduced in *ibid*, p.73.

Contrary to Wedderburn's responsive comments about Indian music and the absence of any reference to Indian music being impacted by political conditions in the country, the Samaj seems to have taken a strongly communal approach to interpreting Indian music history. Thus, in his address at the annual meeting of the Samaj's Madras branch, Rama Row stated:

> Hindu music, after a stage of excessive elaboration, sank under the Mahomedan dynasties into a state of arrested development . . . Under the ordeal of Mahomedan conquest, Hindu music was nearly crushed out of life and the patronage, if at all, afforded was very feeble. Wherever Mahomedans went in India, music became a degraded employment, an accomplishment fit only for the stroller and the dancing-girl. A few learned Hindus preserved in retirement the traditions of their ancient art. Political influences, absence of encouragement and other adventitious circumstances tended to bring about a degeneracy in the noble art of music, and owing to the neglect of this science by persons who were talented enough to foster and develop it, but who either from disinclination to make it their special study, or from want of encouragement, had to give it up, it sank into obscurity with no efforts made to revive, and much less to improve it.[67]

Holding successive Muslim rulers to blame for the ostensible degeneration of Indian music, the speaker went on to shower praise on colonial rule for saving indigenous culture:

> It is fondly believed that in placing this country under the British rule, the All-disposing Providence designed that the civilization of the West should regenerate and renovate the civilization of the East, and that the regeneration of the country was wisely entrusted to that illustrious band of British statesmen to whom this country owes already debt of gratitude.[68]

In an effort to acquaint his readers with the basics of Indian music, Gopal Hari Deshmukh, an important voice among social reformers of the time and a patron of the Samaj, woefully mentioned that ancient music had disappeared, that it had been replaced by the musical rendition of Urdu poetry written under 'Muslim' rule, and that musicians had forgotten the contribution of Narada and other ancient music theorists and had instead proclaimed Tansen, the court musician in Akbar's

67 *Ibid*, pp.82-83.

68 *Ibid*, p.83.

court, as the ultimate guru of musical knowledge.[69] As was the case with the general middle-class critique of professional musicians, Deshmukh also labeled professional musicians as a vice-ridden and intoxicated lot, though in this instance, he did not categorise them as Muslim musicians.[70]

This prejudiced approach was clearly influenced by the colonial writing of Indian history that defined various periods in Indian history on a communal basis.[71] Though there were probably many among the elite who shared this belief, the obvious hybridity of Hindu and Islamic influences experienced in Hindustani music and the fact that many of its practitioners were Muslims did not lend much credibility to this argument or did not seem to have impacted the position of professional musicians in society in a positive or adverse manner. At any rate, Bombay did not seem to share the prejudiced view of the Poona Gayan Samaj. Muslim musicians in the city continued to play an integral role as performers, teachers and composers. Far from 'sanitizing' Hindustani music of its Muslim connections, of its erotic song-texts, or even of its connection with *tawaif*s and *devadasi*s, contemporary literature and oral histories suggest that Bombay experienced the effects of this perspective only marginally.

Some more music clubs like the Arya Gayan Rakshak Mandali, the Shripad Sangit Shala, the Albert Music Club, the Saraswat Gayan Samaj (1896) and the Trinity Club (1904-05), were established in Bombay, perhaps inspired by the success of their predecessors.[72] The Trinity Club was situated in the Mugbhat Lane and continues to have its office premises there to this day.[73] Evidently, the Bombay and Poona experience inspired others to start music clubs in neighbouring areas, apart from the

69 See Gopal Hari Deshmukh 'Lokhitwadi', "*Sangeetshastra*" in Anant Kakba Priyolkar (ed.), *Lokhitwadikrit Nibandhsangraha: Gopal Hari Deshmukh*, (Marathi), Popular Prakashan, Mumbai, 1996, p. 521.

70 *Ibid*, p.524.

71 See James Mill, *op.cit.*; W.W. Hunter, *The Indian Empire: Its People, History, and Products*, Trübner & Co., Ludgate Hill, Second Edition, London, 1886.

72 P.F. Kapadia, *op.cit.*, P.43. See also, Ashok D. Ranade, *Maharashtra: Art Music*, *op.cit.*, pp.66-67.

73 B.R. Deodhar, *Thor sangeetkaar*, *op.cit.*, p.79.

branches of the Poona Gayan Samaj mentioned earlier. For instance, Kolhapur saw significant club activity in the form of the Karveer Gayan Samaj (1883) and the Deval Club (1893). Members of the Deval Club gathered every evening and entertained themselves with music. Gradually, professional musicians also joined the gatherings.[74] The Dharwad Gayan Samaj was established at Dharwad in 1896.[75] Closer to Bombay, the Kalyan Gayan Samaj was started by Kakasaheb Barve in 1926.[76]

It is debatable whether music clubs helped raise the status of musicians in society, but they created awareness about music among members and non-members, and prepared an audience among the urban elite. This in turn democratised the listening experience by paving the way for concerts that were open to the public. Music clubs were thus, responsible for taking early steps to make public patronage of Hindustani music a reality.

---

74 See footnote prepared by N.V. Joshi in Govindrao Tembe, *Maazhaa sangeet vyaasang, op.cit.*, p.52. Also see, http://www.devalclub.org/history.htm

75 Ashok D. Ranade, *Maharashtra: Art Music, op.cit.*, p.67.

76 *Kalyan Gayan Samaj: Amrut Mahotsav (1926-2001)*, Kalyan Gayan Samaj, Kalyan, 2001. Also see, http://www.kalyangayansamaj.org/kgsaboutus_eng.html

MUSIC SCHOOLS

Brought up in a university environment, the educated elite was predisposed to supporting a system of music education that would reflect institutionalized Western pedagogy. Apart from establishing music clubs, they also sought to include music in the curriculum for schools that they set up. In Calcutta, Sourindra Mohan Tagore was actively involved in incorporating music in the regular school curriculum. Thus, a specially appointed teacher paid by Tagore taught boys in the Calcutta Normal School vocal music.[1] Tagore also wrote a book on vocal music in Hindi on the request of C. Browning, the Director of Public Instruction in the erstwhile Central Provinces. This was accepted as a textbook with government sanction.[2]

In Bombay, the Students' Literary and Scientific Society (hereinafter SLSS) formed by the Professors and students of the Elphinstone College in 1848 to spread awareness about education, tried to include music in the academic curriculum of schools established by the Society. The Managing Committee of the SLSS planned to open a special singing class in each of its schools under the superintendence of Narayan

1 Surendra Mohan Tagore, *Public Opinion and Official Communications about the Bengal Music and its President*, *op.cit.*, p.230.

2 *Ibid.*

Vishwanath Shastri.[3] The *Report of the Students' Literary and Scientific Society* described the subject thus, "A simple Educator on singing &c especially adapted to the females of this country."[4] Prizes of Rs.200 were offered for small Marathi and Gujarati treatises on music and drawing.[5]

The SLSS did not stop at introducing music as a subject in its schools, but also encouraged its female students to sing at the school prize distribution functions. One such function was held at the garden-house of Mangaldas Nathubhai on December 13, 1862, and was presided over by Sir Bartle Frere. Girls sang some *garbee*s, of which was one was dedicated to Queen Victoria.[6] In 1874, an exhibition and prize distribution function for the students of the Girls' Schools of the SLSS was held at the residence of Venayekrao Juggonathjee Sunkersett, which was presided over by Maharaja Tukojirao Holkar. Students sang Marathi songs on this occasion.[7]

The emphasis on music education for girls in the SLSS schools came at a time when young girls and women from 'respectable' families were forbidden from learning music and performing. The exact nature of the repertoire that was taught and the teaching methodology in the SLSS schools is not known, but the SLSS schools seem to have focused on teaching songs like *garba*s and Marathi songs. For instance, the Fort School of the SLSS taught *garba*s as part of the school curriculum for Classes I and II.[8] It is not known whether this was a well-planned strategy to introduce repertoire that would have found general acceptance,

3 *Report of the Students' Literary and Scientific Society, and of the Vernacular Branch Societies, together with the Reports of the Girls' Schools for the Session of 1862-63*, Bombay, 1863, pp.7-8. See also, *Report of the Students' Literary and Scientific Society for the Session of 1871-72*, Bombay, 1874, pp.5-6.

4 *Report of the Students' Literary and Scientific Society, and of the Vernacular Branch Societies, together with the Reports of the Girls' Schools for the Session of 1862-63, op.cit.*, p.8.

5 *Ibid.*

6 *Ibid*, pp.10, 22.

7 *Report of the Students' Literary and Scientific Society for the Session of 1873-74*, Bombay, 1875, p.10.

8 *Report of the Students' Literary and Scientific Society, and of the Vernacular Branch Societies, together with the Reports of the Girls' Schools for the Session of 1862-63, op.cit.*, pp.39-40.

but it is possible that these songs may have been overtly religious and may have therefore not provoked the ire of staunch reformists, as would have been the case if *raagdaari* compositions consisting of sacred and profane themes were taught.

Music lessons at the SLSS schools seem to have run into problems in later years, as is evident from the repeated observations in subsequent reports of the Society about the declining quality of singing and the need for a good music teacher. In 1869, examiners mention that while the quality of chanting was maintained well in the Bhau Daji Girls' School at Loharchal, it had fallen below required standards in the Jagannath Sankarsett Girls' School on Palao Road and at the Bhagwandas Purshottamdas Girls' School on Kalbadevi Road.[9] The examination committee further added, "The want of a singing master cannot but be sadly felt."[10] In 1870, examiners commented on the falling standards after the discontinuation of Narayan Vishwanath Shastri's services. They stated:

> Singing has generally declined very much. But the school No.II made an extremely bad appearance in this subject. Since the time the services of Mr. Narayan Shastri as superintendent of singing were dispensed with, it has gradually declined, and we are afraid unless an effort be made to secure the services of a skilful but respectable gentleman to superintend its study, the girls will not make any improvement in that branch.[11]

The direction to engage a 'skilful' but 'respectable gentleman' reflects the prevalent social stigmatization of professional musicians.

There was also a growing concern regarding the lack of funds for music classes. In his report for 1871-72 to the Annual Meeting of the SLSS held at the Elphinstone High School on July 20, 1872, Vishvanath Narayan Mandlik, the Secretary, records:

> The subject of providing a singing master to teach both vocal and instrumental music to the pupils of the Society's schools had occupied the serious attention of the Managing Committee; and they had engaged the services of

9 *Report of the Students' Literary and Scientific Society for the Session of 1868-69*, Bombay, 1870, p.6.

10 *Ibid.*

11 *Report of the Students' Literary and Scientific Society for the Session of 1869-70*, Bombay, 1871, p.6.

> a gentleman of considerable attainments and established reputation to undertake the task in addition to superintending all the schools generally. The Secretary had succeeded in obtaining special pecuniary assistance for this purpose for two years, at the end of which period want of funds alone suspended this portion of the Committee's labours. During the time however that this additional assistance had been procured, this branch was so well attended to, that the pupils made considerable progress in vocal music. A small treatise in Marathi on instrumental music was published by the Secretary at his own expense; but owing to the closing of the singing classes, no further progress has been made in this department. The Committee are most anxious to reopen the singing classes, but want of funds is one of their great difficulties.[12]

The SLSS efforts were remotely linked to a detailed study of Hindustani music, and it was only much later that schools truly incorporated music in their curriculum albeit to a limited extent. There were other schools in the city, which also included music as part of the curriculum, but these were rare instances and did not necessarily incorporate Hindustani music. For example, the Alexandra Native Girls' English Institution established in 1863, included singing and playing on the pianoforte as subjects in the curriculum.[13]

The restricted dissemination of music through clubs and regular academic schools necessitated the formation of special music schools expressly devoted to teaching music. The success of such institutions depended upon their ability to fulfill the interests and expectations of the educated elite that was accustomed to the ways of the Western educational system – a system that was based on a well-defined syllabus, that evaluated students and awarded them degrees, that gave importance to theory and textual sources, that ensured regularity and punctuality in classes, and provided for mass-based training, all of which were pillars of modern education.

In 1880, Maharaja Sayyajirao Gaekwad supported a music school set up in Baroda headed by Maula Baksh Ghisse Khan (1833-1896), a member of a *jagirdar* (landowner) family of Bhiwani and a disciple of Ghasit Khan. Conversant with South Indian and Western musical

---

12 *Report of the Students' Literary and Scientific Society for the Session of 1871-72*, Bombay, 1874, pp.5-6.

13 Zenobia E. Shroff, *op.cit.*, p.144.

systems, Maula Baksh had also made a study of the treatises at Tanjore.[14] Sourindro Mohun Tagore's efforts at setting up a music school in Calcutta have already been mentioned earlier. Relevant to this study, were the paths pursued by Vishnu Narayan Bhatkhande and Vishnu Digambar Paluskar, both of who chose Bombay as a fulcrum for their educational activities. Recognizing the needs of the educated elite and the opportunities afforded by the modern intellectual environment to propagate the study and performance of music among non-professionals, they worked towards standardising musical knowledge, creating teaching institutions and designing frameworks for wider dissemination of music on a national level.

Vishnu Narayan Bhatkhande[15]

Born in Bombay, Vishnu Narayan Bhatkhande began studying music as a child, but his association with the Parsi Gayan Uttejak Mandali gave him an opportunity to listen to and learn from several musicians. Like many of his contemporaries from the English-educated Indian intelligentsia, Bhatkhande was influenced by Western scholarship. Western authors writing on European music demonstrated links between their musical system and ancient Greek culture based on information in old treatises. He felt the need to similarly establish an association between ancient Samvedic music and the music of his times. The lack of easy access to old Indian treatises and the absence of wider comprehension of these texts, made him acutely aware that it was necessary to have a plausible and demonstrable explanation to establish an association between ancient music theory and contemporary practice.

14 See Laxminarayan Garg, *op.cit.*, pp.306-307; B.R. Deodhar, *Thor sangeetkaar*, *op.cit.*, pp.82,84; Vamanrao H. Deshpande, *Indian Musical Traditions: An Aesthetic Study of the Gharanas in Hindustani Music*, *op.cit.*, p.148; Vilayat Hussein Khan, *op.cit.*, pp.13-14. See also http://wahiduddin.net/mv2/bio/Biography_3.htm for a biographical sketch of Maula Baksh. Another source mentions that Maula Baksh's school was established in 1881. See Joep Bor and Philippe Bruguierre, *Masters of Raga, Meister Des Raga, Les Maitres Du Raga*, Haus der Kulturen der Welt, Berlin, p.40.

15 Biographical details for Vishnu Narayan Bhatkhande included here, are from P.N. Chinchore, "*Sangeetoddhaarak P. Bhatkhande meri drishti mein*" in *Bhatkhande smriti granth*, (Hindi), *op.cit.*, pp.52-57, unless otherwise mentioned.

Bhatkhande was a product of times when social reformers revisited Sanskrit treatises and reinterpreted them incisively to bolster their perspective. In Bombay, as mentioned by historian J.C. Masselos, members of the Bombay-based Widow Marriage Association established in 1861, used Hindu Dharmashastras "... to influence and develop key sections of public opinion by using an indigenous framework of argument. The ideas suggested by a Western education may have triggered the debate but their formulation was indigenous".[16] It was not entirely surprising therefore that Bhatkhande chose to republish old Sanskrit treatises and also adopt Sanskrit as a medium for some of his books. Bhatkhande acquired during his first tour to the South, the manuscript of *Chaturdandi Prakashika* by Venkatmakhi, from Subram Dixitar, a descendant of Govind Dixitar and Venkatmakhi. He procured copies of *Raag Lakshana*, Ramamatya's *Swara-mel-kalanidhi*, Tulajendra's *Sangeet Saramrit*, and printed and published them in Bombay making them available to the public for a nominal price of 4-8 annas each.[17] He wrote *Shrimallakshya Sangeetam*, *Abhinava Ragamanjari* and *Abhinava Talamanjari* in Sanskrit, and composed Sanskrit *shloka*s under the pseudonym Bharatpurvakhandanivasi Chaturpandit and published them in *Lakshyasangeet*.[18]

But Bhatkhande discovered a disparity between information provided in ancient treatises and the nature of current performance practice. With a view to understanding contemporary theory and practice of music, Bhatkhande closely observed the grammar that was followed by vocalists. He was of the opinion that though performers did not support their *raag* interpretations with any documentary evidence, they explained the rules and adhered to them.[19] He embarked on tours across the country to establish contact with local musicians and scholars. He prepared a list of patrons, music clubs and libraries, located in these areas before his travels. Armed with preliminary queries, he listened

---

16 J.C. Masselos, *Towards Nationalism*, *op.cit.*, p.92.

17 S.N.Ratanjankar, *Pandit Bhatkhande*, National Book Trust, India, New Delhi, 1967, p.18.

18 *Ibid*, pp.21-25.

19 S.N. Ratanjankar, "*Jeevan charitra*" in *Bhatkhande smriti granth*, *op.cit.*, pp.16-17.

to music, procured the required information and made copious notes, after meeting local patrons, musicians, scholars, and music lovers.

In his lectures held at the Mandali between 1890 and 1905, he stressed the need to modify the existing system of music education.[20] Having experienced university education, Bhatkhande was keen to introduce the same paradigm of standardized mass learning to the study of music. Crucial to modern pedagogic methodology was the creation of textual material that could be put to use in schools and made accessible to the general public. The printed word was in fact an integral part of the nineteenth century intellectual climate that had produced numerous books and periodicals catering to different sections of Indian society and addressing various issues of social significance. For instance, in Western India, the Marathi, Gujarati, and Anglo-Marathi and Anglo-Gujarati press contributed greatly to creating a vibrant intellectual environment in the Bombay Presidency.[21] Obviously influenced by this situation and based on his interactions with different musicians, Bhatkhande sought to draw out the essential characteristics of current musical practice and establish a uniform approach for dissemination. He collected several hundred vocal compositions from various sources such as Ashiq Ali Khan, and his father Muhammad Ali Khan of Jaipur, from the 'Manrang' tradition, Eknath Pandit (c.1870-1950) of the Gwalior tradition, Ganpatibuwa Bhatt (d.1927), disciple of Balkrishnabuwa Ichalkaranjikar, Vasudeobuwa Joshi and Krishnashastri Shukla.[22] He notated these compositions using a new system of notation that he had evolved and codified afresh the grammar of Hindustani music and *raag* rules based on the study of these compositions.

---

20 *Bhatkhande smriti granth, op.cit.*, pp.486-487.

21 J.C. Masselos, *Towards Nationalism, op.cit.*, pp.28, 31-33, 59, 79, 88. Also see, Nowrozjee Sorabji Bengallee *op.cit.*, pp.7-9, 14-15. For more periodicals in the Bombay Presidency, see also *The Bombay Calendar and Almanac for 1853, op.cit.*, pp.274-275. For a detailed discussion on intellectual pursuits as represented in Marathi newspapers and major publications during the first half of the nineteenth century, see J.V. Naik, "The Seed Period of Bombay's Intellectual Life, 1822-1857" in Sujata Patel and Alice Thorner (ed.), *Bombay: Mosaic of Modern Culture, op.cit.*, pp.64-72.

22 S.N. Ratanjankar, "*Jeevan charitra*" in *Bhatkhande smriti granth, op.cit.*, p.41. See also, Laxminarayan Garg, *op.cit.*, pp.135-136.

He was inspired to compile, analyse, notate and publish this material and several compositions that he acquired from the Mandali teachers and other sources in order to provide standardised texts for teaching music to amateurs on a mass-scale.

Thus, in approximately 1915, Bhatkhande started publishing traditional compositions with notations in a series of monthly pamphlets called *Geeta Maalikaa* at a price of 4 annas each. Twenty-three parts of these pamphlets were printed and were published by the Bombay Samachar Press.[23] His six-part textbook series *Kramik Pustak Maalikaa* contained compositions collected and learnt from different artistes and standardized and notated by him. His penname Harrang and Chatur appear in his compositions.[24] Four volumes of *Hindustani Sangeet Paddhati* in Marathi, and two English books entitled *A Comparative Study of the Music Systems of 15th 16th, 17th and 18th Centuries*, and *A Short historical Survey of the Music of India*, written by him were published between the years 1908 and 1933. His unpublished works include travelogues, diaries, letters and some compositions.[25] In 1911, he published his *lakshan geet*s. A booklet of hundred *swar maalikaa* compositions in popular *raag*s and *taal*s was published in 1911.[26]

Informed patrons and musicians had published works on Hindustani music well before Bhatkhande and Paluskar began their work. Nineteenth century Bengal saw the publication of important works on music like *Sangeet Taranga* (1832) by Radhamohan Sen, *Swaralapi Gitimala* in two volumes (1897) by Jyotirindranath Tagore, *Sangitsar, Kanthakaumudi, Ashuranjani, Gitagovinda Swaralipi* by Kshetramohan Goswami (1813-1898), and *Gita Sutrasar* (1885-1886) containing *dhrupad*s and *khayal*s notated in the Western system by Krishnadhan Bandyopadhyay.[27] *Sangita Ragakalpadrum* (1842) by Krishnananda

23 S.N.Ratanjankar, *Pandit Bhatkhande, op.cit.*, pp.21-25.

24 Vamanrao Deshpande, *Between Two Tanpuras, op.cit.*, pp.159-160, 163-164.

25 *Ibid.*

26 S.N.Ratanjankar, *Pandit Bhatkhande, op.cit.*, pp.21-25. It is not clear if Ratanjankar is referring to the book published by the Mandali in 1909. See Mr. Vishnu Narayan Bhatkhande, *Swar Maalikaa, op.cit.*

27 Sukumar Ray *Music of Eastern India: Vocal Music in Bengali, Oriya, Assamese and Manipuri with special emphasis on Bengali*, Firma K.L.M. Private Limited, Calcutta,

Vyas was a compilation of song-texts from multiple languages.[28] S.M. Tagore wrote several books on music like *Kanthakaumudi, Sangita Sara, Yantrakshetradipika.*[29] But, Bhatkhande's compilations of traditional compositions had far-reaching consequences. His work froze a living entity by removing the music from its essential interpretative and improvisatory context, but it was a major contribution as it helped to preserve traditional information and enabled an easier dissemination of musical knowledge on an institutionalised basis.[30] Indeed, Bhatkhande had not claimed that his compilations would enable students to elaborate on the compositions. Besides, the oral tradition had also never completely excluded written sources. Musicians maintained written records of compositions, which had been passed down from generation to generation.[31] However, there were essential differences between these written works and those documented by Bhatkhande. The former were skeletal frameworks of the repertoire, accessible only to those having written them or to members of their family and disciples. Bhatkhande's works were on the other hand open to anyone curious about musical knowledge and equipped to comprehend his system of notation.

Bhatkhande's system of notation was adopted by the Mandali. After 1916, Bhatkhande started a music class called the Shri Sharada Sangit Mandal in the premises of Good Life League, a Parsi organisation situated at Nanabhai Lane, Flora Fountain. His disciple Vadilal Shivram, assisted him in the teaching.[32]

2nd ed., 1985, pp.7-8, 101, 184,185,296. Also see, V.N. Bhatkhande, *A Short Historical Survey of the Music of Upper India, op.cit,*, p.37; http://www.bpedia.org/T_0019.php and http://www.banglapedia.org/HT/G_0176.HTM

28 V.N. Bhatkhande, *A Short Historical Survey of the Music of Upper India, op.cit,*, p.37.

29 *Ibid.* Also see, Laxminarayan Garg, *op.cit.*, p.69.

30 For a detailed discussion pertaining to written texts and their role in Indian society, see Satish Saberwal, "Segmentation and Literacy" in *Economic and Political Weekly*, Vol.XXVI Nos.11 and 12, Annual Number 1991, Sameeksha Trust, Bombay, 1991, pp.723-738.

31 Ashok D. Ranade, *On Music and Musicians of Hindoostan*, *op.cit.*, p.38. Also see N. Jayavanth Rao, *op.cit.*, pp.44-47.

32 S.N. Ratanjankar, "*Jeevan charitra*" in *Bhatkhande smriti granth*, *op.cit.*, pp.16-17, 36.

Apparently, Bhatkhande was instrumental in introducing music as a subject in the regular schools' curriculum. The Bombay Municipality introduced music as a subject for Primary schools following a suggestion from Bhatkhande. The Municipality requested him to train musicians to teach according to his methodology, for which Teachers' Training classes were held at the Mandali.[33] Maharaja Madhavrao Scindia of Gwalior also ordered music classes to be held as per Bhatkhande's system in primary, pre-middle, middle and normal schools.[34]

Bhatkhande hoped to include music as a subject in the University curricula. He stated:

> The first step then in the work of revival of our Northern music has been attempted by me and my labours have so far resulted in a fair measure of success. I feel happy at the thought that I have been able to mould a model for my successors to improve upon and to perfect; and I cannot but hope that in a few years more there will be an easy system for the instruction of our music, which will lend itself to mass education. Then will the ambition of India be fulfilled, for then the Indians will have music in the curricula of their Universities and music instruction will be common and universal.[35]

Around April 1925, Bhatkhande reiterated his hope, in a letter to leading barrister M.R. Jayakar, a member of the Bombay University Reform Committee. Jayakar succeeded in getting Bhatkhande's graded course incorporated in the Report of the University Committee.[36] The women's university set up in Bombay by D.K. Karve offered music as a subject at the degree level. Manjulabai Mehta of Baroda, one of the twelve women who were awarded their graduation degrees in Art in 1926, had opted for music as a subject and Bhatkhande was her examiner.[37]

---

33 S.N. Ratanjankar, *Pandit Bhatkhande*, *op.cit.*, p.34. According to B.R. Deodhar, it was due to the efforts of V.D. Paluskar that music was introduced as a subject in the syllabus of Primary, Secondary schools and colleges. See B.R. Deodhar, *Thor sangeetkaar*, *op.cit.*, p.128.

34 Sobhana Nayar, *Bhatkhande's Contribution to Music*, *op.cit.*, p.185.

35 V.N. Bhatkhande, *A Short Historical Survey of the Music of Upper India*, *op.cit.*, p.50.

36 M.R. Jayakar, *The Story of My Life, Vol. II, 1922-1925*, Asia Publishing House, Bombay, 1959, p.568.

37 Margaret E. Cousins, *The Music of Orient and Occident: Essays towards mutual understanding*, *op.cit.*, pp.169-170.

Arguably, Bhatkhande had his set of supporters and critics from among hereditary practitioners. Many musicians did not welcome his work as they felt the dissemination of music among amateurs was a threat to their professional interests as performers and teachers.[38] On the one hand, steps taken by Bhatkhande could be explained as a democratizing process, which made musical knowledge that was traditionally the preserve of hereditary musicians and courtesan families, now available to the general public. But, it could equally be argued that this was an appropriation of knowledge that rightfully belonged to these families, thus creating a trajectory for Hindustani music that was far removed from that envisioned by its hereditary practitioners and also robbing them of their livelihood as teachers. Their involvement in Bhatkhande's activities was often decided by their patrons, as and when they chose to support Bhatkhande, or was motivated by a need to procure different professional opportunities in the institutionalized framework. For instance, Nawab Ali Khan, *talukdar* of Akbarpur in Uttar Pradesh, sent his employee Kale Nazir Khan to Bombay, to understand Bhatkhande's system and learn his *lakshangeet*s. Nawab Ali Khan learnt these compositions from Kale Nazir Khan and incorporated them in his book *Marif-un-Naghmat*.[39] Similarly, Maharaja Madhavrao Scindia of Gwalior sent six music teachers and one dance teacher to Bombay to have discussions with Bhatkhande and to learn his system, before Bhatkhande set up his first music school called the Madhav Sangeet Mahavidyalaya in Gwalior in 1918 under Scindia's patronage. Not satisfied with the traditional method of oral transmission and the emphasis on performance, Bhatkhande introduced a separate study and examination for theory, a fact that perhaps antagonized practitioners. But hereditary performers took up employment at the Marris College of Music founded by him at Lucknow in 1926, an institution that executed the syllabus drawn up by him.[40]

38 B.R. Deodhar, *Thor sangeetkaar*, *op.cit.*, p.33. Also see Joep Bor and Philippe Bruguierre, *op.cit.*, p.67.

39 Vamanrao Deshpande, *Maharashtra's Contribution to Music*, *op.cit.*, p.42.

40 *Ibid*, pp.36-37,99. See *Bhatkhande smriti granth*, *ibid*, pp.126-127; Vilayat Hussein Khan, *op.cit.*, pp.13-14; Vamanrao H. Deshpande *Between Two Tanpuras*, *op.cit.*, p.160; Sobhana Nayar, *op.cit.*, pp.184-185. See also Susheela Misra, *Music Makers of*

Balkrishnabuwa Kapileshwari reports explicit public action taken by several senior musicians in a meeting held at the Forbes Gujarati Hall, Bombay, in 1936. They had apparently gathered to register their protest against Bhatkhande's statements related to music theory and to condemn the incorrect information included in a Marathi book on music theorists and practitioners entitled *Sangeet shaastrakaar va kalaavant yaanchaa itihaas*. Kapileshwari suggests that the book written by Lakshman Dattatreya Joshi was based on information provided primarily by Bhatkhande. According to Kapileshwari, two resolutions were passed on this occasion. The first one tabled by vocalist Faiyaz Khan, disciple of his maternal grandfather Ghulam Abbas Khan and the latter's brother Kallan Khan, who presided over the meeting, tabled the first resolution regarding Bhatkhande's system of notation and his statements. Manji Khan tabled the second resolution, which urged musicians to seek legal opinion individually in case they found wrong information about their lineage in Joshi's book.[41]

But this reported public protest does not take away from the fact that there were some musicians who supported Bhatkhande and even collaborated with him. For instance, Nazir Khan, employed on the teaching staff of the Parsi Gayan Uttejak Mandali, interacted with Bhatkhande in Bombay. He learnt *lakshangeet*s composed by Bhatkhande and taught them to women performers learning from him, who in turn went on to add them to their concert repertoire.[42] According to vocalist Vilayat Hussein Khan (1895-1962), disciple of Karamat Hussein Khan, Ghulam Haider Khan alias Kallan Khan (1835-1925) and several others, Bhatkhande contributed greatly to Indian music by compiling and publishing notated versions of numerous compositions that he procured from various parts of the country after overcoming several obstacles. Remembering his friendship and meetings with Bhatkhande on

---

the Bhatkhande College of Hindustani Music, Sangeet Research Academy, Calcutta, 1st ed., 1985, for an account on the teachers in the Marris College, which came to be later known as Bhatkhande College.

41 Balkrishnabuwa Kapileshwari, *Shrutidarshan*, (Marathi), Continental Prakashan, Pune, 1963, p.214.

42 S.N. Ratanjankar, "*Jeevan charitra*" in *Bhatkhande smriti granth*, *op.cit.*, pp.15-16,18. See Govindrao Tembe, *Maazha sangeet vyaasang*, *op.cit.*, pp.74-75, 79.

the Chowpatty sands in Bombay, Vilayat Hussein Khan recounts Bhatkhande having often told him that he was merely an author but that music-making was the prerogative of the musicians.[43]

Contrary to this recognition of the practitioners' privilege, Deodhar recounts a conversation that was an overt display of Bhatkhande's prejudice. On being asked by a gentleman to write in English, Bhatkhande had replied that the British never wrote their treatises in Marathi for Marathi-speaking people. Hence, anyone wishing to read and understand his works would need to learn Marathi. The gentleman then requested him to translate his works into Hindi-Urdu. Bhatkhande answered that the Hindus had completely lost the art of music and the art was with the Muslims who would not part with it without service to them, in spite of the fact that the art belonged originally to Hindus. Bhatkhande argued that he had written in Marathi, as he believed that the practical aspect might not have remained among the Hindus, but that they would at least have control over the theory. He felt if Hindus were thus empowered, they would give explanations about *raag* rules and the Muslims would be wary of them. If not as singers, the Hindus would at least be respected as *pandits* – scholars.[44] This seemingly curious juxtaposition of rational thinking and communal bias was also revealed in Bhatkhande's writings. His analysis of Hindustani music history reflected the representation of India's past by colonial historians:

> The most convenient method of dealing with the history of Hindusthani music appears to be to divide the subject into three distinct periods, *viz.*, (1) the Hindu period, (2) the Mahomedan period, and (3) the British period. Each of these periods may again be sub-divided, if necessary, into two divisions, *viz.*, (1) the earlier and (2) the later.[45]

Probably exposed to the colonial interpretation of Indian history, Bhatkhande too upheld the communal periodization of the past. He described the Hindu period as the time from Vedic times to the end of the tenth century AD, the Mahomedan period from the eleventh century AD to the end of the eighteenth century AD, and the British period

43 Vilayat Hussein Khan, *op.cit.*, p.13.

44 B.R. Deodhar, *Thor Sangeetkar*, *op.cit.*, pp.42-43.

45 V.N. Bhatkhande, *A Short Historical Survey of the Music of Upper India*, *op.cit.*, p.3.

from the eighteenth century AD.[46] Believing that the Muslims did not patronize music, he wrote:

> It is not in India alone that the Mahomedan invaders distinguished themselves by their ruthlessness towards music. The history of Persian music after the conquest of Persia by the Musulmans reflects a similar state of things there . . . The Persians, as we all know, had a very ancient civilization and as a civilized nation they possessed a regular music system of their own before the conquest of their country by the Mahomedans in the seventh century.[47]

He believed that Muslim musicians had deviated from earlier musical tradition:

> The Mahomedan rulers naturally patronized at their courts, their own co-religionists as musicians, who knew their tastes much better, and who by pandering to the tastes of their masters commenced to take all sorts of liberties with the orthodox Sanskrit melodies. We are told that many of the first class Hindu Pandits of those times were scared away or ceased in course of time to take the same interest in their science of music as they did formerly . . . A glance at the list of Akbar's principal musicians given in the Ain-i-Akbari will show that among the thirty-six names contained therein, there are not more than four or five which are Hindu.[48]

But curiously he seems to have welcomed changes that were incorporated as a result of foreign influence:

> I shall not deny that the Northern music during those times underwent some vital changes, but I am of the opinion that our music gained considerably from the foreign influence.[49]

Vishnu Digambar Paluskar and the Gandharva Mahavidyalaya[50]

A contemporary of Bhatkhande, Vishnu Digambar Paluskar was a staunch votary of institutionalized music education. His journey was

---

46 *Ibid*, p.4.

47 *Ibid*, p.10.

48 *Ibid*, p.20.

49 *Ibid.*

50 Unless otherwise mentioned, biographical details for Vishnu Digambar Paluskar and information about Gandharva Mahavidyalaya included here, are from B.R. Deodhar, *Gaayanaachaarya P. Vishnu Digambar*, *op.cit.*, and from a biographical sketch on him provided in B.R. Deodhar, *Thor Sangeetkar*, *op.cit.*

challenging as will be seen in the account provided here. While training with Balkrishnabuwa Ichalkaranjikar at Miraj for approximately nine years until 1896, he observed the deplorable, arduous and humiliating situation that musicians faced. He noted that their subsistence depended on support from wealthy patrons and tuition fees procured from women performers. He decided not to approach patrons for seeking performance opportunities and to instead take steps to give music and musicians a respectable status in society and bring them the patronage of the educated urban elite. Influenced perhaps by prevalent social prejudice and probably to cater to the elite, he adopted a high moral ground by emphasising that musicians took to vices because of their proximity to women performers and that it was imperative to train a new set of performers and music teachers who would be vice-free and socially acceptable. In order to gain patronage, he realized the need to establish a system of institutionalized education that met the requirements of the Indian elite.

Paluskar travelled for performances, met influential individuals and gained wide-ranging experience in Aundh, Satara, Baroda, Kathiawad, Gwalior, Aligad, Mathura, Delhi, Jalandhar, Amritsar, Kashmir, Bharatpur, Bikaner, Jodhpur, and in Rawalpindi, Lahore, Okara in present-day Pakistan. He equipped himself with language and oratory skills that he put to use in his educational activities. In Mathura, he studied the grammar and rules of Hindustani music from ancient Sanskrit treatises, but he was convinced that this information was not in consonance with contemporary musical practice, and therefore, did not merit further examination. He devised a system of music notation in 1900, inspired by the Western staff notation that he had studied from James, a bandmaster in Jodhpur.

His first major step in institutionalizing music education came with the setting up of a music school called Gandharva Mahavidyalaya (hereinafter called GM) in Lahore on May 5, 1901. After an initial lukewarm response, more students enrolled and the school received some financial support, enabling Paluskar to set up a printing press, an instrument repair section, and a hostel for resident students. In Lahore, Paluskar set to *raagdaari* music the poems of saint-poets and taught these pieces to young students, to counter any reformist pressure that would criticise the school for teaching traditional repertoire containing erotic content.

In 1907, Paluskar visited Bombay for concerts and to further his educational work. Supported by music enthusiasts and prominent individuals in the city like reformer Sir Narayan Chandavarkar, leading medical practitioner and civic leader Sir Bhalchandra Bhatwadekar (1852-1922), Deshmukh, Bhajekar, Y.V. Nene alias Annasaheb Nene, Treasurer for the Swadeshi motivated Paisa Fund, businessman Sir Muhammad Yusuf Saudagar, Baam Bandhu, S.P. Kapadia, Shrimant Babasaheb Bivalkar, the Dewan of the Alibag Angrias, and Dalal, he established a Bombay branch of the GM in 1908.[51] Soon, the headquarters were shifted from Lahore to Bombay along with the printing press and instrument-making section. Bombay became the epicentre of his educational work, in turn deeply impacting the musical life of the city.

Paluskar was careful in garnering support for his school from the right quarters. He therefore always made an effort to invite influential and respected individuals for all school functions. Thus, Shankaracharya, the Hindu religious head, inaugurated the Bombay branch of the GM. Paluskar's attempts at attracting members of the intellectual elite to his school were apparent in his efforts at restructuring the process of music education by putting in place a series of administrative and teaching policies. Discipline and punctuality were closely monitored. Classes for those not staying in the hostel were conducted from 7 am to 10 am and from 3 pm to 9 pm. Female students were taught only between 3 pm and 6 pm. As Principal, Paluskar remained present in the office and supervised the teachers during teaching hours. Teachers followed a strict dress code. A graded syllabus was put in place, examinations were held at regular intervals, and degrees such as *Sangeetpraveshika* and *Sangeetpraveen* were awarded on completion of the four years and nine years coursework, respectively. Teachers conducted the preliminary examinations and Paluskar conducted the finals. Initially, these examinations met with criticism, but later, they became the order of the day.

51 For information about the Paisa Fund, see *The Paisa Fund Silver Jubilee Number*, Paisa Fund, Poona, n.d.

Gradually, Saraswats, Prabhus, Gujaratis, Parsis, Bohris, and Prarthana Samajists, enrolled as students, as they believed the GM taught music without what they considered were the whims and vices of traditional *ustads*. But the GM faced opposition from orthodox Parsis, who published letters in the Gujarati press claiming that the school carried on immoral activities behind closed doors under the guise of conducting music classes. Paluskar responded publicly that the closed doors prevented classes from disturbing each other, and that this was open for checks with the permission of the Principal. Despite this criticism, Paluskar continued holding classes for women as part of the GM activities.

Paluskar's avowed nationalist stance seen later in his rendition of patriotic songs like *Vande Mataram* at Congress sessions did not seem to cloud his choice of British officials to preside over the GM's convocations. The need to assert the school's stature in the public eye had obviously influenced Paluskar's decision to invite Lord Sydenham, Lord Willingdon and Sir George Lloyd, to preside over convocations held during their tenures as Governors of Bombay. This antithetical approach was noticeable even earlier in 1906, when he sang in Lahore at the public felicitation of George V, during the latter's visit to India as Crown Prince of England. He also decorated part of the GM building in Lahore and played music when George V went by in a procession the next day. Similarly, in 1912, Paluskar received a government order restraining him from performing in Calcutta immediately after the assassination attempt on Lord Hardinge in Delhi. In response, Paluskar announced that the programme was in fact being held to pray for the Viceroy's recovery and for his long life, and that community prayer of this nature had a quicker impact on God. His explanation satisfied the official who had ordered for the closure of the programme. Once again, for Paluskar, such moves perhaps did not seem contrary to his open alliance with the independence movement, and were probably chosen as tactical means to consolidate the GM's position in Indian society.

While in Lahore, Paluskar realized the need to publish and disseminate musical material for easier and wider communication with the educated elite. Accordingly, he established the Sangeet Printing Press, which printed his books and a Hindi magazine entitled *Sangeetamrit-pravaha* started in 1905. The fourteen to sixteen-page magazine containing articles on Sankrit musical treatises, notated compositions, and reports on Paluskar's tours and special programmes held at the Lahore school, had an annual subscription of Re.1/- inclusive of postage, and separate issues were sold for two annas each. But financial constraints forced him to stop this publication in 1916. In 1910, he started a Marathi magazine in Bombay entitled *Gandharva Mahavidyalaya*, but this too was discontinued.[52] Despite his reluctance to rely on textbooks, he introduced them as an aid to teach amateurs, who otherwise would not have been able to learn in the traditional *guru-shishya* format. This was also done to systematize the new pedagogic pattern in the GM and to further consolidate his ties with the intellectual elite. Thus, he published books entitled *Bal sangeet, Bal prakash,* and *Sangeet Bal bodh*, to inculcate an interest in music among children and to teach them *raagdaari* music in a graded manner. His *Swalpaalaap gaayan* was in 3 parts and contained short *aalap*s and *taan*s for compositions that were considered convenient for children to handle. *Mahilaa sangeet* was especially written for women students. Five parts of *Bhajanaamritlahari* had *bhajan*s in Gujarati and Hindi. Twelve parts of *Raag Pravesh* had *raagdaari* music set out in an elementary textbook fashion. *Raag Kalyan, Raag Bhoop, Raag Bihaag, Raag Maalkauns, Raag Bhairav*, were more advanced books on vocal music. Some of Paluskar's publications also reveal his pan-Indian approach to the study of music. For instance, his book entitled *Carnatki Sangeet* contains notated versions of Carnatic compositions that he arranged for some of his students to learn. In Calcutta, he collected some Bengali songs and published them in a book entitled *Bangali Gayan.*

As a performer trying to reach out to a wider audience and as a zealous advocate of the GM activities, Paluskar chose a variety of students' items to precede his recital. Some of these were unusual in the context of conventional Hindustani music concerts. For instance, he engaged the services of a Kathak teacher to train young students to

52 Shankar Ganesh Date and others (ed.), *Marathi niyatkaalikaanchi soochee (1800 to 1950)*, (Marathi), Mumbai Marathi Granth Sangrahalaya, Mumbai, 1969, p.200.

dance on such occasions. Going further, he engaged Manik, a drill instructor from Banaras to train music students in club drill, flag drill and barbell drill, which were then presented with instrumental accompaniment at concerts. He even published the notation of music composed specially to accompany drill, in a book entitled *Vyaayaama ke saath sangeet*. As was his wont, Paluskar maintained strict punctuality during programmes and items were restricted to segments of fifteen to twenty minutes each. The curtain opened at the appointed hour and the concert began with a prayer, obviously in keeping with Paluskar's moralistic approach and his religiosity. This was followed by an array of assorted items like mandolin *jugalbandi*, violin recital, dance, pyramid acrobatics, *mridang* recital, harmonium recital, orchestra, and drill with musical accompaniment. Based on his observations of Western orchestra, Paluskar also composed some *gat*s, which were played in unison by twelve to fifteen instruments. Paluskar's efforts at popularizing Hindustani music did not stop him from incorporating Western instruments and concepts in performances. Clearly, he was open to harnessing every possible tool to attract public attention for his cause. The finale of the concert was an hour-long recital of art music by Paluskar. Once again, his performance also revealed the desire to entertain connoisseurs and lay listeners alike. He did not confine himself to rendition of a single *raag*, but instead, chose Gujarati and Hindi *bhajan*s for a Parsi audience or during Parsi festivals like Papeti, and *abhang*s for Marathi-speaking listeners.

In addition to their performances as part of Paluskar's concerts, students were at times also invited to perform at weddings, thread ceremonies, and feasts, instead of professional women performers who would have otherwise performed on such occasions. For example, impressed by the students' public concerts in 1908-09, Sir Muhammad Yusuf Saudagar decided to invite them to perform at his residence on festive occasions in place of women performers normally featured there.

Through this period, the students' fees and the money collected at concerts increased the school's profits. In a short span of time, the rising number of students could not be accommodated in the GM premises, despite having rented buildings near the Congress House. The success of the Girgaum Backroad classes created a similar demand in other parts. Consequently, a new branch located on the Princess Street was inaugurated by Sir Munmohandas Ramji, the Founder President of the Indian Merchants Chamber on June 30, 1911, at a function held at the Morarji Goculdas Market on Kalbadevi Road.

By 1912, the GM was very successful with support coming from reputable sources. The increase in monthly rent to Rs.500/- compelled Paluskar to explore the possibility of constructing an exclusive building for the GM. The students' fees and the collection from his concert tours took care of the school's expenses, strengthening Paluskar's resolve to develop an independent space. Thus, in 1913, he bought a plot of land for Rs.48,000/- on the Sandhurst Road between Dubash Lane and Angrewadi with a loan from Shrimant Babasaheb Bivalkar. Sir Bhalchandra Krishna Bhatavdekar laid the foundation stone on October 9, 1913 and the building was completed by December 1914. Notwithstanding his nationalist stance, Paluskar invited Lord Willingdon, the then Governor of Bombay to inaugurate the building on January 11, 1915, a strategy that he followed to bring public attention to the GM. The Governor praised Paluskar for his work and urged people to aid this activity.

The planning and design for the new school building accommodated Paluskar's multi-pronged approach to music education, and in many ways, established a norm for similar premises that came up after a few decades. Each floor of the building had a hall, five big rooms, and verandahs in the front and rear. Five rooms on the ground floor housed an exhibition of instruments and classes for instrumental music. The first floor had five rooms for a library, reading room and classes for vocal music. A hall for the prayer assembly was provided on the second floor along with space for the Principal's office and his classes. The third floor had a concert hall equipped with green room facility and a seating capacity of four to five hundred people.

While Paluskar was happy with the new building, he was aware of the amount that had to be repaid to Shrimant Babasaheb Bivalkar. Till 1915, he was confident of repaying the loan amount. The success and prosperity of the school was marked by the fact that the school building was worth Rs. 2,00,000/- and that approximately hundred persons, including teachers and students, were fed daily at the school. But the unforeseen financial crisis during World War I adversely affected the school's financial returns. Bivalkar's amount was returned with the help of engineer N.V. Sukhtankar, who had already supported the school by supervising the construction of the *chhatralaya* in 1916 behind the school, on an honorary basis. Sukhtankar's loan of Rs.70,000/- was in turn repaid with a loan from Vitthaldas Thackersey (d.1923) against a mortgage on the building. By 1920, the loan amount had risen to Rs.1,67,000/-. Hanumanprasad Poddar, a prominent businessman from the Marwari community, collected and presented to Paluskar, a fund of Rs.16,000/- to help the GM tide over troubled times.

The foundation stone of the *chhatralaya* was laid by Narayanmaharaj Kedgaonkar, a religious head, and was inaugurated by Shrimant Babasaheb Ichalkaranjikar. Paluskar's penchant for discipline, regimen and moral values, was even more evident in the day-to-day functioning of the *chhatralaya*. A bell was sounded at 5 or 5.30 am to wake up students in the *chhatralaya*. They had to be ready by 7 am for the group prayer. Attendance at the prayer assembly was compulsory for teachers and students of the *chhatralaya*. Initially, Paluskar led this prayer, but the teachers did so later. The prayer lasted for ten to twelve minutes and thereafter everybody was involved in various tasks. Some taught in the classes, a few taught new students in the *chhatralaya*, and others were involved in *riyaaz*. Paluskar taught senior students. The evening prayer took place at 7 pm. Students in the *chhatralaya* were not aware of the happenings in the music world beyond what happened within the four walls of the GM, as they were not permitted to leave the building, except for specific work. Their sources of information about the outside world were people connected with the GM who would visit them on holidays.

The school trained needy children in a section called the *upadeshakvarg*, and arranged for their accommodation on the GM premises. The students of this section signed a three or six year bond with the school. Paluskar's vision of a holistic education was apparent when students of the *upadeshakvarg* were also required to work for a few hours in the instrument making and repairing section of the school.

Paluskar taught regularly at the GM until 1915, and personally supervised students, with the result that those trained during this period became performers and teachers. Among these were Keshavrao Datar, Narayanrao Khandekar, V.A. Kashalkar, Narayanrao Khare, Raghunathrao Patwardhan, Vinayak Narayan Patwardhan, Shankarrao Pathak, Baburao Gokhale, Vamanrao Padhye, Dhondopant Paluskar, Shankarrao Vyas, Narayanrao Vyas, Vyankatesh Modak, Omkarnath Thakur and Vamanrao Thakar. The successful students were taught and interacted with Paluskar primarily in the *guru-shishya* tradition, despite their enrolment as students in the GM. To that extent, Paluskar had tried to integrate the traditional and modern forms of training. But apparently, there were no students of any significance or repute after 1916-17, as Paluskar was preoccupied elsewhere. Teachers relying on textbooks taught new entrants in the *upadeshakvarg*.

Until 1916-17, annual gatherings for non-residential students were held with much enthusiasm at the Girgaum Backroad GM, with a respected personality presiding over the function. The annual gatherings created a close contact between the school and the outside world.

Paluskar believed students should have the opportunity to learn from any good musician, and it was for this reason that the GM adopted an eclectic approach to music education through its graded syllabus that did not adhere strictly to a particular musical style. This was at variance to the conventional practice of musicians learning from one *guru* for a sufficient period and moving to another only after procuring permission for such a change from the first *guru*. Thus, the GM gave an institutional interpretation and credence to eclectic training. Paluskar employed *sitar* player Ismail Khan, nephew of Barkatullah Khan, on a monthly salary of Rs.100/- and urged the *sitar* students to learn from him. Bhaurav Vatve, disciple of Sardar Ashtewale of Ujjain, also taught *sitar* in the GM. *Shehnai* player Ganpatrao of Baroda was employed for about eight months on a monthly salary of Rs.100/-. Paluskar provided his students with the opportunity of listening to and learning from Gundubuwa Ingle, disciple of Balkrishnabuwa Ichalkaranjikar, and Govindrao Shaligram, disciple of Alladiya Khan. On several occasions, students also heard Bhaskarbuwa Bakhale in concert at the GM.

Paluskar's pan-Indian outlook was once again reflected in his decision to appoint violinist Sundaram Ayyar to teach Carnatic music to students in the *upadeshakvarga*. Ayyar had come to Bombay in 1910 to learn Hindustani music from Paluskar. Paluskar also arranged for some of his students to be taught the *mridangam*. Whether this was a decision driven purely by musical curiosity or if it was the prevalent nationalist sentiment that prompted him to encourage an exchange of musical ideas between practitioners of Hindustani and Carnatic music, is left to conjecture.

Strangely Paluskar's openness in incorporating a variety of influences into the school framework did not extend to any partnership with Bhatkhande, who was working in the same city and for similar goals of standardising music education for mass dissemination. Around 1911-1912, Bhatkhande requested Paluskar to organize weekly lectures delivered by him followed by the GM students' performance of *raag*s that had been chosen by Paluskar and taught to them by Bhatkhande according to his method of *raag* classification. Paluskar agreed to host the lectures, but was skeptical about the number of listeners on such occasions. Always mindful of varying musical tastes, Paluskar wanted the lectures to be interspersed at regular intervals with vocal and instrumental music in order to entertain audiences and familiarize them with the format of the lectures. Bhatkhande disagreed and their differences remained unresolved, but Paluskar maintained that Bhatkhande's research was of great importance. But the nationalistic sentiment they shared, led them to cooperate in foiling an attempt to pass a resolution at a conference, favouring the validity of Western staff notation for Indian music. Edward Charles Clements (1895-1935), a British official appointed in the Judiciary Department of the Indian Civil Service in the Bombay Presidency, and organiser of the conference in Ahmedabad, sought to pass this resolution, but was unsuccessful in his attempt as a result of the two Vishnus collaborating on this occasion.

Aware of the social stigma faced by musicians, Paluskar claimed that he wished to create a band of vice-free and disciplined musicians and teachers. It was perhaps for this reason that Paluskar arranged regular schooling for five students in June 1918 while simultaneously continuing their music training. Of these, B.R. Deodhar (1901-1990), Anantrao Kulkarni, Shankarrao Bodas, completed their matriculation, but Laxman Bodas and Shankarrao Athavale gave up academics and pursued music. It may be noted that a few professional performers also underwent schooling, albeit for a short span of time. Thus, Anjanibai Malpekar was a student at a missionary school at Thakurdwar, where she learnt Marathi and English.[53]

In the course of his stay in Lahore, Paluskar had been introduced to the *Tulsi Ramayan*, and after 1910, he began delivering discourses on the Ramayan across the country. Over the years, he was drawn closer to religion and many regarded him more as a man of God than a singer. Not surprisingly, in 1919, Paluskar gave out part of the GM premises for a *keertan sammelan*. Describing this facet of his life and work, a report that appeared in the *Nizam Vijay*, a weekly published in the princely state of Hyderabad, mentioned Paluskar's weeklong discourse on the *Tulsi Ramayan* at the Gouliguda Ram Mandir, and urged Indians to contribute wholeheartedly to the GM and relieve him of the monetary debts that had confronted him after the initial success of the school. This was followed by yet another weeklong discourse in the Residency Bazaar, which was attended by traders, businessmen, other wealthy individuals and officials. The four to five thousand strong public gathering also included Parsis and Muslims.[54] Paluskar perspicaciously utilized this public space for espousing the cause of music education and in particular the work conducted at the GM. Typically, he would mention the GM's goals and activities during his discourses, and would stress the importance of music education. His students would perform at the same venue in the days immediately following the discourses. Advertisements for these concerts would be displayed and handbills would be distributed. Paluskar would urge audiences to purchase tickets and help the school activities. He would organize a concert in a specially rented theatre or large hall. Reporting on a programme held at

53 From footnote prepared by S.V. Gokhale in Govindrao Tembe, *Maazha sangeet vyaasang*, *op.cit.*, p.64.

54 Reports from *Nizam Vijay* dated 15 January 1924 and 25 January 1924 reproduced in D.P. Joshi (ed), *Kalachya Paddyaad, Vol. 1*, (Marathi), Marathi Sahitya Parishad, Andhra Pradesh, 1992, pp.164-165.

the Vivekvardhini Theatre in Hyderabad on January 4, 1924, the *Nizam Vijay* mentions Paluskar's rendition of patriotic songs and the fact that he urged Hyderabad audiences to attend the forthcoming programme of the male and female students of the GM to be held at the same venue on January 11, 1924.[55] Special programmes were also held in aid of the GM such as the one scheduled at the same venue on January 30, 1924, from 8.30 pm to 10.30 pm.[56]

Paluskar thus established a method for the tours he undertook to spread awareness about music, to raise the status of the art in the eyes of the general public, and to collect funds to support the GM.

Though the public response to Paluskar's work and the GM was good, expenses towards the school activities and the loan amount rose astronomically. Well-wishers offered to help Paluskar, provided the school was registered as a public trust, but Paluskar was against this move. Wishing to remain unfettered, he believed that those sympathizing with his cause had to perforce trust him for the sacrifices he had made since 1896. In 1924, the GM in Bombay had to be closed down due to financial constraints. It was re-established on December 8, 1929, in four rooms rented on the first floor of the Marker Building (later called Govardhan Bhuvan), with Ramkrishna Joshi, a disciple of Paluskar, as the Principal along with four other teachers. But this school did not meet with much success. Later, Dhondopant Paluskar shifted this school to Benham Hall Lane for two to three years, but even that was closed down.

The Gandharva Mahavidyalaya Mandal was started in Ahmedabad in December 1931, by Paluskar's disciples, Narayanrao Khare, V.A. Kashalkar, Shankarrao Vyas and V.N. Patwardhan to continue their *guru*'s work after his death, and its headquarters were based in Bombay. The aim of the Mandal was to conduct examinations for music schools run on the lines laid down by Paluskar, to hold music conferences and to propagate music.

Branches of the GM had been inaugurated in Poona and Nagpur. On June 7, 1912, another branch was opened in Budhwar Peth, Poo-

55 *Ibid*, pp.159-160.

56 *Ibid*, p.166.

na, and the inauguration was presided over by Shrimant Babasaheb Ghorpade, Ichalkaranjikar. The branch was in existence until 1917. In Sept 1913, a branch was opened in Nagpur, and the inauguration was presided over by Sir J. Walker, Financial Commissioner.[57] Inspired by Paluskar's work in the field of music education, other music schools were established elsewhere in India by his disciples and other musicians. These included schools in Karachi, Poona, Kolhapur, Nagpur, Sholapur, Allahabad, Delhi, Jammu, Nasik, Ahmedabad, Amritsar, Kanpur, Banaras and Hyderabad.[58] But in Bombay, it was Deodhar's School of Indian Music, which epitomised the Paluskar model of music education.

School of Indian Music[59]

In 1924, Paluskar prevailed upon his disciple B.R. Deodhar to start a music school in Bombay, despite the latter's initial apprehension. In the following year, Deodhar was requested to compose music for devotional poetry to be sung by children frequenting the Prarthana Samaj in the Rammohan High School building. Later, Deodhar provided organ accompaniment to the children's evening prayers on Sundays. The success of these presentations encouraged Deodhar to request Vasudeorao Bhandarkar, the President of the Samaj, for permission to start a music school in the same building. The Samaj officials granted him permission to conduct classes after 5 pm in three rooms on the first floor.

At the time, Deodhar was also teaching Sunalini Rajam, Sarojini Naidu's sister. He became closely associated with Sunalini Rajam's extended family, and it was during one of Naidu's visits to Bombay that he requested her to suggest an appropriate name for his school. She suggested that the school be called the 'School of Indian Music' (hereinafter SIM).

---

57 B.R. Deodhar, *Gaayanaachaarya P. Vishnu Digambar*, *op.cit.*, p.61.

58 *Ibid*, pp.103-105. Also see, *Pune Swarvishwa '90: Sangeet Mehfil 19 May 1990*, (Marathi), Rotary Club of Pune, Parvati, 1990.

59 This section is based on information provided in B.R. Deodhar, "School of Indian Music", (Marathi), *Deodhar's School of Indian Music, Golden Jubilee Souvenir*, Mumbai, 1975, unless otherwise mentioned.

The school started functioning on July 1, 1925, albeit without a single musical instrument, but Babasaheb Bhajekar helped by giving Deodhar his personal *paay-peti* to begin with. The location of the SIM in a reputed institution like the Prarthana Samaj, inspired confidence among 'respectable' families to enroll their daughters as students, and within a month the school had more than thirty girls learning vocal music. Classes for girls were held every evening from 5 pm to 6 pm, and men were taught from 6 pm to 7 pm and in a special class from 7 pm to 8 pm. Each student was taught thrice a week, with one group attending classes on Mondays, Wednesdays and Fridays, and another on Tuesdays, Thursdays and Saturdays.

Three months later, Shankarrao Athavale, another disciple of Paluskar, offered to teach harmonium at the SIM, a proposition that Deodhar accepted readily, as there was an interest in learning the instrument. He bought five harmoniums for the classes, and soon, several students enrolled for these classes as well. Clearly, the harmonium was rapidly making a permanent space or itself in Hindustani music, despite criticism leveled against it. Interestingly, Deodhar introduced harmonium classes, which was contrary to the stand taken by him and others in 1948 against the instrument later in the context of music education in schools.[60]

The SIM was formally inaugurated by Paluskar at a function held at the Prarthana Samaj Hall on Nov.13, 1925. Those attending the function included several dignitaries, Professors of the Wilson College, and European teachers of the St. Columba High School located at Gamdevi where Deodhar taught for an hour every week. At the inauguration, girls from the SIM presented some songs followed by violin and harmonium recitals by Raghunathrao Patwardhan, a disciple of Paluskar, and Ganeshilal from Nepal, respectively. Paluskar informed the audience about his work and requested them to support Deodhar.

Deodhar seems to have followed Paluskar's technique for bringing publicity to the GM. Thus he maintained close contacts with members of the press during his visits to the Bombay Students Brotherhood, an organization established in 1890 by reformist students of the Bombay

60 For details, see chapter entitled Epilogue.

University. He was particularly close to Sundar Kabaadi of the *Free Press*, who had advised him to invite well-known leaders and dignitaries to the SIM and seek their blessings. Kabaadi prepared and dispatched letters of invitation to such leaders after getting Deodhar to sign them. As a result, within a span of three to four years, several leaders and dignitaries like Sarojini Naidu, Annie Besant, Bipin Chandra Pal, Madan Mohan Malaviya, Babasaheb Jaykar, Sir Govindrao Pradhan, Justice Patkar, Bhulabhai Desai, Sayyad Abdullah Brelvi, visited the school. Deodhar also invited some American correspondents and the interaction with them proved beneficial for his tours of Europe and the USA.

Inspired by the GM's special classes held on Sundays for those who could not afford the fees or for those who were not able to attend on other days, Deodhar conducted a free class from 4 pm to 5 pm every Sunday and publicized it in the press. The class drew twenty to twenty-five students, some of whom went on to enroll themselves as students in the regular school.

Gradually, the number of students and classes increased. Vocal, harmonium and *dilruba* classes had been started. Prahlad Ganu, a student of Deodhar, taught *dilruba*. The SIM retained the services of Nisar Hussein, son and disciple of *been* player Murad Khan, to teach *sitar* for approximately a year. Murad Khan also taught intermittently. Vighneshwar Shastri taught violin in the SIM, and his students V.G. Jog and D.K. Datar became popular performers later.[61]

The SIM celebrated each of its anniversaries with great fervour. Some anniversary functions were held at the Prarthana Samaj Hall, but the growing number of listeners necessitated a larger space. Undoubtedly, until 1932, these programmes were held in the Wilson College Hall, and received press coverage. Deodhar also invited several dignitaries like Sir Govindrao Pradhan, Bhulabhai Desai, Justice Patkar, Justice Mirza Ali, Mirza Ali Muhammad Khan (Vice-Chancellor, Bombay University), Sir A.R. Dalal, McKenzie (Principal, Wilson College), Maharana of Dharampur, Maharana of Porbandar, Pranlal Devkaran Nanji, and Sir George Lloyd, to preside over his school anniversary functions.

61 For more information, see B.R. Deodhar, *Thor sangeetkaar*, *op.cit.*, p.75.

To further propagate music, Deodhar also organized regular concerts under the aegis of the SIM. At first, these concerts featuring vocalists Ganpatrao Purohit, Mehboob Khan 'Daras Piya' of Atrauli, and Vilayat Hussein Khan, *been* player Murad Khan, and harmonium player Govindrao Tembe, were held at the Prarthana Samaj premises. A concert featuring Ramkrishnabuwa Vaze was held at the Brahman Sabha Hall, as a large audience was expected. Thereafter, the SIM held concerts at the Laxmi Baug Hall featuring artistes like Faiyaz Khan and Krishnarao Phulambrikar alias Master Krishnarao. This pattern continued until 1930-1931. The fees offered to the artistes were relatively low, and artistes were apparently satisfied with a fee of Rs.60-Rs.100. But the limited number of listeners forced Deodhar and his students to collect this amount by approaching music lovers individually. Some music lovers liked Deodhar's idea of organizing concerts in this manner, and soon, the Bombay Music Circle was set up headed by Motiram Pai.

In due course, few students including some men and women from 'respectable' families wished to pursue music as a vocation. The restricted duration during the evening classes compelled Deodhar to conduct special classes on Sunday mornings from 8 am to 10 am expressly to train those showing potential to pursue music professionally. Students in these classes included Godavaribai Sathe, Deodhar's elder brother Dattatreya Deodhar, Indu Purohit, Prahlad Ganu and a few others. Shankarrao Deshpande also helped Deodhar in these classes.

The space limitations at the Prarthana Samaj became apparent in a few years, as the three rooms provided by the Samaj were inadequate to accommodate the rising number of students in the evening classes. Classes had to be held even in other rooms of the Rammohan School building. Some Samaj members were not happy with this increased activity and the regular concerts held on the premises. Apparently, the Prarthana Samaj came to be known more as a music school in some quarters. Consequently, the Samaj office bearers moved Deodhar's school to the Sir Narayan Chandavarkar Primary School on Benham Hall Lane in January 1930 and charged a small rent. There was more freedom at the new location and Deodhar started organizing concerts on every Saturday from 5.30 pm to 7.30 pm, featuring the students and staff of the school and some guest artistes. These concerts attracted huge audiences as they were non-ticketed events, but tickets were sold for some performances. Vocalists like Abdul Karim of the Tanras Khan *gharana*, Bashir Khan of Jawra, Master Krishnarao, Rajabhaiyya Poonchwale, S.N. Ratanjankar, and *sarangi* player Bundu Khan, performed here.

During this period, many reputed individuals in the city learnt from Deodhar privately and at the SIM. These included members of the Ruia family, a reputed business household, Leelavati Munshi, wife of educationist Kanhaiyalal Munshi, film actor Devika Rani, and girls from reputed Khoja families who otherwise were in *purdah*. Special classes were conducted for those who were particularly talented. Students like Sumati Oak, Shanta Amladi, Kanchanmala Shirodkar, and others, made progress in vocal music, and Manik Kaabaadi and Leela Samant progressed as mandolin players.

At Benham Hall Lane, the SIM also started *garba* classes conducted by Maniben Manji on Saturdays and Sundays, and *garba* performances also became a part of the school's programmes. This activity was as much an instance of Deodhar's openness to include subjects other than art music, as was it an instance of his making efforts to attract different sections of society to the SIM.

Deodhar would take his students for annual music competitions held at Allahabad. This was probably his way of establishing the SIM credentials as a premier teaching institution in other parts of the country. On one such occasion, the SIM students secured first positions in all age group categories. These students included Chandrashekhar Rele, Atmaram Hardikar, Shanta Amladi, Sheela Pandit, among others. As a result, the SIM's popularity grew outside Bombay.

In 1939, the Sir Narayan Chandavarkar Primary School moved from Benham Hall Lane to Vitthalbhai Patel Road. The SIM also followed suit. However, it was difficult to play musical instruments on small benches in the classrooms. Deodhar decided that it was time to procure an independent space for his music school, rather than conduct classes in other school premises. The monthly rent for the SIM until then was Rs.50/-. In May 1941, Deodhar decided to rent a space on the first floor of the Modi Chambers owned by Manilal Modi. The monthly rent here was Rs.180/-, but it was possible to be seated on the floor in these new premises. Deodhar also moved his residence to a space adjacent to the newly acquired school premises. The new space was inaugurated by Madhobasaheb, the head of the princely state of Kutch. He donated Rs.1000/- to the SIM, which enabled the school to purchase furniture, carpets, instruments and other material. The number of students increased from sixty-seventy to over a hundred and fifty in the span of two months. More teachers were also appointed. In June 1942, Deodhar rented the ground floor of the same building, and the total monthly rent rose to Rs.300/-.

In August 1942, Kumar Gandharva and other disciples of Deodhar decided to observe Paluskar's death anniversary by organizing a large concert. With the help of Vishnudas Shirali, a disciple of Paluskar and the composer for Uday Shankar's ballet troupe, Deodhar invited Ravi Shankar and Ali Akbar Khan to perform for the SIM. Both artistes readily agreed and they performed in a morning concert from 10 am to 1 pm for an audience of hundred or hundred and fifty. This, according to Deodhar, was the beginning of the popularity of these two artistes in Bombay.

The activities of the SIM during the World War II were adversely impacted as Bombay was regarded as a prime target for bomb attacks and annual concerts had therefore to be stopped temporarily. But Paluskar's death anniversary was always observed in a big way. Concerts were held for five days, and vocalists from all *gharana*s were featured here. Vocalists like Vilayat Hussein Khan, Azmat Hussein Khan, Khadim Hussein Khan, Latafat Hussein Khan, and others would gladly perform on these occasions. One year, the programme continued for six days and featured vocalists Bade Ghulam Ali Khan, Bibbe Khan of Hyderabad in Sindh, *dhrupad* singer Tansen Pande, Agra *gharana* vocalists, and *pakhawaj* solo by Makkhan Khan. Ahmed Jan Thirakwa played *tabla* solo four or five times at the SIM and Alla Rakha played *tabla* solo on ten to twelve occasions. The audience response to these concerts was tremendous and speakers had to be placed outside the building at times to accommodate listeners who were standing outside.

Music Classes

Other important music classes in the city included the Maharashtra Sangeet Vidyalaya started at Girgaum in 1926 by Baburao alias Ganesh Ramchandra Gokhale (1893) and the Vyas Sangeet Vidyalaya started in Dadar by Shankarrao and Narayanrao Vyas.[62]

While the Parsi Gayan Uttejak Mandali gradually became less significant in the musical life of twentieth century Bombay, there were other classes catering expressly to Parsis. For instance, Framroze Dhunjishaw Shroff set up The Parsee Music Institute located at Chira Bazar on Girgaum Road in 1921. Shroff played a variety of instruments like harmonium, violin and *dilruba* while at the Coronation Music Club. His Institute therefore included classes for harmonium, violin, *dilruba*, and singing. Separate classes were held for women on Monday, Wednesday and Friday from 6 pm to 7 pm, and on Tuesday, Thursday and Saturday from 11.30 am to 12.30 pm. Classes for men were held from 7 pm to 8 pm. The Institute ran a branch at Dadar exclusively for women students, with classes held on Tuesday, Thursday and Saturday from 4.45 pm to 5.45 pm. Not restricting itself to Hindustani music, the Institute conducted classes for Western instrumental music for men and women from 1932, with Mr. Coutinho of the Universal Band as the teacher. The Institute hosted annual music concerts in addition to conducting regular educational activity. Shroff also taught at Maneck Pardiwalla's Britannia Music Class at Lal Baug since 1934. His classes at the Britannia Music Class were held for women from 6 to 7 pm and for men from 7 to 8 pm on Tuesday, Thursday and Saturday.[63]

---

62 B.R. Deodhar, *Gaayanaachaarya P. Vishnu Digambar*, *op.cit.*, pp.104-105. For biographical details of Ganesh Ramchandra Gokhale, see Arvind Mulgaonkar, *Tabla*, (Marathi), Popular Prakashan, Mumbai, 2nd ed., 1999, p.420. Also see interview with Kaushalya and Dinker Manjeshwar, held on 10 September 1993.

63 See H.D. Darukhanawala, *Parsi Lustre on Indian Soil:-Lives and Portraits of Professionals, Historians, Scholars, Educationists, Parsi Religionists, Philanthropists, Politicians, Officials, Reformers, Pioneers, Industrialists, Merchants and others of The Past and Present, Vol.II*, *op.cit.*, p.234. More information related to the Coronation Music Club and the Britannia Music Club was unfortunately not available. See also, H.D. Darukhanawala, *Parsi Lustre on Indian Soil–Vol.I*, *op.cit.*, p.777.

Thus, the music school paradigm introduced by the GM in Bombay, was well and truly entrenched in the city.[64] Music classes for women started several years after those for men. There may have been many reasons for the increasing number of music classes for women after the 1920s and for 'respectable' women taking to music training in greater numbers thereafter, but obviously, this would not have been possible had it not been for the larger socio-political reality that had transformed the circumscribed public life of elite women to a more open involvement in mass-based movements for national independence. The establishment of formal music schools provided easier access to music education for their social milieu. Be it personal inclination or music becoming a social grace in some circles and a worthy qualification for a woman of marriageable age, elite women joined music schools or learnt in their own homes. For instance, Leelabai Shirgaonkar, daughter of Anantrao Shirgaonkar, an engineer in Bombay Municipal Corporation, initially learnt from Vilayat Hussein Khan and continued her training after 1937 under Alladiya Khan.[65] The late nineteenth century rarely saw professional and amateur women instrumentalists, but after the 1920s, there were some women from elite households who took to learning instruments like the *dilruba*. The *sarangi* was therefore considered profane by the elite, because of its association as an accompanying instrument for professional women performers. There was however the rare case of Lila Mundkur, who learnt the *sarangi* in 1931-1932 from Baburao Kumtakar. In 1940 or thereabouts, she became a student of Hamid Hussein, originally from Rampur-Muradabad, who was her teacher until he migrated to Pakistan in 1947.[66]

---

64 For a brief discussion on early institutionalised music education in Bombay and for a list of clubs and schools involved in Indian music training in the city, see Michael D. Rosse, "Music Schools and Societies in Bombay c.1864-1937" in Joep Bor, Francoise 'Nalini' Delvoye, Jane Harvey and Emmie Te Nijenhuis, *Hindustani Music: Thirteenth to Twentieth Centuries*, Manohar Publishers & Distributors, New Delhi, 2010, pp.313-330.

65 Govindrao Tembe, *Gaayanmaharshi Alladiyakhan yaanche charitra*, *op.cit.*, pp.94-95.

66 Personal communication from Mohini Mundkur, Lila Mundkur's daughter-in-law, sent through Kishore Udipi on 15 January 2000.

Concomitant with Bombay's increasing number of music schools and private classes, similar activities were undertaken in other parts of Western India. This was particularly true in the case of Poona, where the Bharat Gayan Samaj was set up in 1911 with Bhaskarbuwa Bakhale and Govindrao Tembe as the Principal and Secretary, respectively. In 1940, the Poona Gayan Samaj was merged with the Bharat Gayan Samaj. An independent teaching wing of the Samaj called the Bhaskar Sangeet Vidyalaya was started in 1944.[67] Classes like the Gopal Gayan Samaj – Sangeet Mahavidyalaya (1918), the Ghate Sangeet Vidyalaya (1948), and Achpal Music House (1934), were also started in Poona by individual musicians. The Music Department of Poona's SNDT Arts and Commerce College was started in 1944.[68]

---

67 *Pune Bharat Gayan Samaj va Bhaskar Sangeet Vidyalaya: vaarshik vritant (1 April, 1989, to 31 March, 1990)*, Pune, 1990. See also, S.V. Kelkar, *Bharat Gayan Samaj, Pune: San 1911 te 1940 yaa kaalkhandaateel sansthechaa itihaas*, (Marathi), Pune Bharat Gayan Samaj Prakashan, Pune, n.d.; Jayashree Bokil, "*Bharat Samajachi Navvadi*", *Loksatta*, 15 October 2000.

68 *Pune Swarvishwa '90, op.cit.* Also see, Chaitanya Kunte, "*Punyachyasangeetparamparecha ek aitihasik vedh*" in *Punyaswar*, Lalit Kala Kendra, Pune University, Pune, 2009, pp.15-30.

MUSIC CONFERENCES

The restructuring of pedagogy, performance, and musicology, also involved attempts at bringing about a closer dialogue between those working in the three areas through music conferences held in various parts of the country. The conferences sought to bring together musicians and musicologists on a common platform to discuss issues pertaining to the theory and practice of music, at a time when a chasm existed between practitioners and theoreticians. Mirroring in some ways the prevalent political mood and nationalist endeavour, these music conferences aimed at proving to the West and to the Indian intelligentsia that Hindustani music had a scientific basis, that it was on par with Western music, that it was a reflection of a highly sophisticated culture and that it needed to enjoy a prestigious position. Special efforts were made to substantiate that the microtonal intervals in Hindustani music met the standards of Western sciences, and that music presented by bands could be notated with Western staff notation.

Music conferences were positioned as a pan-Indian phenomenon by organisers. Bhatkhande went a step further, favouring a single unified system of music at the Al Indian Music Conference organised by him at Baroda in 1916. He stated:

> And if it please Providence to so dispense that there is a fusion between the two systems of the North and the South, then there will be a National music for the whole country and the last of our ambitions will be reached, for then the great Nation will sing *one* song.[1]

Elsewhere, Bhatkhande stated:

> In my opinion a happy fusion between the two great music systems of the country is most desirable. When it comes on the Hindusthani system will be considerably enriched. Hundreds of beautiful Ragas can be reintroduced here into our system by our leading living experts. The Southern System again will have an opportunity of adopting our northern graces in the Vadi, Samvadi, rules and thereby of making its music much more interesting. All this however, will be the province of Bhavi Sangeet and thus beyond the province of this paper.[2]

But this seemingly pan-Indian approach, bringing together Hindu and Muslim and Northern and Southern musicians and scholars, implied an assumption that Indian music primarily comprised of the two main art music systems, Hindustani and Carnatic. It neglected the plurality that existed in the form of tribal, folk and other musical forms.[3] Women performers also did not largely find representation at conferences. Possibly, organisers of most conferences excluded hereditary women performers because of the social taboo against them.

There are references to a music conference that was held in the 1890s by Shamsher Jang Bahadur, the Maharaja of Nepal. But this seems to have featured a series of concerts without any discussions that were to become an integral part of later-day conferences.[4] The Harivallabh Sangeet Sammelan, started in 1875 as a religious congregation, went on to become one of the leading public platforms for Hindustani music

1 V.N. Bhatkhande, *A Short Historical Survey of the Music of Upper India*, *op.cit.*, p.50.

2 V.N. Bhatkhande, *Music Systems in India (A Comparative study of some of the leading music systems of the 15th, 16th, 17th & 18th centuries)*, S. Lal & Co., Delhi, 2nd ed, 1989, p.108.

3 For a detailed analysis of the different categories in Indian music existing at the present moment, see Ashok Ranade, "Categories of Music" in *National Centre For The Performing Arts, Quarterly Journal, Vol.XIV, No.4*, Bombay, December 1985.

4 Joep Bor and Philippe Bruguierre, *Masters of Raga, Meister Des Raga, Les Maitres Du Raga*, *op.cit.*, p.20.

performance after 1908.[5] However, the conferences held by V.N. Bhatkhande and V.D. Paluskar distinguished themselves from earlier efforts. Bhatkhande organised All India Music Conferences in Baroda, Delhi, Banaras and Lucknow, between the years 1916 and 1925, with financial support from princely patrons and other affluent individuals.[6] Heaping fulsome praise on Sayyajirao Gaikwad for his support to the first music conference held in Baroda in 1916, Bhatkhande said:

> . . . I shall take this opportunity to express my immense gratitude to our noble and enlightened Prince and Ruler H.H. the Maharaja Saheb Gaekwar who takes such keen interest in the matter and has placed the whole of Indian under his obligation by his enabling us representatives to assemble here for this glorious work of the revival of our degenerate art, as also by taking the lead in acknowledging, by doing so, the incalculable value of musical education to humanity.[7]

Of relevance to this study, however, are five conferences or Sangeet Parishads organised by Paluskar at the Gandharva Mahavidyalaya (hereinafter GM) in Bombay between 1918 and 1922 and the provincial music conferences he organised in 1928 and 1929. Paluskar probably decided to organize conferences after witnessing the success of Bhatkhande's endeavour in this sphere. He had reservations about the manner in which Bhatkhande conducted proceedings at conferences, and perhaps wanted to counter this thorugh the GM conferences. According to Vamanrao Deshpande, "Having found that Bhatkhande's innovation of the Baroda Music Conference did not fit in with his own ideas on the subject, Vishnu Digambar proceeded to organize his own music conferences, in which proper justice could be done to the performing musicians, whose position in Bhatkhande's conferences, he thought, was only subsidiary."[8] Among other things, Paluskar observed that English was the chosen language for discussions and resolutions at Bhatkhande's Baroda conference, a language not understood by musicians assembled there. Very few speeches were delivered in Marathi,

5 For history of the Sammelan, see http://harballabh.org/home.html

6 S.N. Ratanjankar, *Pandit Bhatkhande*, *op.cit.*, pp.45-46.

7 Pt. V.N. Bhatkhande, *A Short Historical Survey of the Music of Upper India*, *op.cit.*, p.50.

8 Vamanrao Deshpande, *Maharashtra's Contribution to Music*, *op.cit.*, p.54.

Hindi and Gujarati, and senior musicians seated on stage were directed to raise their hands in support of resolutions. Ashok D. Ranade suggests Paluskar's conferences were not popular in the North. He states, ". . . there was a greater acceptance of Pt. Bhatkhande's views and methods in the north and hence 'his' conferences were largely attended by non-Maharashtrian Hindustani musicians. On the other hand non-English-speaking traditional musicians based to the south of Narmada found a more congenial platform in the five conferences inspired by Pt. Vishnu Digambar during the period 1918-1922."[9] Paluskar's participation in many sessions of the Indian National Congress where he rendered *Van-de Mataram* and other patriotic songs, and his pan-Indian approach to music may have doubly inspired him to organize these conferences.[10]

Gandharva Mahavidyalaya Sangeet Parishad[11]

Paluskar's conferences were held in a specially decorated pandal erected on an open ground in the Shree Ram Chowk at the GM. They had a more or less fixed format with a formal inauguration, an instruments' exhibition, discussions through the day followed by concerts at night. The wide variety of subjects that were discussed included deliberations on:

- the need for a system of notation in Indian music
- the efficacy of Paluskar's system of notation
- the relation of ancient texts to current performance practice
- the existence of harmony in Indian music
- the relation between literature and music
- the shrutis used in Hindustani music
- exploring the possibility of creating Marathi compositions as part of Hindustani music repertoire
- specific *raags*

---

9 Ashok D. Ranade, *Maharashtra: Art Music, op.cit.*, p.62.

10 B.R. Deodhar, "*Sangeet-sevak Shriman Damodardas Khanna, Calcutta*" in *Sangeet Kala Vihar*, Varsha 8, Ank 3, March 1955, Gandharva Mahavidyalaya Mandal, 1955, pp.29-30. See also Vamanrao Deshpande, *Maharashtra's Contribution to Music, op.cit.*, p.54.

11 Unless otherwise mentioned, information about the GM music conferences has been taken from B.R. Deodhar, *Gaayanaachaarya P. Vishnu Digambar, op.cit.*

Evidently, the subjects revealed the predominant trend in contemporary musicological discourse to draw parallels between and establish parity between Indian and Western music.

Paluskar was astute in inviting persons of eminence to his conferences, unmistakably to draw more public attention to the projects he had undertaken. M.R. Jayakar, who presided over the first conference (March 9-11, 1918), notes in his memoirs that many connoisseurs including a good number of Parsi patrons attended the conference and that the Indian and British press in Bombay gave the conference a good reception. He states:

> The Conference had drawn most of the famous singers of India, and the prosperous condition of the institution at that time enabled it to make excellent arrangements for the reception and accommodation of the guests.[12]

In keeping with the underlying nationalist current at conferences, Jayakar spoke in favour of preserving what he considered was the original purity of Indian music and warned younger musicians against looking Westwards. He notes:

> In the speech I made on the occasion as President, I advised a historical study of Indian music, and warned the public against a cheap imitation of European music. I suggested the foundation of an institution in Bombay, which would serve as an asylum for needy musicians from any part of India, and that all the songs popularly current should be published in their original purity. In conclusion I warned the younger musicians to preserve the purity of a trained and unvitiated ear so necessary in Indian music, where we have no aids like tuning forks to set the correct note.[13]

The press supported Jayakar's views, as is demonstrated here:

> Mr. Jayakar's rejection of European music is sure of some support. We notice worthy and educated Indians of all classes and creeds listening by hundreds of an evening to the degraded and unclassical strains of a brass band playing 'If you were the only girl in the world', or 'When the midnight Choo-Choo starts for Alaban'. Also, it is an extremely common thing in Bombay for Indians to hire European music for weddings. Even the cheap three-man native band with a cornet, a clarionet and a drum plays some quaint, simple old

12 M.R. Jayakar, *The Story of My Life, Vol. I, 1873-1922*, Asia Publishing House, Bombay, 1958, p.187.

13 *Ibid.*

> echo of the British past like 'Sweet Dreamland Faces' or 'White Wings' as it heads some middle-class bridal procession or serenades in the bridegroom's garden. If these things go on, we fear for the future of Indian music as advocated by Mr. Jayakar.[14]

On March 10, Sanskrit poet Kshamabai Rao inaugurated an exhibition of musical instruments and discussions began at 4 pm on that day. Solicitor M.V. Gokhale, Narayan Moreshwar Khare and Gajananrao Patankar, addressed the gathering. Discussions on the third day started at 9.30 am and Ketkar, Phadke and Kashalkar, spoke on this occasion. The musicians at the conference included Paluskar's disciples, his *guru* Balkrishnabuwa Ichalkaranjikar and the latter's son Annabuwa and disciples Gundubuwa Ingle and Anant Manohar. Rehmat Khan, Bhaskarbuwa Bakhale, Ramkrishnabuwa Vaze, Ismail Khan, Vilayat Khan and Govindrao Shaligram, performed at concerts that were held every night. On the last day, snacks were provided to all artistes. The income for this conference with donations was Rs.3,750 and 2 annas, and the expenditure was Rs.3,640, 11 annas and 3 paise.[15]

The second conference (May3-5, 1919), was presided over by Balkrishnabuwa Ichalkaranjikar, whose speech was read out at 5 pm on May 3. Bhaskarbuwa Bakhale inaugurated the instruments' exhibition on the eve of the conference. Discussions began on May 4 at 9 am. Keshavrao Datar gave information about the GM, and Shankarrao Pathak, R.K. Khare and Narsimharao of Bangalore participated in the discussion. Sardar Abasaheb Mazumdar and Omkarnath Thakur spoke on literature and music. N.C. Phadke spoke on the notation system and said that symbols should be used in place of letters to represent *swaras*, so as to make the system accessible for non-Devnagari knowing persons. Phadke argued that the system advocated by him was best suited if Indian music was to spread across the world. Kashalkar argued that efforts were being made to make Hindustani the language of the entire country and everyone would therefore be conversant with Devnagari. This discourse reflected the larger contemporaneous debate on recognition and establishment of Hindi/ Nagari as the single

14 As quoted from press report in *ibid*, pp.187-188.

15 B.R. Deodhar, *Gaayanaachaarya P. Vishnu Digambar*, *op.cit*, pp.70-71.

national language and script.[16] Paluskar negated Phadke's arguments in the discussion that followed. The third discussion began at 8 am on May 5. Paluskar and Panshikarshastri spoke about the possibilities of using ancient treatises for contemporary musical practice. N.G. Gore read out his essay on the Hindustani scale, and Sardar Abasaheb Mazumdar read out his essay on *raag* Bhinna Shadja, after which the *raag* is said to have gained popularity. Four concerts took place in the three-day conference. Balkrishnabuwa, Bakhale, Paluskar and his disciples performed. All participants were invited for meals to the Shree Ram Chowk, where arrangements were made to seat hundred people. The seating arrangement typified the existing social climate that maintained strict caste hierarchy and communal separation. Thus, Balkrishnabuwa Ichalkaranjikar, Bhaskarbuwa Bakhale, K.B. Deval and other Brahmins sat in the first row, Paluskar's disciples and accompanists sat in the second row, and the Muslim musicians sat in the third row. Apparently, the communal divide merged when Muslim musicians joined the recitation of *shlokas* by vocalists during the meal.[17]

The presidential address for the third GM conference (December 4-7, 1920) was delivered in English by Babasaheb Ghorpade, ruler of the Ichalkaranji state. In this instance, Paluskar seems to have made a compromise with his earlier consternation at English being used at Bhatkhande's conferences. Well-known painter Madhavrao Dhurandhar inaugurated the instrument exhibition. Many scholars participated in discussions and read out their essays. As was the case with previous conferences, the GM's notation system was discussed and Abasaheb Mazumdar of Poona read out his essay on the subject. Going a step further, the conference deliberated upon the concept of harmony and its usage in Indian music, perhaps hoping to prove that harmony existed in Indian music. Participants opined that harmony existed in Indian music, but it did not manifest itself in the way it did in Western music. Responding to a report of these discussions in the *Times of India*, Gio-

16 For a detailed discussion on the Hindi/Nagari debate, see Alok Rai, *Hindi Nationalism*, Orient Longman Private Limited, (Reprint), Hyderabad, 2002.

17 B.R. Deodhar, *Gaayanaachaarya P. Vishnu Digambar*, *op.cit*, pp.74-75. Also see, B.R.Deodhar, *Thor sangeetkaar*, *op.cit.*, p.78.

vanni Scrinzi (c.1864-1935), an Italian pianist, scholar of Western music and music critic for the *Times of India*, suggested through a series of articles that a person adequately trained in both systems, namely Indian and Western music, would alone be able to decide upon the existence of harmony in Indian music. He offered to teach Western music to a candidate trained in Indian music and chosen by the GM, and instituted a scholarship in his mother's name for this purpose. It was in response to this offer that Paluskar selected his student B.R. Deodhar for this project and taught him at the GM twice a week from June 1921.[18] In the same year, Paluskar also arranged for Dhondiraj Paluskar, another student of the GM, to study violin under Savini, an Italian violinist. For this purpose, he was granted a scholarship of Rs.25/- instituted by Babasaheb Ghorpade of Ichalkaranji.[19]

Balkrishnabuwa Ichalkaranjikar, Bhaskarbuwa Bakhale, Gundubuwa Ingle, Mubarak Ali Khan, Shamsuddin Khan, Ganpatrao Sanaivadak, Dharamdas, Umamaheshwar, Devilalji, and Sureshbabu Mane, performed at the third conference. Paluskar's disciples Vinayakrao Patwardhan, Keshavrao Datar, Shankarrao Vyas, Vamanrao Padhye, Baburao Gokhale and Shankarrao Pathak, also performed.

The fourth GM conference (December 9-12, 1921) was presided over by Ramapati Mishra and the working president of the reception committee was Balasaheb Kher. The instrument exhibition was inaugurated by Sarojini Naidu. Balkrishna Ichalkaranjikar, his son Annabuwa, Gundubuwa Ingle and Anant Manohar Joshi, were present as usual. Bhaskarbuwa Bakhale was one of the performers on the occasion. The fourth conference seems to have deviated from earlier ones in that it featured a recital by a woman performer, namely Hirabai Badodekar (1905-1989). Importantly, Badodekar wished to portray a self-image of respectability in order to distinguish herself from the general public impression of hereditary women performers. To this purpose, she made

18 B.R. Deodhar, *Gaayanaachaarya P. Vishnu Digambar*, *op.cit*, pp.85-86. Also see, B.R. Deodhar, *Thor sangeetkaar*, *op.cit.*, pp.45-67. Another source mentions that Deodhar received a scholarship from the ruler of Ichalkaranji to facilitate his learning of Western music from Scrinzi. See Ashok D. Ranade, *Maharashtra: Art Music*, *op.cit.*, p.64.

19 B.R. Deodhar, *Gaayanaachaarya P. Vishnu Digambar*, *op.cit.*, p.87.

contact with and taught women from elite homes.[20] It was perhaps this portrayal that convinced Paluskar to feature her in the conference. The conference also featured a piano recital by Scrinzi, which was yet another deviation from the focus on Hindustani music. During the discussions and paper reading, Scrinzi proposed that Hindustani music should adopt Western staff notation in order to receive international acclaim.[21]

The fifth GM conference was (December 3-6, 1922) was attended by Balkrishnabuwa Ichalkaranjikar, his disciples, and Paluskar's disciples from across the country. Essays were read out, and discussions and concerts were held at the conference.[22]

Paluskar repeated his strategy of inviting important personalities even in provincial conferences. Held in Bombay (November 1928), the first provincial conference was inaugurated at a hall in Shankarwadi near Prarthana Samaj, Girgaum, by J.V. Deshmukh, the then Mayor. The activities for the next two days were held at the Cowasji Jehangir Hall. The second provincial conference organised at the Jinnah Hall in Bombay (December 1-2, 1929) was presided over by Kanhaiyalal Munshi. The women's music conference (December 3, 1929) was presided over by Shafi Tyebji, a prominent votary of political consciousness among Muslim women.[23] Balkrishnabuwa Kapileshwari reports that the first provincial conference discussed the possibility of translating traditional Hindi, Braj and Punjabi *khayal* compositions to Marathi and notating them accordingly, an idea that proved to be controversial. Apparently, Aman Ali Khan organized a meeting of Hindu and Muslim musicians in Bombay, all of whom resolved to counter any attempt to 'Marathize' (the term *Marathikaran* is used in the source) traditional compositions. Thus, musicians seem to have responded to Paluskar's conferences, not merely as performers on these occasions but also as those concerned

20 Pratibha Gopujkar, "*Hirabai Badodekar*" in *Loksatta*, Mumbai, 15 April 2000. This source mentions that Hirabai Badodekar's debut public performance was at Aryabhushan Theatre, Poona, in 1926, which is five years after her performance at Paluskar's conference.

21 B.R. Deodhar, *Gaayanaachaarya P. Vishnu Digambar, op.cit*, p.92.

22 *Ibid*, pp.94 -95.

23 *Ibid*, p.114.

about traditional knowledge and its public portrayal. Kapileshwari further states that he was given the responsibility to publicly oppose this move, which he accomplished by writing two articles in the Marathi daily *Navaakaal* in October 1928. Kapileshwari argued that the move to 'Marathize' was in fact a threat to Muslim hereditary musicians. His articles were countered by Vinayakbuwa Patwardhan in an article published in the *Kesari* on December 4, 1928. Patwardhan's response speaks of new Marathi compositions and does not mention any translation of traditional compositions. But he emphasized that Kapileshwari's taking up cudgels for Muslim musicians was unwarranted and that this projected them as the sole creators of Hindustani music. Aside from the war of words between Kapileshwari and Patwardhan, in the absence of any documentary evidence left behind by Muslim musicians, it is unclear whether they indeed felt threatened by the new move or that they experienced any communal bias, but they seem to have made their disapproval publicly known as reported by Kapileshwari.[24]

Notwithstanding the debates that stemmed from these conferences, it is clear that the GM Sangeet Parishads, first of their kind in the city, gave importance to the theoretical and the practical aspects of music and were attended by local and visiting musicians and musicologists. They also provided audiences in Bombay with an opportunity to listen to diverse styles of music and to performances of students and maestros.This may have objectively helped in attracting larger audiences to music concerts.

Music conferences (1920s-1930s)

Such was the popularity of the conferences that similar conferences continued to be held in Bombay and elsewhere. In Bengal, the All Bengal Music Conference was started in Calcutta in 1925 by Bhupendra Ghosh, a zamindar, and Damodardas alias Lalababu Khanna. Lalababu had hosted Paluskar during his stay in Calcutta in 1912. Musicians considered it a privilege to be invited to perform at this conference. Lal-

24 Balkrishnabuwa Kapileshwari, *op.cit.*, pp.418-423. Kapileshwari mentions that the first provincial conference was held in Poona in 1927.

ababu exhorted friends in other parts of the country to start similar conferences and even attended these to help the organizers.[25]

According to B.R. Deodhar, until 1925, conferences were held in the country occasionally, but the public realized the importance of these only by 1930. He points out that Bhatkhande's conferences were held due to the financial support from princely patrons and other affluent individuals, but Paluskar was self-reliant and organized conferences in Bombay on his own strength.[26]

After 1933, music conferences were held on an annual basis at Allahabad, Lucknow, and Kanpur. In 1934, Deodhar attended the Kanpur conference where he first heard child prodigy Kumar Gandharva for the first time. Later, in 1934, a conference was organized by Vamarao Deshpande, B.R. Deodhar and Motiram Pai in Bombay, and was presided over by M.R. Jaykar. The Chairman of the Reception Committee and President of the Working Committee was Bhalchandra Sitaram Sukthankar, a solicitor closely associated with Bhatkhande. They organized a second music conference in around 1936 at the Jinnah Hall, presided over by the Maharaja of Dharampur. M.R. Jaykar headed the Reception Committee.[27] On being asked to recommend hitherto unheard of and new artistes for Bombay audiences, Deodhar suggested the names of *shehnai* player Bismillah Khan and vocalist Kumar Gandharva, both of whom he had heard at the Kanpur music conference. The other organizers were initially reluctant to invite these two artistes, but Deodhar managed to convince them.[28]

The conferences played a major role in bringing issues related to Hindustani music on a national platform, but it would be an exaggera-

25 B.R. Deodhar, "*Sangeet-sevak Shriman Damodardas Khanna, Calcutta*" in *Sangeet Kala Vihar, Varsha 8, Ank 3, op.cit.*, p.30. Also see, B.R. Deodhar, *Gaayanaachaarya P. Vishnu Digambar, op.cit.*, p.59.

26 *Ibid*. Also see, B.R. Deodhar, *Gaayanaachaarya P. Vishnu Digambar, ibid*, pp.29-30.

27 Vamanrao Deshpande, *Between Two Tanpuras, op.cit.*, p. 154. See also, G.H. Ranade, "*Sangeet ke aadhunik Bheeshmaachaarya*" in *Bhatkhande smriti granth*, Indira Kala Sangeet Vishwavidyalaya, Khairagarh, M.P., 1966, p.328.

28 B.R. Deodhar, "School of Indian Music", *op.cit.*, n. pag.

tion to conclude that they drastically changed the lives of musicians.[29] Contrary to the belief that there was bonhomie among participants at the conferences, available evidence seems to suggest that the competitive spirit among performers witnessed earlier in princely courts also found its way here and was encouraged wholeheartedly by the organizers.[30] Thus, Faiyaz Khan was conferred with the title 'Sangeet Chudamani' at the All India Music Conference in Lahore. At another conference organized by Bhatkhande, he was chosen as the best *khayal* singer, and he was gifted Rs.33,000/- by the audience at a conference in Indore.[31] As observed by Ashok Da. Ranade:

> A perceptive organizer and a participant in the Bhatkhande conferences, Bhalchandra Sukhtankar ruefully commented in 1938 on the glaring scarcity of medals in conferences organized in Bombay and opined that the fact affected the performers adversely.[32]

Recognition after successful performances at conferences emboldened some performers in princely service to demand higher wages and special concessions from their patrons, but for the vast majority of musicians, conferences did little for them in material terms.[33]

Perhaps, as a response to new pedagogic activity and conferences, and to assert their hereditary hold over the subject, Muslim musicians in Bombay organised a conference in 1937 at the Cowasji Jehangir Hall under the aegis of the Sangeet Pracharak Mandal, an organization that they had established. The conference was presided over by the Maharaja of Dharampur. All expenses during the conference were borne by the Mandal. One could easily slip into the trap of examining the Mandal and its activities only through the prism of communal rivalry. But this would ignore the reality that this was probably a response from hereditary musicians to a situation that seemed to challenge their position as performers and *gurus*. Indeed, this conference witnessed a sense of

29 For an overstated account of the conferences organized by Bhatkhande, see Sobhana Nayar, *op.cit.*, p.282.

30 Ashok D. Ranade, *Maharashtra: Art Music*, *op.cit.*, p.62.

31 Susheela Misra, *Music Profiles*, *op.cit.*, p.49.

32 Ashok D. Ranade, *Maharashtra: Art Music*, *op.cit.*, p.63.

33 Joan L. Erdman, *op.cit.*, pp.109-110.

camaraderie among musicians in the city, when the Mandal requested Omkarnath Thakur, Vinayak Patwardhan, B.R. Deodhar, D.V. Paluskar and Narayanrao Vyas, to collaborate in organising a conference, as these vocalists had decided earlier to host a conference in the city at the same time. There was a general consensus and the conference was said to be a success with performances by celebrated vocalists, and instrumentalists such as *been*, harmonium, *sitar* and *tabla* players, and orchestras. There were some artistes from the GM too. It is not known whether this conference like its predecessors involved discussions on topics concerning musicology, but the Mandal passed the following resolutions on this occasion:

- Efforts were to be made to strengthen the Mandal.
- Funds were to be raised for the Mandal activities.
- A big school or college of music was to be started after the collection of a sizeable sum of money for this purpose.
- Efforts were to be made to enrol more artistes as members.[34]

While conferences became a part of the musical landscape in various cities they also met with some criticism. Writing in the 1940s, commentator S.K. Chaubey castigated the manner in which music conferences were organized:

> An All Indian music conference, today, is neither representative in character nor symbolic of the spirit of classical music. It is neither music nor conference. It is a pompous show organized by some influential organizers who have either power or money at their command. Long-winded patrons and secretaries inaugurate it with long and boring speeches which are exercises in mutual admiration and in which the virtues of our ancient music are described in metaphor, hyperbole and poetic exaggeration. With the veneer of middle class culture is mixed a sufficient quantity of red-tapism and snobbery. In the royal front seats meant for the aristocracy of good taste and good judgement, sit those who either yawn intermittently or gossip quite garrulously in their more lucid intervals. To them music is a luxury, which they think is quite conventional to enjoy once a year. The rest of the audience consists of many mediocre lovers of music whose applause is more worthy than their judgement. The programme is composed of first-rate classical music, third-rate classical music, popular music, unpopular music, no music,

34 Vilayat Hussein Khan, *op.cit.*, pp.16-19.

> classical dances, sacred dances, profane dances, ultra-modern dances, and other items, – all printed on fine paper. The listeners constitute a mob, which enjoys adult franchise in the new democracy of music. Every musician has to cater to it.[35]

Chaubey goes further to warn musicians of their duty towards the audience and the music:

> What can we expect from a music conference which just entertains a mob of ticket-holders? Such a conference, treats musicians as hirelings whose duty it is to entertain people by some means. It also becomes a hot-bed of politics sowing seeds of communalism among the musicians and audiences both. The organizers have never thought of this and willingly or unwillingly, they often fall a prey to vested interests which dominate a music conference. With such serious limitations, no music conference, however honest its intentions may be, can set up any principles of refined taste and solid judgement. It is bound to encourage elements which are detrimental to the cause of music. Musicians should not be judged by the plebiscite of an emotional mob which keeps swaying from one extreme to another. No music conference should attempt to pass a judgement on real musicians because it is too ill-equipped to do so . . . In the same way, musicians should not be expected to stoop down to the level of the listeners. Their primary duty is to lift them up to their level. As wage-earners, as mere paid artisans of a show, they can never enjoy the right of doing so . . . In spite of all its noble pretensions, which it conveniently bolsters up in the public press, it often reduces itself to the level of a carnival or a circus. A conference which lets its audience have the chance of hearing the music of the glamour-girls and show-boys of the screen, is utterly incapable of setting up a corrective of judgement and appreciation. I wish many of these music conferences would not be held at all. They are just an annual epidemic which must be controlled.[36]

Was Chaubey referring to situations like the one seen in Allahabad in 1935? The famous film singer Kundan Lal Saigal was invited to perform at the Allahabad University Senate Hall under the aegis of the Prayag Sangeet Samiti in 1935, during a conference that featured renowned Hindustani vocalists like Omkarnath Thakur, Faiyaz Khan, Narayanrao Vyas, Vinayakrao Patwardhan, and others.[37] At any rate, Chaubey's criticism does not seem to have resonated widely, as Hindu-

---

35 S.K. Chaubey, *Indian Music Today*, Kitab Mahal, Allahabad,1945, pp.120-122

36 *Ibid*, pp.121-122.

37 Raghava R. Menon, *K.L. Saigal: The Pilgrim of the Swara*, Hind Pocket Books (Pvt.) Ltd., 1st paperback ed., Delhi, 1989, pp.20-21.

stani music had evidently begun receiving wider public attention. This was reflected in the formation of music circles that provided a regular public platform for performers and further increased the number of listeners in the city.[38]

38 Aneesh Pradhan, "The Emergence of Modern Concert Platform in Bombay" in *Journal of the Indian Musicological Society, Vol.*25, Baroda, Jan.-Dec.1994, pp.51-55.

MUSIC CIRCLES

Private patronage from the commercial and industrial elite continued well into the twentieth century, with individual patrons hosting recitals for a select gathering of family, friends, business associates and music aficionados. But there were also an increasing number of middle class patrons who had begun hosting such concerts. For instance, a barrister by the name of Mehendale organized Kesarbai Kerkar's concert at his residence near the French Bridge for a select audience of thirty to forty people.[1] Similarly, some families belonging to the Karwari community living in Dr. Bhalchandra's chawl next to the Grant Road Station organised a few of Bhaskarbuwa Bakhale's concerts. Bakhale reciprocated by going beyond his professional commitment and voluntarily sang an additional concert.[2] At times, these concerts exhibited a degree of competitiveness when more than one musician was featured or when the audience consisted of musicians. Four accounts provided below reflect this atmosphere.

In 1927, while praising Alladiya Khan's performance at a private home in Chunam Lane near Lamington Road, Ramkrishnabuwa Vaze compared his singing with other vocalists and criticized Abdul Karim

---

1 B.R. Deodhar, *Thor Sangeetkar*, *op.cit.*, pp.21

2 Govindrao Tembe, *Maazha sangeet vyaasang*, *op.cit.*, pp.71-72. Mangeshrao Telang's year of birth is mentioned as 1856 in Laxminarayan Garg, *op.cit.*, pp.40-41.

Khan (1872-1938), noteworthy vocalist of Kirana and disciple of Kale Khan and Abdullah Khan. His remarks infuriated Abdul Karim Khan's disciple Balkrishnabuwa Kapileshwari, who was also present on this occasion. Alladiya Khan finally brought the argument to a close.[3]

In another concert, *been* player Murad Khan could not tolerate *sitar* player Barkatullah Khan's claim that the authentic *sitar baaj* was played only in his *gharana*. Murad Khan chose not to retaliate on this occasion and instead practised *sitar* with his son Nisar Hussein for a year. After regaining command over the instrument, he requested Vitthaldas, a *shetia*, to organize Barkatullah Khan's concert expressly with a view to challenging the latter. At the concert, no sooner had Barkatullah Khan started than Murad Khan announced that he too felt like playing *sitar* that day and suggested that they play together. This suggestion was accepted and Murad Khan and Barkatullah Khan sat next to each other with Nisar Hussein behind them. The first *raag* went on for approximately two hours with both using all possible methods to 'vanquish' each other in this musical battle. Eventually, Vitthaldas ended the performance by saying that they were both equally matched artistes of a high order and that it was impossible for the audience to decide who was better. Vitthaldas paid both artistes equally. Later, Murad Khan reminded Barkatullah Khan of his anger at the claim the latter had previously made.[4]

In 1928, Baburao Gokhale, a disciple of Paluskar, organized a private concert near the Brahman Sabha to showcase Paluskar's ability as a consummate performer and to dispel all rumours of him having lost form. Alladiya Khan, Agra *gharana* vocalists and other musicians were present in the audience. *Tabla* accompaniment was provided by Dattaram Nandwadkar alias Nandodkar who was known to confuse vocalists with rhythmic intricacies. He tried to puzzle Paluskar by playing a rhythmic pattern to begin the Jhumra *theka* for the *khayal* – *baajat tat bitat ghan*, in *raag* Mia ki Malhar, but Paluskar was unfazed and continued to sing. In fact, Paluskar asked him to improvise more and not restrict himself to playing the *theka* during the *chhota khayal*. Appar-

---

3 B.R. Deodhar, *Thor sangeetkaar*, *op.cit.*, p.116.

4 *Ibid*, pp.74-75.

ently, Nandwadkar acknowledged Paluskar's prowess and everyone appreciated the concert.[5]

There was the rare case of Bawabhai Achalji Dholakia, a reputed Ayurvedic practitioner, who hosted not just concerts but also a discussion at his home in around 1914 or 1915 between Krishnaji Balwant Deval alias Ballal alias Balaji (1847-1931), noted scholar and District Deputy Collector at Ratnagiri, Edward Charles Clements, and Vishnu Narayan Bhatkhande. The dialogue focused on the use of *shruti*s in Hindustani music. Zakiruddin Khan, eminent *dhrupad* performer belonging to the Dagar lineage moderated the discussion. The deliberations were followed by concerts that continued at the same venue for a month.[6] British officials seldom attended Hindustani music concerts in private homes, but Lord Willingdon, the Governor of Bombay, was present for Zakiruddin Khan's performance at Dholakia's residence.[7]

Several such accounts have now become a part of Hindustani music nostalgia and in some cases have even created a new mythology. But more importantly, patronage in the twentieth century underwent a radical transformation, impacting performance space, practice and context. No longer restricted to private homes, concerts moved to public spaces that accommodated larger audiences. Beginnings in this direction had been made in late nineteenth century Bombay, but the formation of music circles in the 1930s was a quantum leap in public patronage, providing the middle class with a formal platform to assert its identity as the new urban patron and provoking musicians to tailor their presentations to appeal to the varied tastes of a mixed audience.[8]

---

5 B.R. Deodhar, *Gaayanaachaarya P. Vishnu Digambar*, *op.cit.*, p.90. See also, B.R. Deodhar, *Thor sangeetkaar*, *op.cit.*, pp.127-128.

6 N.Shukla, "*Maine unhe mehfil mein gaate hue sunaa hai*", in *Bhatkhande smriti granth*, Indira Kala Sangeet Vishwavidyalaya, Khairagarh, M.P., 1966, pp.358 *ka* and *kha*. Shukla mentions Dholakia's first name as Bababhai, but information about him elsewhere mentions his first name as Bawabhai. See http://www.zanduayurveda.com/about-us/history.php

7 N.Shukla, *ibid.*

8 Such organisations continue to dot the urban musical landscape to this day despite a shortage of funds, and musicians look forward to performing under their aegis.

Tickets and subscription

There are differing opinions regarding the immediate source of inspiration for establishing music circles. According to S.N. Ratanjankar (1900-1974), disciple of V.N. Bhatkhande and Faiyaz Khan (1881-1950), the idea of starting music circles in Bombay took shape after some enthusiastic music lovers were encouraged by the success of the three concerts organised by his father featuring Alladiya Khan. Though the concerts were held at the residence of Balwantrao and Krishnarao Madgaonkar, tickets were sold and the proceeds were offered as honorarium to the artiste.[9] On the other hand, B.R. Deodhar has suggested that the first music circle in the city was started by individuals who had drawn inspiration from a concert organised by him in about 1930 featuring Murad Khan, the reputed *been* player. The venue for the concert was the Rammohan High School in Girgaum and tickets were sold at Re.1/- each to approximately seventy or eighty listeners. Some doctors and lawyers volunteered to pay Rs.5/- each. The proceeds from the sale of tickets went to the artiste.[10]

Such conflicting claims make it almost impossible to determine a definite date for the establishment of the first music circle in Bombay. To an extent, this is a non-issue, given the fact that the Parsi Gayan Uttejak Mandali had already initiated the idea of public concerts in the nineteenth century with its formal ticketed *jalsa*s and printed programme notes. Some performers had also taken an initiative to organize ticketed concerts featuring themselves. For instance, Paluskar organized a ticketed public programme as far back as in 1897. Interestingly, this ticketed concert held in Rajkot displeased Paluskar's guru Balkrishnabuwa Ichalkaranjikar, who felt that Paluskar had commercialized traditional knowledge. This response did not perturb Paluskar. On the contrary, he felt his idea of holding ticketed public concerts was to take music to common people and not restrict it to princely patrons. Paluskar believed that Balkrishnabuwa belonged to an earlier era and did not therefore realize the significance of this step. But in the days to come,

9 Shree Shreenath Ratanjankar, "*Sw. Alladiya Khan saaheb*" reprinted in *Alladiya Khan*, Shruti Mandal, Jaipur, 1994, pp.11-12.

10 B.R. Deodhar, *Thor sangeetkaar*, *op.cit.*, p.69.

Paluskar felt his *guru* would ask for similar concerts to be organized for him in Bombay. Indeed, such was the case, as Balkrishnabuwa faced financial problems. His nominal salary in Ichalkaranji did not enable him to repay loans and on informing Paluskar of this situation, Paluskar organized concerts for him in Bombay and apparently arranged for a good fee for his *guru*.[11]

Thus, there were a series of events, rather than a single catalyst that led to the formation of music circles in Bombay. Most music circles functioned on similar lines. They charged a periodic or life subscription fee that covered the costs of periodic concerts held for members. Non-members were permitted to attend on payment of an entrance fee. Tickets were sold in advance and at the venue on the day of the concert, at rates ranging from Rs.2/- to Rs.5/- each.

Fees to the soloists and the accompanists were predetermined and were paid separately in most cases.[12] While information about the exact fee structure existing in the early part of the twentieth century is unavailable, B.R. Deodhar states that in the period prior to the establishment of music circles and probably in a private concert situation, Paluskar demanded a fee of Rs.500/- or more, when other musicians were charging Rs.50/- to Rs.75/- per performance.[13] Fees also varied as per the calibre of the musicians and in relation to the financial resources available to the organizers. The latter was particularly true, according to Vamanrao Deshpande, in the case of concerts organized later by music circles, where fees are said to have ranged between Rs.75/- and Rs.100/- for the main performer.[14] Apparently, Kesarbai Kerkar was the highest paid performer, receiving Rs.1,000/- for each concert in Bombay, an amount that covered her accompanists' fees. Her fee for an outstation concert was Rs.1,500/-, which did not include travel costs and accompanists' fees. Faiyaz Khan is said to have charged Rs.500/- per concert,

11 B.R. Deodhar, *Gaayanaachaarya P. Vishnu Digambar*, *op.cit.*, pp.19, 73-74.

12 Interviews with Batuk Diwanji held on 24 August 1992 and in January 1993, with Sharad R. Mehta held on 29 April 1992, and with Kaushalya and Dinker Manjeshwar held on 10 September 1993. Also see Eklavya, *op.cit.*, pp.90, 123-124.

13 B.R. Deodhar, *Thor sangeetkaar*, *op.cit.*, p.124.

14 Vamanrao H. Deshpande, *Indian Musical Traditions*, *op.cit.*, p.126.

but other main performers were paid approximately Rs.200/-. The *tabla* and *sarangi* accompanists were usually paid Rs.25/-, but better-known accompanists like Bundu Khan on *sarangi* and Kamu Mangeshkar on *tabla* were paid Rs.50/- to Rs.60/- and Rs.70/- to Rs.80/- per concert, respectively.[15]

Typically, concerts held under the aegis of music circles began around 10 p.m. and continued for about three hours with an intermission. Concerts featuring more popular artistes like Faiyaz Khan would continue until 4 a.m. the next morning with two intermissions.

Full-fledged public concerts required bigger performance spaces. Thus, venues for concerts moved beyond private residences to large public spaces. Most concerts organized by the new circles were held at Laxmi Baug Hall in Bhatwadi, while other public concerts were also held at B.R. Deodhar's School of Indian Music, Nana Shankarsheth Hall, Jinnah Hall, Muzaffarabad Hall, Wagle Hall, Marwari Vidyalaya, Forbes' Hall and Blavatsky Lodge. These venues, though accessible to the public, were significantly smaller than present-day auditoria and were not equipped with sound amplification.[16]

Bombay Music Circle

The Bombay Music Circle, one of the earliest music circles in the city, was established in the early 1930s by Govindrao Muley and M.D. Pai. Solicitor Bhalchandra Sitaram Sukthankar was President of the Bombay Music Circle between c.1933 and 1936.[17] The Life Membership fee was

15 Information gathered from private conversation with Sharad R. Mehta on January 7, 1993 and from interview with him held on 29 April 1992. Unfortunately, the exact period when these fees were paid is not known.

16 See interviews with Batuk Diwanji held in January 1993 and on 24 August 1992, and with Kaushalya and Dinker Manjeshwar held on 10 September 1993. Diwanji and the Manjeshwars have contrary versions about the presence of amplification at venues during this period, but based on information available elsewhere, it would be reasonable to conclude that such a system did not exist until after the 1940s or so. Suresh S. Chandwankar, "Preserving The Recorded Sound: 78 RPM", in Balawant Joshi, Dilip Inamdar, Charudatta Bhagwat, S.S. Gore (eds.), *World of Gandharvas*, Sound Library Project of Akhil Bharatiya Gandharva Mahavidyalaya Mandal, New Bombay, 1993. Govindrao Tembe, *Maazha sangeet vyaasang, op.cit.*, p.64.

17 Vamanrao Deshpande, *Between Two Tanpuras, op.cit.*, p.154.

Rs.100/- and Ordinary Members had to pay a quarterly fee of Rs.3/-. Guests were charged a fee of Rs.1.50 per month. Concerts organized by music circles attracted more listeners than were seen earlier at the music clubs, though one source mentions that the membership of the Bombay Music Circle was restricted to eighty and each member was allowed to bring only two guests for the concert. This restriction was probably due to the fact that the Circle was interested in maintaining a certain degree of initiated listenership. In fact, the audience at the time was considered enlightened and perceptive about the subtleties of music.[18] Guests at the Bombay Music Circle had to therefore prove their credentials as initiated listeners before they could be accepted as members.[19] The number of listeners in most music circles around this time did not exceed one hundred and twenty-five. Vamanrao Deshpande states, "As Secretary of the Bombay Music Circle, I still remember the wrangles over increasing its membership from a hundred to a hundred and twenty-five.[20]

The audience would often include eminent musicians like Alladiya Khan, Ramkrishnabuwa Vaze, who had received training from many musicians including Balwantrao Pohare (court musician of Kagal) and Vithaanna Hadap in Malwan (disciple of Balkrishnabuwa Ichalkaranjikar and Vishnupant Chhatre), Umrao Khan, son of Tanras Khan, Vilayat Hussein Khan, Faiyaz Khan, Abdul Karim Khan, and Govindrao Tembe. Thus, performing for such an audience was an onerous task.[21]

The Bombay Music Circle organised several programmes featuring artistes like Ramkrishnabuwa Vaze, Alladiya Khan and Manji Khan.[22] But like music clubs in the past, the Circle also encouraged performances by amateur musicians. A Member's Day was observed, featuring per-

---

18 Vamanrao H. Deshpande, *Indian Musical Traditions, op.cit.*, pp.117-118.

19 Interview with Kaushalya and Dinker Manjeshwar, held on 10 September 1993.

20 Vamanrao H. Deshpande, *Indian Musical Traditions, op.cit.*, p.155.

21 Vamanrao Deshpande, *Between Two Tanpuras, op.cit.*, pp.69,114, 22. Also see Govindrao Tembe, *Gaayanmaharshee Alladiyakhan yaanche charitra, op.cit.*, pp.58-59; Govindrao Tembe, *Maazhaa sangeet vyaasang, op.cit.*, p.162; Eklavya, *op.cit.*, pp.120, 122-123; Vamanrao H. Deshpande, *Indian Musical Traditions, op.cit.*, pp.155-156. Interview with Kaushalya and Dinker Manjeshwar held on 10 September 1993.

22 Vamanrao Deshpande, *Between Two Tanpuras, op.cit.*, p.154.

formances by some members of the Circle. Amateur but highly motivated musicians like Gulubhai Jasdanwala and Vamanrao Deshpande performed at these functions and eminent artistes were invited as Chief Guests.[23] However, the appearance of amateur women performers on the public concert platform continued to remain a distant reality.

Soon, other music circles were set up. These included the Musical Arts Society started by Bhanubhai Trivedi, the Bharatiya Sangeet Samiti presided over by Bhalchandra Sitaram Sukthankar, the Gandharva Sangeet Mandal, the Agra Gharana Sangeet Samiti, and Sangeet Niketan.[24] The trend towards establishing music circles was also followed by vocalist Anjanibai Malpekar, who formed the Bombay Music Art Society with the help of Shursen Karangutkar, a solicitor, and Namdev Manjrekar. Musicians like Faiyaz Khan, Alladiya Khan, Abdul Karim Khan, Ramkrishnabuwa Vaze, Bal Gandharva, Kesarbai Kerkar, Bade Ghulam Ali Khan, Vilayat Hussein Khan, Kumar Gandharva and Mallikarjun Mansur performed under the aegis of this music circle.[25] Later, Anjanibai Malpekar hosted programmes at her own residence and the artistes were paid from the collection made from the listeners on each occasion.[26]

Initial efforts at establishing music clubs and circles were focused around the southern end of the city probably to maintain proximity with patrons of music, most of who lived here. However, music lovers residing in Santa Cruz held an informal meeting on October 20, 1936, and expressed the need to have a music circle in the northern suburbs "with the object of promoting and cultivating the taste for Indian classical music among the residents of the suburbs . . . ."[27] Thus, Indranarayan Brijmohanlal, Chief Judge, Court of Small Causes subsequently inaugurated the Suburban Music Circle at a function, which was also attended

23 Interview with Kaushalya and Dinker Manjeshwar held on 10/ September 1993.

24 From interviews with Batuk Diwanji held on 24 August 1992 and in January 1993. Also see Vamanrao Deshpande, *Between Two Tanpuras, op.cit.*, p.154.

25 Mangala Khadilkar, "*Gaansaadhikaa Anjanibai Malpekar*", *Maharashtra Times*, Mumbai, 23 April 2000.

26 Interview with Batuk Diwanji held on 21 September 1992.

27 A.S. Rao, "About Ourselves", in the *Golden Jubilee Souvenir of the Suburban Music Circle*, Bombay, 1986.

by B.G. Kher, the then Chief Minister of Bombay. A vocal recital by Hirabai Badodekar was held to mark the occasion. The Circle organised eight concerts in a year, which featured musicians from various parts of the country. By the end of the first year the Circle had a membership of 144. In 1945, the membership fees were Rs.1,000/- for Founder Members, Rs.500/- for Patrons, Rs.300/- for Life Members, and Rs.5/- per quarter for Ordinary Members. During the early period, the Circle held its concerts at the Vimalanand Koppikar Hall in Santa Cruz.[28]

Notwithstanding the formal character of concerts organized by music circles, the presence of musicians in the audience provided fertile ground for performers to not only prove their merit, but also to throw challenges at each other. This was reminiscent of contests in private gatherings or in princely courts. To an extent, these contests strengthened professional rivalries that had existed among hereditary musician families. Not to be left out of this competition, even Omkarnath Thakur, a senior disciple of Paluskar not belonging to a hereditary musician family, would often pepper his performances with acerbic or proclamatory comments. His declarations at Laxmi Baug in April 1944 under the aegis of the Indian Musical Society to mark the death anniversary of Bhaskarbuwa Bakhale, demonstrate this facet of his personality. He sang *raags* Hem Kalyan and Darbari in the pre-interval session, followed by a *dhrupad* in Rudra *taal* in the post-interval segment, claiming that he had chosen to sing a composition in a rare *taal* since Bhaskarbuwa Bakhale sang rare *raags*. His next piece in *raag* Malkauns was constantly interspersed with comments.[29]

Candid criticism, challenge and declaration, was also accompanied by an overt acceptance of merit in public concerts. For instance, Faiyaz Khan refused to sing after Siddheshwari Devi (1903-1977) at an All India Music Conference in Bombay, publicly announcing that the crown of *thumri* rested on Siddheshwari Devi's head after Gauhar Jan, the noted *thumri* singer.[30]

---

28 *Ibid.*

29 Ramkrishna Bakre, *Buzurg*, Sadhana Prakashan, Pune, 1990, p.60.

30 Susheela Misra, *Great Masters of Hindustani Music*, *op.cit.*, p.164

A major difference between the music circles and the nineteenth century music clubs was that the newer organisations devoted themselves to holding performances of local and visiting musicians with no diversion into practical teaching. However, Vilayat Hussein Khan took a rare initiative in 1936, when he along with other reputed musicians started the Sangeet Pracharak Mandal, with the twin intention of popularising musical performance and music education in the city. Alladiya Khan was nominated as the President, Azmat Hussein Khan (1911-1975), disciple of Altaf Hussein Khan (1863-1964), Alladiya Khan and Vilayat Hussein Khan, was the Secretary, Shantaram Telang and Anwar Hussein Khan were the Deputy Secretaries, and a disciple of Vilayat Hussein Khan was appointed as treasurer of the Mandal. The Mandal held monthly programmes and members were confident with the progress they had made. They were certain of future success, but problems arose within the organisation due to differences with the treasurer. Eventually, a new music circle called Gayan Vardhak Sanstha was established to carry forward the task that the Mandal had embarked upon, but this according to Vilayat Hussein Khan, did not meet with any success.[31]

Other public concerts

Public concerts also became a part of annual Saarvajanik Ganeshotsavs or public festivities held to worship the Hindu deity Ganesh. The first-ever Saarvajanik Ganeshotsav was held in Poona in 1893, but Lokmanya Tilak introduced an educational angle to the festivities in 1894. The Saarvajanik Ganeshostav took firm roots in Bombay since 1895. Typically, these festivities would take place in chawls and buildings like Keshav Naikanchi Chawl, Goregaonkar Building, Soman Chawl, Shantaramachi Chawl, Zaobachi Chawl, Jintikaranchi Chawl, Natunchi Chawl, Vaidyachi Chawl, Gangaram Kshatriya Chawl, Angryanchi Wadi, Jagannathachi Chawl, Ramathi Pura, Lanke Chawl, Sardargraha, and Shastri Hall. Brahman Sabha in the Shankar Wadi came to play a prominent role in these festivities only much later. In most cases, *kirtans*, *bhajans*, and *powadas* would be presented, and lectures would also be

31 Vilayat Hussein Khan, *op.cit.*, pp.16-19.

held.[32] Later, well-known practitioners of Hindustani music were invited to perform on these occasions. For instance, Bhaskarbuwa Bakhale performed every year during the Brahman Sabha Ganpati celebrations, and Master Krishnarao, disciple of Bhaskarbuwa Bakhale, was also invited to sing at the Brahman Sabha Ganpati celebrations held at the Gandharva Mahavidyalaya.[33] Vinayakrao Patwardhan and Narayanrao Vyas also performed at Sarvajanik Ganeshotsavs. These Ganeshotsavs even featured amateur performers.[34] Apparently, vocalist Mallikarjun Mansoor (1910-1992), originally from the Dharwad region and trained in the Gwalior and Jaipur-Atrauli styles, also gained popularity among the city's music lovers after his recital in 1944 at a Ganeshotsav concert in Bombay.[35]

The public concert culture reached a climax with the seven-day Vikramaditya Sahastrabdi Mahotsav held at the University Convocation Hall in 1944. This unprecedented function began every evening at 6.30 pm and had a morning session on Sunday. It was organised by a Committee comprising of Champaklal Modi, O.D. Vyas, an ophthalmic surgeon, and a few others. The event was presided over by noted barrister Mukundrao Jaykar. Only season tickets were sold in advance and the ticket denominations were Rs.30/-, Rs.50/-, Rs.100/-, and Rs.200/-. The venue was packed to capacity with even the balcony completely booked.

Artistes were allotted an hour each for their performances and they were listed as per seniority as far as possible with juniors preceding seniors. The Mahotsav featured performances of almost all noted male and female vocalists, and instrumentalists like *sitar*, *sarod*, *shehnai*, *pakhawaj*, *tabla* players, practising diverse styles of Hindustani music and belonging to various *gharanas*. Among the notable performances on this occasion, were vocal recitals by Alladiya Khan and Kesarbai Kerkar representing the Jaipur-Atrauli *gayaki*, Faiyaz Khan belonging to the Agra

32 J.S. Karandikar (ed.), *Shreeganeshotsavaachi saatth varshe*, "J.S. Karandikar", Pune, 1953, pp.8-9, 17-18, 150.

33 B.R. Deodhar, *Thor sangeetkaar*, *op.cit.*, pp.78-79.

34 J.S. Karandikar (ed.), *op.cit.*, p.186. Also see interview with Kaushalya and Dinker Manjeshwar held on 10 September 1993.

35 Bhanu Charankar, "*Gelya dashakaateel sangeet kshetraateel padzhad*", in *Naadbrahma*, Madhavi Prakashan, Mumbai, January 1994, p.11.

tradition, Hirabai Badodekar following the Kirana *gayaki*, *sarod* recitals by Hafiz Ali Khan and Sakhawat Hussein Khan, *been* performance by Sadiq Ali Khan, *bansuri* recital by Pannalal Ghosh, *tabla* recitals by Ahmed Jan Thirakwa and Anokhelal Mishra from Banaras, and *shehnai* recital by Bismillah Khan. Other performances that were received well by the audience included vocal recitals by Omkarnath Thakur and *thumri* singers Siddheshwari Devi, Rasoolan Bai and Begum Akhtar. The function began with a *saraswati veena* recital by Venkatgiri Appya, court musician of Mysore, and ended with a vocal recital by Alladiya Khan. This was also perhaps the last time that he was heard in public performance. It was at this festival that Bade Ghulam Ali Khan (1901-1968), reputed vocalist of the Patiala tradition, and Vilayat Khan (1928-2004), eminent *sitar* player of the Itawah tradition, gained wide public acclaim.[36]

Apart from regular concerts, Bombay also saw public events organized by individuals and institutions to mark special occasions. For instance, a condolence meeting for Paluskar was held in August 1931.[37] At another programme presided over by M.R. Jaykar, Alladiya Khan was awarded the titles of Sangeet Samrat and Mount Everest of Music.[38] Two concerts were held at the Cowasji Jehangir Hall, Fort, on 15th and 30th April 1939, in aid of the Abdul Karim Khan Memorial Fund started in 1938. The concerts featured disciples of Abdul Karim Khan and other musicians who had been associated with him.[39] In a rare occurrence, a Nritya Utsav or dance festival directed by Hiten Chaudhury was held at St. Xavier's College on December 15, 1939, in aid of the Bombay Presidency Women's Council. The orchestra consisted of Nandalal Ghosh, Rajen Mukherjee, Gopal Singh, P.D. Sharma, Alauddin Khan, Ram-

---

36 Govindrao Tembe, *Gaayanmaharshee Alladiyakhan yaanche charitra*, *op.cit.*, pp.97-98. Also see Susheela Misra, *Music Profiles*, *op.cit.*, p.81; Balkrishnabuwa Kapileshwari, *op.cit.*, p.214; Batuk Diwanji, "*Ek sangeetkaarnee nondhpothee*", in *Navneet Samarpan*, (Gujarati), Bharatiya Vidya Bhavan, April 2000, pp.45-47. Additional information obtained from interview with Batuk Diwanji held in January 1993.

37 B.R. Deodhar, *Gaayanaachaarya P. Vishnu Digambar*, *op.cit.*, p.17.

38 Vilayat Hussein Khan, *op.cit.*, pp.177-178.

39 Michael Kinnear, *Sangeet Ratna – The Jewel of Music: A Bio-Discography of Khan Sahib Abdul Karim Khan*, Author, Heidelberg, Australia, 2003, pp.142-143.

krishna Udyavar, Chandrakant Naik, Jayanti Shah, Indu Roy, and Sunil Biswas. The singers were Sital Ghose, Sudhira Ghose, and Abha Basu.[40]

Thus, by the 1940s, the public concert platform was firmly entrenched in Bombay's musical landscape. Whether through the network of music circles or by way of other public events, a middle class audience now had easier access to concerts and public patronage to music and musicians became the norm.

40 *Nritya Utsav or Dance Festival in aid of the Rescue Home and Sub-Committees of the Bombay Presidency Women's Council*, BPWC, Bombay, 1939, p. 15.

ADAPTIVE STRATEGIES: PEDAGOGY

Gharana

Different styles in Hindustani music had been referred to by nomenclatures that have changed over centuries. For instance, since the medieval period, *dhrupad* styles were identified as *baani*s, a word derived from *vaani* related to speech, words, language or voice.[1] Terms like *gayaki* and *baaj* were used later to refer to vocal and instrumental styles, respectively. But institutionalized music education challenged traditional pedagogy, necessitating a change. Musicians in Bombay were quick to recognize this, and gradually, the term *gharana* came to be commonly accepted towards the end of the nineteenth century as a defining model for musical styles that could be identifiable to a largely uninitiated urban audience. Originally meaning family or lineage, a *gharana* was identified by the region it originated from or by the founder's place of origin or residence, as was the case with terms like *gayaki* or *baaj*. But *gharana*, going beyond strict norms of genealogy, referred to hereditary musicians from a particular lineage and the tree of disciples and grand-disciples outside the founder's family, all following a specific musical style. For some, this period was the 'golden age' of Hindustani music

1 Ashok Da Ranade, *Music Contexts: A Concise Dictionary of Hindustani Music*, *op.cit.*, pp.87-88.

when music was supposed to have been preserved in its pristine form by generations of accomplished musicians.[2]

Bombay played host to members of many *gharana*s, who continued to practice their respective musical styles and trained other musicians. There were also instances of new *gharana*s that came up in the city. Their founders were trained in established styles, but deviated from them and added features that changed the character of the original style. For instance, Nazir Khan (d.1920), a reputed *sarangi* player and disciple of Inayat Hussein Sahaswanwale and Ghulam Haider alias Kallan Khan Agrewale, and his brothers Sajjad Hussein alias Chhajju Khan and Khadim Hussein started the Bhendi Bazaar *gharana* of vocal music. Originally from Muradabad, Nazir Khan moved to Rampur to seek an appointment as a court musician, after which he shifted to Bombay with his brothers. All three became successful as teachers to several women vocalists in the city and bought an independent house in the Bhendi Bazaar area. Popularly known as Bhendi Bazaarwale, their style of vocal music thus came to be known as the Bhendi Bazaar *gayaki*.[3] The Bambai *gharana* of *tabla* became popular because its founder Munir Khan lived in Bombay for several years and trained a huge number of disciples here. The six major styles of *tabla* playing Delhi, Ajrada, Lucknow, Farrukhabad, Banaras and Punjab, demonstrated separate stylistic approaches and repertoire, but many *tabla* players in the late nineteenth and early twentieth centuries assimilated content from more than one *gharana*. Munir Khan was one of the prominent *tabla* players to have adopted this approach and is believed to have received training in four *gharana*s under twenty-four *guru*s including his father Kale Khan, Hussein Ali Khan, and Boli Bakhsh. He trained several disciples, many of who became path-breaking soloists, accompanists, teachers and composers. Originally hailing from Laliana in present-day Uttar Pradesh, many therefore addressed the lineage of disciples started by Munir Khan as the Laliana *gharana*. But this lineage also came to be

---

2 Vamanrao H. Deshpande, *Indian Musical Traditions*, *op.cit.*, pp.116-117.

3 Anjanibai Malpekar, "*Hum gaayako ka bhaagya khul gayaa*", in *Bhatkhande smriti granth*, (Hindi), Indira Kala Sangit Vishwavidyalaya, Khairagarh, M.P., 1966, pp.322-325; See Govindrao Tembe, *Maazha sangeet vyaasang*, *op.cit.*, pp.74-75, 79.

called the Bambai *gharana*, because Munir Khan spent a large part of his life in Bombay and trained several disciples here.[4]

Munir Khan's assimilative and eclectic approach was found among others who were equally eager to imbibe knowledge from a variety of sources. Clearly, eclecticism was very much prevalent, despite the desire to maintain musical exclusivity and hereditary ownership through the *gharana* model. As observed by B.R. Deodhar, Ramakrishnabuwa Vaze had learnt from several vocalists following various styles. His singing could therefore, not be categorised under the Gwalior *gayaki* in its entirety, although he trained in that style. Thus, Deodhar suggested that his style be called 'Vaze *gayaki*'. In fact, Vazebuwa's eclectic interests were not restricted to vocal music alone, as he also played the fiddle and the *sitar*.[5]

The decision to learn from more than one *guru* was prompted by the disciple's interest in other styles or at times even by the lack of continued guidance available in the same city or town. However, as per convention, a new *guru* could be approached only after the previous *guru* granted permission for such a change. This was therefore largely dependent on the magnanimity of the previous *guru*, as is evident from Bhaskarbuwa Bakhale's experience. Faiz Mohammad Khan, his first *guru* in Baroda, advised Bhaskarbuwa to learn from Natthan Khan Agrewale in order to imbibe elements that were peculiar to the latter's style. After learning from Natthan Khan in Bombay, Bhaskarbuwa was advised by him to learn from Alladiya Khan in the city, once again to enhance his musical spectrum.[6] Even Faiyaz Khan, in his boyhood years was encouraged by his *gurus*, namely, Ghulam Abbas Khan, his maternal grandfather, and Kallan Khan, his maternal grand-uncle, to listen to leading musicians pursuing various styles. His comprehensive musicianship is said to be the result of the tutelage he received and the influences he incorporated in his style. Consequently, he became adept at several diverse forms like *khayal*, *dhrupad-dhamaar*, *tarana*, *thumri*,

---

4 Arvind Mulgaonkar, *op.cit.*, pp. 365-366. See also, Aneesh Pradhan, *Tabla: A Performer's Perspective*, *op.cit.*, pp.32-33.

5 B.R. Deodhar, *Thor sangeetkaar*, *op.cit.*, pp.111,114,118.

6 *Ibid*, pp.86-88.

tirvat, hori, dadra, tappa, rasiya, ghazal.[7] Another classic example of a musician procuring knowledge from a variety of individuals is that of Vilayat Hussein Khan, who lists forty-one such sources.[8]

This eclecticism got a fillip once musicians pursuing different musical styles came together in Bombay and disciples got an opportunity to listen to such a wide variety. The *gharana* ideology was an accepted fact even for those who did not belong to hereditary musician families, but learnt individually from musicians following a particular style. Disciples moved from one *guru* to another across *gharana*s, but even at this stage, this was done while respecting the convention of seeking permission from previous *guru*s. On the other hand, institutionalized music education inculcated a different perspective among amateurs. Music schools standardized their training and repertoire and *gharana* loyalties were therefore not a reality for amateurs learning in such institutions. Thus, *gharana*s at once became a defining feature and also a porous phenomenon in the urban context and musicians were quick to adapt to this logic.

The tuition ethos

The fact that the commercial, industrial and intellectual elite displayed an interest in studying Hindustani music in the comfort of their homes at a predetermined time and that they could provide much-needed patronage by way of a fixed monthly tuition fee prompted musicians to restructure the traditional *guru-shishya* pedagogic format to accommodate this new class of students. The commercialisation of the transmission process that had begun with the financial arrangement between the women performers and their *guru*s was well entrenched in early twentieth century Bombay with this form of exchange growing among amateur *shishya*s. It opened the doors of music learning to amateurs for whom the study of music was only a leisure pursuit. These students did not provide services to the *guru* as was done by disciples who wished to pursue music as a profession. In some cases, these *shishya*s provided the *guru* with extra financial aid and looked after his needs. For instance,

7 N. Jayavanth Rao, *op.cit.*, pp.24-25.

8 Vilayat Hussein Khan, *op.cit.*, pp.128-135.

Madhavdas Gokuldas Pasta (1856-1937), a wealthy mill owner, studied vocal music under Daulat Khan, a *dhrupad* singer, and retained his services until the latter's death. He also engaged the services of *pakhawaj* player Makkhan for a period of twenty-five years. Madhavdas Pasta's brother, Vitthaldas, learnt *khayal* from Alladiya Khan.[9] Alladiya Khan also taught Gulubhai Jasdanwala, a businessman, who had learnt earlier from the former's second son, Manji Khan.[10]

This is not to say that living and working conditions for musicians in the city or the rest of the country improved vastly, due to the modern tuition ethos, as seems to have been concluded by Margaret Cousins. She stated:

> . . . the status of the professional musician in India is being raised. The teacher is being paid according to rates set by government standard similar to those given for other subjects; similarly there is increased appreciation, financial and otherwise, for virtuoso entertainers.[11]

Far from this positive account about the status of musicians in Indian society, musicians had to cope with the challenging circumstances in Bombay. The case of vocalist Khadim Hussein Khan amply demonstrates the manner in which musicians steadily adapted themselves to an environment that was significantly different from the one they were accustomed to under princely patronage. Khadim Hussein Khan travelled by the cheapest mode of transport, the electric tramcar, to teach his first student in the city for a monthly fee of Rs.20/-. Subsequently, other students paid him a fee of Rs.25/- each per month.[12] Natthan Khan, nephew and disciple of Alladiya Khan, received a monthly tuition fee of Rs.30/- from Vamanrao Deshpande between the years 1940 and 1946, with a separate fee for the *tabla* player accompanying the

---

9 From note prepared on Madhavdas Gokuldas Pasta by S.V. Gokhale in Govindrao Tembe, *Maazha sangeet vyaasang*, *op.cit.*, p.166. Also see Arvind Mulgaonkar, *op.cit.*, p.422.

10 Govindrao Tembe, *Gaayanmaharshi Alladiyakhan yaanche charitra*, *op.cit.*, p.95.

11 Margaret E. Cousins, *op.cit.*, p.180.

12 Khadim Hussein Khan came to Bombay in 1925. See N. Jayavanth Rao, *op.cit.*, pp.51,58-61,64-65.

sessions.[13] The tuition format was similarly followed in towns outside Bombay. Unfortunately, there is no exhaustive information, which could allow drawing comparisons between the fee structure in Bombay and elsewhere. But B.R. Deodhar's account of his early lessons in music at Miraj, give some indication of the fees charged in other areas. Thus, Vamanbuwa Chaphekar (1880-1964), disciple of Balkrishnabuwa Ichalkaranjikar, was paid a monthly fee of 8 annas to give daily lessons to Deodhar in 1908/09. Chaphekar and other vocalists in Miraj during this period earned their living by teaching professional women performers, as learning music was taboo in respectable society.[14]

However, the status of the *gurus* was better in the context of disciples training to become professionals. Here, it was the disciples who had to face uncertainties. In addition to the struggle they had to undergo in convincing their *gurus* to impart knowledge, regular guidance from one *guru* was seldom possible, because musicians constantly moved to a region that held promise of patronage or that was a vestige of princely patronage. The difficulty experienced by the *shishya* due to this constant migration is best seen in the case of Kesarbai Kerkar. Her training in Bombay under Barkatullah Khan was intermittent because of his sojourns to the Patiala and Mysore princely courts and to Poona. She then tried learning from Alladiya Khan and Bhaskarbuwa Bakhale and thereafter from Ramkrishnabuwa Vaze, but these efforts also failed due to an absence of any extended period of teaching. It was only in 1920 that she was successful in being accepted as a disciple of Alladiya Khan and the tutelage lasted over a considerable length of time.[15]

Thus, despite the modern urban environment, the *guru-shishya* relation structure continued to be one in which the *guru* could dictate terms, which the *shishya* had to acquiesce to. Even in twentieth century Bombay, there were occasions when the *guru* laid down stringent conditions, which the potential professional had to scrupulously follow.

---

13 Vamanrao H. Deshpande, *Between Two Tanpuras*, *op.cit.*, p.16.

14 B.R. Deodhar, *Thor sangeetkar*, *op.cit.*, pp.152-153.

15 *Ibid*, p.195-200. Kesarbai Kerkar's birthdate is mentioned as 1890 in Susheela Misra, *Great Masters of Hindustani Music*, *op.cit.*, p.134, and as 1893 in Laxminarayan Garg, *op.cit.*, p.128.

The requirements specified by Alladiya Khan before agreeing to teach Kesarbai Kerkar are illustrative. She had to pay a sum of Rs.5000/- at the *ganda-bandhan* in addition to a pre-determined monthly salary. Alladiya Khan specified that he would leave Bombay if he found the climate unsuitable, but he stipulated that Kesarbai would be required to learn at the new place of residence. His salary was to continue even if he was absent due to ill health or other reasons. He also laid down the condition that the training would continue for ten years.[16]

On the other hand, one cannot ignore the rare instance of a *shishya*, who sought legal redress for the *guru* not having kept his promise to teach her. This was the case of the niece of a famous songstress who had her *ganda* tied by vocalist Rajab Ali Khan (1875-1959), for which she had offered him a sum of Rs.1,500/-. Soon thereafter, Rajab Ali Khan moved to Dewas and the teaching was discontinued. The disciple therefore served him with a legal notice on his return from Dewas, demanding the return of the money that had been paid to him at the *ganda-bandhan* ceremony since he had not fulfilled his part of the agreement. The notice further stated that a legal suit would be filed in the event that he did not repay the amount. Though the matter was settled in favour of Rajab Ali Khan, it is evident that a new world-view was emerging among performers. In this instance, the court of law was seen as an arbiter in a dispute that would otherwise have been dealt with through the conventional *panchayat* and *chaudhari/chaudharain* arrangement.[17]

Gurus chose a dichotomous approach in their choice of teaching methodology for the elite and the potential professionals, by making compromises while teaching the former, but remaining firmly grounded in tradition when teaching the latter. They ensured that a strict regimen of *taaleem* and *riyaaz* was followed in the case of potential professionals. For instance, Nazir Khan Bhendibazarwale taught Anjanibai Malpekar at her residence everyday from 5 a.m. His brothers Sajjad Hussein alias Chajju Khan and Khadim Hussein Khan taught Anjanibai at other times during the day. The early part of the training involved

16 B.R. Deodhar, *Thor sangeetkar*, *op.cit.*, pp.21,199-200.

17 *Ibid*, p.138. Unfortunately, the names of the woman performer and her niece are not available.

several vocal exercises that were taught specifically to gain command over voice projection, breathing technique, intonation and rhythm. The traditional method also concentrated on a detailed treatment of the repertoire. Consequently, Anjanibai was taught *raag* Yaman for the first three and a half years, and was then taught *raag* Bhairav for another year and a half. Additionally, Anjanibai was trained in dance, as professional women performers continued to study music and dance through this period. She also studied Urdu and Sanskrit, since this was part of a woman performer's grooming.[18] But in the case of hobbyists, no such regimen could be enforced and the *guru* was forced to compromise.

Their ways of negotiating new teaching requirements in the city did not deter musicians from falling back on the traditional format once outside the urban situation. The teaching methodology followed by Balkrishnabuwa Ichalkaranjikar aptly illustrates that while adapting himself to conditions in Bombay, he remained a staunch believer in the conventional *guru-shishya parampara* during his stay in Miraj thereafter. While in Bombay in the 1880s, Balkrishnabuwa started a music class and a monthly periodical dedicated entirely to music.[19] To that extent, he contributed to the dissemination of music among amateurs along modern lines. But once he settled in Miraj, he went back to age-old practices. His disciples swept his house, spread cow-dung and watered it, washed clothes and utensils, chopped firewood, looked after his children and completed other tasks as directed by him. The *taaleem* took place mainly at night, but at times even in the morning. The training pattern in Miraj demonstrated influences of his stay in Bombay, but it retained the ethos of the traditional style. It is likely that during his days in Bombay, Balkrishnabuwa taught groups of students in his class.[20] In Miraj, he continued teaching his disciples in a classroom situation. They were to sit together in *virasana* (and form semi-circles, with senior disciples in the first semi-circle and juniors behind them. However, Balkrishnabuwa did not permit a spirit of enquiry among the disciples in Miraj. Often, compositions were taught with no mention

18 Mangala Khadilkar, *op.cit.*

19 See footnote 37 for further details.

20 B.R. Deodhar, *Thor sangeetkar*, *op.cit.*, pp.155-156.

of names and rules of the *raags*. Disciples were strictly forbidden from noting down the words of the compositions and there was no standardised method of notation. The choice of compositions was made by Balkrishnabuwa and these were practised innumerable times in order to get them right. His *gayaki* was to be comprehended by singing along with him.[21]

Impact of institutionalised training on musicians

The dichotomous existence of musicians in Bombay was also reflected in their response to institutionalised music education in the city. Most musicians opposed the idea, but some noticed the recognition that this form of training received from the elite. A few of them taught at music clubs in the city.

Gradually, some musicians started conducting their own classes in the city, possibly taking a cue from music clubs. Balkrishnabuwa Ichalkaranjikar's was a remarkable case, as it showed the extent to which a musician was willing and able to adapt himself to new urban conditions. He was one of the first musicians to have started his classes in the 1880s. Eminent personalities from the educated gentry in Bombay like the jurist K.T. Telang (1850-1893), and scholars R.G. Bhandarkar (1837-1925) and V.N. Mandlik (1833-1889), were among who attended these classes.[22] While their response to these classes is not documented, biographer P.M. Lad mentions in his memoir on K.T. Telang, "Literature was the main delight of his life; and he had also acquired a taste for music and even had with his (*sic*) a couple of *Sitars*."[23]

---

21 B.R. Deodhar, *Gaayanaachaarya P. Vishnu Digambar, op.cit.*, pp.4,20-21.

22 Vamanrao Deshpande, *Maharashtra's Contribution to Music, op.cit.*, pp.13-14. Also see B.R. Deodhar, *Thor sangeetkaar, op.cit.*, pp.12-13. Elsewhere, Balkrishnabuwa Ichalkaranjikar has been described as a teacher at the Bombay Gayan Samaj. It is therefore not known whether the individuals mentioned above were learning from him privately or at this Samaj. If the Samaj alluded to here is the Bombay Branch of the Poona Gayan Samaj, then the date of this teaching assignment would be post-1883, which the year when the Samaj was founded in Bombay. See Shankar Ganesh Date and others (ed.), *op.cit.*, p.335.

23 P.M. Lad, *Kashinath Trimbak Telang – 1850-1893*, Telang Centenary Celebration Committee, Bombay, p.15.

Later in the twentieth century, more musicians conducted classes in Bombay, probably inspired by the rising popularity of music schools. In 1917, vocalist Abdul Karim Khan started a music class in Bombay named Arya Sangeet Vidyalaya, a branch of the Arya Sangeet Samaj that he had set up previously in Poona in 1913. Notably, Abdul Karim Khan started the school in Poona after observing Paluskar's work in this area. He admitted needy students who signed a seven-year bond. The school looked after their expenses and they accompanied Abdul Karim Khan on his concert tours. His concerts would feature *jaltarang*, *tabla-tarang*, *ghantitarang*, *shehnai*, and dance, among other items. The concerts would conclude with his performance. He shut the school in 1920 and moved to Miraj.[24] There are several other instances that demonstrate ways in which musicians remoulded their conventional approach and set up music classes in Bombay. For instance, Anant Manohar Joshi (1878-1967), a disciple of his father and Balkrishnabuwa Ichalkaranjikar and Rehmat Khan, was for many years the President of the Guru Samarth Sangeet Vidyalaya in Bombay.[25] Omkarnath Thakur also shifted his music school from Bharoch to Bombay in 1934.[26] Vocalist and *binkar* Krishna Ganesh Mule (1864-1944), disciple of Purshottam Ganesh alias Anna Gharpure (1842-1920), Ganesh Krishna Apte, and Bande Ali Khan started the Veenavadan Sangeet Vidyalaya at Dadar.[27] Likewise, Balkrishnabuwa Kapileshwari and his brother, disciples of Abdul Karim Khan, established the Shri Saraswati Sangeet Vidyalaya in 1920 to teach their *guru*'s vocal style. The Vidyalaya organized peri-

24 Ashok Da. Ranade, *On Music and Musicians of Hindoostan*, *op.cit.*, p.151. See also, Laxminarayan Garg, *op.cit.*, p.85. B.R. Deodhar mentions the name of the Poona school as Arya Sangeet Vidyalaya. See B.R. Deodhar, *Thor sangeetkaar*, *op.cit.*, pp.131-132. For a detailed account of Abdul Karim Khan's life, recordings, and his educational activities, see Michael Kinnear, *Sangeet Ratna – The Jewel of Music: A Bio-Discography of Khan Sahib Abdul Karim Khan*, *op.cit.*

25 Laxminarayan Garg, *op.cit.*, p.83. Joshi's year of birth is given as 1881 elsewhere. See http://www.gajananbuwajoshi.com/anant_manohar_joshi

26 *Ibid*, p.183.

27 See note prepared by S.V. Gokhale in Govindrao Tembe, *Maazhaa sangeet vyaasang*, *op.cit.*, pp.128-130.

odic concerts at Blavatsky Lodge and other venues.[28] Still later, Navrang Nagpurkar (1919-1999) alias Master Navrang, disciple of Krishnarao Shankar Pandit, Narayanrao Vyas, Shankarrao Vyas, Narayan Moreshwar Khare and Aman Ali Khan, started a music class Sangeet Mandir in 1944, which gave preliminary training to numerous students many of whom rose to become well known vocalists in art and popular music.[29] Some musicians also started classes where one teacher trained students in more than one subject. Jaffer Khan, a *been* and *sitar* player also well versed in vocal music, started the Dadar Sangeet Vidyalaya at his residence. He conducted classes for *sitar*, *tabla*, *jaltarang*, harmonium and vocal music, under the banner of the Vidyalaya. These classes did not follow any syllabus and there were no fixed timings for teaching. He used a rudimentary system of notation in Urdu. The fees also varied, but were in the range of Rs.15/- to Rs.20/- per month.[30]

Available information suggests that these classes did not follow a strictly laid down syllabus. Other than the nomenclature and group sessions, there were very few elements that were adopted from the more formally established institutions. These music classes were often conducted to supplement the income that the teachers drew from their performances or from the regular tuition that they gave at the homes of students. Deodhar's School of Indian Music, however, was significantly different in its approach, as has already been discussed earlier.

Sangeet Pracharak Mandal

The impact of institutionalization and the anxiety felt by hereditary musicians to take a more proactive role in this movement, was best seen in an extraordinary case of musicians coming together in 1931 to set up an educational institution and a music circle in Bombay. Their experiences at music conferences held in Bombay also probably motivated them to take steps in this direction. Vilayat Hussein Khan took the lead

28 B.R. Deodhar, *Thor sangeetkaar*, *op.cit.*, p.136. For more details on the Shri Saraswati Sangeet Vidyalaya, see Michael Kinnear, *Sangeet Ratna – The Jewel of Music: A Bio-Discography of Khan Sahib Abdul Karim Khan*, *op.cit.*, pp.73, 97-100.

29 Madanlal Vyas, "*Bahumukhee pratibhaa ke dhanee Master Navrang*", in *Dr. Navrang Nagpurkar Amrut Mahotsav* souvenir, Bombay, 1994.

30 Interview with Abdul Halim Jaffer Khan held on 6 May 1997.

by convening a meeting of some well-known vocalists from various lineages, who were then visiting Bombay or residing in the city, with the intention of convincing them of the necessity to set up a music school and music circle run by musicians. He believed this would bring about greater interaction among these musicians and help in arriving at a consensus for drawing up a syllabus to be followed by the proposed school. According to the account presented by him, Alladiya Khan presided over the meeting and those present included Manji Khan, Faiyaz Khan, Abdul Karim Khan, Aman Ali Khan, Azmat Hussein Khan, Anwar Hussein Khan, and Khadim Hussein Khan. The fact that the participants belonged to Muslim hereditary musician families may suggest a communal response to institutionalized music education propagated by Hindu music educationists. But it is important to note that no Muslim instrumentalists were present, thus demonstrating the hierarchy that still put vocalists on a higher pedestal even among Muslim musicians. Undoubtedly, this proves that Muslim musicians were not a monolithic entity. Indeed, this was not true even of Hindu musicians.

While addressing the gathering, Aman Ali Khan clarified that he would be involved in the project only if the proposed school would adopt the syllabus that he had prepared. Abdul Karim Khan stressed the need for unity among all musicians and stated that he was willing to participate in the venture if titles associated with names of musicians were removed. Vilayat Hussein Khan emphasised the need for the school. Faiyaz Khan said that self-praise would not help and that they needed unity. He spoke in favour of drawing up a common syllabus of popular *raag*s in order to take the theory of music a step further and to help students of music. He felt that *raag*s having commonly accepted structures could be retained as such, but rare *raag*s interpreted in diverse ways needed vocalists from across the country to draw up standardised versions of these. Being a precursor of the *khayal*, the *dhrupad* form was believed to have retained the older version of a *raag*, and *dhrupad*s were considered to be benchmarks of authenticity in interpreting *raag*s, as they were said to encapsulate the image of the *raag*s. Faiyaz Khan therefore recommended that vocalists should present *dhrupad*s from their repertoire, which would then prove the legitimacy of the version that they felt should be accepted.[31] Concluding the meeting, Alladiya Khan held that no syllabus was incorrect as there were different interpretations of each *raag*. He sang one or two compositions in *raag* Malkauns, which according to Vilayat Hussein Khan sounded beautiful despite the fact that they did not display a common character of the *raag*. Though this meeting did not bring about any common ground for agreement, Vilayat Hussein Khan pursued the idea and organised yet another meeting. As many musicians did not respond to his second invitation, he brought together the vocalists of the Agra lineage at his residence and invited Alladiya Khan and Manji Khan to preside over the meeting. They decided to start a music circle to organize programmes and to collect funds for enhancing music-related activities. This led to the formation of the Sangeet Pracharak Mandal.[32]

The Sangeet Pracharak Mandal, despite its failure to achieve consensus, was significant as it brought to the fore concerns and perspectives of hereditary musicians amidst undercurrents of professional rivalry and insecurities.

Looking Westwards – B.R. Deodhar and Giovanni Scrinzi[33]

Circumstances leading to B.R. Deodhar's of study Western art music under pianist Giovanni Scrinzi (c.1864-1935) have been discussed earlier. This singular experiment in pedagogy for a Hindustani music practitioner merits detailed discussion. The dialogue between the two equipped Deodhar with information about the Western musical system and also gave him the opportunity to experience Western teaching methodology. This encounter had no major impact on the musical life of Bombay, and yet, this being a solitary case of extended musical inter-

31 Being a precursor of the *khayal*, the *dhrupad* form was believed to have retained the older version of a *raag*, and *dhrupads* were considered to be benchmarks of authenticity in interpreting *raags*, as they were said to encapsulate the correct portrayal of the *raags*.

32 Vilayat Hussein Khan, *op.cit.*, pp.16-19.

33 This sub-section is based on information provided in B.R. Deodhar, *Thor sangeetkaar, op.cit.*, pp.45-67, unless otherwise mentioned. For more information on the beginnings of Western art music in Bombay, see http://www.tajmahalfoxtrot.com/?p=685

action between practitioners of two systems of music in the city makes it particularly relevant.

A pupil of Begniamino Cesi who in turn studied under pianists and composers, Sigismond Thalberg (1812-1871) and Franz Liszt (1811-1886), Giovanni Scrinzi came to Bombay with his mother in 1889, on the advice of his elder brother who was already working as a secretary to a Belgian lawyer in Bombay. His brother had advised Scrinzi to come to Bombay and take up the job of teaching music as the city lacked a good artiste. In Bombay, Scrinzi devoted all his time to practising piano and refining his command over the English language. He started his first tuition within a period of three to four months of his arrival in the city. His first student, who paid him a monthly fee of Rs.40/-, later introduced several other prospective students through his friends' circle. After staying in Bombay for about ten years, he went back to Italy with his mother. Scrinzi returned to India later and through his earlier contacts, got several tuition assignments in rich Parsi households. He was music critic for the *Times of India*, Bombay. Scrinzi composed works based on certain Indian scales, some of which have been published by Ricordi Ltd. of Europe. He left behind several students among who were many Parsi women, Europeans and Indian Christians. His first student Bhikaji Palamkote started her own school of music and was popular among the Parsis. Cursetjee Wadia and his daughters were other noteworthy students, who belonged to a wealthy family and pursued music as a hobby. His elder daughter, Hillabai sang at many concerts and the younger daughter won acclaim as a pianist in India as well as in Europe. Scrinzi also taught piano for many years at the residence of Justice Coyaji of the Bombay High Court.

Scrinzi asked Deodhar to procure all the books mentioned in the syllabus of the Trinity College of Music, London, and taught him as per the syllabus of the College. Pleased with Deodhar's progress, Scrinzi spoke highly of him to Paluskar. The latter then rented a piano from S. Rose Company at forty rupees per month, to help Deodhar pursue his practice at the GM premises.

Deodhar left the GM in 1922, but continued to learn from Scrinzi twice a week. During their meetings, Scrinzi encouraged Deodhar to read books on music from his personal collection. At times he notated a Hindi song and introduced harmony into it. They also discussed issues related to the *shrutis*, which were employed in Indian music.

Scrinzi took Deodhar to recitals of an Italian Company performing at the Royal Opera House in 1924. He explained the narrative, and provided him with information about the composer and special features of that opera. Deodhar was surprised at the power, volume and emotions expressed by the singers and the orchestra. Deodhar studied the European method of voice training from Scrinzi. Scrinzi felt that voice training in India did not receive requisite importance, which led to faulty vocal technique. He brought this to Deodhar's notice when they attended music concerts.

Scrinzi performed once or twice a year in the programmes held by the Bombay Symphony Orchestra. This orchestra was founded in 1921 with Edward Behr, a German, as its Director and Conductor. Lord George Lloyd, the then Governor and Lady Lloyd were patrons of this Orchestra. The works of European composers like Beethoven, Brahms, Chopin, Bach, were presented through these concerts. The programme note for 13 November 1924, states that the Orchestra hoped to "provide the citizens of Bombay with frequent performances of the finest orchestral music at popular prices so that all classes of every community can have the chance of this valuable intellectual culture".[34] Deodhar on the other hand concluded that many Indians attended these concerts to emulate the ways of the Westerners and would clap with the others after every performance even though they did not understand music.

Scrinzi's recital date was finalized four to six months in advance. Once the items were decided for the concert, he would then start practising the pieces. For the first two to three months, he would practise daily for a minimum of two hours and on Sundays for four to five hours. A month before the programme, he would cancel his tuitions and devote all his time to practising piano. As part of his training Deodhar learnt the Western system of notation and assisted Scrinzi during his

34 *Bombay Symphony Orchestra*, Bombay Symphony Orchestra, Bombay, n.d. For programme notes and schedules of Bombay Symphony Orchestra programmes between 1921 and 1928, see the same source. See also, Naresh Fernandes, *op.cit.*, pp.60-63.

practice sessions by turning the music sheets according to the latter's requirement. Scrinzi made Deodhar aware of the responsibility of the Western musician to interpret the composer's work in a befitting manner taking into account the composer's aesthetic sensibility and inspiration.

Deodhar's interest in Western music and his connection with Scrinzi enabled Deodhar to procure an invitation to the world music conference held at Florence in 1933. While in Prague, Deodhar met Alois Haba, a Czech composer and academic, who had heard of Indian shrutis. He had a discussion with Deodhar on this subject and also showed him a quartertone piano that he had developed.[35]

Printed word

The lack of formal academic education did not deter musicians from writing and publishing works containing theoretical and practical information related to music, as they seem to have been inspired by the manner in which Indian intellectuals published periodicals and books to disseminate modern and traditional knowledge in multiple languages. A detailed study of each of the writings from this period will bring to the fore the authors' concerns, but that is beyond the scope of this book.

Musicians often partnered with intellectuals to publish music-related literature. In Baroda, Maula Baksh and Vishwanath Ramchandra Vakil jointly edited a monthly periodical called *Gaayanaabdhisetu* since April 1870.[36] The popularity exercised by periodicals in Bombay, perhaps motivated Balkrishnabuwa Ichalkaranjikar to bring out *Sangeet Darpan* in 1883, a monthly magazine consisting of information and lessons for *sitar* and vocal music, with the help of *sitar* player Vishwanath Ramchandra Kale. The magazine included theoretical and practical aspects of music.[37] The focus on *sitar* in these publications brings to light the fact that the instrument had gained acceptance in genteel society.

35 For a short bio-sketch on Alois Haba, see http://en.wikipedia.org/wiki/Alois_Hába

36 Shankar Ganesh Date and others (ed.), *op.cit.*, p.75.

37 For a detailed discussion on the book, see Ashok Da. Ranade, "Reflections on Musicology and History" in Special Issue of *Journal of the Indian Musicological Society*, Volume 31, Indian Musicological Society, January-December 2000, Baroda, pp.43-47. Also see, Shankar Ganesh Date and others (ed.), *op.cit.*, p.335; B.R. Deodhar,

The openness to write for periodicals continued even in the twentieth century. For instance, Deodhar was a prolific writer and had also contributed an article on *been* player Murad Khan for the Bombay Chronicle, at a time when articles on music seldom appeared in newspapers.[38] Similarly, Ramkrishnabuwa Vaze (1871-1945) also penned his memoirs in the weekly *Vasundhara* (1933). Vaze had completed four years of schooling with Marathi as the medium of instruction and could single-handedly author books on music. He wrote two volumes of *Sangeet Kalaprakash* (1938), which include compositions in rare *raags* and an autobiographical account.[39] There were other instances of musicians who had undergone academic education. For example, Krishna Ganesh Mule (1864-1944), a *been* player employed in a Bombay textile mill, had undergone school education. He studied the *Natyashastra* and wrote *Bharatiya Sangeet-Bhag 1*, published by N.C. Kelkar under the imprint of the latter's Yashoda-Chintamani Trust. This volume was a history of Indian music from Vedic times to the *Natya Shastra*. The next two volumes remained in manuscript form.[40] Govindrao Tembe (1889-1946), eminent harmonium player, composer and playwright, wrote articles on music. Later, he wrote his memoirs and a biography of Alladiya Khan.[41] G.B. Achrekar (1885-1939), a *sitar* player from Poona, also wrote extensively in Marathi on music.[42] Notably, books on *mridang* or *pakhawaj* and *tabla*, instruments primarily considered for accompaniment, were written by Dattatreya Vasudev alias Gurudev Patwardhan. Patwardhan was Vice-Principal of the Gandharva Mahavidyalaya in

---

Thor sangeetkaar, op.cit., p.13; Ashok D. Ranade, *Maharashtra: Art Music, op.cit.*, pp.68-69; Vijay Tapas, "*Gaanyaachaa aarsaa*", *Loksatta*, Bombay, 30 May 1993.

38 B.R. Deodhar, *Thor sangeetkaar, op.cit.*, p.71.

39 *Ibid*, p.111. See also, Ashok D. Ranade, *On Music and Musicians of Hindoostan, op.cit.*, p.141.

40 Govindrao Tembe, *Maazhaa sangeet vyaasang, op.cit.*, pp.128-130. See also Vamanrao Deshpande, *Maharashtra's Contribution to Music, op.cit.*, pp.49-50.

41 Vamanrao H. Deshpande, *Between Two Tanpuras, op.cit.*, p.33. Also see Govindrao Tembe, *Maazhaa sangeet vyaasang, op.cit.*; Govindrao Tembe, *Gaayanmaharshi Alladiyakhan yaanche charitra, op.cit.* For a comprehensive list of Tembe's other writings, see Govindrao Tembe, *Maazhaa sangeet vyaasang, op.cit.*, pp.180-182.

42 Vamanrao Deshpande, *Maharashtra's Contribution to Music, op.cit.*, pp.48-49.

Lahore and Bombay. His first book called *Mridang-tabla vaadanpaddhati* was published in 1903 and was used as a text for the Gandharva Mahavidyalaya classes in Lahore, but this was later considered more appropriate for advanced students. Consequently, he wrote *Mridang aur tabla vaadan paddhati: mridang aur tablekaa prathambhaag*, which was published in Bombay in 1910 and was used as the primary text for the Gandharva Mahavidyalaya students.[43]

Early writing on Hindustani music in this period also included the works of some intellectuals who possessed musical knowledge. They wrote musicological works and focused on discourses that were a part of the new pedagogical framework. Thus, they provided compositions in notated form, and discussed among other subjects, questions related to the presence and use of *shrutis* in Indian art music. For instance, Krishnaji Balwant Deval alias Ballal alias Balaji (1847-1931), District Deputy Collector at Ratnagiri, wrote prolifically between 1886 and 1908 on the issue of *shrutis* in the Indian scale. His treatise *Hindu Musical Scale and Twenty-two Shrutis* was published in 1910. Deval translated for *Navyug* magazine, five lectures delivered with demonstration by E. Clements in 1926, under the aegis of the Bombay University.[44] Mangeshrao Telang (1856-1949), Assistant Registrar in the Bombay High Court and a *veena* player, wrote *The Twenty-two shrutis of Indian music*, and several music-related articles.[45]

---

43 Sv. Dattatreya Vasudev alias Gurudev Patwardhan, *Mridang-tabla vaadanpaddhati*, (Hindi), Sangeet Natak Akademi, New Delhi, 1962; Shrimaan Gurudev Patwardhan, *Mridang aur tabla vaadan paddhati: mridang aur tablekaa prathambhaag*, (Hindi), Author, Bombay, 1910. For a detailed analysis of Patwardhan's writing, see James Kippen, *Gurudev's Drumming Legacy: Music, Theory and Nationalism in the Mrdang aur Tabla Vadanpaddhati of Gurudev Patwardhan*, Ashgate Publishing Limited, Hants, 2006.

44 Govindrao Tembe, *Maazhaa sangeet vyaasang*, *op.cit.*, pp.144-149; Vamanrao Deshpande, *Maharashtra's Contribution to Music*, *op.cit.*, pp.45-49. The date of publication for K.B. Deval's book *Hindu Musical Scale and Twenty-two Shrutis* is given as 1890 in Mohan Nadkarni, "Musical literature in Maharashtra", *Indian Express*, Bombay, 10 July 1990.

45 Laxminarayan Garg, *op.cit.*, pp.40-41. Mangeshrao Telang's year of birth is mentioned as 1859 in Govindrao Tembe, *Maazhaa sangeet vyaasang*, *op.cit.*, pp.71-72.

The general ignorance about Indian music among non-Indians gave way to more informed writings on the subject from British authors. In fact, there were rare moments when British and Indian authors and musicians worked closely as was the case when Bhatkhande helped Clements in translating and collating certain Indian texts for his book entitled *Introduction to the Study of Indian Music* focusing on the problem of determining the *shrutis* in Indian scales, although Bhatkhande disagreed with some of Clements' views. First published from London in 1913, the book was also aided by K.B. Deval's research in the subject.[46] Abdul Karim Khan joined Clements and Deval in researching the *shruti* problem, but later, he too had a difference of opinion with them.[47] Interestingly, the Philharmonic Society catering originally to Western music in Bombay and revived and renamed in May-June 1912 as the Philharmonic Society of Western India by Clements and Deval, published a three-part book of Dagurbani and Khandarbani *dhrupad* compositions with staff notation called *Ragas of Hindustan*. Later, it also published *Ragas of Tanjavur* and *The Tuning of the Sitar*.[48]

Literature on music was also printed in other parts of Western India, particularly in Poona. The Poona Gayan Samaj published a series of Marathi texts. Beginning with *Svarashastra: The Science of Sound:* in 1878, the Samaj went on to publish *Sataareeche Pahile Pustak* in 1883 written by Purshottam Ganesh Gharpure, the editor of the Marathi magazine *Sangeet Mimansak* (1886). The Samaj also published *Bal San-*

---

46 E. Clements, *Introduction to the Study of Indian Music*, Gaurav Publications, New Delhi, 1st Indian edition, 1981, pp.xiii-xv. For another instance of a Western scholar collaborating with an Indian musician, see A.H. Fox Strangways, *The Music of Hindostan*, Oxford University Press, London, 1914.

47 Ashok D. Ranade, *On Music and Musicians of Hindoostan*, *op.cit.*, p.151. See also, Michael Kinnear, *Sangeet Ratna – The Jewel of Music: A Bio-Discography of Khan Sahib Abdul Karim Khan, op.cit.*, pp.65-67. For a detailed discussion on Abdul Karim Khan's views related to the *shruti* issue, see Balkrishnabuwa Kapileshwari, *op.cit.* Kapileshwari is critical of most other musicians and scholars in this context and is particularly dismissive of Bhatkhande, Paluskar and their disciples, holding forth that it was only Abdul Karim Khan who could practically demonstrate the use of *shrutis* in Hindustani music.

48 There are different opinions on the exact year of its formation. P. F. Kapadia, *ibid*, p. 16, mentions the year 1869, and Govindrao Tembe, *Maazhaa sangeet vyaasang*, *op.cit.*, p.148, provides 1862, as the year in which the Society was established.

geet Bodha that was used in its classes, as well as works on Carnatic music like *Treatise on Hindu Music* by Seshagiri Shastri and a series in Telugu by T. Shringaracharlu.[49] Other publications in Poona included *Rekhaa*, a monthly periodical, which first appeared in January 1938. It was edited by Bal Gangadhar Ghaisas and published by Bhamburde from Poona on behalf of Madhukar Gayan Vadan Vidyalaya. This periodical though not entirely focusing on music, contained articles related to music, apart from stories, poems, horoscope, and other writings. *Bharatiya Sangeet* was a bimonthly edited jointly by Gangadhar Narayan Muzumdar and Keshav Anant Godbole. Published under the auspices of the Bharat Gayan Samaj, it continued from October 1932 to July 1935. It was stated that the aim of this publication was to improve the art of music in all respects, and to do away with the differences of opinion, which were said to exist among musicians. The scope of the periodical was very wide as it contained articles on the science of music, *dhvanichitrapat* (cinema), *Natyashastra*, notation, use of the Marathi language in musical compositions, Sanskrit treatises, *tabla*, *mridang*, the inclusion of music at university level, biographies, and such other topics. It also included compositions with notation.[50]

49 Janaki Bakhle, *op.cit.*, pp.65-67.

50 Shankar Ganesh Date and others (ed.), *op.cit.*, pp.74-75,269. For a detailed list of Marathi books on music published in the late nineteenth and early twentieth centuries, see Anupama Muzumdar (ed.), *Swarsangat Sardar*, Pratap Narayan Muzumdar, Pune, n.d., pp.26-31.

ADAPTIVE STRATEGIES: PERFORMANCE

Musicians met in informal gatherings or *daavat*s even in the twentieth century. Typically, Muslim musicians would meet at a fellow musician's residence after their customary Friday *namaaz* or prayers. Young and old, and junior and senior musicians were heard at these gatherings referred to as *jumma*, as they were held on Fridays. The name was retained even if they were held on any other day of the week. The audience comprised of musicians and connoisseurs.[1] Performances held here were often competitive in nature and challenges were thrown at each other to test creative ability and training. This form of performance was called *dangal* (lit. wrestling place). The competitive atmosphere guided the choice of repertoire and manner of presentation. Professional rivalry notwithstanding, there was a frank acknowledgement and appreciation of those who excelled.[2]

Instrumental music

Before the 1940s, concerts in Bombay featured more vocal performances than instrumental ones. The fact that instrumental solo presentation was still in its formative stages as compared to the rich variety that vocal music had acquired could have been one reason for this phenomenon.

1 Interview with Abdul Halim Jaffer Khan held on 6 May 1997.

2 Information procured during training sessions with Nikhil Ghosh.

This in turn was probably due to the structural limitations of instruments like *sitar* and *sarod* at the time, which did not allow them to use a wider and more developed technique necessary for complete self-expression. The importance that vocal music enjoyed in the eyes of the musicians and the listeners as being the pinnacle of musical expression could have also contributed to this situation.

The lowest position enjoyed by accompanists in the musician fraternity continued well into the twentieth century and is reflected in the lack of any acknowledgement of or information about them on jacket covers or labels of commercial recordings. This was particularly evident in the case of instruments traditionally regarded as accompanying instruments to vocal music such as *sarangi*, *tabla* and *pakhawaj*. In most cities, solo performances of these instruments did not receive as much support as was the case with vocal or other instrumental solo performances. *Tabla* solos were generally witnessed in gatherings like the *daavat* or the *jumma*.[3] *Tabla* players respected for their scholarship and artistry like Nanhe Khan, Natthu Khan (1875-1940), Munir Khan (1863-1937), Kamurao Mangeshkar, Yeshwant Naik alias Valle Mama, Dattaram Nanodkar and Kanta Prasad, and *pakhawaj* players like Makkhanlal (c.1876-1951) and Parvatsingh (1876-1951), were present in the city.[4] Noteworthy among Munir Khan's disciples was well-known soloist and accompanist Ahmed Jan Thirakwa, who had trained earlier under his uncles Sher Khan, Faiyaz Khan and Baswa Khan. Thirakwa had his debut at the age of sixteen in a programme held at Khetwadi.[5] His solo recital at the Vikramaditya Festival was one of the highlights of this event.[6] Parvatsingh, a well known *pakhawaj* player of Gwalior and son and disciple of Sukhdeosingh, came to Bombay at the age of twenty-five and accompanied many noted musicians in the city.[7] Important among the few *pakhawaj* solo recitals in the city is one featuring Makkhanlal, a reputed *pakhawaj* player of Mathura and disciple of Madan

3 Daniel M. Neuman, *op.cit.*, p.70.

4 Interview with Arvind Mulgaonkar held on 4 January 1993.

5 Susheela Misra, *Great Masters of Hindustani Music*, *op.cit.*, p.92.

6 Interview with Batuk Diwanji held in January 1993.

7 Arvind Mulgaonkar, *op.cit.*, p.418.

Mohan, Gangaram and Bhavanishankar of Punjab at a function held in c.1944-45 by many musicians to felicitate Khaprumama Parvatkar (1880-1953), a *tabla* player originally from Goa known for his command over the mathematical intricacies of rhythmic structures.[8] Public concerts featuring *sarangi* solo recitals were even rarer in this period. One of the few exceptions was a *sarangi* solo by Bundu Khan (c.1880-1955), sometime in 1928-1929, under the aegis of Deodhar's School of Indian Music.[9] However, barring these exceptions, it was only later that *tabla*, *pakhawaj* and *sarangi* players received the acknowledgement that had eluded them for many years.

Diversity in repertoire

The increasing number of listeners naturally brought in diverse expectations from listeners that musicians sought to fulfill in the new performance space and context. Musicians widened the scope of conventional vocal music concerts to include various forms like *khayal*, *thumri*, *dadra*, *bhajan* and even stage songs in a single presentation, perhaps to satisfy diverse musical tastes among listeners. In fact, the need to reach out to as many listeners perhaps guided musicians to incorporate what would have been considered unconventional repertoire in a strictly Hindustani music performance. For instance, the rising popularity of Marathi theatre inspired some vocalists like Abdul Karim Khan to incorporate songs from theatrical productions in their music recitals.[10] In fact, Abdul Karim Khan added several musical varieties including folk songs to his repertoire during his days in Baroda.[11] Manji Khan also presented Marathi poems set to music in a concert held by the Bombay Music Circle in 1930.[12]

Women performers from the *devadasi* community seem to have veered away from forms like *thumri* and *dadra*, and were more inclined

8 B.R. Deodhar, *Thor sangeetkaar*, *op.cit.*, pp. 254-255,258.

9 *Ibid*, p.163.

10 *Ibid*, p.134.

11 Michael Kinnear, *Sangeet Ratna – The Jewel of Music: A Bio-Discography of Khan Sahib Abdul Karim Khan*, *op.cit.*, p.29.

12 Eklavya,, *op.cit.*, p.120.

to focus on the *khayal* form. Reasons for this change may be manifold and need to be examined in a separate study. Briefly, the *devadasis* did not have a prolonged exposure in their hometowns to many of the Hindustani music forms. Much of their training took place sporadically when visiting musicians chose to teach them during their temporary residence in the region. Most of these visiting musicians were practitioners of the *khayal* form, and this could therefore have been one reason for the women to continue with their training in this form in Bombay. The fact that there were a greater number of *khayal* teachers than *thumri* specialists in Bombay could also be another reason for their choice of the *khayal* genre. Indeed, their exposure to the *thumri*, *dadra* and allied forms, was lesser than what was available to the *tawaifs* from the north, some of who were also trained in *khayal*. Additionally, the *khayal* had also displaced the *dhrupad* and had established its primacy in a vocalist's repertoire. Competence in *khayal* was probably therefore considered a means of upward mobility within the fraternity, overshadowing forms like the *thumri*, *dadra* and allied genres like *chaiti, hori, jhoola,* and *saavan,* which were conventionally considered the domain of women performers. Those who continued to perform primarily *thumri*, *dadra*, *ghazal* and allied forms, incorporated *ada* and *haav bhaav* to suitably highlight and demonstrate multiple shades of the song-text.[13] Jennifer Post Quinn describes *adaa* as a performance that featured the woman performer singing a *thumri*, *lavani* or *hori-dhamaar* while seated, using gestures that were often directed to attract the attention of a single man in the audience. She mentions *haav-bhaav* as a similar performance, but one that used only facial gestures.[14]

Later, some women performers also gave up dance and restricted themselves to vocal recitals alone. Quinn points out that the term *gayika*, which denoted a woman performer who would sing and dance in late nineteenth century Bombay, assumed a completely different meaning later. It came to mean women performers who had chosen to pursue the study of art music forms, mainly *khayal*, and were publicly

---

13 Jennifer Post Quinn, *op.cit.*, pp.90-92. See also K. Raghunathji, *op.cit.*, pp.166, 170.

14 Jennifer Post Quinn, *op.cit.*, p.92.

respected by the male musicians.[15] The reasons for the departure from dance may be manifold and may be difficult to evaluate in the absence of first hand information. The conscious choice of women performers to distance themselves from dance was perhaps an adaptive strategy to counter the social stigma and reformist pressure they were experiencing. It is equally probable that their decision was prompted by a desire to gain equal status with male musicians.[16] As pointed out by Jennifer Post Quinn:

> As a dancer, a woman was much more actively displaying her body and the seductive nature of the music and story she was interpreting, than the musicians did during a performance. Some women refused to be mere embellishments to programs, to display openly their skills of enticement and to wear clothing which marked their profession as dancers. Instead, they restricted their performances to the more modest act of singing, using no gestures or eye movements. This may have been an effort to lend an aspect of modesty, and therefore, respectability to their performances.[17]

Making a departure from dance that was regarded lascivious or coquettish by reformers, some women performers chose to sit while performing, a practice that was normally followed by male singers. They also gave up the *peshwaj*, a typical costume for dancers.[18] One source mentions that Anjanibai Malpekar was responsible for the decision to abandon the *peshwaj* in Bombay.[19]

While many *devadasi*s were moving away from the *thumri*, *dadra* and allied genres and focusing more on *khayal* rendition, there seems to have been a reversal of roles in cases where some male performers like Moujuddin Khan and Pyara Saheb chose to specialize in *thumri*s or acknowledged *khayal* singers like Abdul Karim Khan, Faiyaz Khan and later Bade Ghulam Ali Khan included *thumri* in their performances. Their decision to render *thumri*s and allied forms may have been purely

15 *Ibid*, pp.90-91.

16 *Ibid*, pp.91-93.However, there were dancers who focused on *Kathak* repertoire alone and included *thumri* only to add another dimension to their recitals.

17 *Ibid*, pp.91-92.

18 For a description of the *peshwaj* and ornaments worn by women performers, see K. Raghunathji, *op.cit.*, p.175. Also see, J.T. Molesworth (comp.), *op.cit.*, p.528.

19 Mangala Khadilkar, *op.cit.*

guided by an aesthetic sensibility, but it may be equally true that they used this as a strategy to add variety to their performances in order to appeal to diverse tastes in public concerts. Thus, audience perspectives and artistic decisions went hand in hand to shape performance practice in the late nineteenth and early twentieth centuries.

Concert repertoire for public concerts seems to have been planned or there was a deliberate sequential choice of pieces in a single concert. Generally, this repertoire was not necessarily practised well in advance for a specific concert, but Kesarbai Kerkar believed otherwise. She chose to perform two months from the date that the organiser approached her and then selected and practised the repertoire that she wished to present.[20]

Experiments with repertoire were seen at other times too. The new trends in music education saw their reflection in the presentation of traditional repertoire in an instructional format. Music circles unlike music clubs had no overt educational programme, but the Agra Gharana Sangeet Samiti was in fact started with a view to not only holding concerts, but also educating the listeners about the subtleties of different *raag*s. The Samiti featured an amateur vocalist in the first half followed by scholar-musicians like Vilayat Hussein Khan, who would explain and demonstrate the structure of *raag*s bearing close resemblance or varieties of a particular *raag*.[21] Individual patrons also hosted thematic programmes, though on rare occasions. For instance, Vitthaldas Sheth organised sixteen consecutive concerts of Manji Khan, son and disciple of Alladiya Khan, at the Nana Shankarsheth Hall between the years 1930 and 1935, with each concert scheduled at different hours of the day to enable listeners to hear *raag*s pertaining to those times.[22]

The response of the audience controlled the progress of a performance as is apparent from the following example. Some listeners having preconceived notions about *been* recitals being excessively lengthy

20 Interview with S.R. Mehta held on 29 April 1992.

21 Unfortunately, the exact period when the Samiti carried on its activities is not known. Interview with Batuk Diwanji held in January 1993.

22 Eklavya, *op.cit.*, pp.123-124. *Raag*s in North Indian art music are associated with the cycle of day and night and the cycle of seasons.

and boring, asked B.R. Deodhar, who had organised a concert featuring *been* player Murad Khan, to limit the exposition of each *raag* to half an hour. Murad Khan was not pleased with this suggestion, but wanted to satisfy the audience. He therefore asked Deodhar to give him a half-hour cue, so as to enable him to change the *raag*. The concert began at 9.30 p.m. and continued for three hours. The venue was packed with listeners among who were reputed musicians like Govindrao Tembe, Vilayat Hussein Khan and Ramkrishnabuwa Vaze, and connoisseurs like Sardar Abbasaheb Mazumdar, N.C.Kelkar, Babasaheb Bhajekar and Gharpure. Many of the listeners did not appreciate the idea of limiting the *raag* exposition to half an hour, as they were very involved in the music. Murad Khan started with the *raag* exposition and played the *aal-aap* on the *been*. This was followed by the *drut gat*, which was presented on *sitar* by Murad Khan and his son Nisar Hussein. This section of the performance was succeeded by compositions, which are popularly identified today as semi-classical renditions. Fulfilling public demand, he also played a Marathi stage song with *tabla* accompaniment. Finally, there was a request for *raag Bhairavi*, a morning *raag*. When Deodhar gave the cue to end the performance after half an hour, the audience wanted the artiste to continue. Deodhar then asked Murad Khan to continue for another twenty minutes.[23]

V.D. Paluskar came up with a novel way of countering audience perception of musicians and asserting his status as a performer. At some concerts, Paluskar noticed that listeners were seated on chairs while musicians were seated on a carpet. He decided instead that he and his ensemble would perform seated on chairs. The accompanying instruments were placed on specially constructed wooden stands. He made this a condition while discussing arrangements for his concerts. Even in case of performances for princely patrons, he would insist on having performers seated at least at the same level as the patrons.[24]

23 B.R. Deodhar, *Thor sangeetkaar*, *op.cit.*, pp.69-71.

24 B.R.Deodhar, *Gaayanaachaarya P. Vishnu Digambar*, *op.cit.*, pp.90-91.

Nationalism and concert repertoire

The nationalist movement in the twentieth century also impacted musicians and instances of this were seen in Bombay. Paluskar's involvement in the Congress sessions and his association with national leaders has been referred to earlier. As a result, the British Intelligence service in India maintained a close watch on his activities.[25] But there were also others who responded to Bombay's political climate. For example, Manji Khan composed and sang *Charkheke karaamatse lenge swarajya lenge* at the Blavatsky Lodge in 1930 in support of the ongoing Swadeshi Movement and taught this song to children participating in the *prabhat pheris*.[26]

Musicians also contributed to the nationalist cause by participating in Marathi theatre productions that used mythological themes as metaphors to depict the contemporary political climate. In 1921, Bombay witnessed an exceptional theatrical event. This was a joint performance of the popular play *Maanapamaan* by Bal Gandharva's Gandharva Natak Mandali and Keshavrao Bhosale's Lalitkaladarsh Natak Mandali, both of which were well-known competing theatre companies. The performance was held to raise funds for the Tilak Memorial Swaraj Fund, which was set up to finance the activities undertaken by the Indian National Congress.[27] Recounting the fervour at the time, M.R. Jayakar states:

> The enthusiasm ran so high that we were able to sell tickets for Rs.100 each. I presided on the occasion in spite of serious illness in my family, and spoke to the public about the necessity of supporting the good aspect of the Non-Cooperation Movement. We collected what was a record figure viz., Rs.16,000, as he proceeds of one night's benefit performance and handed over the amount to Jamnalal Bajaj who was the Treasurer of the Congress at that time. Both the dramatic celebrities did their best and the next day, meet-

---

25 B.R. Deodhar, *ibid*, pp. 37-39, 44, 78-79; Eklavya, *op.cit.*, pp.37-39.

26 Eklavya, *ibid*, pp.119-120.

27 Baburao Deshpande, "*Rangabhoomisaathi zhapaatlelaa avaliyaa*" in *Lokaraajya*, Sangeetsoorya Shri Keshavrao Bhosale Visheshaank – August 1990, (Marathi), Mahaasanchaalak, Maahiti va janasamparka mahaasanchaalaya, Maharashtra Shaasan, Mumbai, 1990, p.12.

> ing them privately at my residence, I conveyed to them in the fullest measure our appreciation of their work.[28]

On the other hand, special concerts featuring Tarabai Shirodkar (1889-1949) were held specifically to raise money for the war-fund during World War I perhaps reflecting the divided Indian response to the war.[29]

Hindustani music and Western instruments

The nationalist movement aside, musicians in Bombay played an important part in turning the interface with the West to their benefit. More precisely, they were proactive in ensuring the entry of Western instruments into Hindustani music performance. Of these, the harmonium, a seemingly simple metal-reed keyboard instrument, was introduced in India in the form of its distant European cousin, the Christian missionary's organ. Introduced initially in the shape of a table-harmonium, it underwent a metamorphosis in the hands of Indian artisans. While the British introduced the instrument in India, they did not appreciate its adaptation to Indian music. Expressing his reservations in the matter, F.W. Gaisberg (1873-1951), the leader of the first recording expedition from Britain to India, stated, "In my search for artists I attended theatres, parties and fetes. Never again will I be able to summon up an equal enthusiasm for Indian music, for one indispensable accompaniment to most songs was a simple missionary's organ . . . I found it produced a dull and uninspiring sound, and I soon came to loathe the instrument."[30] Even more contemptuous of the instrument and its introduction into Indian music, are the following observations made by Margaret Cousins:

> One might travel the length and breadth of Great Britain and France and never see an instrument resembling the kind of harmonium which the Indians mistakenly think is an honourable part of Western music. It is only the equipment of Central European beggars. It has no place as an Indian instrument. It is unworthy of both East and West. It is the most sinister influence in eastern music. It is tuned falsely and contrary to the natural tuning employed

28 M.R. Jayakar, *The Story of My Life, Vol. I, 1873-1922, op.cit.*, p.436.

29 Laxminarayan Garg, *op.cit.*, p.185.

30 F.W. Gaisberg, *Music on Record*, Robert Hale Limited, London, (n.d.), p.56.

> for countless centuries in India. It prohibits all use of quarter-tones. Its harsh, over-loud tone is quite unsuitable for accompanying the human voice which is strained in trying to hold its own against its protagonist. It is sapping all musical self-reliance in the voice so that even a good singer feels helpless unless he is propped up by the harmonium. It is no wonder, it is called the harm-onium, for it works 'harm' wherever it goes![31]

Elsewhere, Cousins says, "It was the tambura which supplied the constant sruti or keynote drone for all singers up to the ill-starred advent of the portable harmonium. There is not yet given out the name of the god or demon to whom this last-named instrument of torture is ascribed, but it wasn't one of the Celestials."[32] Clearly, Cousins had failed to comprehend the distinct roles played by the two instruments. While the *tanpura* maintained a constant drone, the harmonium provided a melodic accompaniment to the vocalist, anticipating and mirroring he latter's musical ideas and at times opening alternative areas of creativity.

Even Ananda K. Coomarswamy, the eminent Indian art historian and aesthetician, in his foreword to Clements' book, has cited the use of the tempered harmonium as one of the causes for what in his opinion was the degeneration of Indian music. He writes:

> The neglect of centuries, as in so many analogous cases, has proved less disastrous than the renewed patronage of a few decades. The constant use of the tempered harmonium; the endeavour to adapt Indian modes to the purposes of tenth or fifteenth-rate brass bands maintained by Indian rajas; the absence of any aesthetic element in modern Indian education; the mania for English accomplishments: all these causes have actively contributed to the degeneration of Indian music. By degeneration, I mean literally confusion, a running together, and destruction of bounding-lines; a process quite distinct from any natural waning of vitality at the latter end of an art cycle.[33]

Interestingly, even national leaders, not otherwise known to comment on music per se, made observations about the harmonium. Stressing the importance of music education in a speech delivered on October 20, 1917 at the Second Gujarat Educational Conference held at Broach, Mahatma Gandhi said, "Our boys learn to sing songs from

---

31 Margaret E. Cousins, *op.cit.*, p.28.

32 *Ibid*, p.66.

33 See Ananda K. Coomarswamy's foreword to E. Clements, *Introduction to the Study of Indian Music*, Gaurav Publications, New Delhi, 1st Indian ed., 1981, p.vi.

popular plays in all manner of tunes and without regard to time and place, and try their hands on noisy harmoniums and other instruments, and this does them harm."[34] In a letter dated July 2, 1918 to G.K. Devdhar of the Seva Sadan, Gandhi once again criticised the harmonium and gave more importance to other instruments when he wrote, "Harmonium is only a stage removed from the concertina. I would give them the *vina* and the *sitar*. These are cheap, national and infinitely superior to the harmonium."[35] That the harmonium was seen as a foreign instrument and was not considered "national" could perhaps have been one of the reasons for Gandhi's perspective. Commenting on the contrast between rural people and urban middle class in their connection with the arts, Jawaharlal Nehru wrote:

> In Bengal, in Gujrat and in the south, one discovers sometimes, with a shock of pleasant surprise, how fundamentally, and yet unconsciously, artistic the mass of the village people are. Not so the middle classes; they seem to have lost their roots and have no aesthetic tradition to cling to. They glory in cheap and horrid prints made in bulk in Germany and Austria, and sometimes even rise to Ravi Varma's pictures. The harmonium is their favourite instrument. (*I live in hope that one of the earliest acts of the Swaraj government will be to ban this awful instrument.*)[36] (emphasis added)

Despite this repeated condemnation of the harmonium, the instrument gained in popularity, and dealers and manufacturers in Bombay and Calcutta made it accessible to musicians and the general public. In 1851, the Narrotamdas family in Bombay started S.B. Ramchunder, harmonium manufacturers and musical instrument dealers, later known as T.S. Ramchunder and Bros.[37] Notably, harmonium players S.B. Ramchunder and his brothers were often engaged to perform at functions organized by the Christian community and churches.[38] Majid

34 Mahatma Gandhi, *The Collected Works of Mahatma Gandhi Vol.14, October 1917-July 1918*, The Director, Publications Division, Delhi, 1965, p.30.

35 *Ibid*, p.465.

36 Jawaharlal Nehru, *Jawaharlal Nehru: An Autobiography*, Allied Publishers Private Limited, Bombay, 1962, p.405.

37 Michael S. Kinnear, *The Gramophone Company's First Indian Recordings, 1899-1908*, Popular Prakashan, Bombay, 1994, p.49.

38 Michael S. Kinnear, "Reading Indian Record Labels: "RAMAGRAPH" – The History of the RAM-A-PHONE and RAMA-GRAPH disc records", in *The Record News:*

& Co, situated on Mohammedali Road also imported and sold harmoniums and accessories like harmonium reeds.[39] Similarly, Parakh and Sons established in 1910 and situated on Kalbadevi Road, stocked harmoniums apart from gramophones, radio and radio gramophones, and records.[40] In Calcutta, Dwarkinath Ghose pioneered the manufacture of harmoniums in Calcutta in 1887 and soon there were other contenders in Calcutta to compete with Dwarkin and Son.[41] Local craftsmen even experimented with indigenous material to make reeds for the instrument. In 1905, Jivanlal Kanji Mistri a hereditary carpenter set up shop for harmonium repairs at Palitana and set up a factory in Palitana to manufacture harmonium reeds, which were until then imported primarily from Paris.[42]

Thus, notwithstanding the revulsion for the harmonium and thanks to the ingenuity of local craftsmen, Indian musicians included the instrument in their performances. The novelty of the instrument brought it criticism, but it was not saddled by the social stigma that was the bane of the *sarangi* and the *tabla*. In fact, its resemblance to the piano probably attracted the Indian elite to it, particularly among those sections that wished to emulate the West. The Western origin of the harmonium and its easy accessibility in shops selling Western manufactured goods such as phonographs and typewriters, perhaps gave it a respectable status and transformed the instrument into a drawing room instrument for middle class homes. Whether harmonium gave its amateur players a feeling of being almost able to play the piano, an instrument of luxury even in those days, and to that extent be closer to Western culture, is anyone's guess, but its relatively simple technique for beginners and its

---

The Journal of the Society of Indian Record Collectors, Vol.20, Bombay, October 1995, p.5.

39 *Ibid*, p.12.

40 H.D. Darukhanawala, *Parsis and Sports and Kindred Subjects*, (n.p.), 1935, p.185.

41 Michael S. Kinnear, *The Gramophone Company's First Indian Recordings, 1899-1908*, *op.cit.*, pp.35-36. Also see, Chhaya Chatterjee, *Sastriya Sangita and Music Culture of Bengal Through the Ages, Vol.I*, Sharada Publishing House, Delhi, 1996, p.273.

42 *Illustrated Catalogue and Price-List of Genuine Palitana Make Harmonium Reeds*, Jivanlal Kanji Mistri & Sons, Palitana, 1956.

greater ability to produce melodies in a rudimentary manner, gave it an edge above traditional Indian instruments. Thus harmonium found a relatively easy entry into middle class homes. The acclaim that the harmonium received in Western India was perhaps due to the popularity enjoyed by Marathi stage music, which used the organ, in some ways a precursor of the harmonium. The initial popularity of the harmonium in Bombay is accredited to the efforts of Zaoba and Laxmikant Sadanand alias Bhachubhai Bhandare (1878-1909). The latter accompanied *kirtans* in the Shenvi Rammandir temple at Thakurdwar owned by his family, and also played a few *raags*, popular tunes and western band songs in solo recitals.[43]

The successful entry of the harmonium into Hindustani music performance was reflected in its widespread use on early gramophone recordings. However, harmonium solos were few and far between. It was Bhaiyya Ganpatrao, scion of the Gwalior princely family, and his disciple Basheer Khan of Indore who brought the instrument into prominence with his solo renditions.[44] Ganpatrao's solo recitals at Lala Dulichand's temporary residence in Bombay would perhaps have been rare cases in this respect. He would be seated with his harmonium in the centre of the performing space and his disciples would sit with harmoniums on either side. He would be accompanied not only by a *tabla* player but also by a *sarangi* player, both of whom would sit behind him and his disciples. *Sarangi* was used in this case not only for aesthetic reasons, but also to probably imply that harmonium enjoyed the status equal to that of vocal music, which used the *sarangi* as accompaniment. At one such concert recounted by Govindrao Tembe, Ganpatrao played an *aalaap-jod* and a composition in *raag* Bihag. This format was possibly an artistic decision, but could well have been a way of establishing harmonium on par with those instruments that had incorporated these sections in their solo presentations.[45] Tembe also describes his own solo appearance at a gathering of the Bombay Students' Brotherhood

43 Govindrao Tembe, *Maazhaa sangeet vyaasang*, *op.cit.*, pp.12, 48, 51. Unfortunately no biographical information pertaining to Zaoba was found.

44 Chhaya Chatterjee, *op.cit.*, p.273.

45 *Ibid*, p.106-109.

at Tribhuvandas Mangaldas' bungalow.[46] Another instance of a harmonium recital in Bombay was that of Nawab Ali, the *talukdar* of Akbarpur, also an accomplished harmonium player. He met Bhatkhande in Bombay in 1912, and performed at the Parsi Gayan Uttejak Mandali during this visit to the city. He is said to have impressed audiences, who had never been exposed to this style of harmonium playing.[47] Similarly, in 1940-41, Vitthaldas Korgaonkar performed harmonium solo at Trinity Club, Bombay. Govindrao Tembe presented a harmonium solo on the following day, which continued for approximately two hours. This programme drew a large audience, although the venue could actually seat only fifteen to twenty persons.[48]

Despite these early efforts at establishing the solo status of the instrument, the harmonium was constantly criticised for its inability to reproduce integral parts of Indian music such as the *shruti*, *meend* and *gamak*. The discourse surrounding the *shruti* formed an important aspect of Hindustani musicology during this period, but the introduction of the harmonium with its tempered scale heightened the debate.[49] Even harmonium players like Govindrao Tembe publicly noted these limitations. But Tembe believed that the popularity of the harmonium was due to its full-bodied and continuous sound. According to him, the tonal novelty and clarity and the relative ease with which the harmonium could be played, allowed it to make inroads into every corner of the country.[50] Meanwhile, G.B. Achrekar (1885-1939), a musicologist, musician and artisan of Poona, attempted to counter critics by building a *shruti*-harmonium and delivered lectures on the subject along with demonstrations at Bombay, Poona and Kolhapur.[51] To rid

46 Govindrao Tembe, *Maazhaa sangeet vyaasang*, *op.cit.*, pp.73-74.

47 S.N. Ratanjankar, "*Jeevan charitra*" in *Bhatkhande smriti granth*, pp.38-39.

48 *Ibid*, p.22.

49 For a detailed discussion on the debate related to the *shruti*, see Suvarnalata Rao and Wim van der Meer, "The Construction, Reconstruction, and Deconstruction of Shruti" in Joep Bor, Françoise "Nalini" Delvoye, Jane Harvey, Emmie te Nijenhuis (eds.), *Hindustani Music – Thirteenth to Twentieth Centuries*, Codarts and Manohar, New Delhi, 2010, pp. 673-696.

50 Govindrao Tembe, *Mazha sangeet vyaasang*, *op.cit.*, pp.82-83.

51 *Ibid*, pp.177-178.

the instrument of its tempered scale, Achrekar constructed in the 1930s a *shruti*-harmonium called *shrutimandalmanjushe*, after making a detailed study of *shrutis* and the tonal intervals between notes. An earlier attempt at building a similar instrument had been made according to the specifications of E. Clements, but its use was restricted to demonstration and could not be employed in performance.[52] Around 1912 or thereabouts, Moore and Moore, a company formed by well-known educationist and musicologist H. Keatley Moore, had attempted to pinpoint exact microtonal differences and had made an organ based on this research. Clements informed Moore of K.B. Deval's research on *shrutis*, after which a few changes were made in the tonal distances and three organs were built. The Philharmonic Society bought each of these for Rs.1200/-. Clements and Deval demonstrated thenceforth on one of these organs. Achrekar's harmonium was a compact version of this organ.[53]

Like the harmonium, other non-Indian instruments like the banjo, the mandolin and the violin, were incorporated in Hindustani music. Though the violin became more popular in Carnatic music, its use was not uncommon in Bombay. The Parsee Music Institute taught Indian music on different musical instruments like the harmonium and the violin.[54] The entry of the banjo was fortuitous when Asadullah Kaukab Khan (1858-1912), a reputed *sarodiya* of the Bulandshahr/Lucknow lineage, played the instrument for the first time in his performance at Paris in 1902, and continued to play it even after his return to India. Primarily residing in Calcutta, Asadullah Kaukab Khan played the banjo in Bombay, sometime between 1903 and 1910.[55] Similarly *bulbultarang*, a new string instrument with a keyboard, was introduced at a music con-

---

52 *Ibid.*

53 *Ibid*, p.148. For more information on research on reed organs and harmonium in the West, see http://tardis.dl.ac.uk/FreeReed/organ_book/node22.html For a detailed discussion on the discourse centring around the entry of the harmonium in Hindustani music, see Birgit Abels, *The Harmonium in North Indian Music*, New Age Books, New Delhi, 2010.

54 H.D. Darukhanawala, *Parsi Lustre on Indian Soil–Vol.I, op.cit.*, p.777.

55 Joep Bor and Philippe Bruguierre, *op.cit.*, p.40. See also Govindrao Tembe, *Maazhaa sangeet vyaasang, op. cit.*, p.91.

ference held in Bombay in 1936.[56] Paluskar also taught some students to play Hindustani music on the mandolin and the banjo, and presented them in concerts.[57]

By the mid-twentieth century, the inclusion of Western instruments in Hindustani music performance became increasingly noticeable. Added to this, the incorporation of amplification and the many changes in performance practice discussed earlier, went a long way in shaping the aesthetics of Hindustani music in this period and later. It is sufficiently clear that practitioners played a key role in charting such a course. This was their way of negotiating the impact of modernity on Hindustani music.

---

56 Ashok D. Ranade, *Maharashtra: Art Music*, *op.cit.*, p.64.

57 B.R. Deodhar, *Gaayanaachaarya P. Vishnu Digambar*, *op.cit.*, p.55. Also see Ashok D. Ranade, *ibid*, p.58.

UNCONVENTIONAL PERFORMANCE EXPLORATIONS

Performance and teaching in the city provided limited and unpredictable means of sustenance to practitioners of Hindustani music. They had therefore to identify other income generating options and to accept challenges that these alternatives posed to their musicianship. Not only were their musical capabilities tested in the process, but they also had to reinvent themselves themselves especially given the changes that were ushered into the field.

Theatre

Theatre was one of the key areas that offered opportunities to musicians since early times. Theatre halls set up in nineteenth century Bombay drew touring theatre companies or *natak mandali*s to the city. The oldest venue for theatre performances called The Bombay Amateur Theatre was started in 1776. It was situated in the Elphinstone Circle opposite the Town Hall. All plays and major programmes for European entertainment took place here.[1] A few Indian patrons donated to

1 M.D. David, *op.cit.*, p.163. Also see, Kumudini A. Mehta, *English Drama on the Bombay Stage in the late Eighteenth Century and in the Nineteenth Century*, Ph.D. Thesis, University of Bombay, March 1960, p.4. For an advertisement of a European performance at the Bombay Amateur Theatre, see *The Bombay Courier*, Tuesday, 21 April 1834, Vol.XLII, No.2329, p.189.

theatre funds and also attended theatrical presentations at this venue. Advertisements were specially inserted in Indian newspapers to attract Indian audiences.[2] This venue was renovated in 1819 and finally auctioned in 1835. The money gathered from this auction was used on the urging of Jagannath Sunkersett and other reputed individuals, to build a new space called the Grant Road Theatre. Set up in 1846, the land for this theatre was donated by Jagannath Sunkersett. Initially, only English plays were staged at this venue. By the mid-nineteenth century, other theatres such as Play House, more popularly known as Pila House, were started in the same vicinity. A separate theatre had been set up at Matunga to entertain British soldiers of the Bombay Artillery based there. The well-known Opera House was set up much later in 1910.[3]

Indian music made an entry into English theatre in nineteenth century Bombay, demonstrating early attempts at collaboration between Indian and European music. Early English theatre in Bombay saw the short interval between two dramatic pieces filled in by music performed by singers who were accompanied by trumpets, French horn, clarinet and kettle drums. The violin substituted the clarinet in 1829. While it is not known whether musicians for these performances were of Indian origin, the programme for the evening at times included Western and Indian musical pieces. Hindustani songs were set to popular English tunes and English songs were translated into Indian languages. Thus, a programme printed by the N.D. Appyakhtiar Parsi Opera Concert and Burlesque Company of Indian Music, included an assorted musical entertainment featuring an Ethiopian Ballet, an Overture from the works of Italian composer Gioacchino Rossini (1792-1868), and songs in *raags* like Yaman, Bhairavi and Jogiya.[4]

2 Kumudini A. Mehta, *ibid*, pp.46-47.

3 M.D. David, *op.cit.*, p.163. Also see, Kumudini A. Mehta, *ibid*, p.4. The Grant Road Theatre has also been referred to as the Royal Theater, situated in Girgaum. It was also known as Badshahi Theater or Shankarshetki Juni Natyashala. See *The Record News: The Journal of the Society of Indian Record Collectors*, Volume–Annual: TRN 2006, Mumbai, 2006, p. 26.

4 Kumudini A. Mehta, *ibid*, p.230. For more instances of musical and theatrical cross-pollination see Naresh Fernandes, *op.cit.*, pp.52-53.

In 1863, Vishnudas Bhave brought his Hindu Natak Mandali to Bombay from Sangli where it had been mainly staging mythological plays since 1843. In Bombay, Bhave staged his plays in tents put up on an open ground in Girgaon, winning the appreciation of well-known citizens like Bhau Daji Lad, Jagannath Sunkersett and Jamshetjee Jeejeebhai. With support from Lad and Sunkersett, Bhave went on to stage his plays at the Grant Road Theatre.[5]

Foreign companies also staged their plays at the Grant Road Theatre and Indian bands provided musical accompaniment to their plays.[6] But since many Indians frequented the Grant Road Theatre, the Europeans chose to maintain their exclusivity by starting the Gaiety Theatre in 1879, which staged English plays catering to European audiences. Later, this theatre was converted into the Capitol Cinema, for screening films. The Novelty Theatre was also set up having the largest stage in those times with a seating capacity of 1400.[7] By 1880, there were four theatres in the Grant Road area, which staged Hindi, Marathi and Gujarati plays. Dahyabhai Dholsajee started a playhouse, which had its performances at the Princess Theatre, built in 1905 by Tribhuvandas Mangaldas Nathubhai.[8]

Several amateur Indian theatrical groups came up in nineteenth century Bombay. Parsi students of the Elphinstone College formed the Parsi Elphinstone Dramatic Society in around 1850.[9] Bhau Daji Lad and Dadabhai Naoroji were associated with the Parsi Theatrical Committee. This Committee and the Hindu Dramatic Company staged their plays at the Grant Road Theatre.[10] Increasingly, professional theatre productions won the appreciation of Bombay's elite. Mention must be made of Jamshetji Framji Madan (1857-1923), who bought the Bombay-based

5 M.D. David, *op.cit.*, p.163.

6 *Ibid*, p.165.

7 *Ibid*, p.164.

8 *Ibid*, p.165.

9 *The Record News: The Journal of the Society of Indian Record Collectors*, Volume–Annual: TRN 2006, Mumbai, 2006, p. 26. See also, Sisir Kumar Das, *A History of Indian Literature (Volume 8): 1800-1910, Western Impact: Indian Response*, Sahitya Akademi, Reprint, New Delhi, 2005, p.183.

10 M.D. David, *op.cit.*, p.164-165.

Elphinstone Natak Mandali, earlier known as the Elphinstone Dramatic Club. This company staged many Hindi, Gujarati and Urdu plays for several years at the Corinthian Theater in Calcutta. The Corinthian Theater had its own brass band and orchestra. Madan also supported the Alfred Natak Mandali established in 1871.[11]

Of the language theatres that co-existed in Bombay, it was perhaps Marathi theatre that absorbed practitioners of Hindustani music the most and also borrowed prolifically from their repertoire. This was Marathi theatre patronized by the city's elite and one that borrowed heavily from the Hindustani music idioms, unlike other Marathi musical theatre productions like the folk form *tamasha* and the *kaamgaar rangbhoomi* or the theatre of the textile mill workers incorporating several influences, both of which provided entertainment for the less privileged.[12] The integral part played by music contributed heavily to the rising popularity of elite Marathi theatre. Describing the public response to Annasaheb Kirloskar's musical plays, Vamanrao Deshpande states:

> Even distinguished political leaders such as Lokmanya Tilak and Vishnushastri Chiplunkar, or leaders of the legal and academic professions such as Justice K.T. Telang, Sir Mahadev Chaubal, Dr. Sir Ramkrishna Bhandarkar, and Dr. Bhalchandra Bhatawadekar were simply fascinated by their performances and some of them went to the length of subscribing their weighty signatures to the Company's advertising handbills.[13]

Primarily from the Maharashtra-Goa-Karnatak region, the Marathi touring companies absorbed many musicians of this area, who joined theatre to supplement the income that they received from performance and teaching. They were required to perform a variety of roles in musical theatre. Reputed musicians were engaged to compose songs

11 "Gramophone Celebrities – 14 – J.F. Madan: Lover of Theater" in *The Record News: The Journal of the Society of Indian Record Collectors*, Volume–Annual: TRN 2006, Mumbai, 2006, pp. 25-26. See also, Michael S. Kinnear, *The Gramophone Company's First Indian Recordings, 1899-1908, op.cit.*, p.18. For a detailed account of Parsi theatre, see Dhanjeebhai N. Patel, *Parsi natak takhtaanee tavaareekh: gayi sadinaa gujar paamelaa Parsi actoro*, (Gujarati), Kaiser-Hind, Mumbai, 1931.

12 Editor's note in Narayan R. Jadhav, "Textile workers' theatre: a cultural perspective" in *Facts & News*, No.14, National Centre for the Performing Arts Project: Theatre Development Centre, Bombay, 1989, p.4.

13 Vamanrao Deshpande, *Maharashtra's Contribution to Music*, *op.cit.*, p.58.

for the plays. Many of them in the early days of Marathi theatre were 'tune selectors', as they chose tunes from traditional art music repertoire and used them for new poetry that was written for the theatrical productions.[14] For instance, Vasudeo Narayan Dongre (1850-1905), founder of the Bombay Royal Opera Company (est. 1881), invited Balkrishnabuwa Ichalkaranjikar to compose songs for plays staged by his Company.[15] Nissar Hussein Khan was attached to the Patankar Sangeet Mandali (est. 1891).[16] Bhaskarbuwa Bakhale was attached to the Gandharva Natak Mandali (est. 1913) and composed music for songs in plays like *Vidyaharan*, *Swayamvara* and *Draupadi*. Stage music until then was considered to be elementary, but Bakhale's tunes based on Hindustani music repertoire are believed to have brought about a major change.[17] During the period 1920 to 1931, Ramkrishnabuwa Vaze was engaged as composer by the Lalitkaladarsh Sangeet Natak Mandali (est. 1908) and the Balwant Sangeet Mandali (est. 1918).[18] Govindrao Tembe composed music for the plays *Manapaman* and *Vidyaharan*, blending elements from *raag* music and the *thumri-dadra* forms.[19]

Some musicians also joined as actor-singers. For instance, Vinayakrao Patwardhan joined the Gandharva Natak Mandali in 1922 as an actor-singer.[20] At a time when women characters in plays were played by male actors, Mogubai Kurdikar worked in the Chandreshwar Bhootnath Sangeet Natak Mandali and the Satarkar Sangeet Mandali, before

---

14 Ashok D. Ranade, *Maharashtra: Art Music, op.cit.*, p.56.

15 See S.V. Gokhale's note in Govindrao Tembe, *Maazhaa sangeet vyaasang, op.cit.*, p.25. There is a reference to a theatre company called Dongre Sangeet Mandali to which Balkrishnabuwa Ichalkaranjikar was attached. However, it is not certain whether this was the same as the Bombay Royal Opera Company mentioned above. See Ashok D. Ranade, *Maharashtra: Art Music, op.cit.*, p.57.

16 Ashok D. Ranade, *ibid*, p.57.

17 Vamanrao H. Deshpande, *Between Two Tanpuras, op.cit.*, pp.57-61. Also see Ashok D. Ranade, *ibid.*

18 Ashok D. Ranade, *On Music and Musicians of Hindoostan, op.cit.*, p.141. See also B.R. Deodhar, *Thor sangeetkaar, op.cit.*, p.117. Also see Ashok D. Ranade, *Maharashtra: Art Music, op.cit.*, p.57.

19 Vamanrao H. Deshpande, *Between Two Tanpuras, op.cit.*, pp.32-33.

20 B.R. Deodhar, *Gaayanaachaarya P. Vishnu Digambar, op.cit.*, p.80.

focusing her complete attention on training in Hindustani music.[21] Mallikarjun Mansoor acted and sang in plays staged by the Vishwagunadarsh Company and the Vani-vilas Natak Mandali.[22] Often, theatre companies enlisted the services of senior musicians to train actor-singers. Thus, Bhaskarbuwa Bakhale taught stage actors like Govindrao Tembe, Narayan Shripad Rajhans popularly known as Bal Gandharva (1888-1967), Master Krishnarao, and Jagannathbuwa Pandharpurkar.[23] The decision to arrange for such training was perhaps prompted not only by musical compulsions, but also by the publicity it would bring to the companies. Theatre advertisements in this period announced 'authentic' musical antecedents of actor-singers, by publicising the training to attract serious music lovers. For example, in 1926-1927, Shankarrao Sarnaik's Yeshwant Natak Mandali advertisements mentioned actor-singer Ganpatrao Dewaskar as a disciple of Alladiya Khan. Dewaskar had also initially learnt from Rajab Ali Khan.[24] Shankarrao Sarnaik became a disciple of Alladiya Khan after offering him Rs.5000/-. Similarly, Keshavrao Bhosale, Bapusaheb Pendharkar and Dinanath Mangeshkar became disciples of Ramakrishnabuwa Vaze, and Sawai Gandharva began receiving training from Abdul Karim Khan. It is believed that most of these actor-singers did not receive intensive training from their *gurus*.[25] But in the case of Dinanath Mangeshkar, Ashok Ranade maintains that the actor-singer "... found his feet by now in slow tempi and he had also acquired a better grip over the art-music techniques of elaboration, improvisation ..."[26]

Musicians like noted *tabla* player Ahmed Jan Thirakwa, and *sarangi* players Qadir Bux and Muhammad Hussein Khan, provided musi-

21 See Suresh Chandwankar, "Mogubai Kurdikar (1904-2001)" in *The Record News: The Journal of the Society of Indian Record Collectors*, TRN 2001, Bombay, pp.90-91. See also, Laxminarayan Garg, *op.cit.*, p.303.

22 Sadanand Kanvalil, *Mallikarjun Mansoor*, (Marathi translation by Prabhakar Deshpande), Satyajit Prakashan, Bombay, 1993, pp.13, 20-21.

23 Vamanrao H. Deshpande, *Between Two Tanpuras*, *op.cit.*, pp.57-61.

24 B.R. Deodhar, *Thor sangeetkaar*, *op.cit.*, pp.21,139.

25 Govindrao Tembe, *Gaayanmaharshee Alladiyakhan yaanche charitra*, *op.cit.*, p.87.

26 Ashok D. Ranade, *Stage Music of Maharashtra*, Sangeet Natak Akademi, New Delhi, 1986, p.78.

cal accompaniment to plays. Thirakwa and Bux were attached to the Gandharva Natak Mandali. Muhammad Hussein Khan joined the same company later and went on to work in the Aryasubodh Natak Mandali, and in Hirabai Badodekar's Natak Mandali.[27]

Performance in theatrical productions came closest to the area of work that the practitioners of Hindustani music were accustomed to. After the initial stages, songs in Marathi theatre were based on or inspired by art music repertoire. Melodic elaboration was permitted, but care was taken that the songs were well rehearsed. There was therefore a mix of spontaneity and rehearsed variation – a mix that was probably new to musicians who were more at ease with the structured improvisation and elaboration that was integral to Hindustani music, but one that they seem to have negotiated successfully given the approbation that their performances drew.[28]

In some cases, musicians joined theatre not necessarily for pecuniary gain and performance opportunities. In a period when the search for a *guru* was fraught with many obstacles, musicians also treated this as an opportunity to travel to various regions with theatre companies and find a *guru* of their choice. Thus, Balkrishnabuwa Ichalkaranjikar joined the Amarchand Vadikar Natak Company in Poona and travelled to Bombay among other places to find a good *guru* under whom he could pursue his musical training.[29] Bhaskarbuwa Bakhale too joined theatre as a young actor-singer to spend time with local musicians at various locations.[30]

Some musicians established theatre companies, though such instances were rare. Pandurang Ganesh Yavateshwarkar alias Pandoba Gurav (c.1840/45-?), a *pakhawaj* player from Goa and a vocalist adept at the *dhrupad*, *dhamar*, *hori* and *tappa* forms, started the Waikar San-

27 From N.S. Phadke's foreword to the book, Mohammad Hussein Khan, *Upaj: Shabd evam swararachanaa*, (Hindi), "author", Pune, 1981.

28 Vamanrao H. Deshpande, *Between Two Tanpuras*, *op.cit.*, pp. 32-33, 57-61. Also see Ashok D. Ranade, *Maharashtra: Art Music*, *op.cit.*, pp.56-57. For a detailed analysis of the various phases in the evolution of music in Marathi theatre, see Ashok Da. Ranade, *Stage Music of Maharashtra*, *op.cit.*

29 B.R. Deodhar, *Thor sangeetkaar*, *op.cit.*, p.5.

30 *Ibid*, p.83.

geet Mandali in Bombay after serving with the Ichalkaranjikar Natak Mandali in Belgaum.[31] Hirabai Badodekar's Natak Mandali was a radical instance of a theatre company started by a woman in a period that excluded women from acting. It was a branch of her mother Tarabai Mane's music class Nutan Sangeet Vidyalaya.[32]

In addition to employing musicians, theatre companies also patronized visiting performers by organizing their concerts on special occasions for the theatre staff and friends. Some companies like the Kirloskar Mandali, based for months in Bombay, even enrolled their employees' children as students at the Gandharva Mahavidyalaya. According to Ashok Ranade, "From 1885 onwards until the third decade of the twentieth century the *mandali*s continued to share their prosperity with artistes etc."[33] The close rapport enjoyed by theatre companies and practitioners of Hindustani music was best exhibited by the fact that Paluskar was nominated to preside over the seventh Natyasammelan held at the Elphinstone Theatre in Bombay on May 22 and 23, 1911, under the auspices of Kolhapurkar Sangeet Natak Mandali. However, theatre lovers did not appreciate Paluskar candid criticism of some stage songs.[34] Paluskar's view embittered theatre persons, and the Kirloskar Mandali countered his critique by establishing the Bharat Gayan Samaj in the same year at Poona to compete with the Gandharva Mahavidyalaya. The Samaj conducted regular music classes with Bhaskarbuwa Bakhale heading the teaching faculty.[35]

In a rare occurrence, Keshavrao Bhosale decided to stage a play written by Heerabai Pednekar, a Bombay-based singer. Entitled *Damini*, the play had been rejected earlier by the Kirloskar Mandali, because it had been written by a *kalavantin*. In her preface to the play, Pednekar writes:

31 See note prepared by S. V. Gokhale in Govindrao Tembe, *Maazhaa sangeet vyaasang*, *op.cit.*, p.13, and Vamanrao H. Deshpande, *Between Two Tanpuras*, *op.cit.*, p.3.

32 Pratibha Gopujkar, *op.cit.*

33 Ashok D. Ranade, *Maharashtra: Art Music*, *op.cit.*, pp.56-57.

34 B.R. Deodhar, *Gaayanaachaarya P. Vishnu Digambar*, *op.cit.*, pp.51-52.

35 *Ibid*, p.52.

> I wrote this play, but it would not have come to public notice had it not been staged. I was anxious about theatrical representation of such an ordinary creation of an uneducated woman like myself. But Keshavrao Bhosale, the owner of the Lalitkaladarsh Sangeet Natak Mandali, and Ganesh Vinayak Veerkar, the Manager of the Mandali, staged the play everywhere. I cannot thank them enough for their courage to undertake this task and for their belief in women's education.[36] (trans.mine)

This instance is illuminating as it proves that the stigma against hereditary women performers also existed even in theatre circles. It also points to the fact that the woman performer in this case had in fact played an extremely unconventional role – the role of a playwright – in a world of theatre that seldom featured women performers and where men played women characters at most times.

These examples demonstrate adequately that theatre provided alternative means of livelihood to professional musicians. Janaki Bakhle believes that senior Muslim musicians abhorred theatre or had scant interest in the area.[37] But the fact that Abdul Karim Khan included stage songs in his performance repertoire and even recorded some of these, or that Muslim vocalists trained actor-singers and enjoyed a close rapport with theatre companies, contradicts Bakhle's statement.[38] While accepting that Ahmed Jan Thirakwa and Qadir Bux played a significant role as instrumentalists employed in theatre, Bakhle argues that Muslim vocalists were deliberately kept out, thus ascribing a communal motive to the selection of theatre personnel.[39] But harmonium player Purushottam Walawalkar, who spent his childhood travelling with his father Madhavrao Walawalkar, an actor-singer serving in the Mandali, remembers Thirakwa receiving a monthly salary of Rs.120/-, a handsome amount at the time. The Mandali also provided him with lodging, boarding, tailoring, and laundry services.[40] Bakhle accepts that Marathi

36 Baburao Deshpande, "*Rangabhoomisaathi zhapaatlelaa avaliyaa*" in *Lokaraajya*, Sangeetsoorya Shri Keshavrao Bhosale Visheshaank – August 1990, (Marathi), Mahaasanchaalak, Maahiti va janasamparka mahaasanchaalaya, Maharashtra Shaasan, Mumbai, 1990, p.9.

37 Janaki Bakhle, *op.cit.*, p.92.

38 B.R. Deodhar, *Thor sangeetkaar*, *op.cit.*, p.134.

39 Janaki Bakhle, *op.cit*, p.92.

40 Interviews held with Purshottam Walawalkar on 9 October 1992, 11 October 1992.

theatre by its very regional nature kept out non-Marathi speaking actor-singers, but she insists that Muslim vocalists "could have been gainfully by this new forum".[41] However, Bakhle fails to consider the limitations that non-Marathi speaking Muslim musicians would have had to face in Marathi theatre. Songs could be included in performance repertoire or recorded, but playing the part of actor-singers to deliver lines in Marathi apart from songs, would have required proficiency in the language. Besides, it was also possible that Muslim vocalists did not feel drawn to playing an active role in dramatic performances, which does not necessarily amount to them abhorring theatre.

Walawalkar insists there were no antagonistic feelings among Muslims and Hindus employed in the Gandharva Natak Mandali. But it would be an exaggeration to state that they were treated equally given the fact that all Mandali employees dined together, but the Muslims sat in a row perpendicular to that of the Hindus using dining utensils exclusively arranged for them. Walawalkar recounts that Muslim musicians participated in Hindu festivals like Ganesh Chaturthi and took part in the *visarjan* processions, but this could well have been a deliberate attempt to conform with the Hindu majority in the Mandali.[42]

Gramophone recordings

Alongside their involvement in theatre, musicians were also presented with fresh professional opportunities and were provoked to reformat their performances, as a result of advances in technology. Bombay played a significant role in providing such alternative and additional opportunities of sustenance to musicians, and created ground for innovation and experimentation in these areas. In 1877, Thomas Alva Edison invented the phonograph, which enabled sound recording on a cylinder that came to be commonly known as *chudi* or *bangdi* in India. Ten years later, Alexander Graham Bell made some modifications to the original phonograph, and in 1888, Emile Berliner replaced the cylinders with single sided flat discs. The first recordings of Indian songs were done in London in 1898. Not before long, European gramophone

41 Janaki Bakhle, *op.cit.*, p.92.

42 Interviews held with Purshottam Walawalkar on 9-11 October 1992.

companies recognising the potential of the Indian market, deputed recording crews to capture Indian music on gramophone records.[43] The advent of gramophone recordings enabled musicians to share their work with a greater number of listeners, redefining the concept of performance that was understood and appreciated until then only by way of its immediacy, spontaneity and acoustic naturalness. On the other hand, gramophone companies recorded a large number of Indian musicians in a bid to expand their markets, but objectively encouraged wider social acceptance and respectability for Hindustani music and its practitioners.

Frederick William Gaisberg led the first gramophone recording tour to India in 1902 as technical recorder and artist advisor to The Gramophone and Typewriter, Ltd. Calcutta was selected as the location for making all the recordings during this tour.[44] According to Gaisberg, the fees paid to musicians were reasonable compared to those paid in Europe, but the expenses were heavy as most of the musicians had to be trained over long periods before they were considered acceptable for gramophone recordings.[45] The Gramophone and Typewriter, Ltd. set up training centres in Calcutta, Delhi, Lahore, Madras and Rangoon, and engaged musicians to train artistes and to set tunes to selected poems. Thereafter, two to three thousand songs were recorded each year across India in almost six hundred dialects and languages.[46] The first music recordings featured primarily professional women performers, because male performers, particularly those attached to princely courts were not open to the idea of having their renditions recorded and made easily accessible.[47]

---

43 Suresh S. Chandwankar, "Preserving The Recorded Sound: 78 RPM", in Balawant Joshi, Dilip Inamdar, Charudatta Bhagwat, S.S. Gore (eds.), *World of Gandharvas*, *op.cit.*, p.162.

44 Michael S. Kinnear, *The Gramophone Company's First Indian Recordings, 1899-1908*, *op.cit.*, pp.11-12.

45 F.W. Gaisberg, *op.cit.*, p.57.

46 *Ibid*, p.58.

47 Allyn Miner, "The sitar: an Overview of Change", in *the world of music, le monde de la musique, die welt der musik India*, Journal of the International Institute for Comparative Music Studies and Documentation (Berlin), Vol.XXXII, No.2-1990, p.53.

According to discographer and recording engineer Michael Kinnear:

> Although the first Far Eastern recording expedition had been organized in a businesslike manner, that experiment with its spirit of adventure which all who took part in must have felt, had been at a disadvantage because of the lack of any appreciation of the cultural life of India. Fred Gaisberg, who was thirty years old at the time, and his nineteen year old assistant, George Dillnutt, were unlikely to have had much experience or appreciation of the complexities of Indian music, let alone an understanding of the artistic abilities of the artists that they were recording.[48]

The second recording expedition of The Gramophone and Typewriter, Ltd. was led by William Sinkler Darby assisted by Max Hampe in 1904 and covered Bombay as a recording location among others. It was decided that the artistes included in this recording schedule would be brought from their hometowns in case they were not residing in the city selected as the recording location, perhaps at the expense of the company. A flat fee was paid for total number of recordings made by each main artiste. During this tour, most of the musicians recorded by Darby were renowned vocalists and instrumentalists from the world of art music and theatre. Some of them were also retainers at princely courts. One of the prominent musicians to have been recorded in the Bombay session was Abdul Karim Khan.[49]

H. Bose Records, Nicole Record and other record labels also recorded several musicians. In the latter part of 1905, Heinrich Bumb and Wilheim Hadert made recordings in Bombay and Calcutta for the Beka Record label. Arrangements for artistes and the location for the recording sessions were made by Valabhdas Lakhmidas and Co., one of the largest firms importing talking machines and records among other goods. Renowned artistes from Lucknow and Banaras visiting Bombay during this period were recorded in the city.[50] T.S. Ramchunder and

---

48 Michael S. Kinnear, *The Gramophone Company's First Indian Recordings, 1899-1908, op.cit.*, pp.21-22.

49 *Ibid*, p.22,24,45.

50 *Ibid*, p.45.

Bros., situated at Kalbadevi Road, brought out the Ram-a-phone and Rama-graph disc records.[51]

There were several noteworthy musicians who were recorded in Bombay. The early recordings of Mushtaq Hussein Khan (1880-1974) were made in 1908 and were issued on Zonophone Record and Gramophone Concert Record.[52] Kesarbai Kerkar cut four records with the Broadcast label, and later, thirteen records with His Master's Voice. Vishnupant Shirodkar and Majid Khan accompanied her on *tabla* and *sarangi*, respectively. Her recordings for the Broadcast label were probably done in 1935-36 at the Blavatsky Lodge.[53] Narayanrao Vyas made his first gramophone recording in 1920. He is said to have risen to popularity as a result of the gold medal that he received for the best sale of his records, apparently this being the first of its kind given to any vocalist.[54] Odeon recorded Sundrabai, Hirabai Badodekar, Abdul Karim Khan, Balabai Kale, Mohammad Bashir Khan and Vilayat Hussein Khan among others in the 1930s.[55]

While the musicians mentioned here were prominent performers of the time, there were many who were not well-known, and yet, were recorded. They found an opportunity to reach out to listeners through this new medium and some of them even acquired popular status as recording artistes. There is little information available regarding artistes' fees for recording sessions, but Gauhar Jan, arguably the best-known

---

51 For a detailed discussion about the company and its record labels, see Michael S. Kinnear, "Reading Indian Record Labels: "RAMAGRAPH". – The History of the RAM-A-PHONE and RAMA-GRAPH disc records", in *The Record News: The Journal of the Society of Indian Record Collectors*, Vol.20, Bombay, October 1995.

52 Michael S. Kinnear, "Reading Indian Record Labels: Part One – "GRAMOPHONE" and ZONOPHONE records", in *The Record News: The Journal of the Society of Indian Record Collectors*, Vol.1, Bombay, January 1991, p.20. The source spells his name as Mustak Hossein.

53 *Ibid*, pp.22-24. Also see Michael Kinnear, "Kesarbai Kerkar: Discography", *The Record News: The Journal of the Society of Indian Record Collectors, Vol. 11*, Bombay, July 1993. Additional information provided in personal communication by Suresh Chandwankar in September 2004.

54 Joan L. Erdman, *op.cit.*, p.120.

55 M. Mistry and Mapla, *Odeon: Gujarati ane Hindustani naveen catalogue, Odeon Electric Records,* (Gujarati), Ruby Record Co., Bombay, January 1935.

woman performer and recording artiste in the early period of the recording industry, was believed to have been the highest paid artiste of her time.[56]

Besides recording solo presentations of musicians, recording companies also recorded ensembles, some of which were led by musicians involved otherwise in art music. The Gramophone Company had released two recordings of B.R. Deodhar's orchestra and another of his solo vocal rendition. He was also recorded on the Odeon label.[57]

Musical renditions for gramophone recordings were restricted by the technology of the time. The short playing length of the 78 r.p.m. records forced musicians to encapsulate their normal rendition in small pieces. Technology restricted the length of the piece and the manner of presentation, and musicians probably tried to highlight what they considered were key areas of their performance and style. Sometimes the regular performances were broken into separate segments of three minutes such as presenting a *drut gat* and *jhala* without the long introductory *aalaap* and slower *gat*.[58] In some instances, successive parts of the performance were recorded over a series of recordings, as was the case with some of the *tabla* solo recordings made by Ahmed Jan Thirakwa.[59]

It is also important to note that recordings made until 1925 or thereabouts used the acoustic method of capturing sound and playing it back on spring wound machines called 'Talking Machines'. Since this method did not utilise electricity in the sound recording or reproduction, musicians had to project their voices and instruments in a forceful manner for the sound to be recorded suitably.[60]

---

56 F.W. Gaisberg, *op.cit.*, pp.55-56.

57 B.R. Deodhar, *Gaayanaachaarya P. Vishnu Digambar, op.cit.*, pp.121-122. Also see Suresh Chandvankar, "*Pahile sangeet digdarshak*", in *Loksatta*, 16 September 2001.

58 Imdad Khan's sitar recital of *raag* Sohini can be accessed at http://www.youtube.com/watch?v=IKw8ZTicp1M

59 See https://itunes.apple.com/in/album/the-genius-of-thirakwa/id212633255

60 Personal communication from Suresh Chandvankar in March 2006.

Film

Cinema was yet another sphere that developed due to the advances made in technology. As in theatre, Hindi and regional films made in Bombay and Calcutta saw musicians working as members of the orchestra, as actor-singers, or as composers. Film productions placed a different set of demands on musicians and developed skills in them that were hitherto unheard of. Here was a space where Indian composers, arrangers and musicians, borrowed from any source that captured their imagination, leading to what could be seen as one of the most successful and early 'fusion' experiments. This was despite the vehement assertion that film music was fundamentally 'Indian' and that orchestration only created an illusion of Westernisation. In the words of composer Naushad Ali:

> . . . the credit for popularising film music must go to the New Theatres Ltd. of Calcutta that introduced orchestra in film songs, and since then orchestration of film songs has been sweepingly gaining ground. All film songs (with rare exceptions) are essentially Indian in their composition – only the accompanying musical instruments are mostly Western. And because orchestra music has come to play a tremendously important part in the composition of film songs, it sometimes creates the illusion, specially to the uninitiated that film-music has become Western in its style.[61]

The early European and American silent films screened in British cantonment areas in India were accompanied by army bands, which entertained soldiers with their favourite songs and dance music. When films were screened for other audiences, they used diverse elements for background music depending upon the region and the kind of instruments that were available there. In general, there were combinations of *ghazal*-harmonium-*tabla*, or violin-*mridangam*, or piano-clarinet and/or voices. In some cases, the piano was backed by an orchestra consisting of *tabla*, *sarangi*, violin and/or harmonium. The exact nature of the music is not known, but these ensembles seem to suggest that musicians were experimenting with a new medium and applying a musical treatment that they were familiar with. At times, stock music was

61 Naushad Ali, *Indian Talkie 1931-1956: Silver Jubilee Souvenir*, Film Federation of India, Bombay, 1956, p.100.

used as background music.[62] As mentioned by J.B.H. Wadia, director from the silent and early talkie era and founder of the Wadia Movietone company:

> One Mr. De Costa used to play the piano in the Empire Theatre, Bombay, showing foreign films; Mr. Patly and Mr. Pirosha Mistry, both Parsees, played the piano and the harmonium respectively in the other cinema houses.[63]

With the advent of the talkies, musicians had to contend with new technology. Music had to be recorded during the filming process, which required the actor-singers and orchestras to be on the set and mindful of any extraneous sounds that could inadvertently creep into the recording. But with the advent of playback in films, producers had the luxury of recording songs well before the actual filming.[64] In Bombay, musicians found an avenue for continued employment at studios like Wadia Movietone, Bombay Talkies, Mohan Studio, Prakash Movietone, Filmistan, and Circo Studio, which undertook film production.[65] Initially, these studios did not follow a uniform system of payments to musicians. Generally, they received Rs.2/- for a rehearsal and Rs.10/- for a

---

62 Bhaskar Chandavarkar, "Indian Film Song", in T.M. Ramachandran (ed.), *70 Years of Indian Cinema (1913-1983)*, CINEMA India-International, Bombay, 1985, pp.246-247. See also J.B.H. Wadia, "The Indian Silent Film", in T.M. Ramachandran (ed.), *70 Years of Indian Cinema (1913-1983)*, CINEMA India-International, Bombay, 1985, p.20; Vasant Karnad, "Meet the Mercurial Mr. Madhu Master", in *Cinema Vision India*, Vol. 2 No. 2, ISSN 0250-6998, pp. 14-15; H.D. Darukhanawala, *Parsi Lustre on Indian Soil:-Lives and Portraits of Professionals, Historians, Scholars, Educationists, Parsi Religionists, Philanthropists, Politicians, Officials, Reformers, Pioneers, Industrialists, Merchants and others of The Past and Present, Vol.II*, (n.p.), *op.cit.*, pp.676-677; Gregory D. Booth, *Behind the Curtain: Making Music in Mumbai's Film Studios*, Oxford University Press, New York, 2008, pp.32-33.

63 J.B.H. Wadia, *ibid*, p.20.

64 For a detailed account of the technological changes and their impact on film music, see Gregory D. Booth, *op.cit.*, pp.34-55.

65 Interview with Abdul Halim Jaffer Khan held on 6 May 1997. Practitioners of Carnatic music were similarly drawn to film productions in Madras. See S. Theodore Baskaran, "Music for the Masses: Film Songs of Tamil Nadu" in *Economic and Political Weekly*, Vol.XXVI Nos.11 and 12, Annual Number 1991, Sameeksha Trust, Bombay, 1991, pp.755-758. For a chronological listing and a discussion related to early Hindi film history, see Ashok Da. Ranade, *Hindi Film Song: Music Beyond Boundaries*, Promilla & Co., Publishers, New Delhi, 2006, pp.88-123.

'take' or a song recording. They were paid Rs.15/- for recording background music. But there were no fixed working hours or shifts and musicians were not graded according to levels of skill and competence. Rehearsals continued for an hour and a half to two hours at a stretch and recordings went on for any length of time. Musicians were at times employed by studios on a permanent basis or for the entire period required in completing the recording for a single feature film. They were allowed to accept other recording work while being permanently attached to a particular studio, since an average of two to two and half hours were required on a daily basis in case of the latter. The Minerva Studio started in Sewri by eminent film personality Sohrab Modi, earlier employed musicians at the rate of Rs.30/- a month. However, broadly speaking, the monthly salary was fixed at Rs.75/- and exceptionally good musicians were paid Rs.100/-.[66]

Most musicians had a foundation in Hindustani music, but Goan and Parsi musicians were largely trained in Western music. Hindustani music practitioners working in the Bombay-based Hindi film productions included *sitar* players S.G. Mohiddin (disciple of Hafiz Ali Khan), Sayyad Saheb, Afaque Hussein, Aziz Khan (son of Wahid Khan of the Etawah-Imdad Khan lineage), Muhammad Shafi (brother-in-law of sitar player Vilayat Khan of Etawah-Imdad Khan lineage; also worked as assistant music director), Ramlal (disciple of S.G. Mohiddin), Abdul Halim Jaffer Khan (son and disciple of Jaffer Khan), *sarangi* players Abdul Rehman Khan and Bashir Khan, Sajjad Hussain (mandolin), *tabla* players Ahmed Jan Thirakwa, Abdul Karim, Jeere Khan and Alla Rakha, *dholak* player Ghulam Muhammad, flautist Pannalal Ghosh, and vocalists Khan Mastana (son of Wahid Khan), Saraswati Rane and Padmavati Shaligram. Musicians like Bashir Khan and Alla Rakha also composed music for films.[67]

---

66 Interview with Abdul Halim Jaffer Khan held on 6 May 1997.

67 *Ibid.* According to Abdul Halim Jaffer Khan, *sarangi* player Bashir Khan residing at Mahim, joined the industry in the absence of music concerts and with the intention of discontinuing *sarangi* accompaniment to hereditary women performers. He also composed music for *Ujaalaa*. Also see Isak Mujawar, *Maharashtra: Birthplace of Indian Film Industry*, Government of Maharashtra, Bombay, 1965, p.34, and Vasant Karnad, *op.cit.*, p. 14.

Some musicians accepted work outside their area of specialisation. Thus, *sitar* player Abdul Halim Jaffer Khan sang a line in a children's chorus song for the film *Bahurani*. The music for this film was composed by Rafiq Ghaznavi, a music composer and *batta been* or *vichitra vina* player. Abdul Halim Jaffer Khan also played *jaltarang* in the films *Marvi*, *Nadan* and *Mahatma Vidur*.[68]

Hindustani music practitioners who joined films as composers included Govindrao Tembe, B.R. Deodhar, R. Ramnathkar, Dilipchandra Vedi, Master Krishnarao, G. Devaskar, Abdul Karim Khan, Shankarrao Vyas, Firoz Dastur, Sureshbabu Mane, Pannalal Ghosh, Alla Rakha alias A.R. Qureshi, Shridhar Parsekar, Sajjad Hussein, Gyan Prakash Ghosh, Ravi Shankar, and Omkarnath Thakur.[69]

Some musicians were also approached to act in films. In his capacity as music director at the Shrikrishna Film Company and on behalf of the Company, B.R. Deodhar requested Vishnu Digambar Paluskar, to play the role of Tulsidas in a film on the saint's life. Paluskar was offered a fee of Rs.5,000/- for a three-month stint. This was at complete variance to the monthly salary of Rs.250/- to Rs.450/- that was usually offered to film actors. Paluskar accepted this proposal, but work had to be postponed as the recording machine in Bombay broke down. He could not act in the film thereafter, due to his travels and indifferent health.[70] Vocalist Siddheshwari Devi received film offers in the 1930s and she acted and sang in a few films like *Suryakumari* under the Usha Cinetone Film Company banner. Her name was advertised as 'the singer from Banaras and the actress of Usha Cinetone – Miss Siddheshwari'.[71]

As was the case with gramophone recordings, film songs were bound by restrictions on duration that were imposed by technology.

68 Interview with Abdul Halim Jaffer Khan held on 6 May 1997. Also see Vasant Karnad, *ibid*, p. 14.

69 Firoze Rangoonwalla, *Indian Filmography, Silent and Hindi Films 1897-1969*, Bombay, 1970, pp.81-246. Also see Vamanrao H. Deshpande, *Between Two Tanpuras*, *op.cit.*, p.8, and Bhaskar Chandavarkar, "The Great Film Song Controversy", in *Cinema Vision, Vol.1, No.4*, October 1980, pp.71-72.

70 B.R. Deodhar, *Gaayanaachaarya P. Vishnu Digambar*, *op.cit.*, p.125-127.

71 Savita Devi, *Maa . . . Siddheshwari*, Lotus Collection Roli Books, New Delhi, 2000, pp.65-66.

Film composer Bhaskar Chandavarkar writes, "The 78 r.p.m. record was the only available format till other means of sound recording came to be invented and the film magazine would not allow very lengthy sequences to be filmed without a break. These factors made it necessary to have songs of about 3 ½ minutes . . ."[72] Ground was thus laid for what later flowered into a separate genre of music called 'film song' with characteristic features that were emulated by some non-film songs too. Film songs and background scores transported musicians from the conventional Hindustani music format to an orchestral arrangement. Some of them even learnt to read notation to be able to cope with the new working pattern.[73]

Experimentation with technology was accompanied by innovative production of various kinds of films. When the talkies made their entry and the silent era gradually drew to a close, many film production companies were in search of novel musical experiments that could form a part of the new talkies. The Krishna Company represented by Shukla, the Manager, was interested in producing films featuring variety programmes presented by Deodhar's School of Indian Music. Accordingly, the first talkie was shot in Bombay in 1931 featuring the school performances and Deodhar was acknowledged as Music Director on screen. Apparently, this was the first time that a person was acknowledged as Music Director in Bombay.[74] Wadia Movietone also produced a series of short films in the 1930s featuring practitioners of art music like Ahmed Jan Thirakwa.[75] These were probably some of the earliest instances of live art music performances recorded on film format.

Broadcasting

Broadcasting was yet another technological boon to Hindustani music that benefitted its practitioners hugely. Coming on the heels of pro-

---

72 Bhaskar Chandavarkar, "Indian Film Song", in Ramachandran, T.M. (ed.), *70 Years of Indian Cinema (1913-1983)*, *op.cit.*, p.249.

73 Interview with Abdul Halim Jaffer Khan held on 6 May 1997.

74 B.R. Deodhar, "School of Indian Music", (Marathi), *op.cit.*, n.pag..

75 For a film featuring Ahmed Jan Thirakwa produced by Wadia Movietone, see http://www.youtube.com/watch?v=StWrVL6SHL4

gress made in recording technology, broadcasting in India began with amateur efforts in the 1920s. Private enterprise soon took the cue and the Radio Club of Bombay broadcast its first programme in June 1923. The Calcutta Radio Club began broadcasting in November 1923 and the Madras Radio Club began transmitting in July 1924. However, the service of the Radio Clubs were closed down in 1927 due to financial difficulties. Thereafter, organised broadcasting began in India with the inauguration of the first station of the Indian Broadcasting Company in Bombay by Lord Irwin on July 23, 1927. The Calcutta station was inaugurated on August 26, 1927. Lionel Fielden took over as the first Controller of Broadcasting on August 30, 1935, and it was due to his initiative that the broadcasting service adopted All India Radio (hereinafter AIR) as its new nomenclature when it came under the control of the Government of India in 1936.[76] According to Balkrishnabuwa Kapileshwari, the Bombay radio station was established in 1925 by the Chenoi brothers, who were noted businessmen. He mentions that the inaugural programme featured a vocal recital by Faiyaz Khan, as Abdul Karim Khan who had been approached earlier for this purpose declined from performing in front of a machine.[77]

The first Advisory Committee called the Delhi Station Advisory Council was formally recognized on August 21, 1936. Later, other stations had their Advisory Committees. In Bombay, the Committee was constituted sometime after March 1939, with the Controller of Broadcasting as the President, the Station Director as Secretary, and Sir Rahimtoolah Chinoy, V.N. Chandavarkar, Lt. Col. Sir Richard Temple, Rani Laxmi Bai Rajwade of Gwalior, and B.S. Sukthankar, as Members.[78]

Nineteenth century colonial perceptions about Indian music and dance were reflected in the lack of British patronage to Indian perform-

76 U.L. Baruah, *This is All India Radio-a handbook of radio broadcasting in India*, Publications Division, Ministry of Information and Broadcasting, Government of India, New Delhi, 1983, pp.1,8. Also see, Sumati Mutatkar, "Music and the Radio (looking Back and Beyond)" in the *Akashwani Sangeet Sammelan 1998* brochure, Prasar Bharati Broadcasting Corporation of India, Ministry of Information & Broadcasting, Government of India, New Delhi, 1998.

77 Balkrishnabuwa Kapileshwari, *op.cit.*, p.68.

78 Lionel Fielden, *Report on the Progress of Broadcasting in India: Up to the 31st March 1939*, Manager of Publications, Delhi, 1940, pp.76-78.

ing arts. Musicians found limited official patronage only when concerts were broadcast on the colonial radio network. The basis for including music in radio broadcasts was not part of an overall official policy geared towards the arts. Music was in fact considered of secondary importance, but it was an exigency that the government could not escape, as was obvious from Lionel Fielden's remarks:

> Music, which must necessarily fill about seven-eights of any broadcasting programme, is naturally a factor of considerable importance. It may be said that music is, to some extent, 'padding', because it does not instruct or inform, and that it is, therefore, actually of less significance in broadcasting than talks or news. Nevertheless, it is obvious that for a large percentage of listeners, music will be the chief source of entertainment and possibly also the general factor governing popularity or unpopularity.[79]

Bombay was broadcasting Hindustani music since the early days, even before the Government established its control over the medium. For instance, Murad Khan broadcast his *been* recital on the Chenoy Company's privately owned radio station in 1928, despite his initial refusal to broadcast.[80] But barring such exceptions, senior musicians largely did not accept the idea of broadcasting their art to one and all, as had been their initial response to gramophone recordings.

In this situation, the example of the Homji sisters is noteworthy. Monthly broadcasts of the Homji Sisters orchestra since the early days of the radio consisted of vocalist and organ player Khurshid Minocher-Homji (d.1980) later known as Saraswati Devi and her sisters who played the *sitar*, mandolin and *dilruba*. This came at a time when amateur women musicians were forbidden from performing in public. This was true even in the Parsi community, which is why the Homji sisters stand out as examples of fortitude and courage in the city. Khurshid Minocher-Homji had her training at the Sharada Sangeet Vidyalaya under Bhatkhande, and later joined the Marris College in Lucknow, as a student at first and then as a music teacher. She went on to become India's first woman film music director and worked with the Bombay Talkies between 1935 and 1941. Her sister Manek (d.1981) alias Chandraprab-

---

79 *Ibid*, p.21.

80 B.R. Deodhar, *Thor sangeetkaar*, *op.cit.*, p.68.

ha, was also an actor-singer in films. They assumed aliases as conservative Parsis were against their decision to pursue careers in film.[81]

In general, however, amateurs were not inclined to performing in public. Consequently, as was the case with the recording industry, most music broadcasts featured performers from the salon district, so much so that the Delhi radio station was nicknamed 'Sarkari Chawri Bazaar', after the well-known street where singing and dancing women carried on their profession.[82]

In his report on the progress made in the Indian broadcasting service, Lionel Fielden enumerated the problems associated with broadcasting Indian art music, which according to him made it difficult to formulate a standard policy for broadcasting. He mentioned that music was regarded as inherently immoral because of its association with people whom he referred to as 'prostitutes and *mirasis*'. He felt that Indian music had a limited system of notation and few universally accepted standards for songs, compositions, and voice production. He further stated that the different schools of Indian music adopted rigid and uncompromising attitudes towards any change or progress in indigenous music and towards the impact of Western music on the Indian system. In his opinion, the distinction between what he considered classical and light music was the lyrics that they employed. He therefore believed that the real difference was between religious and erotic poetry. He also stated that the younger generation found greater pleasure in films and gramophone recordings. He concluded:

> To add to the difficulties of the situation, communal bias plays a large part in the likes and dislikes of listeners, and many Indian listeners have actually advocated that a communal percentage should be observed in the choice of artists as it is observed in the choice of recruits to Government service.[83]

While Fielden's concerns are apparent here, clearly he was ill-informed about the intricacies of Indian music and was prejudiced by the prevalent colonial perspective on Hindustani music.

---

81 See Shashikant Kinikar, "Lasting Lady, Khurshi-Saraswati" in *Cinema Vision India*, Vol. 2 No. 2, ISSN 0250-6998, pp. 70-72.

82 Daniel M. Neuman, *op.cit.*, p.172.

83 Lionel Fielden, *ibid*, pp.21-22.

With the passage of time, musicians agreed to broadcast with the result that eminent artistes like Faiyaz Khan performed from Bombay, Delhi, Calcutta and Lucknow AIR stations. Rampur-Sahaswan vocalist Mushtaq Hussein Khan performed from many stations of AIR, but was heard most frequently from Lucknow-Allahabad and Delhi.[84] Special programmes were also scheduled other than regular music broadcasts. Thus, Dattatreya Vishnu Paluskar (1921-1955), son of V.D. Paluskar, sang his first radio concert in 1938 at the Bombay station in a programme held in memory of his father.[85] From January 1938, broadcasts of public concerts were organised. These included major events like the Abdul Karim Khan Anniversary from Miraj, and relays from the Wagle Memorial Hall and from a programme held by Bombay Music Circle featuring Omkarnath Thakur and Abdul Karim Khan of Delhi, respectively. Such broadcasts also extended to Western music, when the fourth concert of the Bombay Symphony Orchestral Society held at the Cowasji Jehangir Hall was relayed.[86] Orchestral works by students of Deodhar's SIM were greatly appreciated by officials from the AIR. These recitals were part of the school's annual gatherings and prize distribution functions held at the Cowasji Jehangir Hall in the presence of a large audience. Consequently, special programmes featuring the students were recorded three to four times each year for the next eight to ten years.[87]

Fees and duration for broadcast were directly negotiated between the station and the individual artiste. Distinguished musicians were paid a fee of approximately Rs.100/-, and in exceptional cases they received a fee of more than Rs.150/-. Every radio station annually prepared a list of artistes indicating the fee and grading of approved artistes, and this list was circulated among all stations. According to available information, stations tried to maintain uniform standards and booked artistes from other zones as well.[88] Apart from notable professional musicians, tal-

---

84 Susheela Misra, *Music Profiles*, *op.cit.*, pp.49,57.

85 Laxminarayan Garg, *op.cit.*, p.173.

86 Lionel Fielden, *op.cit.*, p.60.

87 B.R. Deodhar, "School of Indian Music", *op.cit.* n.pag.

88 G.C. Awasthy, *Broadcasting in India*, Allied Publishers Private Limited, Bombay, 1965, p.38.

ented young artistes were also encouraged to perform on the All India Radio. Auditions were arranged by the Programme Assistant in charge of music and heard by one senior officer like the Assistant Station Director or Station Director.[89]

Radio broadcasts of music were not restricted by the short recording length of a gramophone recording, but depended on the duration of the broadcast. Commenting on the necessity of broadcasting art music, despite majority of listeners wanting popular music, Fielden believed that variety had to be introduced to widen the scope of listeners' tastes. He stated, "Thus we find, in most broadcasting organizations, that classical music gains a place which a majority vote would not actually give it and it is undoubtedly true that the taste for classical music has, in many countries, been considerably strengthened by this policy."[90]

In terms of programme content, the early radio broadcasts reflected the emphasis given to vocal music in comparison to instrumental music in live concerts.[91] The length of transmission in 1937-38 for various types of programmes provided by Fielden, mentions Indian vocal music enjoying maximum time followed by European instrumental music. Indian instrumental music enjoyed the sixth position followed by European vocal music. In 1938-39, Indian vocal music continued to enjoy maximum transmission, but Indian instrumental music had risen to the fourth position, and European instrumental music and European vocal music enjoyed the fifth and eight positions, respectively.[92] Thus, the overall bias towards vocal music seems to have reflected the same tendency seen in live concerts at the time.

In May 1938, an exhaustive questionnaire relating to listeners' musical preferences, was issued to 17,000 listeners in the Bombay Presidency. Of the replies received, 3000 were in favour of broadcasting European music, 2700 wanted it abolished, and 1300 remained neutral. The question related to the length of time to be allotted to a single artiste at a stretch drew opinions that tended towards 30-45 minutes with

89 *Ibid.*

90 Lionel Fielden, *op.cit.*, p.21.

91 *Ibid*, p.20.

92 *Ibid.*

1200 voting for less than 15 minutes, 1500 for less than 30 minutes, 1200 for less than one hour, and 1100 for more than one hour. Regarding the total length of time in a day for any artiste, 850 were in favour of less than 30 minutes, 3500 were in favour of one hour or more, thereby suggesting that listeners were open to listening to more than one performance of the same artiste.[93] A total of 11,000 listeners declared that they listened to all three types of music mentioned in the questionnaire, namely, classical and light Indian music and European music, or to two of these. Of these, 4,800 listened to light Indian music, 3,900 to classical Indian music, and 2,100 to European music. In terms of the comparative number of hours, listeners heard two hours of light Indian music in comparison to 98 minutes of classical Indian music and 53 minutes of European music.[94] Of the three hours allotted to music in evening programmes, listeners were asked to allot durations for Indian and European music. Some refrained from answering, but 4,674 were in favour of two hours or less of Indian music whilst 969 wanted all three hours for the same. For European music, 4,198 voted for 1½ hours or less as against 690 who wanted 2 to 3 hours.[95] Notably, access to radio broadcasts during this period was limited to the upper strata of society. It is clear from these figures that Indian music broadcasts had several listeners who were yearning for more. This was also perhaps one of the early official attempts at giving a nomenclature to non-art music. Thus was born, the term 'light music', borrowed obviously from Western music.

Fielden mentions the AIR policy regarding European music. Broadcasting European music programmes was found to be difficult as talent was restricted and European musicians were not easily available for selection, rehearsal and arranging programmes, except at high salaries. It was however believed that funding for European programmes was justifiable because of the large listenership for such programmes.[96] European programmes were restricted to larger stations, namely, Bombay, Calcutta, Delhi and Madras. At these stations, one hour was to be devoted to European music at lunch time for which there was a per-

93 *Ibid*, pp.72-74

94 *Ibid*, p.74.

95 *Ibid.*

96 *Ibid*, p.24.

ceived demand. One hour of European music was also to be set aside from 10 pm to 11 pm on one wavelength, but with an alternative Indian music programme on the other wavelength.[97]

Lionel Fielden was also keen to retain the services of regular ensembles for Indian music. He noted:

> Three to four Indian musicians must be engaged everyday to provide a modicum of variety, their fees ranging from Rs.20 to Rs.300 per artist. A European orchestra which fills an hour or so, may cost anything from Rs.50 to Rs.150. Indian orchestras have to be maintained at all stations for accompaniments, rehearsals and for performance. Such orchestras consist of 8 to 15 instrumentalists and cost on the average Rs.500 to Rs.1,000 a month or Rs.17 to Rs.34 a day.[98]

Apart from the policy to retain an in-house orchestra, the Bombay station also featured B.R. Deodhar's orchestra every Sunday.[99]

The engagement of Indian orchestras was encouraged by Fielden, notwithstanding the concept of orchestral music being a Western one. On the other hand, he strongly condemned the inclusion of the harmonium on radio broadcasts. His stance reflected the European displeasure and contempt for the harmonium, and finally culminated in the decision to ban the instrument from the All India Radio broadcasts after March 1, 1940. The matter had been discussed in 1939 at the Station Directors Conference, but Lionel Fielden took this initiative after John Foulds (d.1939), a well-known practitioner of European music heading the Western music section on the Delhi All India Radio station in the 1930s, stated in an article that the harmonium was not suited for Indian music since it could not produce the microtones that formed the basis of Indian music.[100]

The experiences gained and policies drawn up during Fielden's time greatly influenced the manner in which Indian music was represented

97 *Ibid*, p.25.

98 *Ibid*, p.134.

99 B.R. Deodhar, *Gaayanaachaarya P. Vishnu Digambar*, *op.cit.*, p.122.

100 U.L. Baruah, *op.cit.*, p.8. Also see Lionel Fielden, *op.cit.*, p.25; Daniel M. Neuman, *op.cit.*, p.184. Thus, the notion that Jawaharlal Nehru was responsible for the ban on the harmonium is erroneous, despite his unfavorable remarks about the instrument cited earlier.

on radio in later years. The listenership for music broadcasts grew and musicians were eager to reach out to newer audiences through this medium.

The quality of music featured broadcasts on radio was a matter of concern to some, and at times even to those placed at the highest level, as is demonstrated in correspondence exchanged in February 1947 between Sardar Vallabhai Patel, the Minister for Information and Broadcasting and for Home in the Interim Government and Maulana Abul Kalam Azad, the Minister for Education. Commenting on music broadcasts on the All India Radio, Azad wrote:

> You perhaps do not know that I have always taken a keen interest in Indian music and at one time practiced it myself. It has, therefore, been a shock to me to find that the standard of music of All India Radio broadcast is extremely poor. I have always felt that All India Radio should set the standard in Indian music and lead to its continual improvement. Instead, the present programmes have an opposite effect and lead one to suspect that the artistes are sometimes chosen not on grounds of merit.[101]

Azad offered to advise the Secretary of Broadcasting in the matter.[102] Patel's response to Azad's comments is equally forthright, when he stated:

> While I make no apology for such defects as exist in the quality of these broadcasts, I think it would be a mistake to ignore the patent fact that the artistic talent at the disposal of each radio station in limited, and that they have to make the best of whatever talent is available to them. We have also to take note of the fact that the remuneration which we can give to these artistes is not sufficiently attractive, and having regard to the present financial difficulties of which you are no doubt aware, it does not seem possible to make any improvement in that respect.[103]

Critics found AIR policy falling short of expectations in its contribution to art music. S.K. Chaubey remarks:

> I grant that the A.I.R. has not failed to popularize Indian music and Indian musicians. Apart from making them presentable, it has entertained its listeners too. But this is hardly satisfactory. The Radio in India has made no solid

101 Ravindra Kumar (Chief Editor), *The Selected Works of Maulana Abul Kalam Azad: Vol.III–1947-48*, Atlantic Publishers & Distributors, New Delhi, 1991, p.28.

102 *Ibid*, p.29.

103 *Ibid*, p.53.

> contribution to the development and progress of Indian music. Like the film company, the Radio knows how to entertain its listeners. But in doing so it shapes their lies and dislikes. It teaches them to develop a habitual indifference towards classical music. It does not care for that negligible minority which shouts the slogans of classical music.[104]

> On the whole, Radio music is detrimental to taste and judgement. In its actual working, it is a free innovator indifferent to the voice of the tradition and the genius of our music . . . It treats music as a marketable commodity whether it is classical or popular. With its limited mental equipment, it widely avoids making excursions into the realm of higher music.[105]

Suggesting ways in which AIR could contribute, Chaubey says:

> It can teach music to its listeners and help them to appreciate it better. It can engage first-rare musicians whose duty would be to train a small group of promising and talented musicians and also broadcast special music on special occasions according to an intelligent plan. It can do immense propaganda for it and also raise public opinion on this issue.[106]

It is not evident if such criticism applied to broadcasts from Bombay, but musicians and listeners from this region always reminisced about the high quality that was maintained by the local radio station until the 1980s or thereabouts.

---

104 S.K. Chaubey, *op.cit.*, p.135.

105 *Ibid*, pp.135-136.

106 *Ibid*, p.136.

EPILOGUE

In his speech at the Madras Music Academy in 1955, Jawaharlal Nehru, the then Prime Minister, commented on the status of music and dance in sovereign India. He stated:

> We know very well how the people in my own generation to some extent, and even more so the one that had preceded mine, were rather ashamed of anything Indian. They thought that there were some virtues in Indian dancing, but it should not be encouraged too much. It should not be considered the right thing. So it is well known that in India many of our own arts were allowed, not to perish, but certainly not to flourish. I am not talking of the last six or seven years but of 20 or 30 years ago. I know that here in Madras, attempts were made with considerable success to revive it and in other parts of India too this has happened. During the last seven or eight years, that is, since Independence, it is natural that much more attention has been paid to these things. In spite of my ignorance, I feel a certain pride in the great development of dancing, music and other arts in India, and I respect greatly those who today are star performers in these.[1]

The politics of government and non-government policies that were put in place in independent India merit a separate detailed discussion that will need to consider the social and political dynamics of the colonial period impacting many of these decisions. Despite the ostensible

---

1 H.Y. Sharada Prasad and A.K. Damodaran (eds), *Selected Works of Jawaharlal Nehru II Series, Vol.30,* (September 1-November 17, 1955), Jawaharlal Nehru Memorial Fund, N. Delhi, p.218.

regeneration in the arts referred to by Nehru and the fact that political independence gave definite shape to social transformation that had begun several decades earlier, the stigma associated with hereditary women performers was reduced only marginally. That it was not totally wiped out is evident from the fact that children of women performers seldom took to music and dance.

> After Independence a ban prohibiting anyone 'whose private life is a public scandal' was introduced by Sardar Patel when he became Minister of Broadcasting. This opened the way for 'non-professional' artistes to offer themselves for broadcast engagements.[2]

In Bombay, most hereditary women performers continued to reside in the same locality they had inhabited since the nineteenth century. In their survey of prostitution in the city, S.D. Punekar and Kamala Rao note the residential quarters of professional women performers thus:

> The private prostitute is one who remains in the exclusive 'keep' of one man and it is only when he gives her up or she leaves him that she takes another man. Most of the singers, dancers, *tamasha* girls and *naikins* hailing from the Karwar district and Goa, fall in this category. The singing and dancing girls of Bombay have settled on Foras Road and near the Kennedy Bridge (opposite to the Congress House) for generations. The Naikins, though scattered all over central Bombay, are mainly in the Khetwadi, Girgaon, Thakurdwar and Charni Road areas.[3]

Hereditary women performers continued to entertain patrons at their residences along the Kennedy Bridge. This area was called the N.B. Compound or 'Compound' for short, and performances held here came to be called 'time'. Held in the *divaankhaanaa*, the performances were open to all and listeners could pay any amount for this entertainment. Liquor was served during the performances. The 'time' started at 8 or 9 p.m. and continued over several hours. Mammi Jan, Neelam Bai, Zohra and Munni, were some of the popular performers in this area. Women performers from other parts of the country stayed for short periods with those residing permanently in the city. Apparently, some women practitioners presented *qawwali*, and were therefore addressed

---

2 Daniel M. Neuman, *op.cit.*, p.172.

3 S.D. Punekar, and Kamala Rao, *A Study of Prostitutes in Bombay (With reference to Family Background)*, Allied Publishers Private Limited, Bombay, 1962, p.202.

as *qawwaliwalis*. However, it is not known whether the *qawwalis* presented here pertained to Sufi mystic philosophy that was the mainstay of a traditional *qawwali* presentation.[4] From all accounts, the kind of music performed here and the environment that surrounded this area changed vastly in over the years. Later the 'Compound' sported a signboard that read 'Bombay Sangeet Kalakar Mandal', one of the few indicators of its musical past.[5]

Avenues for public performance grew in the post-independence period. New music circles were set up and public concerts became an integral part of Bombay's musical climate. The popularity of the Deodhar School concerts lasted until 1956-57, with more than hundred musicians and connoisseurs gathering to listen to some of India's best-known musicians.[6] Musicians' fees were roughly between Rs.75/- to Rs.100/- before World War II, but apparently, they increased twenty-fold in the post-war period and in independent India.[7]

Large festivals of music such as the Swami Haridas Sammelan began in this period. B.N. Anklesaria, the General Secretary of the fourth Sammelan, in his report published in the souvenir proudly claimed:

> It is the privilege of the Sur Singar Samsad to serve our public with a Dance and Music festival of a type and on a scale never held before in this country. This Conference is an advance on the previous ones in many ways . . .
>
> The Sur Singar Samsad legitimately claims to have played an important part in helping to bring about the changed atmosphere. The atmosphere of our social values has so much altered that the present Sammelan will be organised for a full 18 days' programme. Night after night, in the heart of our city, the *Urbs Prima in Indias'* graced by the highest and the choicest from our society, artist after artist will come before you and will be given the recogni-

4 Interview with Batuk Diwanji held on 24 August 1992. Also from interview with Shalini Narvekar, held on 14 December 1992. Though Shalini Narvekar speaks of the presentation of *qawwalis*, it is not known whether the poetic content was pertaining to Sufi mystic philosophy or had incorporated other themes. Unfortunately, no biographical information about these performers is available. For a detailed analysis of *qawwali* in the context of Sufi mystic philosophy, see Regula Burkhardt Qureshi, *Sufi Music of India and Pakistan: sound, context and meaning in Qawwali*, University of Chicago Press, Chicago, 1995.

5 Interview with Batuk Diwanji held on 18 September 1992.

6 B.R. Deodhar, "School of Indian Music", *op.cit.* (n.pag.)

7 Vamanrao H. Deshpande, *Indian Musical Traditions*, *op.cit.*, p.126.

> tion he or she deserves. Not only for the first time a conference of such long duration as 18 days is to be held in this country; it is also for the first time that top-notch artistes in dance are taking part side-by-side our ace musicians with (*sic*). For the first time, such a big conference is to be held in an open air theatre with accommodation for some 4,000 persons.[8]

The next Sammelan was held from April 2 to 21, 1957, at the Mumbadevi Tank Maidan.[9]

Similar festivals of music and dance started in other parts of the country. Many of them were organised in Calcutta and ran over several days. For example, the All India Music Conference was an annual feature started in the 1940s presenting music, dance and dance-dramas.[10] The annual Dover Lane festival started in 1952 with limited time dedicated to art music, but the popularity of this particular segment led organisers to hold an entire festival devoted to art music in subsequent years, featuring top-notch Hindustani music performers. Patrons of these and many other festivals across the country included the commercial, industrial and intellectual elite, and a few *zamindars* and members of the erstwhile Indian royalty.[11] A special All India Women's Music Conference was also held in Calcutta in 1954, to mark the birth centenary of Saradamani Devi, the wife and spiritual counterpart of Ramakrishna Paramhansa. Notably, this conference featured several women performers, who did not belong to hereditary *tawaif* or *devadasi* families, but had undergone training with hereditary practitioners. Many performers were academically qualified and had even been awarded degrees by the Gandharva Mahavidyalaya or other institutions. Their selection made by the organising committee signalled the changed perspective of organisers, audiences and non-hereditary women performers, with regard to public performance by 'respectable'

8 B.N. Anklesaria, "March of Music", in Sur Singar Samsad, *Sangeet Nritya Mahotsava – Swami Haridas Sammelan – 4th in series*, Bombay, 1956, n.p. For more details about the festival, also see, Sur Singar Samsad, *Sangeet Nritya Mahotsava – Swami Haridas Sammelan – 5th in series*, Bombay, 1957.

9 For more details about the festival, see Sur Singar Samsad, *Sangeet Nritya Mahotsava – Swami Haridas Sammelan – 4th in series*, Bombay, 1956, and Sur Singar Samsad, *Sangeet Nritya Mahotsava – Swami Haridas Sammelan – 5th in series.*

10 *All-India Music Conference*, All India Music Conference Trust, Calcutta, 1954.

11 *The Classical Music Soiree*, Dover Lane Festival, Calcutta, 1954.

women. It also demonstrated a departure from the earlier patronage to professional women performers.[12] Was this done deliberately to give 'sanctity' to the occupation, since the conference was being held in honour of Saradamani Devi?

Numerous private and public concerts in Bombay, Calcutta and other parts of the country, continued to feature hereditary women performers, but the dwindling number of women performers specialising in *thumri-dadra*, suggests that genteel society had chosen to patronise the 'classical' as against 'semi-classical' or the 'sacred' as against the 'profane'. This was despite the fact that these genres, known as they were for their decidedly erotic import, were layered with meanings that stretched from the sacred to the profane, as were many *khayal* compositions.

The emerging Indian nation was also reiterating its unified status by emphasizing national integration in different ways, and music conferences also reflected this stance. Reporting on a speech made by R.R. Diwakar, Minister of State for Information and Broadcasting, Government of India, at a music festival held by the Sri Shanmukhananda Fine Arts & Sangeetha Sabha, Matunga, in the Don Bosco School compound on 11-13 January 1952, *The Times of India* states:

> Paying a tribute to the efforts made by the Sabha to popularise Carnaric music in Bombay, Mr. Diwakar said that music, whether Hindustani or Carnatic, was a divine art. There were many who wrongly differentiated between South Indian and North Indian schools of music. He added that music was essentially common for the entire country. If both the types of music were made popular throughout the country, it would greatly contribute to the cultural oneness of the nation, he said.[13]

But an advertisement that appeared in the same newspaper was telling in its portrayal of the two major systems of art music in the country. The festival featured well-known musicians from the north and the south and a Bharat Natyam dancer. But while the musicians from the south included respected names from the Carnatic fraternity, namely, flautist T.R. Mahalingam, violinist T.N. Krishnan and mridangam player C.S. Murugabhoopathy, the musicians from the north mainly includ-

12 *All-India Women's Music Conference on the occasion of Holy Mother Birth Centenary*, All-India Women's Music Conference Sub-committee, Calcutta, 1954.

13 *The Times of India*, Bombay, January 11, 1952, p.7.

ed leading singers from the film world like Geeta Roy, Meena Kapoor, Lakshmi Shankar, Sharda Nadkarni, Durrani, Talat Mahmud, Mohammad Rafi and Surendra.[14] Was this yet another way of attracting more listeners? Was it pre-empting our times when Indian music has become synonymous with film music and is for many a homogenized entity that has lost touch with the multiple strands of music making that have co-existed and overlapped since centuries?

The number of music festivals increased in the decades to follow. Festivals of this magnitude could be held only due to the presence of the amplification system, as venues were not designed to rely on natural acoustics for several hundred. The introduction of amplification changed the aural perspective for musicians and listeners. Musicians had in the past used pitch and volume in a manner that helped project their voices or instruments to every member in the audience in the absence of amplification, but this had at times adversely affected the tonal quality of their medium.[15]

Noting the rise in music festivals, Vamanrao Deshpande, who commented extensively on modern trends in Hindustani music, lamented the change in the quality of listeners:

> Some of the consequences of the process of industrialization certainly cannot be said to be conducive to the development of music. One important consequence was the emergence of the newly rich and the industrial tycoons. They started squandering the vast amount of their unaccounted wealth recklessly. Before the War the number of listeners was limited to barely a hundred and fifty or so; and it comprised mostly singers or real lovers of music. Sometimes this audience also included members of the privileged and the traditionally wealthy class of the society who felt a genuine concern for music. But the newly rich lacked not only the cultural background, but had on the contrary a taste for only cheap, loud and aggressively eccentric sort of things. They patronized music only with the idea that attendance at music concerts added to their social status. Hardly a few among them had a real innate passion for music. The difference in this changed audience can be seen not only in their standard as listeners but also in their numbers. The pre-War music concerts attended by a small number of connoisseurs have been transformed during the last two decades into *mehfils* (concerts) attended by many times larger number of listeners. Many times these concerts are turned into music

14 *Ibid*. Of these, it was probably only Lakshmi Shankar, who pursued Hindustani music professionally.

15 Ashok D. Ranade, *On Music and Musicians of Hindoostan*, *op.cit.*, p.142.

festivals – mistakenly described as music conferences – attended by a vast concourse of the so-called listeners.[16]

Deshpande believed that this change in audience profile motivated musicians to bring in a variety to their concert repertoire. He pointed out that in doing so a predictable sequence of items emerged:

In the old days, the audience, small in numbers, consisted of connoisseurs, who could gauge an artist's erudition. But the years after, the Second World War and the post-Independence decades saw an increase in the sixe of audiences and artists felt that they were called upon to entertain this large mass of listeners. A *khayal* at the start, then a *thumari*, followed by *natya-sangeet* before the intermission. Once again, a *khayal*, a *thumari*, *natya-sangeet* or *bhajan*, culminating in a Bhairavi. That became the pattern of a performance.[17]

However, trends in colonial Bombay examined here prove conclusively that the desire to introduce variety in concert repertoire existed even in the late nineteenth century and was in fact driven by the exigencies of an urban situation that had offered a new set of patrons not necessarily conversant with the subtleties of Hindustani music.

The advances in technology provided greater opportunities to record, broadcast, and work in film ensembles, aiding widespread dissemination of music and in the process moulding public tastes. But the radical change in forms of dissemination was met with criticism from certain quarters. Once again, Vamanrao Deshpande bemoans:

The benefits of new technology, e.g., the record-player, radio, cinema and the loud-speaker, have now reached the common man. Its obvious consequence was the disappearance, at one stroke, of the harmony and the rapport between the audience and the singer. And it at once opened for the common people a new vista of entertainment through an altogether new medium – the mechanical . . . even those who attended music concerts as a fashion were now able to listen to music very easily. Mechanical auditory contrivances have created this new kind of audience, vastly numerous. This process of technology has only contributed to the lowering of the quality of music.[18]

Broadcasting made significant strides in post-independent India. By August 1947, the All India Radio network had nine stations at Delhi,

16 Vamanrao H. Deshpande, *Indian Musical Traditions*, *op.cit.*, pp.118-119.

17 Vamanrao H. Deshpande, *Between Two Tanpuras*, *op.cit.*, pp.36-37.

18 Vamanrao H. Deshpande, *Indian Musical Traditions*, *op.cit.*, pp.119-120.

Calcutta, Bombay, Chennai, Lucknow, Tiruchi, Lahore, Peshawar, and Dacca.[19] Low power radio stations in princely states of Mysore, Trivandrum, Hyderabad, Aurangabad and Baroda, were taken over by All India Radio, when they were integrated with India and became a part of the network by 1950.[20] B.V. Keskar, Minister of Information and Broadcasting (1953-1961) inducted well respected writers, poets, musicians and dramatists, into AIR as 'Producers', on staff-artists' contract, rather than keeping them confined to the earlier label of 'performers'.[21] The first National Programme of Music was broadcast on July 20, 1952. In October 1952, the National Orchestra of AIR was setup in Delhi with Ravi Shankar as Conductor. T.K. Jairama Iyer joined as second Conductor. The first Radio Sangeet Sammelan was broadcast in October 1955.[22]

However, the early 1950s saw a rare occasion in the history of Indian music, when musicians rallied together for a cause common to the fraternity. This was an unprecedented opposition to All India Radio's new policy of grading musicians irrespective of their public stature, by a specially appointed audition panel that pursued a procedure considered draconian and disrespectful by performers. Bombay was the epicenter of this agitation. A musicians' organization called Bharatiya Sangit Kalakar Mandal was set up in 1953 with eminent vocalist Vilayat Hussein Khan as its President and vocalist Kausalya Manjeshwar as Secretary and *sitar* player Arvind Parikh as Joint Secretary. Musicians collectively decided to stop broadcasting and picketed outside the Bombay radio station until a policy more respectful of musicians was in place. The confrontation grew exponentially across the country, with well-known artistes participating and openly voicing their grievances. The agitation ended in 1955 and a settlement was reached. Apparently, the audition policy was altered to incorporate a screening process that was not demeaning to performers.[23]

---

19 U.L. Baruah, *op.cit.*, p.8.

20 *Ibid.*

21 *Ibid*, p.10.

22 *Ibid*, pp.9-10.

23 Interview with with Kaushalya and Dinker Manjeshwar held on 10 September 1993, and with Dinker Manjeshwar held on 30 March 2011. See also, Balkrishnabu-

The gramophone recording industry grew in the post-independence era, breaking new ground with indigenous record labels taking over the reigns of the market from foreign labels. The number of recordings rose to incorporate all manner of music, opening doors to experimentation and collaboration unheard of until then. The number of Hindustani music recordings rose and long playing records took the place of the 78 rpm recordings, allowing musicians to explore their recitals in greater detail. Naturally, the long-playing discs also had restricted duration, and to that extent, gramophone recordings continued to fall short of the live concert format. But it was definitely an improvement from the 78 rpm duration.

The new genre of film music became one of the best examples of musical collaboration across genres, cultures and systems of music. The ground prepared during colonial times for Indian and Western musical collaborations was consolidated in the post-independence era. However, the long-playing discs did not impact the duration of the film song. Keeping to the earlier duration, songs had three to four verses interspersed with interludes played by Indian and Western instruments in unison or in polyphonic arrangement.

Music education in Bombay in the post-independence era found government recognition and steps were taken to facilitate the shaping of a standardized teaching methodology at the schools' level. The Education and Industries Department of the Government of Bombay appointed a Music Education Committee (hereinafter MEC), as per a resolution dated March 24, 1948, to survey the field of music education in the erstwhile Bombay Province.[24] The resolution accepted the reality that music did not find a definite place in the syllabi for primary and secondary schools except in the case of girls' schools. It stated that

---

wa Kapileshwari, *op.cit.*, pp.219-221.

24 *Report of the Committee for Music Education, 1948-49*, Government of Bombay, Education & Industries Department, Bombay, 1949. Information related to this Report is based on the same source. For a brief analysis on the state of institutionalized music education in Hindustani music, past and present, see Aneesh Pradhan with additional inputs from Shubha Mudgal, "Institutionalized Music Education in North India: Some observations", in *Sangeet Natak, Vol XLIII, Number 2*, 2009, Sangeet Natak Akademi, New Delhi, 2009, pp.23-34.

the Government was desirous of promoting the study and appreciation of music in educational institutions and that it was keen to formulate the curriculum for schools in this respect. The Report that was subsequently published included observations and recommendations for the erstwhile Bombay Province, and are therefore pertinent to this study, as they set the tone for institutionalized music education in Bombay in subsequent years.

The non-official members of the MEC appointed by the Government included G.B. Jathar as Chairman, S.A. Deshpande, K.G. Phulambrikar alias Master Krishna, V.N. Patwardhan, B.R. Deodhar, S.R. Tatti, Kanchanlal Mamawala, D.G. Vyas, and G.H. Ranade as Member and Secretary. Their observations and recommendations were therefore, influenced by their training, background and experience in Hindustani music, and to that extent the exercise was limited only to this system of music. Sub-committees were formed to examine subjects like music notation, music courses and syllabuses, and qualifications and pay scales of music teachers. Oral evidence was recorded by conducting interviews at Dharwar, Poona, Bombay, Ahmedabad and Baroda, with music teachers from these cities and other areas in the Bombay Province. A questionnaire was also sent to primary and secondary schools, training colleges, district and municipal school boards, women's schools and colleges and to music scholars, institutions and musicians belonging to the different parts of the Bombay Province numbering 406, of which, 220 replied.

Despite the fact that institutionalized music education had been consolidated by then, the Committee declared in no uncertain terms that its survey proved that music education in the Bombay Province was unsatisfactory and inadequate. Discussing the condition of musical instruction, the Committee stated, "In the regular schools the provision made is of the most perfunctory nature, while in the special schools conducted by private individuals or institutions, the approach to the problem is professional rather than cultural and there is great diversity in their standards".[25] It was noted that special music teachers were not appointed in most places in the Province. They were appointed in larger

25 *Report of the Committee for Music Education, 1948-49*, *ibid*, p.10.

cities, but their salaries were abysmally low and they were not encouraged enough. There was no uniformity in course-work and methodology, and the music teacher decided the framework in consultation with the Principal. The MEC therefore, urged the Government "to give serious consideration to the question of according to music its proper place in the scheme of education in all its stages, prescribing uniform courses and methods of instruction in all Government and Grant-in-Aid Institutions and helping to remedy the present chaotic state of music education in the Province, and to spread the taste for good music among the public".[26]

The MEC made the following recommendations regarding music courses after examining courses followed by Government schools, private schools and institutions, and the matriculation syllabi of the Patna and Andhra Universities:

- Music should be a compulsory subject at the primary school level and until the first three years of the secondary school, but that it should be a voluntary subject thereafter. The Committee explained:

  > The object of music education in ordinary schools . . . is not to turn out professionals but to prepare discerning listeners and develop an aesthetic sensibility in sound, the possession of which should be a vital influence throughout the life of the pupil. Our view is that by making music a compulsory subject during the four years of the primary stage of school teaching and by carefully suiting the manner and matter of music instruction to the tender age and natural environment and aptitude of the pupil, he can be taught the fundamentals of music which should give a healthy direction to his taste in after-life. Although the broad aim on music education will continue to be the same in the Higher Standards, music can no longer be made compulsory there, if only because special aptitude will be required in the stages of music instruction above the elementary, and not all students can be expected to possess such special aptitude".[27]

---

26 *Ibid.*

27 *Ibid*, p.4.

- Music should be taught by the 'Listen and Imitate' method at the primary level and technical terms and explanations should be avoided at this stage. Such terms should be introduced in higher classes. Folk songs and songs in the mother tongue should be taught at the primary level.
- Music should be a compulsory subject in the primary Teachers' Training College for men and women.
- Government should start special schools for advanced training in music at major centres in the Province, and entry to such schools should be granted after students passed an entrance examination.
- Music teachers should be equipped with Sangeet Visharad certificates from various established institutions like the Gandharva Mahavidyalaya other than certificates from Teachers' Training Colleges. The Sangeet Visharad certificates should also be made mandatory for those who wish to teach in special schools set up by the Government.
- A music notation system recommended by the MEC should be adopted in schools after the Primary level. The MEC had arrived at this system after studying eighteen existing systems.

The MEC also laid down specifications for administration, class-management, teachers' qualifications and salaries, and recommended that museums and libraries pertaining to music should be started with periodic lectures on the theory and practice of music. It was suggested that a general course for the arts should be introduced as a compulsory subject in the final year of schooling and that music appreciation should be a part of this course. Graduate and post-graduate degree courses in music were recommended at the University level in the Province.

The MEC displayed a dichotomy in its approach to changes in the world of Indian music. The harmonium and film music came under severe criticism from the Committee for their supposed corrupting influence on the ear. Welcoming the All India Radio ban on the harmonium, the MEC stated, "By banning the harmonium, the All-India Radio has given proof of its concern that our music should be conveyed to listeners in its full beauty unspoilt by an accompaniment which makes it impossible for its finer points being properly appreciated."[28] The Committee's acceptance of the harmonium was at best a conditional one, when it recommended:

> The Harmonium, being a tempered instrument is unsuitable for Indian Music. It has to be tuned again from time to time. Even if used as an instrument to give only the Drone-Notes its effect is not as smooth, pleasant or rich as that of the Drone of the Tambura. It is poor in point of the combination notes and upper-partials contributed by the Drone of the Tambura.
>
> Therefore, the Committee is of opinion that as far as possible the Harmonium should not be used in the Schools. If the volume of the Drone of the Tambura is not sufficient to provide a fairly audible note for the Drone, a Tambura-Box may be used for the purpose. In exceptional cases, however, for reasons of economy and convenience of management, the Harmonium may be used, only to give the Drone notes; but not to accompany or guide the Music. The general opinion for banning the used of the Harmonium is so strong that it is a matter for serious consideration whether there is any justification for using the instrument anywhere for the purposes of Indian Music.[29]

Conversely, the Committee encouraged the use of gramophone records for testing appreciation skills, or playing records of prescribed songs in classrooms to illustrate good music to students. The contribution of All India Radio in developing public taste was praised.

Though at some level, music education in schools got a formal status, it was guided by the vision of the MEC members. Their perspective centred around art music, inspite of the initial prescription to use rhymes and children's songs. They were seemingly progressive in their prescription of using modern technology in the form of gramophone records to acquaint students with various kinds of music, but continued to be guided by their experiences with the Gandharva Mahavidyalaya syllabus. Even when the Bombay University introduced music in its curriculum in June 1949, it followed the Gandharva Mahavidyalaya syllabus. The fact that some of them were erstwhile students of the GM and were actively conducting classes according to its syllabus must definitely have guided their choices. The *Sangeet Kala Vihar* published by

28 *Ibid*, p. 3.

29 *Ibid*, pp.50-51.

the Gandharva Mahavidyalaya Mandal in Bombay and edited by B.R. Deodhar, advertised 'easily accessible teaching' imparted by Deodhar's School of Indian Music and Narayanrao Vyas' Vyas Sangeet Vidyalaya.[30] The *Sangeet Kala Vihar* contained biographical sketches of musicians, reviews, and letters, in Marathi, Gujarati and Hindi, and at times even in English, but it catered to a growing number of teachers and students by way of publishing notated compositions, examination syllabus and questions and answers pertaining to the Gandharva Mahavidyalaya coursework.[31] Little wonder, therefore, that the MEC members recommended GM graduation as a basic qualification for job opportunities as music teachers in schools. Largely, this has set the tone for music education in schools to the present day.

However, these developments and the general changing social environment made the learning of music less of a taboo. Vilayat Hussein Khan concluded that there were more than a hundred to hundred and twenty-five music classes and schools in Bombay in the 1950s, which catered primarily to men and women from non-musician families.[32] But the rampant institutionalization drew criticism from various quarters. Writing in the *Sangeet Kala Vihar*, N.R. Marulkar opined that contemporary music education had become more like a market-place, where music teachers were preoccupied with publicizing their work and their institutions, and were desirous of finding more avenues of income, rather than being involved in actual educational activity. He believed that their motives made them lose sight of their development as artistes and their commitment to making students aware of the seriousness of the art. Marulkar further pointed out that many individuals declared themselves music teachers with few years of training and hid their inadequacies by falling back on textual material related to music. He believed their lack of practice adversely affected the quality of students who they taught.[33]

30 *Sangeet Kala Vihar*, Varsha 8, Ank 3, March 1955, (n.pag.)

31 Shankar Ganesh Date and others (ed.), *op.cit.*, pp.334-335.

32 Vilayat Hussein Khan, *op.cit.*, p.15.

33 N.R. Marulkar, "*Aajche shikshan-satra aani tyaachi saangataa*", in Princ. B.R. Deodhar (ed.), *Sangeet Kala Vihar, Varsha 8, Ank 3*, Gandharva Mahavidyalaya Man-

Echoing Marulkar's feelings, Deodhar in his Presidential Address at the Madhyaprant Sangeet Parishad held at Amravati, from 4 to 8 February, 1955, said:

> The past 25 to 30 years has seen music spreading widely. Most provinces (prantaat) now have music taught at the primary and secondary (duyyam) schools. At least 15 universities have given the subject a respectable status. Music circles have been started in many places. At least 4000 music teachers are now employed around the country. The presence of the radio has enabled people to listen to programmes of good artistes. But good artistes are not being produced in recent times. The only reason for this is the absence of good teachers and diligent students. The students of today wish to become performers with little efforts or practice.[34]

Though Deodhar was one of the members of the MEC, and to that extent, influenced policy during this period, his observation seems to suggest that the ground reality left much to be desired. It is also pertinent to note that few students opted for music at the Secondary School Certificate (SSC) level. This was partly due to the fact that barring Nagpur and SNDT (Bombay) universities, no other universities in Bombay Province included music as a subject in their curriculum. This made it difficult for students who had opted for the subject at the SSC level to get admissions to colleges. Hence, only few interested students appeared for the music examination at this level. The syllabus was also very unwieldy for students who had to cope with other subjects too. 33 *raag*s were to be covered with 5 *bada khayal*s. All examinees had to appear for a vocal examination even if they were not endowed with good voices. Thus, out of over one lakh students appearing at the SSC level only hundred would opt for music. However, the situation seems to have changed marginally over the next few years. More students are believed to have opted for music at the SSC level after March 1959 when changes were introduced in the music syllabus. The new rules allowed those not endowed with a good voice, to play violin, *dilruba*, *sitar*, for the exams.[35]

---

dal, Miraj, March 1955, p.12.

34 B.R. Deodhar (ed.), *Sangeet Kala Vihar, Varsha 8, Ank 3*, *ibid*, p.36.

35 "*S.S.C. chaa 1959 March paasun amlaat yenaaraa sangeetaachaa navaa kaaryakram*", in B.R. Deodhar (ed.), *Sangeet Kala Vihar, Varsha 11, Ank 8*, Gandharva

But institutionalized music education attracted criticism from some quarters. For instance, S.K. Chaubey held:

> A system which is completely divorced from the traditions of the creative art of music, and which aims at mere propaganda, is incomplete and insufficient both. Institutions of music are good in their own way as far as they give a smattering of music to the younger generation. But their self-sufficiency shuts out all progress. They begin to live in their accustomed grooves of thinking and hate to be shocked out of them. They develop narrow visions and serve limited interest. They often become centres of vested interests and are sustained by the poison of provincialism. They set up their own theories of music and pronounce their own separate judgements on music. The result is that music institutions in this country, have no vital common interests, the only common interest being the granting of certificates to dozens of candidates every year. None of these, for instance, have tackled the problem how to teach music to children. Instead of becoming means they become an end in themselves . . .[36]

Chaubey vehemently believed that the modern education system was detrimental to the tradition of art music:

> It is my contention that the modern system of music-education through notation is fundamentally hostile to the tradition and heritage of classical music. The subtle manner in which certain erroneous ideas are inculcated into the minds of the students should be marked. Among many of these myths which are made fashionable by the educated man whose sons and daughters receive training in liberal arts, are: (*a*) that the training given by the professional Ustads is unscientific, (*b*) that they are 'uneducated' and unimaginative, (*c*) that they occupy an inferior social status, and (*d*) that they are behind times and cannot keep pace with the progressive music of the modern man. I do not think any lies could be more convenient than these. It is definitely a kind of malicious propaganda launched against our professional musicians.[37]

On the other hand, Vamanrao Deshpande, writing on music education in the period between 1931 and 1981, was more generous in his observations. He believed that music schools and private tuitions catering to amateurs had not produced artistes, but had created a huge listenership for music.[38] He further stated:

Mahavidyalaya Mandal, Miraj, August 1958, p.362.

36 S.K. Chaubey, *op.cit.*, p.112.

37 *Ibid*, pp.112-113.

38 Vamanrao H. Deshpande, *Indian Musical Traditions*, *op.cit.*, p.149.

> We must admit that in these fifty years, curiosity and even a critical attitude towards music have increased and the audience in general has developed the faculty of listening to music critically. A very important benefit from all this was that, with the introduction of music in schools and colleges, the students began to get at least some technical knowledge of quite a few subjects related to music, e.g., the Psychology of Music, Aesthetics, Voice Culture and subjects directly useful to music, viz., Physics, the Southern (Karnatak) and the Western systems of music etc. As a result of this, the present generation of music students may not have music artists among them; but they have certainly acquired considerable information and knowledge of quite a few *raga*-s that they can sing.[39]

Although institutionalized education made rapid strides, the *guru-shishya parampara* continued. Those wishing to take up music as a profession continued to undergo challenges that the traditional relationship posed. But the changing social environment encouraged more people not belonging to hereditary musician families to learn music in the traditional format, and some of them even became professional performers and teachers.

Bombay saw an experiment in combining features of the *gharana* system and the institutionalized format, when the University of Bombay set up the Music Centre under the Directorship of Ashok Ranade, reputed scholar and musician. The Centre's teaching faculty had representation from major *gharana*s of Hindustani vocal music, and students were placed under the tutelage of specific teachers who taught them the stylistic features of their chosen *gharana*.[40]

The post-independence era saw a rise in popularity of instrumental music, and it gradually achieved an equal performance status with vocal music, due to the contribution of charismatic musicians and the structural development of the instruments brought about by performers and craftsmen. However, the concert arena continued to be restrictive for accompanying instruments like the *sarangi*, harmonium, *tabla* and *pakhawaj*. In fact, to this day, barring a few exceptions, there are few festivals of music that feature solo recitals of these instruments on a

---

39 *Ibid*, pp.149-150.

40 See sleeve notes for the audio album *Sanchay: Bandish Sangraha*, Underscore Records Private Limited, New Delhi, 2007. Also see, http://www.mu.ac.in/arts/fine-arts/music/profile.html

regular basis. Concert tours to the West placed Hindustani music on the world map and brought into focus accompanying instruments too. This phenomenon resonated in India and accompanying musicians began gaining recognition as was evident from the mention of their names on the jackets of later commercial recordings. On the other hand, the All India Radio continued to ban the harmonium for several decades, although the instrument gained more ground in live concerts and commercial recordings. The ban was later opposed in some quarters, but this was not a concerted effort. A petition was filed in the court of law to ensure the lifting of the ban through legal channels. In Bombay, the Dadar Matunga Cultural Centre, a music club established in 1953, took an active part in the agitation against this ban.[41] Constant arguments among those outside official circles for and against the instrument, led the All India Radio to organise a special seminar focusing on various aspects of the harmonium.[42]

Bombay continued to be integral to Hindustani music in the post-independence period. Over time, prospects for performing, teaching and learning music in Bombay became better than elsewhere in the country, primarily due to the advances made here in the audio-visual recording industry and mass media. In the altered setting, performers and those working in areas closely associated with music, made strides in new directions.[43] Since the 1950s, government and private patronage to audio-visual media networks, the increase in public patronage, and corporate sponsorship of music events, have changed the performance space and context. Hindustani music concerts continue to be organized by local music circles situated in different parts of cities and towns, but many of the larger concerts are planned and executed by Event Management companies that liaise between sponsors and artistes. Naturally,

---

41 *Dadar Matunga Cultural Centre Golden Jubilee Souvenir*, Bombay, 2003, (n.pag.)

42 For papers presented at this seminar, see *Journal of the Sangeet Natak Akademi-20*, New Delhi, April-June 1971.

43 For a brief overview of those who made a significant contribution to Hindustani music since the 1950s, see Aneesh Pradhan, "Music from North India: The Dynamics of Changing Traditions and Trends" in *Pathfinders: A Journey through Art & Culture over the last sixty years of the Indian Republic*, Ace Publications and Promotions Pvt. Ltd., Mumbai, 2010, pp.25-35.

young aspirants, foreign students and established professionals continue to be drawn to the city, in the hope of pursuing successful careers.

This may seem like a golden opportunity for Hindustani music and its practitioners, but the reality is far removed. The number of performers and teachers has increased manifold, bringing an uncertainty to performance and teaching opportunities. Given the revenue involved in film music, it is not unnatural to find this genre receiving maximum publicity and advertising. Indeed, popular music by its very nature is bound to attract greater public attention. But the excessive emphasis given to film music on all platforms seems to eliminate exposure to other genres and breeds a sense of musical homogeneity. In such a situation, it is a wonder that Hindustani music continues to draw students from various sections of society and that many among them aspire to becoming professionals. Like their predecessors, they strategize ways to negotiate rapidly changing times. A look into the past would strengthen their resolve and help them appreciate their situation better.

INTERVIEWS

Interviews with Sharad R. Mehta

Sharad Mehta (d.2000), was a connoisseur of Hindustani music, a scholar of *haveli sangeet*, the form of music performed in Krishna temples of Northern India, and one of the leading collectors of old gramophone records. He retired as Principal of a college in Nadiad, Gujarat.

29 April 1992

Association with Hindustani music

I started listening to Hindustani music with a proper understanding of its subtleties since 1946. My family was interested in music, but wanted me to complete my education, take up a job, and thereafter pursue my interest in music. I had therefore attended some *jalsa*s during this period without the knowledge of my family members.

In the course of my stay in Bombay, I was permitted to attend sessions of Vilayat Hussein Khan of the Agra *gharana*. In addition to this, I had the opportunity of being associated with musicians like Faiyaz Khan, Kesarbai Kerkar, Laxmibai Jadhav and Bade Ghulam Ali Khan. I also learnt a few compositions from Laxmibai Jadhav in Ahmedabad.

Later, I played host to some of the artistes visiting Ahmedabad for performances, and also organised some of their concerts.

Influx of musicians to Bombay

The influx of musicians did not start in the 1850s. Among the Agra *gharana* vocalists, Natthan Khan came to Bombay in the last decade of the nineteenth century. During his stay in Bombay he taught Ganpatrao Manerikar, a drawing teacher at the Elphinstone High School, among others. Vilayat Hussein Khan, the son of Natthan Khan learnt a little from Ganpatrao as also from Alladiya Khan of Jaipur.

Among the Sehaswan-Badayun-Gwalior lineage, Nissar Hussein Khan's grandfather Haider Khan saheb, father of Fida Hussein Khan, was the first to come to Bombay. He gave *taaleem* to Indira Wadkar's grandmother Bayabai Wadkar. Nissar Hussein Khan's grandfather later probably went to Nepal and other places. He was in Bombay in the decade prior to that of Natthan Khan Agrewale. When the former went to the princely states, he handed over his *taaleem* sessions to Vilayat Hussein Khan's elder brother Muhammad Khan, and others.

Abdul Karim Khan came to Bombay by about 1931. During that period, he had done several recordings, for example for Odeon. The two purposes, which brought him to Bombay, were to impart *taaleem* and to start having ticketed programmes. In 1931, Abdul Karim Khan experimented with the idea of a ticketed show in Bombay.

Faiyaz Khan used to come to Bombay from Baroda after the Second World War, five to six times in a year. Mr. Shirgaonkar had a great fascination for him and would arrange his programmes at his residence. He presented Faiyaz Khan with a Chevrolet car.

Among the Jaipur *gharana* musicians, Alladiya Khan stayed in Bombay towards the end of the first decade and during the second decade of the twentieth century. He stayed in the Janmashthami Building adjacent to the morgue room of Harkissandas Hospital. Later he went to Kolhapur but returned to Bombay within a short time. Kesarbai Kerkar's *taaleem* started in Bombay by 1912-1913 and continued until 1940. Mogubai Kurdikar also learnt from Alladiya Khan but she learnt some compositions from his brother Hyder Khan.

Laxmibai Jadhav, a disciple of Hyder Khan, younger brother of Alladiya Khan, was appointed state musician in Baroda in 1931. The first record brought out by HMV by the electrical process was Laxmibai's Bahar and Nat Kamod, in 1931. Thus by 1931, Laxmibai was popular in Bombay. She lived until about 1963-64 having completed a singing career of about thirty years.

Bade Ghulam Ali Khan came often to Bombay from Lahore, between 1941 and 1950. He stayed with a *tawaif* Ganga Bai on the top floor of a building near Kennedy Bridge, next to Congress House. I heard many private concerts of Bade Ghulam Ali Khan during this period. His first public concert establishing permanent residence in Bombay was at the Indian Merchants Chamber in 1952. He stayed in an apartment on Doongersey Road. He had performed in the Vikramaditya Festival at the University Convocation Hall. Alladiya Khan also performed at the same Festival.

Patrons in Bombay

People belonging to different communities and social classes patronised musicians in Bombay in many ways. There were some patrons who learnt music by employing musicians to come and teach them at their homes, and there were others who did not learn music and yet invited musicians to their homes for performances.

Among the patrons not learning music and yet hosting music concerts at their residences, were those involved in business. They organised concerts and invited people involved in similar commercial activities. This was solely a means to maintain good public relations and to consolidate business ties. It was not with a view to prove to the audience their knowledge of the art form. There were perhaps other patrons who organised such *jalsa*s as a status symbol to increase their dignity.

There were some patrons, who had a genuine interest in music and could understand the subtleties of the art. The latter was especially so in the case of those learning music from teachers, who were knowledgeable and generous in imparting musical knowledge.

The rich patrons were mainly from the Bhatia, Parsi, Khoja communities, and from among professionals like lawyers, doctors, or Chartered Accountants earning a sizeable income.

Prominent among the professionals patronising music and musicians was the Welingkar family; members of this family were involved in the academic and legal professions. Welingkar, the Principal of Podar College, organised concerts in the Gomantak Samaj and at his residence. Moghe learnt vocal music from Eknath Pandit in Khar, Bombay. The Shirgaonkar family also organised concerts at their residence. Mrs. Shirgaonkar, the mother of the present Shirgaonkar sisters, was receiving *taaleem* from Vilayat Hussein Khan in the second decade of the twentieth century. Her husband was an ardent fan of Faiyaz Khan, and even presented Faiyaz Khan with a Chevrolet car in the 1920s costing a little less than Rs.2,000/- (ref. Mohan Nadkarni's article in Economic Times entitled "Who is Shirgaonkar?"). Thus, many of the professionals in Bombay could appreciate the subtleties of the music.

The businessmen, who organised performances, were those involved in selling textile machinery, colours, and allied products, and those who were wholesale dealers of cloth.

The important wealthy patrons of music were Khataus, the Ishwardas family, and the Kilachands. Khatau Vallabhdas, a CIBA agent residing near Teen Batti, organised concerts at his residence. He organised concerts of Siddheshwari Devi and Kesarbai Kerkar once a year here. I have attended concerts held at Khatau's residence. Kilachand Devchand held performances at the Kilachand House on V.P. Road, adjacent to Anand Bhavan and opposite Sikka Nagar. Among the artistes invited to perform at his residence was Faiyaz Khan.

In 1907, Gouhar Jan in a performance at the Town Hall in Bombay, showered *dua* (good wishes) on seven to eight Bhatia patrons present at the venue. This performance was recorded and published. The names mentioned include those of the successors of Harkissandas (of the Harkissandas hospital) and of Karamsi Damsi (owned property opposite Bharatiya Vidya Bhavan), Mathurdas Goculdas (son of Goculdas Tejpal), and Mathurdas Vissanji (father of C. Vissanji). These Bhatias were prominent patrons of music in this period.

Students of music

Students of music in Bombay came from different communities and classes, but the training always took place at the residence of the students. Vilayat Hussein Khan had an interesting experience during the Hindu-Muslim riots in Bombay in 1929. He was teaching women like Shrimatibai Narvekar and Jambhorikar in Navalkar Lane at Girgaum. Although most of the people in this area knew and respected Vilayat Hussein Khan, he decided to wear a tie and coat during the riot period so that people would not be able to tell whether he was Hindu or Muslim.

One category of students was that of the "Goawalis" (Kothawalis). Another group had students from the Bhatia community. The third group consisted of women belonging to the Maharashtrian families residing in the area from Girgaum Police Court to C.P. Tank, and from Thakurdwar Junction to Lamington Road. These Maharashtrian families came originally from Poona and Kolhapur. The women of this third group of students, learnt music in order to entertain clients during the day when their husbands were working elsewhere; they could earn some money in this manner. The fourth group of students came from the Muslim community, belonging primarily to the Khoja section of Muslims. Race punters like Gulubhai Jasdanwala and Muhammad Baba or Baba Muhammad, learnt music. Gulubhai learnt from Alladiya Khan. The fifth group consisted of students from the Parsi community, like Freni Cama and Shirin Doctor. They engaged senior musicians as teachers. Yet another category consisted of students who wished to learn music with the sole intention of clearing music examinations, which would then enable them to be appointed as music teachers in schools. There were also some families, which employed musicians to teach their daughters so that the latter would have an added qualification for their marriage proposals.

Most of the musicians employed to teach were only interested in earning as much as was necessary to take care of their family expenses. Students paid the musicians an additional sum on special occasions like the marriage of their son or daughter.

It was the possibility of having such fixed and regular *taaleem* sessions in the city that drew musicians to Bombay. Their migration to the city was not with a view to have many concerts. Thus the *taaleem* sessions provided the main part of the musicians' income in Bombay.

Taaleem

Taaleem was of two types – (a) the same *cheeza* in the same *raag* was taught in four of five *taal*s; (b) the same *cheeza* in the same *taal* was taught in another *raag*. This type of *taaleem* was carried out in all *gharana*s. For instance, Anjanibai Malpekar told me that her *guru* Nazir Khan of Bhendi Bazaar taught her a Bhairavi *thumri* in sixteen *taal*s. This type of *taaleem* carried out earlier was to make the student comfortable in any *raag* or *taal*. Kesarbai used these methods to mislead certain members in the audience, who she thought would otherwise imitate her by memorising compositions during her concerts. She would therefore make structural changes, which would wipe out the earlier image of a certain piece heard by particular members in the audience. This was, however, not done by other musicians, although *taal*s may have been changed unconsciously in order to make a *tabla* player feel at ease during a performance in the event that he was not accustomed to playing certain *taal*s.

Fees for performances

Kesarbai Kerkar was the highest paid artiste in her time. She charged Rs.1,000/- for performances in Bombay and Rs.1,500/- for performances out of Bombay. These rates were all inclusive and she continued to receive these fees until 1965. Faiyaz Khan charged Rs.500/- per performance, but he also sang free of cost if he thought that the organiser could not afford his fees. I have organised concerts of Faiyaz Khan in Ahmedabad, where he was paid Rs.500/- for each performance. Artistes like Siddheshwari Devi and Rasoolan Bai performed for a fee of approximately Rs.500/- each. The next category was of artistes like Gangubai Hangal who performed for a fee of Rs.200/- to Rs.300/-. Gauhar Jan received amounts to the tune of Rs.1,500/- to Rs.2,000/- per concert. The popularity of Janki Bai was such that during some concerts she even received an amount as high as Rs.75,000/-.

The actual increase in fees of artistes started in an organised manner with Bade Ghulam Ali Khan charging Rs.3,000/- to Rs.4,000/- for his concert at the Indian Merchants Chamber in 1952. Even Ravi Shankar, who earlier agreed to play for a fee of Rs.75/- began charging colossal fees along with Ali Akbar Khan.

Accompanists were paid separate fees by the organiser or paid by the main artiste.

Social hierarchy among musicians (soloists and accompanists)

The hierarchical order among the musicians continued even in the urban situation with accompanists occupying a lower position. The payment made to accompanists was low as compared to the main artiste. Even prominent *sarangi* players like Bundu Khan and Abdul Majid Khan were not paid highly. Abdul Majid Khan residing in the last building before the open ground at the Gowalia Tank, always accompanied Kesarbai Kerkar. He was paid Rs.300/- per month, for accompanying Kesarbai for her daily practice. Yeshwant Kerkar and his brother Vishnu Kerkar were also employed by Kesarbai on a monthly basis, for daily practice. Yeshwant Kerkar's brother later accompanied Kesarbai on harmonium, as he had suffered a paralytic attack. Faiyaz Khan always asked for Kamu Mangeshkar's tabla accompaniment when he came to Bombay for a concert. In this manner, many soloists had regular *sarangi* and *tabla* players for performances. These accompanists were paid separate fees for concerts; these fees were not included in their monthly salary.

Abdul Majid Khan also accompanied Alladiya Khan when the latter desired so. Dattaram Parvatkar accompanied Mogubai Kurdikar on the *sarangi*. Lalji Gokhale and Chandrakant Kamat provided *tabla* accompaniment to artistes in and from Poona.

In the past, the distinction between accompanists for vocal and instrumental music did not exist. The distinction probably started with Kishan Maharaj accompanying Ravi Shankar and Ali Akbar Khan, and Mohammad Ahmed Khan accompanying Vilayat Khan. In the earlier generation, *tabla* players like Kanthe Maharaj and Habibuddin Khan played with both vocal and instrumental music and did justice to the performance. Instrumentalists were particularly controlled when they were accompanied by Ahmed Jan Thirakwa. Playing a song on *tabla* or making such noise started with Kishan Maharaj, and was continued by Samta Prasad and others. I have heard Kanthe Maharaj and Kishan Maharaj accompanying Siddheshwari Devi and Rasoolan Bai.

Allauddin Khan of Maihar was often accompanied by Jehangir Khan. I heard Allauddin Khan at Ahmedabad in 1956, but he was accompanied there by Sudhir Saxena. This concert was part of the chain booking for concerts held by All India Radio.

Music circles and venues for concerts

In the pre-1947 period, Suburban Music Circle was an important organiser of concerts. Mr. Ghia and Arvind Parikh ran a music circle each. The Gomantak Samaj had its own music circle. But in the earlier period from the later nineteenth to the early twentieth centuries, there were no music circles; performances took place at the residence of the patron.

Planning repertoire for programmes – Kesarbai Kerkar

Kesarbai always selected a date for a programme two months from the date that the organiser had approached her. In the two months prior to the programme, she would select and practise the repertoire for the forthcoming concert. The practice of planning the repertoire for a concert was followed only by Kesarbai and not by other musicians.

In a night concert, Kesarbai would sing any *prakaar* of Kalyan like Hem Kalyan or Savani Kalyan or Nat like Savani Nat or Shuddha Nat, and a light *cheeza*, before the intermission. The light *cheeza*, whether *thumri* or *bhajan*, was either in Kafi or Khamaj. After the interval, she would start with a Kanada or Jaijaiwanti. At times she would also choose to sing Basant Bahar or Basanti Kedar or Rageshri in the post-intermission session. She never sang Marathi stage-songs. After finishing her repertoire as selected for the concert, she would sometime ask if the audience had any *farmaish*. During the monsoon, she would sing Goud Malhar or Meerabai ki Malhar.

In the morning session, she would start with Lalit or Todi, followed by one Bilawal *prakar* or Husseini or Desi Todi, and then have an intermission. After interval, she would sing Sughrai.

This meticulous chalking out of items for concerts was experienced by me from 1946 to 1965. But she did so even as early as 1935.

She was very observant during programmes and after a quick look at the audience, could remember where every person had been sitting even when the turnout was as large as 1,500. She had a powerful stamina and could perform immediately on arriving at the venue (even half an hour after getting out of a train).

Kesarbai had blacklisted some people and if they were present in the audience, she would mislead them or wipe out the earlier mental picture that they had of her compositions by making changes in the *taal* or *raag*. She did this, as she did not want any unauthorised people to imitate her.

I visited her at her residence at Shivaji Park. Her discipline was evident in her promptness at replying to letters. The replies were typed out by her secretary.

Tawaifs and prostitutes

A *tawaif* entertained clients by singing or dancing. A client could be permanent or there could be many clients. There was no physical association with the client, but in the event that physical association did take place, she would be termed as a prostitute.

There were two prostitute classes among those involved in private prostitution:

- Those attached to one man (the man may have had a family of his own). A prostitute of this class would remain a widow after the death of the client. The client would make provision for maintenance in the event of his death.
- These prostitutes invited other clients as they were not satisfied physically by their aged clients (these aged clients also led a family life).

One of the earliest *tawaifs* coming to Bombay was Bablibai or Chanda Karwarkarin. She was a disciple of Natthan Khan Agrewale, and had been appointed as state musician of Bhavnagar. She stayed in Bhavnagar and came to Bombay for concerts.

Menakabai Shirodkar stayed in Ishwardas Mansion, "C" Block, 1st Floor, Nana Chowk.

The *tawaifs* normally entertained a group of fifteen to twenty clients from 8 p.m. to 9.30 or 10 p.m. This duration was referred to as "time *par baithna*". When the *tawaif* was not engaged on "time", she was entertaining a single client. The "time" period changed in every city but it was about 8 p.m. to 10 p.m. in Bombay.

During the Second World War, *tawaifs* were earning Rs.2,000/- to Rs.2,500/- per month on an average from one or more clients. The *sarangi* and *tabla* accompanists (harmonium was used at times) were paid about Rs.100/- on a monthly basis. If the *tawaif* was a dancer, a *pakhawaj* player or *khula-bol* (*baaj*) *tabla* player was employed.

25 May 1992

Association with musicians in Bombay

Although I was not a *ganda bandh* disciple of Vilayat Hussein Khan as was the case with some of his students in Bombay, I was permitted to attend and listen to the *taaleem* that he gave to his students at his residence at Ruby Mansion, Forjett Street.

Important programmes in Bombay

The Bombay State Festival was held in April 1956 at the Elphinstone Technical Institute Compound. Siddheshwari Devi and Rasoolan Bai performed on the first day of this Festival.

The first Swami Haridas Festival held by Sur Singar Samsad, took place in April 1955 at the Mumbadevi Compound.

Patrons of music in Bombay

Shantibhai Gujjar – A barrister by profession and a knowledgeable connoisseur of music, he also played the *been*, which he had learnt from the successors of the Seniya tradition. He resided at Worli, adjacent to the

Mahalaxmi compound. He was also a connoisseur of Western music and had a good collection of Western classical music records. His patronage to Indian music began around 1930 and continued until 1970.

Vinayarao Dada Mulgaonkar (b.1898 or 1901) – A wealthy man, he was an investor in the share market. He could always be found between 2 p.m. and 3 p.m. in the office of Harkissandas and Lakhmidas firm in the share market. He was the brother of surgeon Mulgaonkar.

As a connoisseur of music, he had heard several live performances of artistes like Gauhar Jan. He related an incident to me, which took place in Bombay in about 1928-29. It was a performance of Pyara Saheb organised probably by Rose and Co., a shop dealing in musical instruments, situated at Rampart Row. Gauhar Jan attended the programme and sat next to Vinayak Dada in the audience. During the pre-interval session, Pyara Saheb sang a Khamaj *thumri* "*Chab dikhalaa jaa*". In the intermission Pyara Saheb paid his respects to Gauhar Jan, but the latter criticised him for having sung that particular *thumri*. This incident went to show that she did not consider it correct for anybody to sing the compositions that she normally sang. She considered it her privilege to sing particular compositions.

Khatau Vallabhdas – A contemporary of Vinayak Dada Mulgaonkar, Khatau Vallabhdas had heard artistes like Gauhar Jan. He was an enlightened music listener possessing a large collection of records. He invited artistes like Kesarbai Kerkar, Siddheshwari Devi, and Abdul Halim Jaffer Khan's father, to perform. His father was also a connoisseur of music.

Muhammad Baba – A race punter, Muhammad Baba was a generous man. He told me that Gauhar Jan was his father's mistress. He had heard a great deal of music and although he had not learnt music formally, he would sing Gauhar Jan's *thumri*s.

Gulubhai Jasdanwala – A disciple of Alladiya Khan, his brother Yahya Khan also claimed to know music.

Patel – He retired as an officer in the Secretariat and stayed in Ganpat Bhavan, Girgaum.

Shirin Doctor and Freni Cama – Both were disciples of Vilayat Hussein Khan and were connoisseurs of music. They attended all programmes in Bombay. Freni Cama wrote a book *Saraswati Gayan Sangraha* in Gujarati.

Bhaghubhai Gandhi (b.1895) – He stayed in Ishwardas Mansion and retired as an Income Tax officer. He played *paay petee* and at times accompanied artistes. Musicians also stayed with him. He had heard V.D. Paluskar. He was busy with the races from Thursday.

Payment to musicians

Before Bade Ghulam Ali Khan, all artistes did not accept fees more than what they normally charged, even if more was offered.

As regards tuition, Batuk Diwanji paid Rs.100/- per month to Vilayat Hussein Khan and Rs.25/- per month to the tabla accompanist for the *taaleem* sessions. Diwanji and a few other students learnt at Vilayat Hussein Khan's residence.

Residence of musicians

Alladiya Khan stayed in the Janmashtami Building in the first decade of the twentieth century. He stayed at Babulnath during World War I. He received financial help from Gulubhai Jasdanwala and Shirgaonkars. Gulubhai learnt at Alladiya Khan's residence.

Abdul Karim Khan of the Tanras Khan *gharana* (Delhi *gharana*) was also in Bombay.

Harmonium and violin in Indian music

The earliest prominent harmonium players were Bhaiyya Ganpatrao, his disciple Basheer Khan, and Govindrao Tembe. Basheer Khan of Indore had a solo record and had provided accompaniment to several records of Gouhar Jan.

Sensitive harmonium players could produce *shrutis* by controlling the air from the bellows. Harmonium players performed solo as well as accompanied vocal music. Even among accompanists not all could play with singers of different *gharanas*. The prominence of harmonium as an accompanying instrument was only after the World War II. Before that, *sarangi* was important.

The type of harmonium that was imported into India was called Casreil having French or German reeds. The German reeds were better.

Violin was never used as an accompanying instrument. It was introduced to Hindustani music when Gajanan Joshi and V.G. Jog took to this instrument.

Interview with Batuk Diwanji

January 1993

A senior music critic, author, connoisseur, and collector of compositions and recordings, Batuk Diwanji (1918-2014) began his musical journey as an avid concertgoer and student of music. He went on to forge close ties with many eminent musicians some of whom were his seniors and others who were his contemporaries. In the years to follow, he also organised concerts featuring them. His rich experience made him a raconteur *par excellence*. Added to this were his views on the state of music-making in the past and present. The four interviews included here, were carried out at different points of time. The interviews have not been reproduced here in strict chronological order.

Tutelage

In 1935, I started learning from Ramkrishna Joshi, a disciple of V.D. Paluskar, who conducted classes at Khetwadi under the auspices of Gandharva Mahavidyalaya. I was then in the first year of my college education and was staying close by. I did not opt for the course in the class and chose to study on an individual basis from Joshi. He was not a performer but was a teacher and knew many rare *raga*s. The fees were approximately Rs.20-25/- per month. I gave up learning in this class after three to four months, as I did not like the style. During that period, Narayanrao Vyas, Wamanrao Padhye and B.R. Deodhar also conducted their own classes.

Between 1935 and 1942, I did not learn but I was attending concerts of Vilayat Hussein, Faiyaz Khan and Kesarbai Kerkar, regularly.

Later on in around 1942-43, I started learning from Ghulam Qadir Khan at my home. According to an article written by Madhura Jasraj in a Gharana Sammelan souvenir, Ghulam Qadir Khan had been adopted by the founder of the Mewati Gharana called Ghagge Nazir Khan. I think I paid him approximately Rs.25/- per month and the teaching sessions were held twice a week. I learnt from Ghulam Qadir for about a year after which he moved to Rajkot.

I learnt from Sharadchandra Arolkar thereafter. He would teach me twice a week at my residence after teaching the proprietor of West End Cinema.The proprietor wanted to learn *bhajan*s. I paid Arolkar Rs.25/- per month as tuition fee. I told him that I wanted to learn *thumri*s and *tappa*s, as I wanted to learn classical music from the Agra style. I learnt some *thumri*s and five to six *tappa*s from Arolkar. I also learnt *khayal* compositions in some *raag*s but did not learn the manner of elaborating them. I stopped learning thereafter.

I then told my friend Narendra Shukla, a student of Vilayat Hussein Khan and Faiyaz Khan, who later became Chief Producer of AIR, that I wished to learn from Vilayat Hussein Khan. Shukla advised me that I should learn first from Muley, a student of Vilayat Hussein Khan, to get a good grounding. Consequently, I started learning from Muley at my residence in Khetwadi and paid him Rs.25/- per month for two sessions a week. A *tabla* player accompanied the sessions and his fees were Rs.10/- per month. Although Muley was a student of Vilayat Hussein Khan, he sang in a typically Maharashtrian style. He had not picked up the real style. His voice was also not very good and after some time I got fed up and thought of discontinuing him. His training continued for one year.

I started learning from Vilayat Hussein Khan thereafter. His fees in that period were Rs.50/- per month for sessions held twice a week at the residence of the student. Sitaram Phatarphekar, an old student of Vilayat Hussein Khan, but not a very good singer, told the latter that I was not financially very well off and requested him to reduce the fees. Vilayat Hussein Khan agreed and charged me Rs.40/- per month and Kamanna, the *tabla* accompanist, was paid Rs.10/- per month.

The term *taaleem* was used then. *Taaleem* lasted for one hour or more; the old erratic *guru-shishya* format where time and duration was solely decided by the *guru*, had stopped. Vilayat Hussein Khan was very regular, punctual and open-minded about his teaching. I learnt some rare *raag*s also from him and later many from Anwar Hussein Khan. Vilayat Hussein Khan taught me at my residence for some time but later asked me to go to his residence for daily *taaleem*. I therefore went almost daily to his residence at Ruby Mansion. The payment was the same i.e. Rs.40/- per month, but there was no *tabla* player. Most of the time, his son Yakub Hussein and I would have *taaleem* together and at times the other son Yunus Hussein Khan had *taaleem* with me. Subsequently, Vilayat Hussein Khan had a severe attack of arthritis and stayed in Agra for six months to recuperate.

I then started learning from Anwar Hussein Khan, disciple of Kallan Khan, Vilayat Hussein Khan and Khadim Hussein Khan. At first, I was learning from him at Ruby Mansion, but later learnt from him at Vilayat Hussein Khan's student's residence in the same building. I paid Anwar Hussein Khan Rs.40/- per month, but I also helped him when he was in financial need. I was not very well off during this time. I joined the police department only after doing four to five jobs.

The radio boycott resulted in the exemption of A grade artistes from radio re-audition. All other artistes had to appear for re-audition. I did not appear, as I was not too happy with the irregular nature of programmes, i.e. they would offer me a programme after four, six or even on one occasion after eight months. I somehow came to the conclusion that I had no future in music however much I would try and practise, so I gave up and stopped learning. Anwar Hussein Khan died during this period.

After a gap of fifteen years, I met Khadim Hussein Khan and he asked me to learn from him in about 1978 at his classes in Bhulabhai Desai's bungalow called Hasman at Warden Road. Between 1950 and 1960, I also learnt a few *thumri* songs from Siddheshwari Devi. In 1960, I would go to Hiradevi Mishra's residence in Khar and would pick up many songs from her.

Music Circles

Agra Gharana Samiti – I do not remember the exact period when the Samiti carried out its activities. Vilayat Hussein Khan and Azmat Hussein Khan were on the Committee and Madhu Haldankar (Baban Haldankar's brother) and I were Secretaries. Madhu Haldankar learnt a little from Azmat Hussein Khan. The Samiti programmes were held every month featuring a student in the first half of the programme and a reputed artiste in the latter half. The initial idea for organising these programmes was to educate people. Students of Vilayat Hussein Khan like Ragini Phandke and Balsekar would sing and were followed by knowledgeable musicians like Vilayat Hussein Khan who would sing two parallel *raag*s, e.g. Barwa and Sindhura, or two *prakaar*s, along with explanation. The invitation cards for the Agra Gharana Samiti programmes at times had the names of the *raag*s mentioned that were going to be explained, e.g. Bhupali and Shuddha Kalyan. Musicians from all *gharana*s were invited to perform. The Samiti programmes were held at Laxmi Baug. The funds for the Samiti came from membership fees, which were Rs.2/- per month. Many Parsi ladies were also members of Agra Gharana Samiti. The Agra Gharana Samiti had one patron, Madan Mohan Ruia, who would donate Rs.100/- for every programme. This was in addition to the membership fees, which the Samiti already received. Gulubhai Jasdanwala's brother Yahyabhai would donate Rs.25/- per programme. The artistes' fees were as follows – Rs.100/- to the main artiste, Rs.25/- to the accompanist (*tabla* and harmonium or *sarangi*). Students who performed were not paid anything. Faiyaz Khan, whose charge was normally Rs.500/-, gave back the money as a presentation to the Samiti. No students sang on Faiyaz Khan's concert day in the Samiti. Muley, a past student of Vilayat Hussein Khan, also attended the concerts. Vilayat Hussein Khan did not like Muley taking down notes during his performance and explanation and hence, he later on said that they would not have any more lectures and would have only performances. Brij Narayan, his wife and a friend would attend the Samiti programmes regularly and he was a member of the Samiti. Brij Narayan was employed by Podar but had to leave Podar later on. Brij Nrayan wanted me to include him on the Committee. I asked Vilayat

Hussein Khan whether we should involve Brij Narayan in the Committee, as I thought the latter being a Marwari, could provide funds to keep the show going. But Vilayat Hussein depended on Azmat Hussein Khan's advice. Azmat Husein Khan was his brother-in-law (wife's brother). Azmat Hussein was against the idea of including an outsider as he felt that outsiders would ask the Samiti to organise a particular artiste's programme. During that period (around 1946), Ravi Shankar had once attended a concert of Vilayat Hussein Khan organised by the Samiti at the Marwari Vidyalaya Hall. I do not remember the exact organiser. Vilayat Hussein Khan was singing a *dhamar* in *raag* Sindhura then and Ravi Shankar was complimenting the performance. We were later introduced to each other. I then met Ravi Shankar at the HMV office where he was serving as music composer with a salary of Rs.150/- per month. When I was asked by a friend to organise a concert featuring Ravi Shankar, I told Ravi Shankar that the Samiti was to be closed down due to financial difficulties. Ravi Shankar therefore agreed to give free programmes for the Samiti and performed four times for the Samiti without any remuneration. He performed *prakaar*s of Gauri like Chitra Gauri and many rare *raag*s. The Samiti closed down due to financial difficulties resulting from non-payment of membership fees.

Sangeet Niketan – I started it after Agra Gharana Samiti because an individual said that he had some money for a music circle. Madhu Haldankar and I were secretaries of Sangeet Niketan. This was a music circle but it closed down later due to financial difficulties. Membership was six-monthly or yearly and membership fee was Rs.2 per month. Members were sent invitation cards for each programme.

Sangeet Kalakar Mandal – During the time of B.V. Keskar, a rule was announced in the All India Radio that every artiste should appear for an audition. The Sangeet Kalakar Mandal was formed to oppose this rule. Vilayat Hussein Khan was made President and Kausalya Manjeshwar was made Secretary of this organisation. Musicians boycotted radio broadcasts for one year. Gajanan Joshi sang during this period on the radio and was therefore given the post of Sangeet Salahkar as a reward. I too boycotted the radio broadcasts along with other musicians. The Mandal was formed some time after the formation of the Agra Gharana Samiti.

Haridas Sammelan – The first Haridas Sammelan was held by one Sunderji Monji and not by Brij Narayan. But there was some controversy regarding money involved in the programme. So, the second Sammelan was held by Brij Narayan.

Music circle for *ghazal*s – In the 1960s there was a music circle devoted mainly to *ghazal*s featuring concerts of Begum Akhtar and others. These concerts were mainly held at Laxmi Baug. Rangwala was the secretary of this circle. It had a regular membership and guest fees were about Rs.10/- per programme.

Bharat Sangeet Sabha – It was started by Kanti Desai, Babubhai Raja and others in the 1960s. Kanti Desai (s/o Morarji Desai) was associated with the organisation only on paper. This Sabha would have concerts of Ravi Shankar, Ali Akbar Khan, Kesarbai Kerkar and others. Babubhai Raja surreptitiously recorded these programmes. Later, Rangwala's circle and Bharat Sangeet Sabha were amalgamated. I was also co-opted on this Sabha Committee by Soli Batliwala. Jaichand Seth, son-in-law of K.M. Munshi, was also on the Committee. The Sabha also gave scholarships to young artistes like Habiba Rehman, Sucheta Bhide. But the Sabha was wound up when the amount was exhausted and members did not pay regularly.

Patrons

Most of the patrons did not understand music but they liked to listen to music. Programmes organised by the rich in their houses were open to select friends of the organisers. There were not many in the audience who could really understand music. No drinks were served. Vissanji's father had programmes at his house. Some perhaps had an understanding of music but most had just a liking. To some extent, these patrons organised programmes at their houses as a status symbol. Mr. Sikka sometimes (very rarely) organised programmes at his residence featuring performers like Swami Vallabhdas. Faiyaz Khan sang at his wedding held at Sikka Nagar. Vilayat Hussein Khan also taught Shivdas Sikka at the latter's residence. I first heard Vilayat Hussein Khan when he was teaching Sikka *raag* Desi.

Yahyabhai Jasdanwala – Yahyabhai had a hardware and iron and steel business. He had amassed a lot of money during the war. Another brother Abu Jasdanwala was president of the Cricket Club of India. Yahyabhai was the eldest. Some people, who have succeeded in one line, want to show that they are very cultured. Yahyabhai had employed a ghost poet to write *ghazal*s in his name – the name Yahya would appear in the *ghazal*. Begum Akhtar had sung these *ghazal*s on an EP. These *ghazal*s were also published. Yahyabhai would also show that he was a good *tabla* player by making statements like "Mohammad Ahmed *maaru tabla vagaadech*" ((trans. Mohammad Ahmed follows my style of tabla playing)).

Gulubhai Jasdanwala – He would perform on rare occasions, for example, Bombay Music Circle had a member's programme once in a year on which occasion Gulubhai would sing. His rendition was poor although he knew many rare *raag*s and was a disciple of the great Alladiya Khan.

Shantibhai Gujjar – He was a patron of music and a close friend of mine. We would often practise together. He would play the *been* or *surbahar* and I would sing some new *raag*s, which he would then set for himself. He was a disciple of Mohammed Khan, father of Rais Khan. Shantibhai first took up *sitar* and would play well but later on gave it up and took up *surbahar* and *been*. He used to organise many programmes at his residence. Before the Vikramaditya Festival, Shantibhai Gujjar's maternal uncle had organised a programme of Vilayat Khan at Chowpatty. Shantibhai also recommended his name to music circles and gave him several tuitions. Shantibhai arranged for Dhondutai's stay in Bombay by asking Manju Modak, daughter of Aptes of Kohinoor Mill, to learn from her and also accommodate her in her house. Shantibhai was thus a patron and helped artistes.

Babubhai Banker – He organised concerts at his residence and at Anjanibai Lolekar's residence. Artistes like Vilayat Hussein Khan, Thirakwa, Sitara Devi performed in these concerts. Babubhai Banker stayed in Adenwala Building at Chowpatty. Virendra Kumar Mathur, a *sarod* player, also played here. These programmes were probably after 1947. Babubhai was an accomplished harmonium player.

Important concerts

I first heard Alladiya Khan in 1937 at a concert arranged at Laxmi Baug by the Bombay Music Circle. The Circle had presented three programmes featuring Alladiya Khan over a period of three months and each of these was scheduled at different times of the day (morning, evening and night). I had attended the night concert in which Abdul Majid Khan accompanied him on *sarangi*. Alladiya Khan's *taan*s were superb, very intricate with no halts till the time-cycle was completed. He did not elaborate the *raag* extensively and went to the *taan*s within a short time.

In the 1950s, programmes were held at Anjanibai Malpekar's residence with monetary contributions coming from the audience. Musicians like Hiradevi Mishra, Begum Akhtar, Siddheshwari Devi, Ali Akbar Khan, Allauddin Khan and Ravi Shankar, performed in these contribution programmes.

Keramat Khan of Jaipur (he had taught dhrupad-dhamar to Vilayat Hussein Khan) sang in a concert held at Jinnah Hall. He was ostensibly 110 years old at the time. His voice was absolutely in tune. He sang Basant and some other *raag*s.

At a concert featuring Faiyaz Khan, Sharafat Hussein Khan, a thirteen-year old boy then, accompanied on *tanpura*. Faiyaz Khan sang *raag* Marwa followed immediately by *raag* Shri. During this concert, he asked Sharafat Hussein Khan to come forward and sing solo for ten minutes. His performance was very good.

My first concert took place in the Martandeshwar Utsav organised by Nandanikar, an Ayurveda praticitioner in about 1946. Nandanikar would organise this Utsav every year at Jinnah Hall. C.K. Naidu, the great cricketer, was also present at one Utsav.

Baban Haldankar's father organised programmes on one day of the five-day Ganapati festivities at his house. These programmes continued even after his death. At these programmes, musicians like Mogubai Kurdikar, Anwar Hussein Khan, Vilayat Hussein Khan and Khadim Hussein Khan would be invited to sing.

The Vikramaditya Festival was held during the winter of 1944. It was organised by a Committee comprising Champaklal Modi, O.D. Vyas (ophthalmic surgeon) and some others. Though the University Convocation Hall was the venue, the University did not play a role in organising the Festival. Leading artistes from all over India were invited to perform. Each artiste was given one hour and the artistes were listed as per seniority as far as possible, with the juniors preceding the seniors. This was a week-long Festival with one Sunday morning session and the rest of the days with evening programmes starting at 6.30 p.m. The artistes were paid by the Committee. The programme was ticketed with only season tickets –no daily tickets. Tickets had to be booked in advance. The ticket denominations were Rs.30/-, Rs.50/-, Rs.100/-, and Rs.200/-. I bought a Rs.30/- ticket. This was the first Festival to have been organised on such a grand scale and for so many days. It was the best and most representative. In normal circumstances, concerts were organised for one evening or one morning by music circles. The house was packed to capacity with even the balcony completely booked. The artistes who impressed the most were Bismillah Khan, Vilayat Khan, Ahmed Jan Thirakwa, Alladiya Khan. Alladiya Khan sang Ramkali and Bibhas and received vocal support from Bhurji Khan and Kesarbai Kerkar. Bade Ghulam Ali had specially come from Lahore to perform and had two sittings in this Festival. He sang *raag* Marwa, Punjabi *thumri* and other pieces. Siddheshwari Devi, Kesarbai Kerkar, Heerabai Badodekar and Rasoolan Bai, performed in the Festival. Kesarbai sang Bihagda and a *thumri*. Siddheshwari Devi sang Basant, *thumri* and *bhajan*. She was accompanied by Gopal Mishra (*sarangi*) and Anokhelal (*tabla*). Anahat Nath Bose, who sang in male and female voices, was also featured. Faiyaz Khan and Omkarnath Thakur also sang. Mushtaq Hussein Khan sang *raag* Sagar, but the riff-raff among the audience started clapping and hooting. He then sang *raag* Bihag but the people again started hooting. He followed this with the composition "*Jhanana*" in *raag* Chhayanat, but the people continued clapping and so he stopped and staged a walk out telling the audience that they did not understand anything except clapping. Eminent flautist Pannalal Ghosh also performed here. Hafiz Ali Khan presented a *sarod* recital with *pakhawaj* accompaniment. Sadiq Ali Khan and Sakhawat Hussein Khan, presented *been* and *sarod* recitals, respectively. A *veena* player from Mysore and one or two other musicians presented South Indian music here, but the North Indian music formed the major part of the Festival. Ahmed Jan Thirakwa played *tabla* solo and provided *tabla* accompaniment to some artistes. Other *tabla* solos were featured and *tabla* players like Habibuddin Khan and Anokhelal Mishra also performed on this occasion.

Jhabwala arranged Annapurna Devi and Ravi Shankar's programme at Marwari Vidyalaya in about 1947. Annapurna Devi began with *aalaap*, *jod*, without *pakhawaj* accompaniment and Ravi Shankar performed after interval.

Jhabwala and I had also organised many programmes featuring Latafat Hussein Khan as Jhabwala liked Latafat Hussein Khan's singing. The ticket rate was Rs.2/- and after deducting the expenses for accompaniment and others, the rest was given to Latafat Hussein Khan. These programmes were sometimes held at Laxmi Baug, Talmakiwadi, and also at private residences.

In 1951, a year after Faiyaz Khan's death, a very big programme was organised at Talmakiwadi where Lacchoo Maharaj, Kanwar Singh, Shamshad Chhamiya (mother of actress Naseem Bano) performed. Shamshad Chhamiya sang a *thumri* here and Lacchoo Maharaj did the *bhaav*. I was one of the organisers of this programme. All Agra vocalists also sang. Birju Maharaj had also attended this programme.

Agra vocalists sang without any remuneration at programmes held to mark birth or death anniversaries of Paluskar, Bhatkhande and others.

I first met Latafat Hussein Khan when he sang behind Khadim Hussein Khan at Shivdas Sikka's sister's marriage.

Musicians

Alladiya Khan – Alladiya had approached Mubarak Ali Khan, court singer of Jaipur belonging to the Kawwal Bacche gharana, for *taaleem* but Mubarak Ali refused to teach him with the reason that he only taught his family members. Thereafter, Alladiya Khan would stand on the street outside Mubarak Ali's house and listen to the latter's practice. Mubarak Ali's style influenced Alladiya Khan's *taan*s. When asked about Mubarak Ali's style, Alladiya Khan said that if Mubarak Ali's singing was equal to Re.1/- then his own was not equal to even one *paisa* compared to him.

Muley – Muley was a paying guest in a place at Opera House and had some other business, with two or three tuitions. Vilayat Hussein Khan was very fond of him and took him along when he gave *taaleem* at his students' residences. He even took him along when he taught Mogubai Kurdikar. But Muley fell into disfavour because of something he had said to Vilayat Hussein Khan.

Kamanna – Originally a *tabla* player from Goa, Kamanna would visit his hometown during the Ganpati festivities and make Ganpati idols. He only accompanied *taaleem* sessions and never played in concerts.

Khadim Hussein Khan learnt from Kallan Khan for six years, six hours daily in addition to his own practice.

Vilayat Hussein Khan came to Bombay for some time after he recovered from his bout with arthritis. Sangeet Kala Kendra, a Delhi-based institution, later appointed him teacher. He resigned from here when he was offered the post of Sangeet Salahkar by Delhi AIR. The Sangeet Salahkars got a monthly salary and had to stay in Delhi. He was a court musician of Mysore for one year or so and then at Kashmir (he taught Karan Singh, scion of the royal family of Kashmir), where he had gone from Bombay. Vilayat Hussein Khan was earning Rs.3,000/- per month just by tuitions, in around 1932. His earnings through *taaleem* were quite good, but this was an exception. Other musicians could hardly meet their expenses.

Anwar Hussein Khan performed from the Delhi radio station and not from Bombay as Delhi radio paid more. Anjanibai Lolekar was learning from him at her residence, but she and some other students would not pay his tuition fee on time. Consequently I would have to help him out.

Siddheshwari Devi – At first she would stay in Kashmir Hotel when she came to Bombay but later she stayed with Anjanibai Malpekar on her visits to Bombay.

Anjanibai Malpekar – Anjanibai Malpekar learnt from Nazir Khan, uncle of Aman Ali Khan. She owned a house at Kennedy Bridge.

I met her there when she was seventy and would visit her every evening for some years.

Anjani Jambavlikar – a student of Vilayat Hussein Khan, stayed in Navalkar lane but changed residence after her *seth* bought her a new place elsewhere. She stopped singing as her *seth* placed restrictions on her singing and asked her not to allow any *sarangi* and *tabla* players and musicians to come to her residence.

Latafat Hussein Khan – I helped him by giving him Rs.125/-, which he needed for his trip to Allahabad for a concert, at a time when my bank balance was Rs.350/-.

Kamurao Mangeshkar – a *tabla* player from Goa accompanied both vocal and instrumental music. He accompanied artistes regularly in Bombay.

Krishnarao Kumthekar accompanied artistes regularly in Bombay.

Vilayat Khan was then staying with Muhammad Khan. He later bought his own flat. At one tuition, the people complained to Shantibhai about Vilayat Khan irregularity in teaching despite his charging them a handsome amount (it was Rs.1,000/- per month for Arvind Parikh). When Shantibhai told Vilayat Khan of the complaint, the latter stated that he was an artiste and went to teach as per his mood. Shantibhai thereupon flared up and retorted that Vilayat Khan was not an artiste but doing music to earn a living; on the contrary he said, we students of music were artistes for sacrificing time and money to learn the art. From then on, Shantibhai broke off relations with Vilayat Khan.

Ravi Shankar – His charge for music circle programmes was Rs.100/- and Rs.75/- at times for private programmes.

History

It was Sher Khan of the Agra *gharana*, who started music in Bombay. The Agra people sang free of charge at all *barsi* programmes like Paluskar *barsi* organised by Deodhar and Navrang. Scope for performing in this period was limited and performers came from families professionally involved in music and did not include amateurs.

The first available hall with microphones was Laxmi Baug. The hall rent was Rs.28/- originally for the entire evening with no closing time.

This amount did not include charges for sound system hire, which were about Rs.25-30/-.

The programme of Faiyaz Khan that I heard between 1935 and 1937 was with mikes. All programmes that I heard from the beginning had mikes. Faiyaz Khan's or Kesarbai Kerkar's concerts were always packed to capacity with 300 people in the audience. The ticket rates were Rs.5/- for Faiyaz Khan and Kesarbai's programmes. For lesser-known artistes, they were Rs.2/- or Rs.3/-. Coffee was included in the ticket rate. The tickets were sold at a flat rate with first come first serve policy regarding seating. The demand for tickets for Faiyaz Khan or Kesarbai Kerkar's concert was the most and so people coming after the house was full, would be turned away. Seating arrangement was *baithak* style with one row of chairs near the wall. Laxmi Baug also had a gallery and so in the event the lower part was full, one had to go to the gallery.

Concerts started generally at around 10 p.m. though the scheduled time was 9.30 p.m. Kesarbai normally sang for about two and half-hours. Faiyaz Khan would start at about 10 p.m. and would sing until interval and then continue thereafter. He would sometimes have two intervals in a single programme. I remember some concerts, which lasted until 4 or 5 a.m. the next day. But normally, the concerts did not continue for such a long duration.

Till 1950, there were no tape recorders. There were wire recorders with wire moving over two spools. The tape recorders were costing about Rs.2,500/- in 1950 or so. Grundig was regarded the best. I had to wait a long time till I could buy a machine for myself-a second hand Philips recorder for Rs.500/-. Nagra was high quality but very costly-Rs.1,200/-.

According to an episode related to me by Vinayak Mulgaonkar, a childhood friend of Anjanibai's, Bhatkhande was once asked in private why he had not mentioned the name of Nazir Khan in his work as one of the musicians who had given him *cheeza*s. Bhatkhande replied that he did not do so because Nazir Khan and his brother were basically *sarangi* players and hence others would question the authenticity of the vocal compositions.

Connoisseurs

Vinayak Mulagaonkar lived to an age a little over 90 years. He died in 1983 or so. He had good relations with Kesarbai Kerkar and was a close friend of mine.

Jhabwala – a police prosecutor (f/o Justice Lentin) was a friend of mine. My first encounter with him was at Tripathi Booksellers shop. He sang *nainan so dekhe* and asked me to name the *raag*. He disputed my answer that it was Sughrai but later accepted it as the correct answer. Later, we became friends and at many concerts he would even purchase my ticket. He wrote a book of *bandish*es. He always wore saffron clothes.

The head of the Swaminarayan sect had a bungalow at Mount Abu and as he was fond of Agra vocalists, he would invite Faiyaz Khan, Vilayat Hussein Khan, Latafat Hussein Khan to Mount Abu for concerts. He even recorded them.

Nandanikar – an Ayurveda praticitioner had his dispensary in Parekh Building next to Madhavashram at Prarthana Samaj. We would all gather at his place every day during a certain part of my life. He would give free medicines to musicians and would organise Martandeshwar Utsav every year at Jinnah Hall.

Current state

The level of music has gone down very much nowadays. The main reason for this is the dearth of *samarth guru*s who can give proper guidance to the students. The students also lack a sense of dedication and it is also difficult for them to get enough time for rigorous practice. Besides, the organisers of music programmes do not bother about search for new talents with the result that many promising musicians are lingering in the limbo of oblivion.

24 August 1992

Both Agra and Jaipur *gharana* families were neighbours in Surveyor Building opposite Babulnath Market between 1935 and 1939. Muhammad Ahmed Khan, *tabla* player, later stayed in the same building probably in the 1960s. Vilayat Hussein Khan moved to Ruby Mansion but Alladiya Khan remained there.

Ibrahim Seth was a rich Khoja and owner of Datu Manji Padamsee Surmawala Company. He learnt music as a hobby. In 1937 or so, he was given the title of "*Taan Talwaar*", as a joke by Alladiya Khan. I attended a concert in around 1937 in the compound outside the Surveyor Building. Khadim Hussein Khan sang *raag* Sunderkali. Shivdas Sikka, son of the owner of Sikka Nagar, who had a tobacco business and was involved in *satta* and gambling, learnt from Vilayat Hussein Khan. I stayed at Sikka Nagar. I also heard Swami Vallabhdas at the Sikka residence in around 1937. In 1937-38, I heard Faiyaz Khan at Bombay Music Circle. The concert was held at the Laxmi Baug Hall and he presented *raag*s Paraj, Kafi and others. I was learning then but had an impression of music through listening to recordings. I had gone to this concert with Shivdas Sikka. Abdul Karim Khan also performed on the same day (probably at Gujarati Forbes Hall). Programmes were normally held at Forbes' Hall, Laxmi Baug, Muzzafarabad Hall (near Grant Road) and later at Wagle Hall (Kandewadi). Bhanubhai Trivedi was the Secretary of Musical Arts Society, which was the second best music circle. The best music circle was the Bombay Music Circle. In third position was Gandharva Sangeet Mandal. One of the organisers of this circle was Mr. Lad and Wagle was the Secretary. The Musical Arts Society had booked in advance artistes who were scheduled to perform at the Vikramaditya Festival in 1944. The Society had programmes by Mushtaq Hussein Khan, Bade Ghulam Ali Khan and probably also Hafiz Ali Khan.

18 September1992

Satyendra Trivedi

My keen interest in music started much after 1947, but I was attending concerts with Sikka even before that. I have never met any man in the field of music with a memory as good as that of Satyendra Trivedi, a close friend of mine. He was ten years my senior and belonged to the Nagar community. He was a cashier in the Harkissandas Lakhmidas share broker's firm.

Anecdote regarding Vishnu Narayan Bhatkhande

Vinayak Mulgaonkar related to me an incident that he had witnessed. In a private *mehfil* of Mia Jan of Patiala, Bhatkhande had some doubts about the rendition of the *raag*. Mia Jan saw that Bhatkhande was discussing this with his neighbour so he told Bhatkhande, "*Aapko jo kahana hai woh gaa kar bataaiye.*" Bhatkhande had to be silent after this.

Hereditary women performers and 'time'

Most of the singing girls were Muslims; some were Hindus from Goa. There were girls along the Kennedy Bridge involved in 'time' during which time anybody was allowed to attend and enjoy the music and after that pay any amount. The venue at Kennedy Bridge was called 'compound'. The duration of 'time' was stretched from 9 p.m. to any hour. They had to stop at midnight after Morarji Desai brought a ban on entertainment after 12 at night. Sometimes the word *divaankhaanaa* was used to describe the room where the 'time' took place. Until 1960 or so, they sang *thumri*s and other forms, but then public taste changed and listeners demanded film songs. As a result the *thumri* singers moved to other cities.

Ganda bandhan of a *tawaif*

A *tawaif* had her *ganda bandhan* from Khadim Hussein Khan in her room opposite Congress House. I had started learning from Vilayat Hussein Khan by this time and was present at this function. Bade Ghulam Ali Khan sang at this function and was accompanied by Barkat Ali Khan on *tanpura*. Bade Ghulam Ali Khan started with Marwa and followed this with *thumri*. The audience at this function included Vilayat Hussein Khan, Azmat Hussein Khan, Khadim Hussein Khan and all other Agra vocalists, Aman Ali Khan of the Bhendi Bazaar *gharana*, Alladiya Khan of the Jaipur *gharana* and many others. Khadim Hussein later told me that Faiyaz Khan was also present at this function but I do not remember this.

Relations between male and female hereditary musicians

Bade Ghulam Ali Khan and Ahmed Jan Thirakwa stayed with *chaudharain* Ganga Bai when they came to Bombay. Anwar Hussein Khan also taught one of the girls. However, most of the *ustad*s were riff-raff, although they had grounding in classical music. Some of the girls depending on their desire learnt classical music but most learnt *thumri*s, other related forms and *ghazal*s.

Radio

Old radio recordings were done on zinc discs, which were worn out after they had been played for four or five times. They started using spools after 1950.

21 September1992

*Seth*s as patrons

Hereditary women performers had *seth*s as their patron. Kesarbai Kerkar's *seth* was Gopaldas, a businessman and Anjanibai Malpekar's *seth* was Vissanji Ved. Most of the *seth*s were elderly and so the young girls would carry on surreptitious relations with younger men who were called *thokia*s. These young men were in fact employed by the women for the latter's satisfaction. Most *thokia*s came from the Goan community.

Mujra

The Bhatias and Kapol Banias held *mujra*s during wedding ceremonies. Gauhar Jan's patrons in Bombay were also Bhatias and Kapols. When I was in college, Mr. Gandhi, a retired Income Tax officer, told me that the ladies performing at such events stood and sang. Mr. Gandhi had also heard Kesarbai Kerkar standing and singing in a *mujra*. He described a *mujra* to me. At many *mujras*, there would often not be enough room to sit, as there would be a great rush of guests. In such circumstances, the host would give a coconut to the listeners, which was a signal for them to leave the hall to make place for others who were waiting to listen and witness the event.

Anjanibai Malpekar

Anjanibai Malpekar was beautiful and sang well. These qualities brought her patronage as a result of which she was financially very well off. She, unlike many other Goan women performers, did not have any other paramour. Her *seth* was, in fact, carrying on relations with many others. Vinayakrao Mulgaonkar accompanied him at times on his romantic rendezvous.

Anjanibai owned a building called Narayan Ashram next to Vihar restaurant at Opera House. She stayed on the first floor of this building. I visited her here. She was given a bungalow at Khadki by her *seth* but it was sold to meet financial needs. The building at Opera House was also sold. It is now Mistry Hospital. She then purchased another building next to Laxmi Baug, a portion of which was let out. She stayed on the first floor of this building. Later, to meet financial needs, she sold that too and also sold her expensive saris and jewellery, which had earlier been presented to her. Geetaben Sarabhai nee Mayor bought some of her saris. Geetaben learnt vocal music from Vadilal Naik on Anjanibai's recommendation and learnt *pakhawaj* from Govindrao Burhanpurkar. She also learnt *thumris* from Siddheshwari Devi and Rasoolan Bai of Banaras.

Contribution programmes were held at Anjanibai's Narayan Ashram residence and later at the Bhatwadi building. The guests would pay any amount voluntarily and this would go the artiste. Abdul Aziz Khan, a *sarangi* accompanist of Anjanibai and other *tawaifs*, played the *vichitra veena* on about three occasions at her residence. He took to playing the *vichitra veena* after he had been insulted by two *tawaif* sisters while he was accompanying them on *sarangi* in a programme. He therefore vowed not to play *sarangi* ever again. Allauddin Khan, Ravi Shankar, Bade Ghulam Ali Khan, Siddheshwari Devi, Begum Akhtar and others also performed at Anjanibai's residence. Smaller artistes like Swaruplata, daughter of Gangabai *chaudhrani* preformed at Anjanibai's residence. Durgesh Nandini and Heeradevi Mishra also presented vocal recitals there.

Neelam, a rich Muslim *tawaif* and owner of Neelam Manzil next to Lamington Road police station attended concerts at Anjanibai's house. Neelam acted in films when she was old. She had a *thokia* who stayed with her. He was her *tabla* accompanist and was a dance teacher to Roshan Kumari. He also accompanied Neelam when she attended the concerts at Anjanibai's residence. The listeners at these concerts included Satyendra Trivedi, Ambalal Patel, Narendra Shukla (later Chief Producer of All India Radio), Geetaben Sarabhai, Mahmud Ahmedbhai (a rich Khoja having several race horses and an amateur singer; main contributor at Anjanibai's residence who claimed to have learnt from Gauhar Jan and later learnt a little from Latafat Hussein Khan), Sardar Abasaheb Mazumdar from Poona, Vinayakrao Mulgaonakar, Shantibhai Gujjar, at times Leela Mulgaonkar. A total of around fifty to sixty people attended these concerts.

*Tawaif*s

New *tawaif*s had to pay *nazrana* to *chaudhrani* Ganga Bai before starting their business and she decided on any dispute arising among the *tawaif*s.

Patrons in Surat and Ahmedabad

Kanchanlal Mamawala, a patron in Surat, was a rich and cultured man with an interest in music, poetry, literature and painting. Top artistes like Omkarnath Thakur performed and stayed at his residence in Surat. Kanchanlal lost a lot of money in the share bazaar later.

In around 1948, I accompanied Ravi Shankar, Allauddin Khan and Nudo Bhattacharya to Surat and Ahmedabad, as a manager to look after the financial aspect, ticketing and such other matters. Ravi Shankar's earlier *tabla* player in Bombay was Nodu Bhattacharya who stayed with him and other Bengali boys in a flat at Khodadad Circle. Nodu also knew *jawari* and repairing techniques. Ravi Shankar had taken him to the USA and he then stayed there permanently. I was not paid for this work. The fees for a concert were Rs.300/- or so. Geetaben Sarabhai hosted a private programme and so did Kanchanlal. Geetaben paid for our air tickets on our return (Rs.55/- per ticket) instead of paying the concert fees.

Narayan Menon the then Station Director of Maharaja of Baroda's radio station was present at the concert at Geetaben's residence in Ahmedabad.

Interview with Shalini Narvekar

Translated from Marathi

Shalini Narvekar (1926-2012), was trained in vocal music by Balkrishnabuwa Banavali, Vilayat Hussein Khan and her maternal aunt Shrimatibai Narvekar. A resident of Bombay since her early childhood, Shalini Narvekar performed in many prestigious concerts all over the country and was a regular broadcaster on the All India Radio. A number of reputed music institutions awarded her in recognition of her achievements. A performer with an experience spanning several decades, Shalini Narvekar was witness to changes in performance practice, context and space. This interview focused primarily on her aunt Shrimatibai Narvekar, an eminent vocalist of the Agra tradition.

14 December 1992

My aunt Shrimatibai Narvekar was born around 1906 and died in 1989. She and my mother's family were staying in Ankola village, Karwar, at the time. Our ancestral house still exists there. My aunt started learning at a very young age from Balkrishnabuwa Banavli, a disciple of Muhammad Khan (elder brother of Vilayat Hussein Khan.) After completing her training from Balkrishnabuwa Banavli Shrimatibai's mother who had a deep liking for music was advised by Banavli to take Shrimatibai to Bombay for advanced training. This was around 1918-19. My grandmother brought Shrimatibai to Bombay and stayed near the Congress House in a rented house. The house was owned by a Muslim.

There were women performers residing and conducting their business opposite the Congress House. Their performances were called 'time'. Popular among these women were Mammijan, Neelambai, Zohra, and Munni. They would often have women visiting from other parts of the country and staying with them for six months or so. The 'time' was at night, starting from 8 p.m. and continuing into the early hours of the next morning. Rich men visited these places to listen to these these women performers. This place was opposite my aunt's house and she related these accounts to me. These women mainly sang *khaandaani thumri*s, *ghazal*s, *qawwali*s, and at times classical compositions. They were taught by *ustad*s in the afternoons and their practice would continue for a couple of hours or so. They were also termed as *qawwaliwali*s.

I had seen these performances from our terrace when I was around 13-14 years old. These women did *adaa* with the singing. *Sarangi*, *tabla* and at times harmonium, accompanied the singing. There was a bar in the neighbourhood, which supplied the liquor during the *baithak*s. The *divaankhaanaa* at the women's homes was the venue for the 'time'. It was decorated with flowers. I continued seeing these women performing till I was 18-19. My aunt would at times have *baithak*s at her residence after getting the idea from 'time' ladies.

Thereafter, we shifted residence to a place opposite Ajinkya Hospital in Girgaum near the Portuguese Church. I attended school until matriculation at Sharada Sadan in Girgaum. This was a school run by the Aryan Education Society. I did not continue to the college level after school as I started performing and my mother advised me to concentrate on singing. I completed the Sangeet Visharad degree from the Allahabad University in 1966. Nobody in my family pursued music other than my aunt and myself, but my grandmother was extremely fond of music. In fact, *thumri* singers like Ram Pratap and Pyarelal were called to our Girgaum residence to teach Shrimatibai Narvekar. Ramkrishnabuwa Vaze also visited us.

Shrimatibai Narvekar presented Rs.1,000/- to Vilayat Hussein Khan when he tied the *ganda* to her. The entire sum was offered in coins, which were kept in a silver vessel on a *thali*. There was no payment made to him during the six months prior to this *ganda bandhan* as this was considered to be a trial period for Shrimatibai. After the *ganda bandhan* ceremony perhaps Rs.50/- was paid on a monthly basis. The *tabla* player was paid separately.

I was born in 1926. My first guru was Balkrishnabuwa Banavli of Karwar. He came to Bombay for his *ganda bandhan* with Muhammad Khan and learnt in the city from him. After his training he went back to Karwar.

In around 1934-36, I would accompany my aunt Shrimatibai Narvekar to the princely state of Jawra for her concerts. There were many occasions when I could not accompany her, as I was very young then. At such times her sister would accompany her. We constantly played gramophone records of Faiyaz Khan and Narayanrao Vyas.

Interview with Kausalya and Dinker Manjeshwar

A senior disciple of Mogubai Kurdikar, Kausalya Manjeshwar (1922-2007) was amongst those who did not make music their profession and yet pursued it with same zest. She imparted her knowledge to a few disciples. Her husband Dinker Manjeshwar (1918-2012), a connoisseur of music, provided constant support and encouragement to her through her years of learning and performing.

10 September 1993

Family environment and early lessons in music

Kausalya Manjeshwar (hereinafter **KM**) There was a love for music in my family. My maternal grandfather played the *sitar* a bit, but not professionally. He had moved to Bombay at a very young age and was working at Thomas Cooke. My mother attended vocal music classes at the Gandharva Mahavidyalaya in c. 1916-17. My father had not learnt music formally, but he played a few *theka*s on the *tabla* and also provided flute accompaniment to *bhajan*s at events like Gokulashtami held by Kanara Saraswat Association.

I did not attend many concerts as a young girl, as we were not allowed to remain out of the house late into the evening. The music was mainly heard on radio and gramophone records. Hirabai Badodekar was the idol then. I had a liking for vocal music right since my childhood. My mother's friend would ask me to sing at her house and would note down verbatim the words of the songs that I sang with all the peculiar pronunciations that had crept in at that early age. We were then staying at Gamdevi.

We moved to Lalbaug when I was four as my father was Manager in a mill in this area called the Bombay (Union) Dyeing Mills. We were staying on the lower floor of the proprietor's bungalow. In 1929-30, I began attending New Era, a Gujarati medium school at Gowalia Tank, with the proprietor's children. This school encouraged extracurricular activities like music and art. The school had a separate shed amidst beautiful trees, which housed various instruments. A gentleman by the name of Pathak from the Gandharva Mahavidyalaya was a music teacher at this school. On being asked to sing in school, I sang a song taught by my mother. They liked my singing and I received a great deal of encouragement at this school. However, Pathak died early and was followed by a Bengali teacher from Calcutta. Both these teachers taught *raagdari* music and while there was a syllabus, it was very elementary. The Bengali teacher left and was followed by Kulkarni, a nephew of Narayanrao Vyas. Kulkarni told my father that he would teach me privately for a fee of Rs.25/- per month. We could not afford this fee and my father also wondered how this learning would help me. I could not sing in public, as those were the days when women from non-musician households did not take up music as a career. Besides, it was also uncertain whether my husband's family would have appreciated this fact when I got married. The idea was therefore set aside.

Thereafter, one of my father's friends, a Parsi gentleman studying music with R.B. Kale, a *dilruba* player residing next to Congress House, suggested that I learn from the latter. I started learning from Kale at weekly sessions for a fee of Rs.10/- per month. During the course of these sessions I learnt a few compositions, some *aalaap*, and a few *taans*. He taught me music notation, which proved useful in my future years of learning, particularly in learning *taans*. I also learnt to play *thekas* on the *tabla*.

Tryst with Manji Khan

KM In c.1932-33, we moved from Lalbaug to Raghav Wadi on French Bridge. Manji Khan stayed on the lower floor of the same building. Alladiya Khan would stay with him when he visited Bombay from Kolhapur. I was twelve or thirteen then and had no knowledge of the status of Manji Khan in the music world. Programmes were not as frequently held in those days and I heard only one concert of Manji Khan at Laxmi Baug Hall. Manji Khan had friends like Gulubhai Jasdanwala and Dr. Samsi, a dentist. I think someone from the Shirur family also began learning from Manji Khan after being introduced to him by Dr. Samsi. My mother and I would visit Manji Khan's family and I would join his family on some Sundays for a drive in his car. He had also taken us to a play staged by Bal Gandharva. I would visit their home and play with his daughters, but I never sang there. I would sing at home with my mother accompanying me on the organ. The organ had been given to us by a Gujarati friend who wished to have it removed from his place.

Musical environment in husband's family

KM I got married on January 26,1939, when I was sixteen and my husband was 21. He was extremely interested in music. My husband's family was very interested in music and my husband was already a member of the Bombay Music Circle.

Dinker Manjeshwar (hereinafter **DM**) My father was interested in North and South Indian music. He played violin and other instruments like *tabla*, harmonium and *sitar* as a hobby. Bhoogandharva Rehamat Khan would come with Chhatre's circus to Manjeshwar, our hometown. We had an outhouse in Manjeshwar where we had a tank and a mosque nearby. Chhatre would arrange for Rehamat Khan's accommodation here. I think Rehamat Khan sent a musician by the name of Vilayat Ali from Hyderabad to teach my father in Manjeshwar. We were landlords then and Vilayat Ali stayed at our place. My father and paternal aunt learnt from him. Vilayat Ali is said to have invented the *bulbultarang* and to have sold it to some Japanese firm for a few thousand rupees. Bhimsen Joshi would visit Manjeshwar several times. My father liked Kesarbai Kerkar's music the most. Thus, my family was musically inclined and my father had told me to listen to certain musicians while in Bombay. Consequently, I would attend Bombay Music Circle programmes.

KM Music in South India was encouraged as the compositions were related to God.

DM My mother also played the *tabla*.

KM Music was not looked down upon in the South.

DM I wanted to do a degree in medicine after my Intermediate and therefore came to Bombay. However, I did my Bachelor's degree in Science at St. Xavier's College. My brother-in-law U.B. Rao was then the Assistant Editor of *Times of India*. He later went to Delhi, became the Parliamentary Correspondent of All India Radio and subsequently migrated to England. As he too was a lover of music, he and I would attend Bombay Music Circle and Musical Arts Society programmes. Most of the programmes in Bombay were held in Laxmi Baug and at times at Wagle Hall and Muzaffarabad Hall.

Tutelage after marriage

KM Since my husband was interested in music, he suggested that I learn vocal music. I too was keen to do so. We had to decide upon the teacher. Along with my training before marriage from Kale, I also learnt some tunes on a mandolin, which we had at our home, from Vasant Choudhary who stayed near our house. Choudhary had learnt violin from Gajananrao Joshi, and was performing on the All India Radio. During this period, D.R. Nimbargi, a disciple of Anant Manohar Joshi alias Antubuwa Joshi, would visit Vasant Choudhary. Nimbargi performed at functions held in the municipal gardens, at marriages or thread ceremonies. He would also provide vocal support to eminent vocalists. He had a good voice and had broadcasts. Though a vocalist, Nimbargi also played the violin.

My younger sister was attending music classes at Maharashtra Sangeet Vidyalaya in Girgaum run by Baburao Gokhale (the classes shifted to Gamdevi thereafter) after some Saraswat women like Shashikala Karikatti, Mukta Padbidri and Shanta Amladi took to singing in the changing environment. Later, she stopped attending these classes and began learning privately from D.R. Nimbargi. He was staying near Central Cinema and would come home and teach. He charged a fee of

Rs.10/- per month. He would play the *tabla* in these sessions. He had learnt *tabla* from Vinayakrao Ghangrekar.

While teaching my sister, my husband said that it would be a good idea for me to also learn from Nimbargi but the latter said he would not be able to come to Matunga where we were staying after marriage. I would therefore learn from Nimbargi at Raghav Wadi after returning from St. Xavier's College where I was a student. Nimbargi would arrive at 4 p.m. and I would return to Matunga after the session ended. The duration of each session was not fixed. This routine continued thrice every week for a fee of Rs.10/- per month. This was also a huge sum in those days when we could buy twenty coconuts in Re.1/-. I think I learnt in this manner from him, from 1940 to 1947. Sometimes there were gaps in the learning when we would go out of town or he would.

In the meanwhile I had performed in a programme held in Bombay by Nandnikar, an Ayurveda practitioner. Bhurji Khan heard me at this programme and asked where I was learning. I reminded him that I had stayed in the same building as Manji Khan earlier on. He recollected this, as he would also visit the place at times. In 1949, he invited us to Kolhapur for the unveiling of Alladiya Khan's statue there. I was asked to sing here but I replied that I would not be able to come, as I felt apprehensive about singing on the same platform featuring maestros like Mogubai and Kesarbai. Bhurji Khan sent Gajananbuwa Joshi to our place to insist that we come to Kolhapur. Gajananbuwa was learning from Bhurji Khan then and offered to arrange for our accommodation at his own home. We knew Gajananbuwa as Nimbargi was learning from him at the former's Bombay residence in Soman Building. We attended the function at Kolhapur for a day. Among the performers were Mogubai, Gulubhai, Laxmibai, Ram Marathe, Lilutai Shirgaonkar and others. At Kolhapur, I felt the need to learn from Gajananbuwa. Even though there was progress when I was learning from Nimbargi, I had an urge to learn more. Consequently, I requested Gajananbuwa to teach me when we stayed with him in Kolhapur. He informed me that he visited Bombay for a fortnight at a stretch and agreed to teach me for twelve consecutive days every time he came.

DM Gajananbuwa had shifted to Kolhapur only to learn from Bhurji Khan.

KM Thus, he started teaching me for twelve consecutive days every time he came to Bombay. In fact, on one occasion he taught me twice everyday (morning and evening) for twelve consecutive days, as he was not going to visit Bombay in the following month.

DM He was charging a fee of Rs.50/- per month and would play the *tabla* himself.

KM He taught me really well. In the year 1951-52, I sang at Haldankar's Ganeshotsav celebrations. We had close relations with Haldankars and he asked me to sing at this function. Kishori Amonkar was also to sing here. I had heard that Kishori was singing well and so I asked Haldankar to let me sing first though Kishori was younger than me. Mogubai Kurdikar (Mai) was also present on this occasion but when I began she went inside probably so as to not let me feel uneasy in her presence. After two to three days, Mogubai came over to our place and spent a long time with us. My mother was also present and both she and Mogubai sat talking. After my mother left, Mogubai asked me to bring out the *tanpura*. I was taken aback and was very scared. She said that the *cheez* I had sung in Basant at Haldankar's had some incorrect words and she had come to rectify these mistakes. The compositions I had learnt of the Gwalior style had some words which seemed incorrect or which could not be understood. I would therefore get them corrected from Deodhar later on. She then asked me to sing the corrected version and told me that she only wanted me to correct the words but that I should continue to sing the rest as I always did. After a few days, Gajananbuwa came to our place and I reported this development to him. He did not mind it and accepted that very often compositions had words which could not be understood or which were incorrect. He was happy with this development and even advised me that if I ever had the opportunity to learn from Mogubai I should immediately do so. He told me that he had wanted to learn from her, as she had a good repertoire. His magnanimity and large heartedness were thus clear. He said I should not feel inhibited to learn from her because I was learning from him. However, when the All India Radio agitation started in 1953,

Gajananbuwa broke away from the organisation of the agitating artistes of which I was an integral part as the Secretary, and therefore, he felt uneasy about coming to teach me. Everyone wondered about the future of my training.

DM Vilayat Hussein Khan, Amir Khan and Azmat Hussein Khan, offered to teach her.

KM I was however not in favour of females singing with a masculine voice projection. I would listen to Kesarbai and would like her singing but was never driven to singing like that. It was more masculine. I met Mai (Mogubai Kurdikar) at this point.

KM I wanted to learn from her, but her fee was said to be very high for a person like me.

DM We had also heard that a car had to be arranged for her travel from her residence to the student's home and back.

KM I was therefore hesitant about asking her whether I could study under her. My training in music had discontinued for three to four months, as Gajananbuwa would not come home to teach me. Meanwhile, we had begun visiting Mogubai and she would always ask whether he had been teaching me. Our answer was always in the negative. In this period of dilemma about my future studentship, Satyendra Trivedi suggested that I should request Mogubai to teach. I replied that I was afraid to do so because she was such a respected personality and I had heard about her high fees. I felt our visits to her place would stop if she were not in favour of teaching me. However, Trivedi insisted and we agreed on the condition that he accompanies us for the meeting. Trivedi accepted this condition and when we reached, Mogubai once again inquired about Gajananbuwa. When I informed her that he had not come, she asked me what I had decided about my future training. I then hesitantly requested her to teach me, though I was unable to afford her high fees. She said that she had never expected any fee from me, that I was just like a daughter to her, and that I could learn from her at any time. Thus, the teaching began almost immediately and she would call whenever she had the time. My sessions were thrice a week and at times she would even call me twice a day. The sessions were held at her home in Asher Building on Forjett Street. My father-in-law requested me to concentrate on the *gayaki ang* rather than on collecting *cheeza*s and *raag*s. He said that *gayaki* could be acquired only from the *guru-mukh* (acquired directly from the *guru*), a *guru* of Mai's stature.

Since 1957, I had to visit our hometown often and as a result there were several interruptions in my training. During this period, I would visit Mai whenever we returned to Bombay and would learn some *cheeza*s but this was not a regular affair. My father-in-law died in 1961 and on the ninth day after his death, my sister-in-law also died. This loss shook me emotionally and I almost stopped singing. My mother also died in 1964. In December that year, we happened to visit Mai on a day when Sitaram Phaterphekar, was present there. Sitaram Phatarphekar and Ratnakant Ramnathkar were both disciples of Vilayat Hussein Khan. Those were the days when disciples were very loyal to the *guru*. Phatarphekar would organise a programme at Thakurdwar on every Datta Jayanti.

DM All leading musicians would perform at this Datta Jayanti.

KM Phatarphekar would take care of the day's expenses at the Datta Jayanti programme. Every Jayanti featured an amateur performer followed by a senior artiste. He had come to invite Mai for the programme and asked me to perform at the function. I told him not to insist that I sing, as I was not in good form. Mai said that since the programme was held in service of God, I should sing even if it was for a short while. I agreed and performed for fifteen to twenty minutes. The next day, Mai came to our place at 3-3.30 p.m. and asked me to bring out the *tanpura*. I was surprised and I asked whether I had sung wrongly at the Jayanti programme. She said that was not the case but that I had lost practice.

DM From that time onwards, she said that I should record the *taaleem* sessions. Thus, I started recording from 1964.

KM I was emotionally disturbed that she came home to teach me and taught me for the next ten to twelve days while we were in Bombay. I felt I must really have committed some mistakes, and that Mai must have taken the trouble to come to our residence to guide me properly. She came to my place because I was not going to her regularly. She taught me two *cheeza*s in the *raag*s Sampurna Malkauns and Basant Bahar during these sessions. I then told her that I felt ashamed that she had to come to our place to teach me. We were happy that she visited us but I did not want her to come all the way just to teach me. I therefore told her that once we returned from our hometown, I would learn at her residence. My husband also told her that he would send me to her residence whenever she desired. She then told me to come every evening at 6.30-7 p.m. She would teach Kishori in the mornings but would ring me if she had more time during the day and ask me to come over. I was always taught separately. Kamal Tambe and I were taught without payment of any fees.

Teaching methodology

KM The foundation under Nimbargi was sound. His style was that of pure Gwalior and the compositions were mainly set to *taal*s like Tilwada, Jhumra, Ektaal and Jhaptaal. Teentaal was not used as often in the *vilambit khayal*s and Ada Choutala was also employed on rare occasions. Nimbargi would first explain the *chalan* of a *raag* and sing the notation if it were difficult to grasp. This was a good teaching device. He would teach three to four compositions in each *raag* to familiarise me with the various aspects of the *raag*. I would not note down anything immediately, though I would write the *cheez* after I had memorised it. He would very often write for me, but this too was only the *cheez* without any notation. Nowadays, students are dependent on written material, but this is good only as a reference. I can still sing a *cheez*, which I was taught twenty-five years ago in the same manner in which I was taught, whereas students today have to refer to their books. Even if I forget a word or some *chalan*, I can still recapitulate it, so clearly has it been etched in my memory. However in Gajananbuwa's singing, there were some strains of Jaipur *gayaki*. I had a lot of musical problems when I began learning from Gajananbuwa. In the Gwalior style, I was allowed to sing freely, joining diverse pieces and negotiating the *sum*. In this case however, it was a little calculated. I did not understand why they would prolong or cut short the time spent on a particular note. I was really perturbed and could not come up with any musical ideas. I could not comprehend why I could not sing for even ten minutes in this new style when I could sing for half an hour to forty-five minutes earlier on. However, I gradually got accustomed to this style. When I started learning from Mai, she told me not to forget what I had learnt earlier, as that too was good material according to her. Thus, there was mutual respect for *gharana*s and love for each other's music. Mai decided to start with Jaitashree, a *raag* that I had not learnt. That was the best thing she did. She said I would automatically get used to the new style, as I had not done this *raag* earlier. If she had continued with the *raag*s I had already learnt, it would have been difficult for me to grasp the new style immediately. Subsequently, she taught me several *raag*s in a short span. She provided the *raag* information, *chalan* and then advised students to explore their path accordingly, but all such exploration had to fit properly within the framework of her *gayaki*. There was no writing. Mai was against it. Words of the *cheez*as were written but no notation. I will tell you from my experience that if we notate a *taan* in the book, we depend on that and do not try to explore further. In the Jaipur *gayaki*, we continue developing the same pattern right through the *taal* cycle. This pattern changes if the original speed of the cycle changes and consequently we have to then think of how to complete the cycle within the given number of remaining *matra*s. Written patterns dampen the creative process and stop us from experimenting with more note-combinations. Mogubai played the *theka* on the *dagga* if there was no *tabla* player present during the *taaleem* session.

DM Mogubai had studied *tabla* under Layabhaskar Khaprumama Parvatkar as well and hence her *laya* was perfect.

KM At first, when my husband asked for her permission to record the sessions she was not in favour of this, but later on insisted on it.

DM It was on her insistence that I would carry the recording equipment to her place for recording the tuition. This was a spool recorder.

KM All my teachers taught me a single *raag* for two to three months. Later, this time was reduced.

DM Thereafter, Kausalya also went to Deodhar for training in voice culture.

KM I did ten sessions with him and also continued doing the exercises at home. They helped me a little but only marginally.

DM She also learnt some compositions from him. He was very happy with her quick grasp, which he could not find in many others.

KM Mai knew about this and encouraged it. She was open to the idea of learning from any source. Ramrao Parvatkar and then Laxman Kalgutkar (Mogubai's *tabla* accompanist) provided *tabla* accompaniment to me when I practiced at home. Laxman Kalgutkar came to my residence for almost thirty years. Later, I started having lot of problems with my health and voice and tried various forms of medication. I finally started recovering due to the treatment prescribed by Dr. Vengsarkar, an eminent neuro-surgeon. I have also reverted to voice culture techniques taught to me by Deodhar's.

Radio broadcasts

KM I started performing for radio broadcasts in 1942 and have broadcast over hundred recitals. The atmosphere was very different. There was no grade system. I appeared for the audition, which was then just locally held. I would get a broadcast every two months and the pattern was three half-hour broadcasts in one day – morning, afternoon and night. There weren't so many artistes then and the programmes were also fewer. The accompanying artistes then included Tufail Ali (*tabla*), Alla Rakha (*tabla*), Mumtaz Hussein (*tabla*), Amir Bux (*sarangi*), and Hamid Hussein (*sarangi*). They were on the staff of the All India Radio. We were then amateur artistes and not professionals. They would therefore treat us affectionately, as we were involved in music despite not pursuing it professionally. After the broadcast, they would also give suggestions regarding *raag* development or other aspects of presentation. The atmosphere on radio was also very good at the time. I think Deodhar was on an Advisory Committee then and Dholekar was a Programme Executive. Dinkar Amembal alias D. Amel was also on the staff. The officials would meet the artistes after the broadcast and established good relations by inquiring about tutelage, years of training. They would compliment us on our performance. We therefore felt a strong bond with the All India Radio. At first I received Rs.10/- as a broadcast fee, which was increased in stages to Rs.25/-, Rs.40/- and then to Rs.50/-. Thereafter, the gradation policy was introduced.

DM Everyone was at par and everything was decided by the local station and not from Delhi.

KM The radio authorities would increase the fee on their own. It was only once that I wrote to them, since someone had informed me about the fees that others were getting. We were however not really bothered about the payments made.

DM The radio authorities would decide the fees. Bukhari, the then Station Director, was a great lover of music. He enrolled the services of Alla Rakha and others. He would guide these artistes and would meet amateurs to encourage them.

KM I sought Nimbargi's permission when I started performing for radio broadcasts, as I needed to know whether I was musically fit to do so. Being my teacher, I did not want his name to be blemished by my performance. He permitted me and I then appeared for the audition. I had a fair repertoire by then, though some repetition would take place over a year or so. We received much encouragement from the radio authorities and the musical accompaniment was also good. The programmes were broadcast live without any recording.

Performances

KM I never had the desire to perform. I loved music and just wanted to study it. I never felt that people should hear me and praise me. However, as amateurs, we enjoyed a good status and were encouraged. For instance, we were invited to sing at Ganapati functions, for our Saraswat Association programmes or at Punyatithis. Satyendra Trivedi would come to our place almost daily. Once, he wanted me to sing at a twenty-four hour programme organised by Nandnikar, a reputed Ayurveda practitioner. This was in the year c.1944-45, when I had not yet performed in public. I told Trivedi that I did not know anyone there and could not therefore ask anyone to feature me. He said he knew the organisers and arranged for me to perform there for half an hour in the morning session. I was then very much a beginner and did not know who would accompany me. The veteran Kamurao Mangeshkar said he would accompany me on the *tabla*. The *tabla* players then never thought it below their dignity to play with any artiste, as is the case today. Baburao Kumthekar played *sarangi* in several programmes with me. I never asked for or received a fee for my programmes in Ganapati festivals but the professionals were paid. I was not performing so frequently and would do so only when someone known to me would ask me to perform. For instance, I was asked to sing at the Ganapati festival organised by the Mahila Kala Mandir where I was studying. The Ganapati festivities were held in private and public (*saarvajanik*) but I did not sing in the *saarvajanik* ones. I either performed in the Ganapati festivities held in our building compound or class.

In 1944-45, I was going to perform somewhere. One of our friends said that he would arrange for Alla Rakha to accompany me on *tabla*. He accompanied me in five to six programmes.

DM He would come home for *riyaaz*.

KM If he had some programme of his near our place, he would even borrow our *tabla* pair. His accompaniment to vocal music was also good, as he had learnt vocal music. I had heard him sing a *thumri* and had even started learning one from him. However, I stopped the sessions, as they were irregular.

DM Yeshwant Kerkar would also volunteer to play on *tabla*.

KM The times were very different then. I did a few programmes in Calcutta and Indore. I was not inclined to performing outside Bombay, as I did not want to leave home for so many days.

DM She had refused to sing in Lalababu's Conference at Calcutta but Kesarbai sent word and she had to accept.

KM In Indore too, I had refused the concert but they prevailed upon me through Gajananbuwa. In Bombay, I was accompanied on *tabla* by Shripad Nageshkar and Gurudas Borkar. Alla Rakha had also played earlier in radio programmes and some private concerts.

Concert environment

KM When we would attend concerts at Bombay Music Circle, among the audience were Mogubai, sometimes Kesarbai and Faiyaz Khan.

DM Alladiya Khan, Vazebuwa and Govindrao Tembe would attend these concerts. Consequently, performers had to sing with added responsibility. Commercial people were not at all there. Gulubhai and

Yahyabhai Jasdanwala were also permanent listeners at the Bombay Music Circle, and Shirgaonkars also attended.

KM They would celebrate Member's Day but I somehow missed that occasion. Besides, I was not so advanced as a performer.

DM Gulubhai Jasdanwala (vocal), Vamanrao Deshpande (vocal), Vasant Choudhary (mandolin), and others would perform on this Member's Day as members of the Circle. Bade Ghulam Ali and other artistes were invited as Chief Guests. Among the many concerts I have heard, the maximum number of programmes (almost fifty) featured Faiyaz Khan both in Bombay and in Madras. In Madras, the programmes were organised in Gokhale Hall by a gentleman from Mangalore. I heard twenty-five to thirty programmes featuring Kesarbai Kerkar. I also heard Abdul Wahid Khan, Mushtaq Hussein Khan of Rampur, Altaf Hussein Khan of Khurja, Vazebuwa and Haribhau Ghangrekar. Baba Nasser Khan of Delhi was exceptionally good. Jaddan Bai, who was always present in the audience, sang *thumri*s in her performances. I was Life Member of Bombay Music Circle. The Life Membership fee was Rs.100/- and Ordinary Members had to pay Rs.3/- per quarter. Guests had to pay Rs.1.50 p.m. The total membership of the Circle was maintained at eighty and each member was allowed to bring only two guests. I had to qualify first before they could accept me as a member. They would test me when I would attend as a guest, by asking me to recognize the *taal*s and *raag*s. All the members were thus initiated listeners. Suburban Music Circle of Santacruz was started by Shri Shantaram Ullal and others in 1944 or so. This is running well.

KM Artistes were also not receiving high fees.

DM The performing musicians were paid meagre fees, but they loved to perform in the few music circles that existed then as reputed musicians and connoisseurs attended these programmes and the performers had to give their best with responsibility in the presence of such a learned audience. It was a matter of pride to have performed in such music circles. This was in the years 1936 to 1939. The same range of fees continued even later, though after independence, the fees increased because commercial people started organising programmes and music festivals and paid high fees to the artistes. M.D. Pai, Vamanrao Deshpande and Mr. Wagle, a good harmonium player, were the Secretaries of Bombay Music Circle. When the artistes started charging high fees, M.D. Pai was against this. He was a strong-willed man and was against commercial people entering the music circle. He said that these people would spoil Indian music and that undeserving people would get priority over deserving ones. Conferences like the Vikramaditya Conference also changed the fee structure. I attended the Vikramaditya Conference and heard Alladiya Khan perform with vocal support from Kesarbai Kerkar and Bhurji Khan. Faiyaz Khan was the announcer when Alladiya Khan sang. Faiyaz Khan and many other artistes from outside Bombay performed here. Film related song-dance sequences were also included in this festival. Champaklal Mody and B.D. Trivedi were among the organisers. This was a three-day festival, but I attended only a day or two. Jhabwala started *jugalbandi*s featuring Ravi Shankar and Gajananbuwa, Alla Rakha and Kishan Maharaj. Karsandas Vissanji, a patron with a liking for music, would organise programmes at his residence followed by dinner. He would encourage artistes like Hirabai Badodekar. He had also asked Kausalya to sing in one of these concerts. He was fond of Marathi dramas and Bal Gandharva and Hirabai were his favourite artistes. The earliest music circles were Gayan Uttejak Mandali started by the Parsis, Bombay Music Circle, Musical Arts Society and a few others. I was associated with Sur Singar Samsad as one of the Secretaries of Haridas Sangeet Sammelan organised by them in 1954. It made sizeable profits in this Sammelan. But later, I dissociated myself from this organisation for personal reasons.

The rent of the Laxmi Baug Hall was Rs.30/- and no mikes were used. Hence, we could hear good music directly. Questions would be directed to the artiste from the audience sitting on the mezzanine floor. The audience would demand to know why the artiste was performing in a particular manner or why a particular *sur* was introduced in a *raag* that was being presented.

Mogubai Kurdikar

DM Mogubai lived close to Vilayat Hussein Khan's residence at Ruby Mansion. We would see Vilayat Hussein Khan at times at her residence.

They would discuss music related topics, which was such a treat for us. I wish I had recorded those sessions.

KM Mai had learnt from Vilayat Hussein Khan. She had started in Sangli from Alladiya Khan and had moved to Bombay when he moved here but could not continue her training with him due to certain circumstances. In this period, she learnt from Vilayat Hussein Khan and then from Bashir Khan, his nephew.

DM I have heard Bashir Khan and Ata Hussein provide vocal support to Faiyaz Khan.

KM Mai was more inclined to the Jaipur style, so Alladiya Khan arranged for his brother Hyder Khan to teach her. She learnt from Hyder khan for five to six years until his death and then continued with Alladiya khan. There was a difference between the singing styles of Hyder Khan and Alladiya Khan. Hyder Khan's singing was mellower. Mai developed her unique style under his tutelage.

Bharatiya Sangeet Kalakar Mandal

KM I took active part as the Secretary of this Mandal, in the agitation carried out by the musicians all over India in 1953 against the All India Radio, for the injustice done to the established and performing musicians because of the unfair method of auditions conducted by the Audition Committee. During that time I came in close contact with almost all the top musicians of India who extended full cooperation and support to the agitation. This agitation has made history in creating a sense of awareness among the musicians about their real status and position in the society. This has also, directly or indirectly, contributed to a large extent to the present recognition that the musicians are receiving from the Government and the public, belated though. After a settlement was reached and this agitation withdrawn, I devoted most of my time quietly, to the study and practice of music under the esteemed tutelage of Gana Tapaswini Smt. Mogubai Kurdikar.

Some memorable events in my life

KM I sometimes used to sing devotional songs at Mahatma Gandhiji's prayer meetings in Bombay. On the last day of Mahatmaji's *asthi* immersion, the organisers requested me to sing *Vaishanava jana to* – Mahatmaji's favourite *bhajan* – near the *asthi kalash*, which was kept in the Town Hall for the public to pay their homage. The great Bal Gandharva sang *bhajans* there and when my turn came, he asked my *sur* for tuning the *tanpura*. When I told him about it he immediately tuned the instrument for me and continued to play it. But when I requested him and begged of him to hand over the *tanpura* to me, he merely continued playing it and said "*Baal tu gaa, me vaazavto*", meaning "You sing child, I shall play the *tanpura*". I was compelled to sing with the great person playing the *tanpura*, as time was running short. I fell to his feet after singing and he blessed me. This is a typical example of the humility of the really divine personalities. He was a personification of humility. When Mani Bhavan Building at Gamdevi was to be taken over by Mahatma Gandhi Peace Foundation or some such organisation, Shri Devdas Gandhiji, son of Mahatmaji, visited us at our residence at Raghav Wadi, French Bridge, and requested me to sing *bhajans* from the early hours of the next morning at Mani Bhavan and also at the public function to be held on Laburnum Road, in front of Mani Bhavan. I performed accordingly throughout the function and felt blessed for God giving me this opportunity in my life, which I shall always cherish.

Interview with Arvind Mulgaonkar

An eminent scholar in the field of ***tabla*** and author of the widely acclaimed book ***Tabla***, Arvind Mulgaonkar (b.1937), received his training from Amir Hussein Khan. He also spent some time under the tutelage of Ahmed Jan Thirakwa and Ata Hussein Khan. The information he has kindly provided is primarily based on discussions he had several years ago with Amir Hussein Khan.

4 January 1993

Munir Khan (*tabla*) – He stayed in Akbar Manzil to the right of Play House, which became more popular as Pila House. Among his many disciples were Ahmed Jan Thirakwa, Ayub Miyan, Nazir Khan (Panipatwale), Mushtaque Hussein, and his nephew Amir Hussein Khan. The latter and *sarangi* player Chhote Khan alias Chhote Miyan stayed with him along with twenty other *tabla*, *sarangi* and harmonium players. Amir Hussein Khan and Chhote Miyan cooked for Munir Khan and others. Chhote Miyan was Munir Khan's favourite *sarangi* player, especially for playing the *nagma*.

Qureshi *jamaat* – Bachubhai ki Badi, a two-storey chawl on the Foras Road primarily houses *tawaifs*. *Tawaifs* and *veshyas* are not synonymous as *veshyas* indulge in flesh trade whereas *tawaifs* sing and dance to entertain clients. Previously these *tawaifs* would have a firm foundation in art music due to their tutelage under famous *ustads*. They would then sing semi-classical forms like *thumri*, *dadra*, *hori*, *chaiti*, *ghazal* along with *ada*. From the money that was collected after each performance, four *annas* in a rupee would be paid to the *tabla*, *sarangi* or harmonium players. This pattern of payment was also followed in *kathak* dance recitals. Many disciples of Manna Master of the Jaipur *gharana* or Ghulam Hussein Khan came to the limelight. Thus, these *gurus* would train the *tawaifs*. However, in due course of time, the audience began losing interest in forms from art music repertoire and consequently frivolous film songs and film dances replaced these forms.

Professional musicians from among the Muslims and associated as accompanists to the *tawaifs*, belonged to the Qureshi *jamaat*. The title of *chaudhari* is conferred upon a musician chosen by popular vote, after the completion of the *pagadbandh* ceremony. Elders or respected members in the *jamaat* tie the *pagadi*. Disputes arising among the members of the *jamaat* are resolved by the *chaudhari* with the help of the *panchayat*, thus avoiding recourse to the court of law. In the event of an offender not mending his ways even after three warnings, he is ostracised from this *jamaat* throughout the country and this order is strictly adhered to. A nominal amount is collected from each of the members of the *jamaat* in lieu of which they are helped to establish themselves in the event they migrate to a new city. Every city or district has a large room owned by the *jamaat*, which is called *ustadkhana* or *jamaatkhana*. During the period that Amir Hussein Khan was the *chaudhari*, a nominal sum of Rs.5/- was charged for each bed. Many Muslim artistes have risen to popularity from these *ustadkhanas*. These artistes provide accompaniment at predetermined places from 7 p.m. to 3 or 4 a.m. each day. This accompaniment is called *time bajaanaa*. They return to the *ustadkhana* and begin their *riyaaz* the next morning after rising late. As a custom, only *ganda bandh* students of the *jamaat* were taught consistently and others were not taught with as much concern.

***Tabla* and *pakhawaj* players in Bombay** – Among the noteworthy percussionists in the city at different points of time were *tabla* players Nanhe Khan, Natthu Khan, Munir Khan, Kamurao Mangeshkar, Yeshwant Naik alias Valle Mama, Dattaram Nanodkar and Kanta Prasad, and *pakhawaj* player Makkhanlal. Bhaskarrao Chougule was employed as *tabla* player in Gandharva Company before Ahmed Jan Thirakwa.

Music classes in Bombay – Manhar Barve started his class at Dadar TT in approximately 1940. Though primarily a vocalist, Barve also played *ghungroo tarang, kach tarang, jaltarang, kashtarang.* He also taught *tabla* in his class. Professor Tendulkar's conducted the Shrikrishna Sangeet Vidyalaya music class near the bridge on the western side of the Dadar station. He too was a vocalist but taught *tabla* and harmonium as well. I took my primary lessons in *tabla* in Professor Tendulkar's class in 1953-54 from Deshpandebuwa who was approximately 80 years old at that time. Professor Surendra Rao conducted classical vocal music classes at Gokhale Road, Shivaji Park. Initially, Chhote Ahmedjan of Lucknow would teach advanced *tabla* in this class. After sometime he was replaced by Babalal Islampurkar, a disciple of Munir Khan. I took advanced lessons from him for about six months. He recommended me to Amir Hussein Khan with a note. *Tabla* player Narayanrao Indorekar also conducted a class in Dadar.

Interview with Abdul Halim Jaffer Khan

Translated from Hindi and Urdu

A name that took the world of Hindustani music by storm, Abdul Halim Jaffer Khan (b. 1929) evolved an inimitable style of sitar playing in the second half of the twentieth century. A recipient of the coveted national awards Padma Shri and Padma Bhushan, he has authored the book accompanied by a CD ROM entitled Jaffer Khanibaaj: Innovation in Sitar Music. His experiences in the field of film music have also been rich and varied. This interview carries some of his memories of the early days of this form of music as well as his thoughts on music education and performance, with particular reference to the time he spent in recording sessions for films.

6 May 1997

I came to Bombay with my father at the age of one. My father Jaffer Khan had a command over *been*, *sitar* and vocal music. We stayed in Khoka Building (next to Arab Galli near Grant Road), until I was eight or nine. At the time, other musicians like Aman Ali Khan Bhendi Bazaarwale, Ashraf Khan (a distant uncle of mine and spiritual *guru* of Dinkar Amembal), Ashiq Hussein alias Bhure Khan (a Kathak dancer from Rajasthan), Ram Dulari, Amanat Khan (nephew of Rajabali Khan of Devas), also stayed in this building. Among the musicians who visited us were Mohammad Khan Desai Faridi, a *beenkaar*, and Babu khan, a *beenkaar* and *sitariya* and a disciple of Murad Khan. I was very influenced by Babu Khan's style of playing the *sitar* and started focusing my attention on *sitar* after listening to him. By this time, I had already had some training from my father in vocal music, *jaltarang* and *sitar*.

Our family moved to Gokhale Road a little before 1935, after having stayed for short intervals at Grant Road, Bombay Central, Dongri and Bhendi Bazaar. My father started the Dadar Sangeet Vidyalaya at our residence on Gokhale Road. The Vidyalaya later shifted to Shivaji Park above Azad Restaurant. Under the banner of this Vidyalaya, he conducted classes for *sitar*, vocal, *tabla*, *jaltarang* and harmonium. My elder brother also taught in these classes. There was no syllabus in these classes and the hours for teaching were also not fixed. My father used a rudimentary system of notation in Urdu. The fees also varied, but were approximately Rs.15/- to Rs.20/- per month. In addition to these classes, my father continued to give private tuition at the residence of his students. Among these students were, Shyamalabai Mazgaonkar and her sister Hirabai. He also taught *sitar* to Shri Achyut, who was B.R. Deodhar's brother. The fees for private tuition also varied.

Deodhar would visit us at our Gokhale Road residence to discuss issues related to music with my father and to exchange vocal compositions with him.

Film Career

I moved to Mahim after my father passed away in 1942-44. In the absence of regular concerts, I saw the film industry as a means to earn a livelihood. I started my career in the film industry, at the age of sixteen. I was one of the youngest musicians in the industry then. My performing career as a classical musician began with private concerts, a year or two after this, that is in around 1945.

The studios in Bombay during the early days were Wadia Movietone (later became Rajkamal Studio), Bombay Talkies, Mohan Studio (at Andheri), Prakash Movietone (at Andheri), and Circo Studio (later became Kardar Studio).

At the time, the remuneration to musicians was Rs.2/- for a rehearsal and Rs.10/- for a song recording or what was commonly referred to as a 'take'. The background music was normally recorded at night to avoid disturbance from sounds outside the studio (those were days when recording technology in India was still in its infancy); musicians received Rs.15/- for this recording. There were no shifts of working hours as they exist now and the payments to all musicians were not made according to any system of gradation. There were no fixed hours of work; rehearsals lasted for an hour and a half to two hours at a stretch and the take continued for any length of time. Musicians would shrewdly increase the number of rehearsals to get more money. The pattern of paying musicians per song was introduced much later. In addition to these pay scales, musicians were at times employed by studios on a permanent basis or for the period required to complete the recording for a single feature film. The monthly salary was fixed at Rs.75/-, though exceptionally good musicians were paid Rs.100/-. The Minerva Studio started in Sewri by Sohrab Modi, earlier employed musicians at the rate of Rs.30/- a month. Musicians were allowed to accept other recording work while being permanently attached to a particular studio, since the hours of work in the latter case were two to two and half hours daily, on an average.

I was paid Rs.75/- per month for my first film *Yaadein*, the music of which was composed by D.P. Korgaonkar alias Dada Korgaonkar. I was paid Rs.10/- for each song recording, when I was working with Damodar Master, a permanent music director at Mohan Studio, Andheri, and with Madholal Master. Apart from these music directors, I also worked with others like Ghulam Haider, Naushad Ali, C. Ramchandra, Jhande Khan (music director for Urdu-Hindi theatre before he joined the film industry), Madan Mohan, Vasant Desai, Shankar-Jaikishan, Khurshid Anwar, Khurshid Zafar, Anil Biswas, Rafiq Ghaznavi (*batta been* or *vichitra vina* player, singer and harmonium player; composed music for the film *Bahurani* in which I sang a line in a children's chorus *Chali jae jeevan ki rail, pha ka pha ka pha ka*). I also played in the Marathi film *Annapurna*, which had Snehal Bhatkar as its music director. I played *jaltarang* in the film *Marvi* the music for which was composed by Madholal Master and in *Nadan* and *Mahatma Vidur* both of which had Dada Korgaonkar as the music director.

The musicians in the film industry were primarily from Bombay and some who had migrated from Goa and other regions. Most musicians had a base in Indian classical music. The Goan musicians were Christians who had been trained in Western music. Among the *sitar* players in the industry before I joined were S.G. Mohiddin of Dhaka, (disciple of Hafiz Ali Khan), Sayyad Saheb and a little later Afaque Hussein (originally from Lucknow; played in *Ujala* which had Bashir Khan Sarangiwale as its music director). Other sitar players to follow were, Aziz Khan, (son of Wahid Khan), Muhammad Shafi (brother-in-law of Vilayat Khan who also worked as assistant music director) and Ramlal (disciple of S.G. Mohiddin). Khan Mastana, another son of Wahid Khan also joined the industry as a singer. This was a period when Saraswati Rane, sister of Hirabai Badodekar, sang *Veena madhur madhur kacchu bol* in the film *Ramrajya* based on the *raga* Bhimpalasi at Prakash Studio, Andheri.

Albuquerque (cello), Ram Singh (saxophone), and Peter (violin), were three of the highly paid musicians in the industry. Popularly known as 'ARP', the trio was employed by the Bombay Talkies. Ram Singh also was an arranger and was closely associated with music director Anil Biswas. Other well-known musicians in that period were Nathuram, a student of Ram Prasad (trumpet player and father of Pyarelal of the famed Laxmikant Pyarelal team of music directors), Gajanan Karnad and Narvekar (violin), V. Balsara (piano, composer and assitant to Ghulam Haider, Khemchand Prakash and Dada Korgaonkar).

Of the other musicians in the industry with whom I interacted were, the three brothers Ghulam Muhammad (*dholak* player who later composed music as well), Ibrahimbhai (harmonium player) and Abdul Karim (*tabla* player). Jeere Khan (*tabla* player) was a permanent employee of Minerva Studio. The Minerva Studio had Meer Saheb, the paramour of Jaddanbai, as its permanent music director, on a monthly salary of Rs.90/- to Rs.100/- (Meer Saheb was the music director for the film *Pukaar* with Chandramohan and Naseem, in the lead roles). Abdul Rehman Khan, brother of Ashiq Hussein alias Bhure Khan mentioned earlier, played *sarangi* in films. His family had moved to Bombay from Rajasthan in 1925. Bashir Khan Sarangiwale, a *sarangi* player residing in Mahim, joined the industry in the absence of music concerts and with the intention of discontinuing his *sarangi* accompaniment to high caliber courtesans. He also composed music for the popular film *Ujaalaa*. (He is not to be confused with Bashir Khan Gudiyaniwale, a vocalist of repute, who resided in Bombay for a while. I have heard from my elders of the *jugalbandi*, which took place in the Mysore durbar between Bashir Khan Gudiyaniwale and Faiyaz Khan Agrewale; Bashir Khan emerged successful in this *jugalbandi* when he sang a *taan* from the *madhyam* of the lower octave to the *pancham* of the higher octave). Pannalal Ghosh (*bansuri*) and I played in the film *Parvana*, the music for which was composed by Khurshid Anwar. The film had Suraiyya and K.L. Saigal in the lead roles. Alla Rakha also played the *tabla* in films. In fact, he and I played the title music for a Punjabi film for which he had composed music. This music was recorded by Mr. Patil, the recordist at Shree Sound Studio.

While I was still in the industry, other *sitar* players occasionally played in films. For instance, Vilayat Khan played in music director Madan Mohan's film. Ravi Shankar played in *Nicha Nagar* and *Kalpana*. Nikhil Bannerjee also played in a few film songs. Rais Khan joined the industry after I left.

By the time I left, the payment to musicians in the industry had risen to Rs.15/- for a rehearsal and Rs.75/- for a take. I had by then also begun demanding special fees per take. I was a member of the Cine Musicians' Association (CMA), formed a little before I left the industry. Goody Servai (accordion), Sumanta Raj (flute) and I, had been nominated for the post of President of the *ad hoc* committee of the CMA, but I refused the offer.

Though I was never a music director for any film, I may have composed a few songs for films. I did however compose *vadya vrind* (instrumental ensemble) pieces for the All India Radio. Similarly, I also composed songs for All India Radio, which were sung by Nirmala Arun in Bombay and by Indra Narayan Sharma in Delhi.

In retrospect, I consider film music recordings to have been one of the most challenging tasks, not only for me but also for other musicians. This was especially so for musicians who were not using notation during the recordings. I too memorised the pieces and did not use notation. I learnt western staff notation from music director Pyarelalji's father Ramprasadji, an excellent trumpet player, but I could not continue this since I was not putting it to use on a regular basis.

Social Organisation of musicians

I cannot give a detailed description of the social organisation of musicians, as I never frequented the place where most musicians lived in Bombay. Most *sarangi* and *tabla* players lived here and I have heard from my elders that these *sarangi* and *tabla* players nominated a senior member from amongst themselves to accept the position of *chaudhari*. I have also heard that the *tawaif*s had a *chaudharain* as the head of their group.

This organisation was pertaining only to *sarangi* and *tabla* players and to those soloists, whether vocalists or instrumentalists, who belonged to hereditary *sarangi* or *tabla* player families. The *sarangi* and *tabla* players had a stigma attached to them as they were considered providers of accompaniment behind *tawaif*s. It was due to this that there was a seperation between this group and the rest of the musicians.

The *pagadbandh* ceremony that is spoken of in connection with the nomination of the *chaudhari* could have been influenced by the *dastarbandi* ceremony performed by Sufi spiritual heads to nominate their spiritual heir and *deeksha* in Hindu spiritual lineage.

The term *mirasi* actually refers to those who have inherited musical skills from their ancestors (*miras mein mili*). It has been misconstrued as those accompanying *tawaif*s. *Deredar*s were those belonging to families of women who sang and danced professionally in marriage functions or on such other festive occasions. I am not aware whether these and other categories of musicians existed in Bombay or whether these terms were used in the city. I am equally unaware about the situation in the hometowns of musicians as I grew up in Bombay.

Musicians would meet at a fellow musician's residence on Fridays where young and old, and junior and senior musicians, were heard. These gatherings were referred to *Jumma* as they were held on Fridays, but the name was retained even if they were held on any other day of the week. They were attended by musicians as well as connoisseurs. It was in one such gathering that Habibuddin Khan is said to have challenged

Ahmed Jan Thirakwa, but was not successful in his attempt; Habibuddin Khan had been trained by his father, popularly known as Hakeem, to outshine Ahmed Jan Thirakwa. I too have performed at these *Jumma* gatherings. Many *dantkatha*s are attributed to musicians who have performed here.

Thoughts on music education and performance

The contribution of V.N. Bhatkhande, Thakur Nawab Ali and V.D. Paluskar is praiseworthy. Bhatkhande's contribution is particularly good for creating *kansen*s and qualified pupils who could teach in schools of music. His work made the knowledge from the old texts available to everybody. His textbooks teach both the teacher and the taught. The *seenaa-baseenaa taaleem* and the institutional training, both have their place in music education.

As these Sanskrit lines mention:

ethdhdheshaprasoothasya sakaashaadhagrajanmanah
evam svam charithram shikSheran pRithivyaam sarvamaanavaah
(from *Manusmriti*, Ch.II, verse 20.)

(trans.: All men on this earth must learn their respective codes of conduct from the elders – Brahmins – born in this land.)

Words fail to describe how music would appeal to a listener and at what point of time or season. It is extremely difficult to set a standard for maintaining a balance between creating music that pleases the performer and that which pleases the listener. According to me, that music is successful which pleases the performer's mind and heart and also reaches out to the audience.

Forms in classical music will never lose popularity if there is *shuddha mudra* and *shuddha baani*, with perfect frequencies of pitch, correct intonation and reasonable *layakari*. There are many forms in our music, there is no lack of purity in these and there will always be listeners for every aspect. Changes in music take place because of aesthetic choices made by the musicians and audience. Change is welcome provided *swar* and *laya* are intact.

The scope of *tabla* accompaniment has increased in the past fifty to sixty years. This is mainly due to the musical decision made separately by Ravi Shankar, Ali Akbar Khan and myself. Among vocalists, Vilayat Hussein Khan, Latafat Hussein, Nissar Hussein Khan and Vinayarao Patwardhan, also gave the *tabla* an important place in their music. The last two mentioned particularly executed this when they sang *tarana*s.

Our music is an endless subject and we have no idea of the beginning or the end. It is like the book described in this Persian couplet –

> maaze aagaazo ze anjaam jahaan bekhabare
> awwaloaakhir ee kohona kitaab uftaad ast
>
> (trans.-We are unaware of the beginning and the end of a book, as the first and last pages are missing. However, the middle remains intact.)

There is magic in music and it is not possible to attain perfection in a single lifetime. The success of a musician is largely dependent on his or her good fortune.

Interviews with Purushottam Walawalkar

As a child, harmonium exponent Purushottam Walawalkar (1923-2014) travelled for theatrical productions with his father, an actor-singer in the Gandharva Natak Mandali. Later, he became one of India's much sought-after harmonium accompanists.

9-11 October 1992

Gandharva Natak Mandali

Ahmed Jan Thirakwa was paid Rs.120/- per month in addition to lodging and boarding, tailor and launderer, provided by the Gandharva Natak Mandali. Thirakwa's practice in the Mandali focused on sound production among other things. He emphasised on more volume and better sound quality in the absence of microphones, so that the singers and audience could hear the tabla clearly from the music pit.

The instruments used in Mandali performances were two *sarangis*, one *tabla*, three organs (two in the wings and one in the pit). Music started with the organs giving the *swar* for minor tuning, then the melodic refrain joined later by two *sarangis*, and finally the *tabla* entered with an *utthaan* landing on the *sam* for the vocalist to start the song from there.

Nazir Khan of Panipat played at the Mandali premises (Nana Sunkersett temple precinct) in Bombay in order to challenge and defeat Thirakwa. His performance was followed by Thirakwa's. Nazir Khan played for 1 ½ to 2 hours. Thirakwa got an applause right from the beginning which was not liked by Nazir Khan. Due to their exchange of words, the programme had to be aborted right there.

My father Madhavrao Walawalkar was paid the maximum – Rs.210/- per month, as he played the hero's part. While Thirakwa did not have his family with him during his travels with the Mandali, we stayed in the Mandali and so did the families of Master Krishnarao and Vinayakrao Patwardhan. When we travelled to other places for staging the plays, the entire entourage would be transported and accommodated in the new town for the next two to three months or for as many days as were required for the performances. Plays were staged on Wednesday and Saturday evenings and Sunday afternoons. The rest of the week was spent in rehearsals, individual practice and other actitivities.

The coronation of Pratapsingh of Baroda was held in 1936. Gandharva Natak Mandali was invited to perform on this occasion. All artistes visited patrons and performed at their residences.

There were no communal feelings among Muslims and Hindus in the Gandharva Natak Mandali. They sat together for lunch and dinner, but while the Hindus sat opposite each other and behind each other, the Muslims sat perpendicular to them. The vessels used for the Muslims were also different. The Muslim musicians participated in Hindu festivals like Ganpati by taking part in the *visarjan* processions in Poona.

Bal Gandharva towards the end of his life stayed with Gohar Bai at Mahim (junction of Cadell Road and Sitladevi Road). I came to Bombay in 1957-58 for permanent residence with my family, following the advice of Bal Gandharva. He had told me that staying in Belgaum would not help my career, as Belgaum was a small town. Bombay on the other hand would provide several professional opportunities.

Menakabai Shirodkar

Menakabai's first *seth* was Dhanrajgiri and then Bacchubhai (textile mill owner). Shobha Gurtu was born in Belgaum when Menakabai was 14-15. Menakabai was paid around Rs.5000/- to Rs.10,000/- per private programme. Menakabai had been invited to perform at a programme organized at Belgaum station by Station Master Phadke in around

1949. There were performances by other artistes like Bhimsen Joshi and Manik Varma. Nearly 50,000 people gathered to witness Menakabai's recital and the programme had to be cancelled due to this huge gathering. However, Menakabai performed for a private gathering on the same day in a room at the Raja Lakham Roda Law College, where she danced and sang. She would be accompanied everywhere by Ghamman Khan on harmonium (he was originally a *tabla* player, who taught her *thumris*), Yeshwant Kerkar on *tabla*, and her mother Krishnabai (she died in Bombay at the age of 116).

Menakabai was staying earlier at Ishwardas Mansion.

Jaipur-Atrauli *gharana*

Hyder Khan's voice was much better than Alladiya Khan's. I heard Hyder Khan accompany Alladiya Khan at Laxmi Baug sometime between 1935 and 1937, at a concert organized by Bombay Music Circle (Secretary-Mr. Pai). This morning concert was followed the next day by Faiyaz Khan's morning concert. Faiyaz Khan sang Ramkali, Desi and other *raags*. Alladiya Khan's son Manji Khan sang a large variety of *taans* without any repetition. His pitch was F (*safed* 4). He was not on good terms with his father after the latter started teaching Kesarbai Kerkar according to a contract, which also stated that he was not to teach anyone else. Manji Khan sang *natya sangeet* and *bhaavgeets* in his concerts.

M.G. Chandrachud heard Faiyaz Khan a lot in Baroda, as he studied there. Chandrachud's brother was a civic surgeon attached to the Baroda Court. I was teaching V.V. Gokhale in about 1963. He owned the Srikrishna Boarding House opposite Kohinoor. Mallikarjun Mansoor's *ganda bandhan* from Manji Khan was done at this Lodge and he learnt from him for 6 months to a year.

Kesarbai Kerkar

In 1946, I heard Kesarbai Kerkar at the Mahila Vidyalaya Hall, in a concert organized by the Belgaum Arts Circle. Narayan Nath Gurtu was the President of the Circle and Krishnarao Harihar looked after the administration. Kesarbai had stipulated that the programme was only for members and therefore no tickets were sold at the gate. She was accompanied by Maseet Khan (*sarangi*) and Shirodkar (*tabla*). She sang Behagda and had not yet gone to the *antara* when a little disturbance started at the venue. The disturbance was because Shivrambuwa Vaze entered the hall and sat right in front of the stage. Kesarbai stopped and sought his permission and then resumed her performance. Shivrambuwa left early but Kesarbai requested him to sing for at least five minutes the next day. The next day, Vazebuwa sang Shree for ten to fifteen minutes with Narayan Chikodi (disciple of Mehboob Khan) on *tabla* and me on harmonium. After fifteen minutes, Kesarbai told Shivrambuwa to stop as she felt she could not hear such profound music without the feeling of giving up music herself. She offered some money to Shivrambuwa, but he did not accept it.

Patrons

Among the noteworthy patrons in Western India were:

Abbasaheb Sambhare was a reputed and wealthy *vaid* in Sangli. Alladiya Khan was also attached to him.

Nandanikar was a *vaid* in Belgaum.

Baburao Deshmukh was a landlord in Nagpur.

Munshi in Baroda – I have heard Faiyaz Khan four to five times at Munshi's place in Baroda in around 1936.

Hun was a Bengali mill owner and a student of Natthan Khan Agrewale.

Vikramaditya Festival

I travelled from Belgaum to Bombay with Krishnarao Harihar alias Raosaheb, a theatre owner in Belgaum and other places, to attend the Vikramaditya Festival.

GLOSSARY

aalaap	slow introductory melodic prelude in vocal and instrumental music without percussion accompaniment that creates the mood of the *raag*
adaa	pertaining to hand gestures and facial expressions
asthi	ashes
baaj	instrumental style
baithak	a kind of musical performance
bandish	composition encapsulating the seed-idea of any *raag*
basphor	a caste of musicians
batta been/ vichitra vina	a stringed instrument played with a slide
beenkaar	a musician who plays the *been* or *rudra veena*, a frette stringed instrument
been	fretted stringed instrument
bhajan	a religious song-form
bulbultarang	a plucked stringed instrument with keys
chatrang	a form of vocal music incorporating four distinct elements in the song-text. Typically, the song-text begins with lyrics, and goes on to include *sargam* and syllables used in *tarana* and those used in *pakhawaj* repertoire.
chaudhari/patel	the chief of a trade or caste
daavat	invitation, but also signifies a specific performance context

dadra	a form of vocal music from the Hindustani system, closely associated with *thumri*, but it is distinct from the latter in its pace, longer song-text and manner of elaboration. Like thumri, *dadras* are composed in particular raags, but performers can exercise liberty in moving out of the original *raag* without compromising the aesthetic of the composition.
dagga	the base drum of the *tabla* pair. It is also called *bayan*
dangal	a performance context featuring musical challenges exchanged by musicians
dant katha	legend
dhamaar	a form of vocal music from the Hindustani system, closely associated with *dhrupad*. Set to a particular *raag*, it normally employs song-text referring to Holi, the festival of colours, and is sung in Dhamaar *taal*, a rhythmic cycle of fourteen counts.
dharhi	a caste of musicians
dhrupad/ dhruvapada	a form of vocal music, regarded as the oldest existing form of the Hindustani music tradition. Typically, it contains four stanzas composed in a particular *raag* and *taal*.
divaankhaanaa	living room
drut gat	fast-paced melodic instrumental composition in a particular *raag* and *taal*
gamak	rapid oscillation of a *swar*
ganda-bandhan	a ceremony marking the initiation of a *shishya* into learning music and signifying a bond between the *guru* and the *shishya*. A consecrated thread called *ganda* is tied by the *guru* to the *shishya*'s wrist to indicate this bond.
ganihari	a caste of musicians
garba	A song-dance form from Gujarati in praise of the Mother Goddess.
gaunharin	a caste of musicians
gayaki	vocal style
gharana	literally household, but in musical parlance signifies individual musical styles pursued by hereditary musicians, their progeny and disciples

ghazal	a poetic form, originally in Persian and Urdu, but presently seen in many languages like Hindi, Marathi and Gujarati. It is also considered as a form of vocal music from the Hindustani system, when composed to *raag* and *taal*.
ghikari	a caste of musicians
guru	mentor, teacher and guide
haav-bhaav	pertaining to hand gestures and facial expressions
hori	a song-form describing Holi, the festival of colours, and the exploits of the mythological figure Krishna, his friends and consorts. Also called *holi*, this song-form is found in folk music of northern India, but variants exist in Hindustani art music repertoire that include similar imagery in the song-text, but are elaborated upon according to the parameters of *raag* and *taal*.
jagirdar	landowner
jalsa	a kind of musical performance, but also used to describe a performance context
jaltarang	a percussive rhythmic-melodic instrument comprised of a set of ceramic bowls filled with water that are struck by sticks
jamaat	sect, but also used to signify a congregation or assembly
jawari/jiwari	the vibration of the string that creates resonance
jod	melodic section succeeding the free-flowing *aalaap* section in the presentation of a *raag*. It is rhythmic, but does not employ any percussion accompaniment.
jumma	literally denotes Friday in Urdu, but in musical parlance signifies a specific performance context that was held primarily on Fridays
kalash	urn
kalavant/ kalawant	a caste of musicians
kalavantin/ naikin	hereditary woman performer of a particular caste, from Goa and neighbouring areas
kawaltapi	a caste of musicians
kanchan	a caste of musicians

kathain/utak	a caste of musicians
kathak	a caste of musicians
khaandaani	hereditary; used in the context of music to refer to repertoire that has been inherited, indicating its antiquity and implying quality.
khayal/ khyal	a form of Hindustani vocal music composed in a particular *raag* and *taal*. The song-text has two parts called *sthyai* and *antara*.
laggi/laggi-chanti/laggi-nada	rhythmic section in tabla accompaniment to *thumri*, *dadra* and allied forms
lavani/lavni	a form of vocal music from Maharashtra. Some *lavani*s include dance as an integral part of the presentations. Conventional song-texts of *lavani*s describe amorous dalliances and have erotic overtones.
layakari	complex cross-rhythms and mathematically intricate musical phrasing
matra	lit. amount. A count or unit of time in a taal ordinarily considered synonymous with the English term 'beat'. However, matra refers not just to the beat but also the space between the two beats. It is the duration of space between consecutive matras that determines the tempo.
mirasi	a caste of musicians
mohalla	locality
mujra	a kind of musical performance
munj	a Hindu ceremony, also called *upanayana*, that marks the initiation of an upper-caste male into a phase that focuses on the quest for knowledge.
meend	gradual unbroken glide from one to the other *swar*
nach	a kind of musical performance
nagma/naghma	melodic refrain maintaining the canvas of the *taal* during a *pakhawaj* or *tabla* solo or a Kathak recital
nautch	performance featuring singing and dancing by hereditary women performers
pachamba	a kind of musical performance

pagadbandh	a ceremony nominating a member of a caste or group to head it
pagadi	turban
pakwaj/ pakhawaj	twin-faced horizontal drum primarily used to accompany *dhrupad-dhamaar*, but also used in forms of religious music found in Krishna temples of North India and in temples dedicated to the god Vitthal in Maharashtra
panchayat	an assembly of arbitrators, usually five, heading a village community or caste
patra	a caste of musicians
peshwaj	a flowing robe-like upper garment also worn by dancers
qawwali	a form of religious music integral to Sufism from the Indian subcontinent
qawwaliwali	a nomenclature at times used in mid-twentieth century Bombay to describe hereditary women performers residing in the city
raag	term denoting the melodic framework of art music in India. Briefly, every *raag* is said to create a mood with the help of specific *swar*s that are used in a predetermined manner but are open to elaboration and spontaneous improvisation, provided the ground rules of the *raag* are not broken. Forms of music have evolved over centuries to encapsulate the seed-idea of every *raag*, and each of these forms has its grammar, rules and conventions, which allow or restrict the freedom of interpreting the *raag*.
ramjana	a caste of musicians
ramjani	a caste of musicians
ranganli	a caste of musicians
rasiya	a form of vocal music describing Holi and the exploits of Krishna.
riyaaz	practice
saarvajanik Ganeshotsav	public observance of the Ganesh festival
safed	lit. white. In the context of harmonium, it refers to the white keys on the keyboard
saki	a poetic meter

sam/sum	first and most accentuated count of any *taal*, which is the point of resolution of most musical ideas, particularly in rhythmic exploration
samarth	competent
sargam	solfège
saringi/sarangi	a fretless bowed instrument with a skin-top sound board, used to accompany vocal music but also featured as a solo instrument.
sarod	a fretless stringed instrument with a metal finger board and a skin-top sound board
satta	a form of lottery
seenaa-baseenaa taaleem	one-to-one individual instruction
shetia/seth/shet/sethia	merchant prince or member of the commercial and industrial elite in colonial Bombay
shishya	disciple
shruti	micro-tone
shuddha baani	perfect singing style
shuddha mudra	perfect posture
sitar	a fretted stringed instrument
sitariya	a sitar player
suravartana	a form of vocal music set to *raag* and *taal*, using solfège as song-text
swar malika	a form of vocal music set to *raag* and *taal*, using solfège as song-text
taal	term denoting the cyclical pattern of rhythm in Indian music represented by mnemonic syllables that can be reproduced on various drums
taan	virtuosic swift melodic passage used while elaborating a *raag*
tabla	a pair of upright twin hand drums primarily used in northern India to accompany vocal and instrumental music and Kathak performances. It also possesses a rich solo repertoire.
taleem	teaching

tappa	a form of vocal music set to *raag* and *taal* that originated towards the latter part of the eighteenth century in Punjab. Said to be the creation of Ghulam Nabi alias Shori Miyaan, the form employing Punjabi song-text, became a part of Hindustani vocal repertoire.
tarana	a form of vocal music set to *raag* and *taal*, using syllables like ta, na, ra, diri, dani, nom, in the song-text. Persian couplets and *pakhawaj* syllables were used in the second part of the composition.
thali	a metal plate
thumri	a form of vocal music that incorporated dance and gesture. Thumri song-texts speak of romance, union and separation of lovers, and also incorporate the sensuous and erotic.
tillana	a form of vocal music from the Carnatic system, similar to tarana
tirvat/trivat	a form of vocal music set to *raag* and *taal*, using tabla or pakhawaj syllables in the song-text.
upadeshakvarg	a section in the Gandharva Mahavidyalaya for needy children
utthaan	literally act of rising. In musical parlance, a composition or short piece marking the entry into a section of the performance
vaidya	an Ayurveda practitioner
vastadji	dance teachers
veena	Typically, a fretted stringed instrument, the *veena* has many variants across India. *Veena* was also used as a generic term to signify stringed instruments.
veerasana	a specific seated posture that forms a part of Yoga
vida/beeda	betel leaf mouth freshner

BIBLIOGRAPHY

ENGLISH

Primary Sources

A Brief Account of the Framjee Cowasjee Testimonial and the Principal Correspondence relating to the Framjee Cowasjee Institute, (n.p.), Bombay, 1871.

Ali, Naushad, *Indian Talkie 1931-1956: Silver Jubilee Souvenir*, Film Federation of India, Bombay, 1956.

All-India Music Conference, All India Music Conference Trust, Calcutta, 1954.

All-India Women's Music Conference on the occasion of Holy Mother Birth Centenary, All-India Women's Music Conference Sub-committee, Calcutta, 1954.

Anklesaria, B.N., "March of Music", in Sur Singar Samsad, *Sangeet Nritya Mahotsava – Swami Haridas Sammelan – 4th in series*, Bombay, 1956.

Bate, Mrs. J.D. (compiled by), *The North India Tune-Book, containing Bhajans and Ghazals with Native Tunes, as usually sung*, North India Tract and Book Society's Depot, Allahabad, and Alexander and Shepheard, London, 1886.

Bentley, Richard, *Life in Bombay, and the Neighbouring Outstations With Illustrations*, "author", London, 1851.

Bhatkhande, V.N., *Music Systems in India* (A Comparative study of some of the leading music systems of the 15th, 16th, 17th & 18th centuries), S. Lal & Co., Delhi, 2nd ed, 1989.

——, *A Short Historical Survey of the Music of Upper India*, "B.S. Sukthankar", Bombay, 1934.

Bharat Sangeet Sabha, *Music and Dance Festival*, Bombay, 1958.

Bombay Symphony Orchestra, Bombay Symphony Orchestra, Bombay, n.d.

Census of the Town and Island of Bombay, taken on the 9th February, 1906, with the sanction of Government and of the Municipal Corporation for the city of Bombay accorded under Section 454 of the Bombay Municipal Act III of 1888, by the Municipal Commissioner.

Chaubey, S.K., *Indian Music Today*, Kitab Mahal, Allahabad, 1945.

Clements, E., *Introduction to the Study of Indian Music*, Gaurav Publications, New Delhi, 1st Indian ed., 1981.

———, *Lectures on Indian Music, (Delivered in the University of Bombay in January 1926)*, "Mr. Fardunji M. Dastur", Registrar, University of Bombay, Bombay, 1927.

Cousins, Margaret E., *The Music of Orient and Occident: Essays towards mutual understanding*, B.G. Paul and Co., Publishers, Madras, 1935.

Das Gupta, Amlan and Urmila Bhirdikar (trans. with introd.), *Sangeet Samrat Khansaheb Alladiya Khan: My Life*, Thema, Calcutta, 2000.

Douglas, James, *Bombay and Western India, Vol. I*, Sampson Low, Marston & Company, Limited, London, 1893.

———, *Glimpses of Old Bombay and Western India*, Sampson Low, Marston And Company Limited, London, 1900.

Dubois, Abbe J.A., *Hindu Manners, Customs and Ceremonies*, (trans. from the author's later French MS. and ed. by Henry K. Beauchamp), Clarendon Press, Oxford, 3rd ed., 1906.

Dumasia, Naoroji Maneckji, *A Short Biographical Sketch of the Late Shet Varjivandas Madhavdas*, (n.p.), Bombay, 1896.

Edwardes, S.M., *The Gazetteer of Bombay City and Island (Facsimile Reproduction), Vol.I*, (Originally printed in 1909), Gazetteer Department, Govt. of Maharashtra, Bombay, 1977.

——— *The Gazetteer of Bombay City and Island (Facsimile Reproduction), Volume II*, (Originally printed in 1909), Gazetteer Department, Govt. of Maharashtra, Bombay, 1978.

——— *The Gazetteer of Bombay City and Island (Facsimile Reproduction), Volume III*, (Originally printed in 1909), Gazetteer Department, Govt. of Maharashtra, Bombay, 1978.

Enthoven, R.E., *The Tribes and Castes of Bombay, Vol.I*, Government of Bombay, Bombay, 1920.

—— *The Tribes and Castes of Bombay, Vol.II*, Government of Bombay, Bombay, 1922.

—— *The Tribes and Castes of Bombay, Vol.III*, Government of Bombay, Bombay, 1920.

Fielden, Lionel, *Report on the Progress of Broadcasting in India: Up to the 31st March 1939*, Manager of Publications, Delhi, 1940.

Framjee, Firoze, *Encyclopedia of Hindustani Music*, " author", Poona, 1927.

Fourth Report of the Students' Literary and Scientific Society, and of its Vernacular Branch Societies, Bombay, 1853.

Gaisberg, F.W., *Music on Record*, Robert Hale Limited, London, (n.d.).

Gandhi, Mahatma, *The Collected Works of Mahatma Gandhi Vol.14, October 1917-July 1918*, The Director, Publications Division, Delhi, 1965.

Grant, Sir A., *Catalogue of Native Publications in the Bombay Presidency up to 31st December 1864*, (n.p., prepared under Orders of Govt), 2nd ed., Bombay, 1867.

Gune, V.G. (ed.), *Gazetteer of the Union Territory: Goa, Daman and Diu, District Gazetteer Part 1: Goa*, Gazetteer Department, Government of the Union Territory of Goa, Daman and Diu, 1979.

Hunter, W.W., *The Indian Empire: Its People, History, and Products*, Trübner & Co., Ludgate Hill, Second Edition, London, 1886.

Illustrated Catalogue and Price-List of Genuine Palitana Make Harmonium Reeds, Jivanlal Kanji Mistri & Sons, Palitana, 1956.

Jayakar, M.R., *The Story of My Life, Vol. I, 1873-1922*, Asia Publishing House, Bombay, 1958.

—— *The Story of My Life, Vol. II, 1922-1925*, Asia Publishing House, Bombay, 1959.

Jeejeebhoy, J.R.B., *The Parsees in Bombay*, Reprinted from the Kaiser-I-Hind Nowroze Number, 1940.

Jehangir, Sorabji, *Representative Men of India: A Collection of Memoirs with Portraits, of Indian Princes, Nobles, Statesmen, Philanthropists, Officials, and Eminent Citizens*, Messrs. W.H. Allen & Co., London, 1889.

Kaikini, L.V. (ed.), *The Speeches and Writings of Sir Narayen G. Chandavarkar Kt.*, Manoranjak Grantha Prasarak Mandali, Bombay, 1911.

Keskar, B.V., *Indian Music: Problems and Prospects*, Popular Prakashan, Bombay, 1967.

Khan, Hazrat Inayat, *The Divine Symphony or Vadan*, Sufi Movement, Geneva, 2nd ed., 1931.

—— *Notes form the Unstruck Music from: The Gayan*, N.V. Publishing Co., Holland, 4th revised ed., 1936.

—— *Nirtan or The Dance of the Soul*, N.V. Publishing Co., Holland, 2nd ed., 1938.

Manshardt, Clifford (ed.), *Bombay: Today and Tomorrow*, D.B. Taraporewala Sons & Co., Bombay, 1930.

Mill, James, *The History of British India*, (first pub. in 1818), Vols.I & II, Notes by Horace Hayman Wilson, "Introduction" by J.K. Galbraith, Chelsea House Publishers, New York, 1968.

Mulji, Karsandas, *History of the Sect of Maharajas, or Vallabhacharyas, in Western India*, Trübner & Co., London, 1865.

Nehru, Jawaharlal, *Jawaharlal Nehru: An Autobiography*, Allied Publishers Private Limited, Bombay, 1962.

Nichols, Beverley, *Verdict on India*, (n.p., n.d.)

Nritya Utsav or Dance Festival in aid of the Rescue Home & Sub-Committees of the Bombay Presidency Women's Council, BPWC, Bombay, 1939.

Peile, J.B., *Catalogue of Native Publications in the Bombay Presidency from 1st January 1865 to 30th June 1867, and of some Works omitted in the previous Catalogue*, n.p. prepared under orders of Govt.), Bombay, 1869.

Pingle, Bhavanrao A., *Indian Music*, (n.p.), Bombay, 2nd ed., 1898.

Prasad, H.Y. Sharada and Damodaran, A.K. (eds), *Selected Works of Jawaharlal Nehru II Series, Vol.30*, (September 1-November 17, 1955), Jawaharlal Nehru Memorial Fund, N. Delhi, 2002.

Proceedings of the Students' Literary and Scientific Society, Bombay, for the years 1854-55 and 1855-56, Bombay, 1856.

——, *during 1856-57, 1857-58, and 1858-59*, Bombay, 1860.

Rao, A.S., "About Ourselves", in the *Golden Jubilee Souvenir of the Suburban Music Circle*, Mumbai, 1986.

Report of the Committee for Music Education, 1948-49, Government of Bombay, Education & Industries Department, Bombay, 1949.

Report of the Students' Literary and Scientific Society, and of the Vernacular Branch Societies, together with the Reports of the Girls' Schools for the Session of 1862-63, Bombay, 1863.

——*for the Session of 1863-64*, Bombay, 1864.

Report of the Students' Literary and Scientific Society for the Session of 1865-66, Bombay, 1867.

—— *1866-67*, Bombay, 1867.

——*1867-68*, Bombay, 1869.

——*1868-69*, Bombay, 1870.

——*1869-70*, Bombay, 1871.

——*1870-71*, Bombay, 1872.

——*1871-72*, Bombay, 1874.

——*1872-73*, Bombay, 1874.

——*1873-74*, Bombay, 1875.

——*1874-75*, Bombay, 1876.

——*1875-76*, Bombay, 1876.

——*1877-78*, Bombay, 1880.

——*1879-80*, Bombay, 1880.

Sahasrabuddhe, Balwant Triumback, *Hindu Music and The Gayan Samaj*, The Madras Jubilee Gayan Samaj, Madras, 1887.

Sherring, Rev. M.A., *Hindu Tribes and Castes, Vol.I*, Thacker, Spink, and Co., Calcutta, (n.d.).

——, *Hindu Tribes and Castes together with an Account of the Mahomedan Tribes of the North-West Frontier and of the Aboriginal Tribes of the Central Provinces, Vol.II*, Thacker, Spink, and Co., Calcutta, 1879.

Steele, Arthur, *Summary of the Law and Custom of Hindoo Castes*, "Honorable The Governor in Council", Bombay, 1827.

Strangways, A.H. Fox, *The Music of Hindostan*, Oxford University Press, London, 1914.

Sur Singar Samsad, *Sangeet Nritya Mahotsava – Swami Haridas Sammelan – 4th in series*, Bombay, 1956.

——*5th in series*, Bombay, 1957.

Tagore, Raja Sir Sourindro Mohun, *Universal History of Music: Compiled from diverse sources together with various original notes on Hindu music, The Chowkhambha Sanskrit Studies, Vol.XXXI*, The Chowkhambha Sanskrit Series Office, Varanasi, 2nd ed., 1963.

—— *Yantra Kosha or A Treasury of the Musical Instruments of Ancient and of Modern India, and of Various Other Countries*, "Aubhoy Churun Ghose", Calcutta, 1875.

Tagore, Surendra Mohan, *Public Opinion and Official Communications about the Bengal Music and its President*, "Panchanun Mookherjee", 1876.

Telang, K.T., *Selected Writings & Speeches*, Gaud Saraswat Brahmin Mitra Mandal of Bombay, Bombay, 1916.

The Bombay Almanac, Directory and Register for the year 1842, Bombay, 1842.

The "Bombay Times" Calendar and Almanac for 1851, Bombay, 1851.

The Bombay Calendar and Almanac for 1853, Bombay, 1853.

The Bombay Chronicle: Founded by Sir Pherozeshah Mehta, 3rd March, 1913, Silver Jubilee, 1913-1938, The Bombay Chronicle, Bombay, 1938.

The Classical Music Soiree, Dover Lane Festival, Calcutta, 1954.

The Paisa Fund Silver Jubilee Number, Paisa Fund, Poona, n.d.

Trust Deed of the Students' Literary and Scientific Society, Bombay, dated 15th April, 1878, Bombay, 1881.

Wadia, J.B.H., "The Indian Silent Film", in Ramachandran, T.M. (ed.), *70 Years of Indian Cinema (1913-1983)*, CINEMA India-International, Bombay, 1985.

Willard, Augustus N., *Music of India*, Sushil Gupta (India) Private Ltd., 2nd revised ed., Calcutta, 1962.

Secondary Sources

Abels, Birgit, *The Harmonium in North Indian Music*, New Age Books, New Delhi, 2010.

Angle, Prabhakar, "Indian Music", in Mário Cabral E Sá, *Wind of Fire: The Music and Musicians of Goa*, Promilla & Co., Publishers, New Delhi, 1997.

Awasthy, G.C., *Broadcasting in India*, Allied Publishers Private Limited, Bombay, 1965.

Bakhle, Janaki, *Two Men and Music: Nationalism in the Making of an Indian Classical Tradition*, Oxford University Press, Oxford, 2005.

Ballhatchet, Kenneth, *Race, Sex and Class under the Raj: Imperial Attitudes and Policies and their Critics, 1793-1905*, Vikas Publishing House Pvt. Ltd., New Delhi, 1979.

Banerjee, S.G., *The Princes and the Dancing Girls (In terms of Music and Dance)*, "author", Varanasi, 1967.

Banerjee, Sumanta, *The Parlour and the Streets: Elite and Popular Culture in Nineteenth Century Calcutta*, Seagull Books, Calcutta, 1989.

Baruah, U.L., *This is All India Radio-a handbook of radio broadcasting in India*, Publications Division, Ministry of Information and Broadcasting, Government of India, New Delhi, 1983.

Bengallee, Nowrozjee Sorabji, *The Life of Sorabjee Shapoorjee Bengallee, C.I.E.*, "author", (n.d.).

Bhagwat, Neela, *Krishnarao Shankar Pandit: A Doyen of Khayal*, Popular Prakashan, Bombay, 1992.

Bhattacharya, Jotin, *Ustad Allauddin Khan And His Music*, B.S. Shah Prakashan, Ahmedabad, 1979.

Bhyrappa, S.L. and Ranade, Ashok D., *Gangubai Hangal*, Academy of Performing Arts Prakashana, Hubli, 1988.

Booth, Gregory D., *Behind the Curtain: Making Music in Mumbai's Film Studios*, Oxford University Press, New York, 2008.

Bor, Joep and Philippe Bruguierre, *Masters of Raga, Meister Des raga, Les Maitres Du Raga*, Haus der Kulturen der Welt, Berlin.

Buckland, C.E., *Dictionary of Indian Biography*, Indological Book House, Varanasi, 1971.

Carlyle, Thomas, *On Heroes Hero-Worship and the Heroic in History*, Oxford University Press, London, 1974.

Carr, E.H., *What is History?*, Penguin Books, London, 1964.

Catanach, Ian, "'Who are your leaders?' Plague, the Raj and the 'communities' in Bombay, 1896-1901" in Peter Robb (ed.) in collaboration with K.N. Chaudhuri and Avril Powell, *Society and Ideology: Essays in South Asian History*, Oxford University Press, Second Impression, Delhi, 1994.

Chandavarkar, Bhaskar, "Indian Film Song", in Ramachandran, T.M. (ed.), *70 Years of Indian Cinema (1913-1983)*, CINEMA India-International, Bombay, 1985.

Chandavarkar, Ganesh L., *A Wrestling Soul: Story of the life of Sir Narayan Chandavarkar*, Popular Book Depot, Bombay, 1955.

Chandwankar, Suresh S., "Preserving the recorded sound: 78 RPM", in Balawant Joshi, Dilip Inamdar, Charudatta Bhagwat, S.S. Gore (eds.), *World of Gandharvas*, Akhil Bharatiya Gandharva Mahavidyalaya Mandal, New Bombay, 1993.

Chatterjee, Chhaya, *Sastriya Sangita and Music Culture of Bengal Through the Ages, Vol.I*, Sharada Publishing House, Delhi, 1996.

Chaudhuri, Shubha, "Aspects of Documentation and Mass Media. A Viewpoint from India." in Baumann, Max Peter (ed.), *World music, musics of the world: aspects of documentation, mass media and acculturation*, Florian Noetzel Verlag, Wilhelmshaven, 1992.

Conlon, Frank F., "Vishnubawa Brahmachari-A Champion of Hinduism in Nineteenth Century Maharashtra", in A.R. Kulkarni and N.K. Wagle (ed.), *Region, Nationality and Religion*, Popular Prakashan, Mumbai, 1999.

Dadar Matunga Cultural Centre Golden Jubilee Souvenir, Bombay, 2003.

Darukhanawala, H.D., *Parsi Lustre on Indian Soil – Vol.I*, G. Claridge & Co., Ltd., Bombay, 1939.

——, *Parsi Lustre on Indian Soil:-Lives and Portraits of Professionals, Historians, Scholars, Educationists, Parsi Religionists, Philanthropists, Politicians, Officials, Reformers, Pioneers, Industrialists, Merchants and others of The Past and Present, Vol.II*, (n.p.), 1963.

——, *Parsis and Sports and Kindred Subjects*, (n.p.), 1935.

Das, Sisir Kumar, *A History of Indian Literature (Volume 8): 1800-1910, Western Impact: Indian Response*, Sahitya Akademi, Reprint, New Delhi, 2005.

Desai Devangana, *Erotic Sculpture of India: A Socio-Cultural Study*, Tata McGraw-Hill Publishing Co., New Delhi, 1975.

Deshpande, Vamanrao H., *Between Two Tanpuras*, (trans. by Ram Deshmukh and B.R. Dhekney from Marathi original *Alapini*, with addition of piece on Bhimsen Joshi), Popular Prakashan, Bombay, 1989.

—— *Indian Musical Traditions: An Aesthetic Study of the Gharanas in Hindustani Music*, Popular Prakashan, Bombay, 2nd revised & enlarged ed., 1987.

—— *Maharashtra's Contribution to Music*, Maharashtra Information Centre, New Delhi, 1972.

Devi Savita, *Maa . . . Siddheshwari*, Lotus Collection Roli Books, New Delhi, 2000.

Dhond, M.V., *The Evolution of Khyal*, Sangeet Natak Akademi, New Delhi, (n.d.).

Dhume, Anant Ramkrishna Sinai, *The cultural history of Goa from 10000 B.C.-1352 A.D.*, the University of Michigan: Ramesh Anant S. Dhume, 1986.

Dutta, K.K., *Survey of India's Social Life and Economic Conditions in the Eighteenth Century, 1707-1813*, Firma K.L. Mukhopadhyay, Calcutta, 1961.

Dyson, Ketaki Kushari, *A Various Universe: A Study of the Journals and Memoirs of British Men and Women in the Indian Subcontinent, 1765-1856*, Oxford University Press, Delhi, 1978.

Eminent Orientalists: Indian, European, American, G.A. Natesan & Co., Madras, 1st edition, (n.d.).

Erdman, Joan L., *Patrons and Performers in Rajasthan: The Subtle Tradition*, Chanakya Publications, Delhi, 1985.

Farooqui, Amar, *Opium City: The Making of Early Victorian Bombay*, Three Essays Collective, Gurgaon, 2006.

Farrell, Gerry, *Indian Music and the West*, Clarendon Press, Oxford, 1997.

Fernandes, Naresh, *Taj Mahal Foxtrot: The Story of Bombay's Jazz Age*, Roli Books, New Delhi, 2012.

Ganguly, Rita, "The Tradition of Thumri", in Mutatkar Sumati (ed.), *Aspects of Indian Music: A Collection of Essays*, Sangeet Natak Akademi, New Delhi, (n.d.).

Great Men and Women of India, Publications Division, Ministry of Information and Broadcasting, Government of India, New Delhi, 1973.

Gordon, A.D.D., *Businessmen and Politics: Rising Nationalism and a Modernising Economy in Bombay, 1918-1933*, Manohar Publications, 1978.

Gorekar, N.S., *Glimpses of Urdu Literature*, Jaico Publishing House, Bombay, 1961.

Jogan, Shankar, *Devadasi Cult: A Sociological Analysis*, Ashish Publishing House, New Delhi, 1990.

King, A.D., "Colonialism and the Development of the Modern South Asian City: Some theoretical considerations", in Ballhatchet Kenneth and Harrison John (ed.), *The City in South Asia: Pre-modern and Modern*, Curzon Press, London, 1980.

Kinnear, Michael S., *The Gramophone Company's First Indian Recordings, 1899-1908*, Popular Prakashan, Bombay, 1994.

——, *Sangeet Ratna – The Jewel of Music: A Bio-Discography of Khan Sahib Abdul Karim Khan*, Author, Heidelberg, Australia, 2003.

Kippen, James, *Gurudev's Drumming Legacy: Music, Theory and Nationalism in the Mrdang aur Tabla Vadanpaddhati of Gurudev Patwardhan*, Ashgate Publishing Limited, Hants, 2006.

Kopf, David, *British Orientalism and the Bengal Renaissance: The Dynamics of Indian Modernization 1773-1835*, University of California Press, Berkeley, 1969.

Kosambi, Meera, *Bombay and Poona: A Socio-Ecological Study of Two Indian Cities 1650-1900*, "author", Stockholm, 1980.

Kulke, Eckehard, *The Parsees in India: Minority as Agent of Social Change*, Vikas Publishing House Pvt. Ltd., Delhi, 1974.

Kumar, Ravinder, *Western India in the Nineteenth Century: A Study in the Social History of Maharashtra*, Routledge & Kegan Paul, London, 1968.

Kumar, Ravindra (Chief Editor), *The Selected Works of Maulana Abul Kalam Azad: Vol.III–1947-48*, Atlantic Publishers & Distributors, New Delhi, 1991.

Kuppuswamy, Gowri and M. Hariharan, *Royal Patronage to Indian Music*, Sundeep Prakashan, Delhi, 1984.

Lad, P.M., *Kashinath Trimbak Telang-1850-1893*, Telang Centenary Celebration Committee, Bombay, 1950.

Lederle Mathew, *Philosophical Trends in Maharashtra*, Popular Prakashan, Bombay, 1976.

Maciszewski, Amelia, "Nayika ki Yadgar: North Indian Women Musicians and Their Words" in Amlan Das Gupta, *Music and Modernity: North Indian Classical Music in an Age of Mechanical Reproduction*, Thema, Kolkata, 2007.

Masselos, J.C., *Towards Nationalism: Group affiliations and the politics of public association in nineteenth century Western India*, Popular Prakashan, Bombay, 1974.

——, *Indian Nationalism: An History*, Sterling Publishers Private Limited, New Delhi, 1985.

McNeil, Adrian, *Inventing the Sarod: The Marketing of a Musical Tradition*, Seagull Publications, Calcutta, 2004.

Menon, Raghava R., *K.L. Saigal: The Pilgrim of the Swara*, Hind Pocket Books (Pvt.) Ltd., 1st paperback ed., Delhi, 1989.

Miner, Allyn, *Sitar and Sarod in the Eighteenth and Nineteenth Centuries*, Motilal Banarsidass, Performing Arts Series 7, Reprint, New Delhi, 1997.

Misra, Susheela, *Great Masters of Hindustani Music*, Hem Publishers Pvt. Ltd., New Delhi, 1981.

—— *Music Makers of the Bhatkhande College of Hindustani Music*, Sangeet Resarch Academy, Calcutta, 1st ed., 1985.

—— *Music Profiles*, (n.p.), 1955.

Mohan, Jag, *Twenty-Five Years of Indian Independence*, Vikas Publishing House Pvt. Ltd, Delhi, 1973.

Mujawar, Isak, *Maharashtra: Birthplace of Indian Film Industry*, Government of Maharashtra, Bombay, 1965.

Mujeeb, M., *The Indian Muslims*, George Allen & Unwin Ltd., London, Second Impression, 1969.

Mujtabai, Fathullah, *Aspects of Hindu Muslim Cultural Relations*, National Book Bureau, New Delhi, 1978.

Mukerji, Dhurjati Prasad, *Modern Indian Culture: A Sociological Study*, India Publishers, Allahabad, 1942.

Mukherjee, Bimal, "Jaipur Binkar/Sitar Gharana", in *Seminar on Sitar*, Sangeet Research Academy, 1990.

Mutatkar, Sumati, "Music and the Radio (looking Back and Beyond)", in *Akashwani Sangeet Sammelan 1998* brochure, Prasar Bharati Broadcasting Corporation of India, Ministry of Information & Broadcasting, Government of India, New Delhi, 1998.

Naik, J.V., "Intellectual Basis and Ideological Premises of Maharashtrian Response to British Colonial Rule", in Heidrich Joachim (ed.), *Changing Identities: The transformation of Asian and African societies under colonialism, Studien 1*, Verlag Das Arabische Buch, Berlin, 1994.

—— "Perceptions of the British Rule in Maharashtra: A Selective Study", in Quaisar, A.J. and Verma, S.P. (ed.), *Art and Culture: Endeavours in Interpretation*, Abhinav Publication, New Delhi, 1996.

—— "The Seed Period of Bombay's Intellectual Life, 1822-1857" in Patel Sujata and Thorner Alice (ed.), *Bombay: Mosaic of Modern Culture*, Oxford University Press, Bombay, paperback edition, 1996.

Naik, Vasant N., *Kashinath Trimbak Telang*, G.A. Natesan & Co., Madras, (n.d.).

Nayar, Sobhana, *Bhatkhande's Contribution to Music*, Popular Prakashan, Bombay, 1989.

Neuman, Daniel M., *The Life of Music in North India: The Organisation of an Artistic Tradition*, Manohar Publications, New Delhi, 1980.

O'Hanlon, Rosalind, "Historical approaches to communalism: perspectives from Western India" in Peter Robb (ed.) in collaboration with Chaudhuri, K.N. and Avril Powell, *Society and Ideology: Essays in South Asian History*, Oxford University Press, Second Impression, Delhi, 1994.

Patel, Sujata and Alice Thorner (ed.), Bombay: *Mosaic of Modern Culture*, Oxford University Press, Delhi, 1995.

——, *Bombay: Mosaic of Modern Culture*, Oxford University Press, Bombay, paperback edition, 1996.

Panikkar, K.N., Presidential Address, Section III: *Modern India, Proceedings of the Indian History Congress*, 36th Session, Aligarh, 1975.

Past Times, The Times of India Sesquicentennial Publication, 1992.

Pinto, Jerry and Naresh Fernandes (eds.), *Bombay Meri Jaan*, Penguin Books India, New Delhi, 2003.

Pradhan, Aneesh, "Cultural Interaction and Social Change: The Contribution of the Parsi Gayan Uttejak Mandali to North Indian art music in Mumbai", in Dossal Miriam and Maloni Ruby (ed.), *State Intervention and Popular Response*, Popular Prakashan, Mumbai, 1998.

—— "Music from North India: The Dynamics of Changing Traditions and Trends" in *Pathfinders: A Journey through Art & Culture over the last sixty years of the Indian Republic*, Ace Publications and Promotions Pvt. Ltd., Mumbai, 2010.

—— *Tabla: A Performer's Perspective*, "author", Mumbai, 2011.

Punekar, S.D., and Kamala Rao, *A Study of Prostitutes in Bombay (With reference to Family Background)*, Allied Publishers Private Limited, Bombay, 1962.

Purohit, Vinayak, *Arts of Transitional India: Twentieth Century, Vol.2*, Popular Prakashan Pvt. Ltd., Bombay, 1988.

Qureshi, Regula Burkhardt, *Sufi Music of India and Pakistan: sound, context and meaning in Qawwali*, University of Chicago Press, Chicago, 1995.

Raghuvanshi, V.P.S., *Indian Society in the Eighteenth Century*, Associated Publishing House, New Delhi, 1969.

Rai, Alok, *Hindi Nationalism*, Orient Longman Private Limited, (Reprint), Hyderabad, 2002.

Ranade, Ashok Da., *Indology and Ethnomusicology: Contours of the Indo-British Relationship*, Promilla & Co., Publishers, New Delhi, 1992.

—— *On Music and Musicians of Hindoostan*, Promilla and Co., Publishers, New Delhi, 1984.

—— *Stage Music of Maharashtra*, Sangeet Natak Akademi, New Delhi, 1986.

—— *Maharashtra: Art Music*, Maharashtra Information Centre, Government of Maharashtra, New Delhi, 1989.

—— *Hindi Film Song: Music Beyond Boundaries*, Promilla & Co., Publishers, New Delhi, 2006.

—— *Some Hindustani Musicians: They Lit The Way!*, Promilla and Co., Publishers, in association with Bibliophile South Asia, New Delhi, 2011.

Rangoonwalla, Firoze, *Indian Filmography, Silent and Hindi Films 1897-1969*, Bombay, 1970.

Rao, N. Jayavanth, *Sajan Piya: A biography of Ustad Khadim Husain Khan*, Sajan Milap, Bombay, 1981.

Rao, Suvarnalata and Wim van der Meer, "The Construction, Reconstruction, and Deconstruction of Shruti" in Bor Joep, Delvoye, Françoise "Nalini", Harvey Jane, te Nijenhuis, Emmie (eds.), *Hindustani Music – Thirteenth to Twentieth Centuries*, Codarts and Manohar, New Delhi, 2010.

Rao, V.K.R.V., "Dadabhai Naoroji", in Zakaria Rafiq (ed.), *100 Glorious Years*, Reception Committee of the Congress Centenary Session, Bombay, 1985.

Ratanjankar, S.N., *Pandit Bhatkhande*, National Book Trust, India, New Delhi, 1967.

Ray, Sukumar, *Music of Eastern India: Vocal Music in Bengali, Oriya, Assamese and Manipuri with special emphasis on Bengali*, Firma K.L.M. Private Limited, Calcutta, 2nd ed., 1985.

Rosse, Michael D., "Music Schools and Societies in Bombay c.1864-1937" in Bor Joep, Delvoye, Francoise 'Nalini', Harvey Jane and te Nijenhuis Emmie, *Hindustani Music: Thirteenth to Twentieth Centuries*, Manohar Publishers & Distributors, New Delhi, 2010.

Satow, Michael and Desmond Ray, *Railways of the Raj*, Scolar Press, London, 1980.

Singer, Milton, *When a Great Tradition Modernizes: An Anthropological Approach to Indian Civilization*, Vikas Publishing House Pvt. Ltd., Delhi, 1972.

Spear, Percival, *A History of India – Volume Two*, Penguin Books, London, 1990.

Srinivas, M.N., *Social Change in Modern India*, Orient Longman, Bombay, 1972.

Srivastava, S.K. (ed.), *Tradition and Modernization*, Indian International Publications, Allahabad, 1976.

Stokes, Eric, *The English Utilitarians and India*, Oxford University Press, Delhi, 1982.

Subramanian, Lakshmi, *From the Tanjore Court to the Madras Music Academy: A Social History of Music in South India*, Oxford University Press, New Delhi, 2006.

Umar, Muhammad, *Urban Culture in Northern India during the eighteenth century*, Munshiram Manoharlal Publishers Pvt. Ltd., Delhi, 2001.

Woodfield, Ian, *Music of the Raj: A Social and Economic History of Music in Late Eighteenth Century Anglo-Indian Society*, Oxford University Press, Oxford, 2000.

MARATHI

Primary Sources

Acharya, Balkrishna Bapu, and Shinge, Moro Vinayak, *Mumbaichaa vritaant* (ed. Naik Bapurao), Maharashtra Rajya Sahitya Ani Sanskriti Mandal, Mumbai, 1980.

Bhatkhande, Vishnu Narayan, *Hindusthaanee sangeet paddhati: kramik pustakmaalikaa, paheele pustak,* (ed. Shivram, Pt. Vadilal, Ratanjankar, Shrikrishna Narayan and Sukthankar, Bhalchandra Seetaram), "Dr. Malinibai Bhalchandra Sukthankar", Mumbai, 9th ed., 1940.

—— *Hindusthaanee sangeet paddhati kramik pustakmaalikaa: chouthe pustak*, (ed. "Bhalchandra Seetaram Sukthankar"), Mumbai, 3rd ed., 1939.

—— *Hindusthanee sangeet paddhati kramik pustakmaalikaa, paachve pustak*, (ed. Shrikrishna Narayan Ratanjankar, Vadilal Shivram, and co-ed. "Bhalchandra Seetaram Sukthankar"), Mumbai, 1st ed., 1937.

—— *Hindusthanee sangeet paddhati kramik pustakmaalikaa, sahaave pustak*, (ed. Shrikrishna Narayan Ratanjankar, Vadilal Shivram and co-ed. "Bhalchandra Seetaram Sukthankar"), Mumbai, 1937.

Deodhar, B.R., "School of Indian Music", *Deodhar's School of Indian Music, Golden Jubilee Souvenir*, Mumbai, 1975.

Eklavya, *Sangeetache maankaree*, G.P.Parchure Prakashan-Mandir, Mumbai, 1st ed., 1949.

Gaayanprakaar praarambhee, (n.p.), Mumbai, 1862.

Joshi, Narayan Vishnu, *Pune shaharaache varnan*, "author", Mumbai, 1868.

Kalyan Gayan Samaj: Amrut Mahotsav (1926-2001), Kalyan Gayan Samaj, Kalyan, 2001.

Kelkar, S.V., *Bharat Gaayan Samaaj, Pune: san 1911 te 1940 yaa kaalkhandaateel saunsthyechaa itihaas*, Pune Bharat Gayan Samaj, Pune, 1965.

Khan, Allauddin, *Majhee kahaanee* (trans. from Bengali by Shahane Ashok; Bengali version - Ghosh Shubhamaya, *Amar kathaa-anulekhan)*, by "author", Mumbai, pahili khep ashadhi 1900.

'Lokhitwadi', Gopal Hari Deshmukh, "*Sangeetshastra*" in Anant Kakba Priyolkar (ed.), *Lokhitwadikrit Nibandhsangraha: Gopal Hari Deshmukh*, (Marathi), Popular Prakashan, Mumbai, 1996.

Madgavkar, Govind Narayan, *Mumbaiche varnan*, Itihas Sanshodhan Mandal, Mumbai Marathi Granth Sangrahalaya, Mumbai, 1961.

Mahatme, Suryaji Sadashiv, and Kale, Vishwanath Ramchandra, *Tantuvaadya: sataar shiknyaache paheele pustak*, (Marathi), "authors", 2nd edition, Mumbai, 1881.

Muzumdar, Anupama (ed.), *Swarsangat Sardar*, Pratap Narayan Muzumdar, Pune, n.d.

Tembe, Govindrao, *Maazhaa sangeet vyaasang*, (Marathi), Maharashtra Rajya Sahitya Sanskriti Mandal, Mumbai, 2nd ed., 1984.

Vishnusharma, P., *Hindusthaanee sangeetpaddhati: bhaag dusraa*, "Bhalchandra Seetaram Sukthankar", Mumbai, 1914.

Secondary Sources

Bakre, Ramkrishna, *Buzurg*, Sadhana Prakashan, Pune, 1990.

Date, Shankar Ganesh and others (ed.), *Marathi niyatkaalikaanchi soochee (1800 to 1950)*, Mumbai Marathi Granth Sangrahalaya, Mumbai, 1969.

David, M.D., *Aik Mumbai tujhee kahaanee*, (Marathi-trans. Purshottam Dhakras), Priyank Prakashan, Thane, 1993.

Deodhar, B.R., *Gaayanaachaarya P. Vishnu Digambar*, Akhil Bharatiya Gandharva Mahavidyalaya Mandal, Mumbai, 1971.

——, *Thor sangeetkaar*, Akhil Bharatiya Gandharva Mahavidyalaya Mandal, Mumbai, 1973.

Deshpande, Baburao, "*Rangabhoomisaathi zhapaatlelaa avaliyaa*" in *Lokaraajya*, Sangeetsoorya Shri Keshavrao Bhosale Visheshaank – August 1990, (Marathi), Mahaasanchaalak, Maahiti va janasamparka mahaasanchaalaya, Maharashtra Shaasan, Mumbai, 1990.

Joshi, D.P., *Kaalaachyaa paddyaad, Vol.1*, Marathi Sahitya Parishad, Andhra Pradesh, Hyderabad, 1992.

Kanvalil, Sadanand, *Mallikarjun Mansoor*, (Marathi translation by Prabhakar Deshpande), Satyajit Prakashan, Mumbai, 1993.

Kapileshwari, Balkrishnabuwa, *Shrutidarshan*, Continental Prakashan, Pune, 1963.

Karandikar, J.S. (ed.), *Shreeganeshotsavaachee saath varshe*, "author", Pune, 1953.

Karnatki, Shrinivas Narayan, *Naamdaar Nyaayamurtee Kashinath Trimbak Telang yaanche charitra*, Bharat-Gaurav-Granthmala, Mumbai, 1929.

Kelkar, S.V., *Bharat Gayan Samaj, Pune: San 1911 te 1940 yaa kaalkhandaateel sansthechaa itihaas*, (Marathi), Pune Bharat Gayan Samaj Prakashan, Pune, n.d.

Kunte, Chaitanya, "*Punyachya sangeetparamparecha ek aitihasik vedh*" in *Punyaswar*, Lalit Kala Kendra, Pune University, Pune, 2009.

Mulgaonkar, Arvind, *Tabla*, Popular Prakashan, Mumbai, 2nd ed., 1999.

Pune Bharat Gayan Samaj va Bhaskar Sangeet Vidyalaya: vaarshik vritant (1 April, 1989, to 31 March, 1990), Pune, 1990.

Pune Swarvishwa '90: Sangeet Mehfil 19 May 1990, Rotary Club of Pune, Parvati, 1990.

Satoskar, B.D., *Gomaantak: prakriti aani sanskriti, Vol 1–Samaaj rachanaa va samaaj jeevan*, Shubhada-Saraswat, Pune, 1979.

Tembe, Govindrao, *Gaayanmaharshi Alladiyakhan yaanche charitra*, (ed. Vamanrao Deshpande and Baburao Joshi), Maharashtra Rajya Sahitya Sanskriti Mandal, 2nd ed., Mumbai, 1984.

HINDI

Primary Sources

Bhatkhande, P. Vishnu Narayan ('Vishnu Sharma'), *Bhatkhande sangeet-shaastra [Hindusthaanee sangeeta-paddhati] [bhaag 1]*, (Hindi translation- Bhatt Vishwambharnath and Dubey Sudamaprasad), Sangeet Karyalaya, 5th ed., Hathras, 1981.

Bhatkhande, P. Vishnu Narayan (Vishnu Sharma), *Bhatkhande-sangeetshaastra [Hindusthaanee sangeet-paddhati] [Triteeya bhaag]*, (Hindi translation-Garg Prabhulal and ed. Garg Laxminarayan), Sangeet Karyalaya, 5th ed., Hathras, 1981.

Jaini, Mister S.P. (compiled by), *Hindi gramophone record sangeet-Pratham bhaag*, "author", Calcutta, n.d.

Khan, Mohammad Hussein, *Upaj: Shabd evam swirararachanaa*, "author", Pune, 1981.

Khan, Vilayat Hussein, *Sangeetagyon ke sansmaran*, Sangeet Natak Akademi, New Delhi, 1959.

Malpekar, Anjanibai, "*Hum gaayakon ka bhaagya khul gayaa*", in *Bhatkhande smriti granth*, Indira Kala Sangeet Vishwavidyalaya, Khairagarh, M.P., 1966.

Patwardhan, Shrimaan Gurudev, *Mridang aur tabla vaadan paddhati: mridang aur tablekaa prathambhaag*, (Hindi), Author, Bombay, 1910.

Vasudev, Sv. Dattatreya, alias Gurudev Patwardhan, *Mridang-tabla vaadan-paddhati*, (Hindi), Sangeet Natak Akademi, New Delhi, 1962.

Secondary Sources

Chinchore, P.N., "*Sangeetoddhaarak P. Bhatkhande meri drishti mein*", (Hindi), in *Bhatkhande smriti granth*, Indira Kala Sangeet Vishwavidyalaya, Khairagarh, MP, 1966.

Deodhar, B.R., "*Do Vishnu ki char bhujaaon*", in *Bhatkhande smriti granth*, Indira Kala Sangeet Vishwavidyalaya, Khairagarh, M.P., 1966.

Garg, Laxminarayan, *Hamaare sangeet ratna*, (*pratham bhaag*), Sangit Karyalaya, Hathras, 1957.

Ranade, G.H., "*Sangeet ke aadhunik Bheeshmaachaarya*" in *Bhatkhande smriti granth*, Indira Kala Sangeet Vishwavidyalaya, Khairagarh, M.P., 1966.

Ratanjankar, Shree Shreenath, "*Sw. Alladiya Khan Saheb*", reprinted in *Alladiya Khan*, Shruti Mandal, 1994.

Ratanjankar, S.N., "*Jeevan Charitra*", in *Bhatkhande smriti granth*, Indira Kala Sangeet Vishwavidyalaya, Khairagarh, M.P., 1966.

Shukla N., "*Maine unhe mehfil mein gaate hue sunaa hai*", in *Bhatkhande smriti granth*, Indira Kala Sangeet Vishwavidyalaya, Khairagarh, M.P., 1966.

Vyas, Madanlal, "*Bahumukhee pratibhaa ke dhanee Master Navrang*", in *Dr. Navrang Nagpurkar Amruta Mahotsava* souvenir, Mumbai, 1994.

GUJARATI

Primary Sources

Batliwala, Firozeshah Rustamjee, *Sarode avastaa*, (n.p.), Mumbai, 1886.

Bhatkhande, Mr. Vishnu Narayan, *Swar maalikaa*, Mumbai Gayan Uttejak Mandali, Mumbai, 1909.

Gayan Uttejak Mandali: taa. 28 mee April 1871 thee taa 18 mee December 1886 sudhee jalsaaomaa gawaaelaa gaayanono sangraha, Gayan Uttejak Mandali, Mumbai, 1887.

Kapadia, Pestanjee Firozeshah, *Gayan Uttejak Mandali: tenee ponee sadinee tawaareekhno ahewaal*, "Mrs. Freni M. Cama", Mumbai, 1946.

Mistry M. and Mapla, *Odeon: Gujarati ane Hindustaanee navin catalogue, Odeon Electric Records*, Ruby Record Co., Mumbai, January 1935.

Patel, Dhanjeebhai N., *Parsi natak takhtaanee tavaareekh: gayi sadinaa gujar paamelaa Parsi actoro*, Kaiser-Hind, Mumbai, 1931.

Patell, Bomanjee Byramjee, *Parsi Prakaash, Vol.II*, "Dinbai Byramjee Patell", Mumbai, 1910.

Doctoral Dissertations

Albuquerque, Teresa, *History of Bombay 1840-1865*, University of Bombay, 1980.

Chari, Nithya K., *History of Bombay 1918-1939*, University of Bombay, 1983.

Kobayashi, Eriko, *Hindustani Classical Music Reform Movement and the Writing of History, 1900s to 1940s*, The University of Texas at Austin, Austin, 2003.

McNeil, Adrian, *The Dynamics of Social and Musical Status in Hindustani Music: Sarodiyas, Seniyas and the Margi-Desi Paradigm*, Department of Music, Monash University, Melbourne, 1992.

Mehta, Kumudini A., *English Drama on the Bombay Stage in the late Eighteenth Century and in the Nineteenth Century*, University of Bombay, March 1960.

Quinn, Jennifer Post, *Marathi and Konkani speaking women in Hindustani music, 1880-1940,* University of Minnesota, UMI Dissertation Information Service, University Microfilms International, Ann Arbor, Michigan, June 1982.

Rao, Pragnya Ram, *History of Bombay 1818-1840*, University of Bombay, 1975.

Rosse, Michael David, *The Movement for the Revitalization of "Hindu" Music in Northern India, 1860-1930: The Role of Associations and Institutions*, University of Pennsylvania, Philadelphia, 1995.

Shroff, Zenobia E., *Contribution of the Parsis to the Development of Education and Social Change in Bombay City (1820-1920)*, Dept. of History, Wilson College, Bombay, 1987.

Lexicons

Molesworth, J.T. (comp.), *A Dictionary, Marathi and English*, Asian Educational Services, 2nd ed. (reprint), New Delhi, 1989.

Scholes, Percy A., *The Oxford Companion To Music*, Oxford University Press, London, 10th ed., 1970.

Joshi, Shripad and Gorekar, N.S., (ed.), *Urdu-Marathi Shabdkosh*, Maharashtra Rajya Sahitya-sanskriti Mandal, 1st ed., Mumbai, 1968.

Ranade, Ashok Da., *Music Contexts: A Concise Dictionary of Hindustani Music*, Promilla & Co., Publishers in association with Bibliophile South Asia, New Delhi, 2006.

Periodicals

Aslesha, Ram, "Seshadri Gawai", *Shruti*, Issue 81/82, Madras.

Aslesha, Ram & K.R. Rajagopalan, "The Harmonium in Indian Music", *Shruti*, Issue 81/82, Madras.

A.S.S., "Harmonium's Popularity in North India", *Shruti*, Issue 81/82, Madras.

Atre, Prabha, "*Hirabai Badodekar*", *Ravivarchi Loksatta*, Mumbai, 25 May 1980.

Baskaran, S. Theodore, "Music for the Masses: Film Songs of Tamil Nadu", *Economic and Political Weekly*, Vol.XXVI Nos.11 and 12, Annual Number 1991, Sameeksha Trust, Bombay, 1991.

Bokil, Jayashree, "*Bharat Samaajaachi Navvadi*", *Loksatta*, October 15, 2000.

Bor, Joep, *The Voice of the Sarangi: An Illustrated history of bowing in India*, National Centre for the Performing Arts, Quarterly Journal, Vol.XV, 324; Vol. XVI, 1, Sept., Dec.'86 and March '87.

Bose, Sunil, "Thumri in Hindustani Music", *Sangeet Kala Vihar-Indian Music Quarterly English Supplement, Vol.1. No.2*, April-June 1970.

Capwell, Charles, "Sourindro Mohun Tagore and the National Anthem Project", *Ethnomusicology*, Fall 1987.

—— "Musical Life in Nineteenth-Century Calcutta as a Component in the History of a Secondary Urban Center", *Asian Music, Vol. 18, No. 1 (Autumn-Winter, 1986)*, University of Texas Press, Austin, 1986.

Chandavarkar, Bhaskar, "The Great Film Song Controversy", *Cinema Vision, Vol.1, No.4*, October 1980.

Chandvankar, Suresh, "*Thumriche Badshah: Moujuddin Khan*", *Sangeet Kala Vihar*, Akhil Bharatiya Gandharva Mahavidyalaya Mandal, Miraj, March 1994.

—— "*Pahile sangeet digdarshak*", *Loksatta*, September 16, 2001.

—— "Mogubai Kurdikar (1904-2001)", *The Record News: The Journal of the Society of Indian Record Collectors*, TRN 2001, Bombay.

Charankar, Bhanu, "*Gelya dashakaateel sangeet kshetraateel padzhad*", *Naadbrahma*, Madhavi Prakashan, Mumbai, January 1994.

Deodhar, B.R., "*Sangeet-sevak Shriman Damodardas Khanna, Calcutta*", *Sangeet Kala Vihar, Varsha 8, Ank 3,* March 1955, Gandharva Mahavidyalaya Mandal, 1955.

Dighe, V.G., "The Renaissance in Maharashtra: First Phase (1818-1870)", *Journal of the Asiatic Society of Bombay, New Series, Vols.36-37*, 1961-62.

Diwanji, Batuk, "*Ek sangeetkaarnee nondhpothee*", *Navneet Samarpan*, Bharatiya Vidya Bhavan, April 2000.

Gopujkar, Pratibha, "*Hirabai Badodekar*", *Loksatta*, Mumbai, 15 April 2000.

"Gramophone Celebrities – 14 – J.F. Madan: Lover of Theater", *The Record News: The Journal of the Society of Indian Record Collectors*, Volume – Annual: TRN 2006, Mumbai, 2006.

Head, Raymond, "Corelli in Calcutta: Colonial music-making in India during the 17th and 18th centuries", *Early Music, 13(4)*, Oxford University Press, November 1985.

Humane, Rajaram, "*Adhyayanaache zhapaatlele divas*", *Ravivarchi Loksatta*, Mumbai, 25 May 1980.

Jadhav, Narayan R., "Textile workers' theatre: a cultural perspective", *Facts & News*, No.14, National Centre for the Performing Arts Project: Theatre Development Centre, Bombay, 1989.

Journal of the Sangeet Natak Akademi-20, New Delhi, April-June 1971.

Karnad, Vasant, "Meet the Mercurial Mr. Madhu Master", *Cinema Vision India, Vol. 2 No. 2, ISSN 0250-6998*, Cinema Vision India, Bombay, January 1983.

Khadilkar, Mangala, "*Gaansaadhikaa Anjanibai Malpekar*", *Maharashtra Times*, Mumbai, 23 April 2000.

Kinikar, Shashikant, "Lasting Lady, Khurshi-Saraswati", *Cinema Vision India, Vol. 2 No. 2, ISSN 0250-6998*, Cinema Vision India, Bombay, January 1983.

Kinnear, Michael S., "Reading Indian Record Labels: Part One – "GRAMOPHONE" and ZONOPHONE records", *The Record News: The Journal of the Society of Indian Record Collectors*, Vol.1, Bombay, January 1991.

—— "Reading Indian Record Labels: "RAMAGRAPH" – The History of the RAM-A-PHONE and RAMA-GRAPH disc records", *The Record News: The Journal of the Society of Indian Record Collectors*, Vol.20, Bombay, October 1995.

—— "Kesarbai Kerkar: Discography", *The Record News: The Journal of the Society of Indian Record Collectors, Vol. 11*, Bombay, July 1993.

Kramisch, Stella, "Artist, Patron, and Public in India", *Far Eastern Quarterly XV*, 1955-1956.

Lamb, Helen B., "The Indian Business Communities and the Evolution of an Industrialist Class", *Pacific Affairs, Vol.XXVIII, No.2*, June 1955, Institute of Pacific Relations, New York.

Mani, V.S., "Subrahmania Dikshitar", *Shruti*, Issue 81/82, Madras.

Marulkar, Datta, "*Gaantapasvinee*", *Loksatta*, Mumbai, 10 july 1993.

Marulkar, N.R., "*Aajche shikshan-satra aani tyaachee saangataa*", *Sangeet Kala Vihar, Varsha 8, Ank 3*, Gandharva Mahavidyalaya Mandal, Miraj, March 1955.

Masselos, Jim, "Spare Time and Recreation: Changing Behaviour Patterns in Bombay at the turn of the nineteenth century", *South Asia: Journal of South Asian Studies, New Series Vol. VII, No.1*, June 1984.

Miner, Allyn, "The sitar: an Overview of Change", *the world of music, le monde de la musique, die welt der musik India*, Journal of the International Institute for Comparative Music Studies and Documentation (Berlin), Vol.XXXII, No.2-1990.

Misra, Smt. Susheela, "The Thumri", *Sangeet Research Academy Journal, Vol.2 No.1*, September 1981.

Murthy, H.V. Krishna, "A. Arunachalappa", *Shruti*, Issue 81/82, Madras.

Nadkarni, Mohan, "Harmonium & Raga Music: A Critical Look", *Shruti*, Issue 81/82, Madras.

——, "Musical literature in Maharashtra", *Indian Express*, Bombay, 10 July 1990.

Naik, J.V., "An Early Appraisal of the British Colonial Policy", *Journal of the University of Bombay, Arts No. Vol.XLIV & XLV No.80-81*, 1975-76.

—— "Early Anti-Caste Movement in Western India: The Paramhansa Sabha", Kulkarni, V.M. (ed.), *Journal of the Asiatic Society of Bombay*, Asiatic Society of Bombay, Bombay, 1979.

—— "Raja Rammohun Roy, Swami Dayananda Saraswati and Indian Renaissance", Bhattacharjee, Nirmal Kanti (ed.), *Granthana: Indian Journal of Library Studies*, Quarterly Vol.1, Number 2, January-March 2005.

Pradhan Aneesh, "The Emergence of Modern Concert Platform in Bombay", *Journal of the Indian Musicological Society, Vol.25*, Baroda, Jan.-Dec.1994.

—— "Perspectives on Performance Practice: Hindustani Music in Nineteenth and Twentieth Century Bombay (Mumbai)", *South Asia: Journal of South Asian Studies, n.s., Vol.XXVII, no.3, December 2004*, Carfax Publishing, Taylor and Francis Group.

Pradhan, Aneesh with additional inputs from Shubha Mudgal, "Institutionalized Music Education in North India: Some observations", in *Sangeet Natak, Vol XLIII, Number 2*, 2009, Sangeet Natak Akademi, New Delhi, 2009.

Raghunathji, K., "Bombay Dancing Girls", Jas. Burgess, *The Indian Antiquary: A Journal of Oriental Research, Vol.XIII-1884*, reprinted by Swati Publications, Delhi, 1984.

Ranade, Ashok D., "Categories of Music", *National Centre For The Performing Arts, Quarterly Journal, Vol.XIV, No.4*, Mumbai, December 1985.

—— "Reflections on Musicology and History", Special Issue of *Journal of the Indian Musicological Society*, Volume 31, Indian Musicological Society, January-December 2000, Baroda.

Redfiled Robert, "The Social Organization of Tradition", *Far Eastern Quarterly XV, 1.*

Anandhi, S. "Representing Devadasis: 'Dasigal Mosavalai' as a Radical Text", *Economic and Political Weekly*, Vol.XXVI Nos.11 and 12, Annual Number 1991, Sameeksha Trust, Bombay, 1991.

Saberwal, Satish, "Segmentation and Literacy", *Economic and Political Weekly*, Vol.XXVI Nos.11 and 12, Annual Number 1991, Sameeksha Trust, Bombay, 1991.

Sangeet Kala Vihar, Varsha 8, Ank 3, Gandharva Mahavidyalaya Mandal, Miraj, March 1955,

Sastry, B.V.K., "H.K. Seshagiri Rao", *Shruti*, Issue 81/82, Madras.

Sethuraman, R., "Ghulam Rasul Khan", *Shruti*, Issue 81/82, Madras.

Shirgaonkar, Kunda A., "*Sangeetkaaraanchi kadarkartee*", *Loksatta*, Mumbai, 21 December 1996.

—— "*75 varshaanpurviche Mumbaiteel sangeet kendra*", *Sanj Loksatta*, Mumbai, 20 December 1996.

Singer, Milton, "The Great Tradition in a Metropolitan Center: Madras", Singer Milton (ed.), *Traditional India: Structure and Change*, The American Folklore Society, Philadelphia, 1959.

Singh, Jaideva, "The Evolution of Thumri", *National Centre For The Performing Arts- Quarterly Journal, Volume V, Number 2*, June 1976.

Srinivas, M.N., "A Note on Sanskritization and Westernization", *Far Eastern Quarterly XV, 4*, 1955.

"*S.S.C. cha 1959 March paasoon amlaat yenaaraa sangeetaachaa navaa kaaryakram*", *Sangeet Kala Vihar, Varsha 11, Ank 8*, Gandharva Mahavidyalaya Mandal, Miraj, August 1958.

Tapas, Vijay, "*Gaanyachaa aarsaa*", *Loksatta*, Mumbai, 30 May 1993.

The Bombay Courier, Tuesday, 21 April 1834, Vol.XLII, No.2329.

The Record News: The Journal of the Society of Indian Record Collectors, Volume – Annual: TRN 2006, Mumbai, 2006.

The Record News, Society of Indian Record Collectors, Volume: Annual, TRN 2010, Mumbai, 2010.

The Times of India, Bombay, January 11, 1952, p.7.

Tyabji, F.B., "Social Life in 1804 and 1929 amongst Muslims in Bombay", *Journal of the Bombay Branch of the Royal Asiatic Society, New Series, Vol.VI*, London, 1930.

Whitehead, Clive, "The Historiography of British Imperial education policy, Part I: India", *History of Education, May, 2005, Vol.34, No.3, Journal of the History of Education Society*, tandfonline, October 30, 2013.

Web sources

Frembgen, Jürgen Wasim, "The Scorpion in Muslim Folklore", *Asian Folklore Studies, Volume 63, 2004*, http://nirc.nanzan-u.ac.jp/nfile/631, October 31, 2013.

http://www.devalclub.org/history.htm

http://www.kalyangayansamaj.org/kgsaboutus_eng.html

http://wahiduddin.net/mv2/bio/Biography_3.htm

http://www.bpedia.org/T_0019.php

http://www.banglapedia.org/HT/G_0176.HTM

http://harballabh.org/home.html

http://www.zanduayurveda.com/about-us/history.php

http://www.gajananbuwajoshi.com/anant_manohar_joshi

http://www.tajmahalfoxtrot.com/?p=685

http://en.wikipedia.org/wiki/Alois_Hába

http://tardis.dl.ac.uk/FreeReed/organ_book/node22.html

https://itunes.apple.com/in/album/the-genius-of-thirakwa/id212633255

http://www.youtube.com/watch?v=IKw8ZTicp1M

http://www.youtube.com/watch?v=StWrVL6SHL4

http://www.mu.ac.in/arts/finearts/music/profile.html

Audio albums

Sanchay: Bandish Sangraha, Underscore Records Private Limited, New Delhi, 2007.

Interviews

Interviews with Sharad R. Mehta, music lover, held on 29 April 1992 and 25 May 1992, and from private conversation with him on 7 January 1993.

Interviews with Batuk Diwanji, music lover and critic, held in January 1993, and on 24 August, 18 September and 21 September 1992.

Interview with Shalini Narvekar, vocalist, held on 14 December 1992.

Interview with Kausalya Manjeshwar, vocalist, and Dinker Manjeshwar, connoisseur, on 10 September 1993.

Interview with Arvind Mulgaonkar, scholar in the field of *tabla*, on 4 January 1993.

Interview with Abdul Halim Jaffer Khan, *sitar* player, held on 6 May 1997.

Interview with Purushottam Walawalkar, harmonium player, held on 9-11 October 1992.

Personal communication from Mohini Mundkur, Lila Mundkur's daughter-in-law, through Kishore Udipi on 15 January 2000.

Personal communication from Suresh Chandvankar in September 2004 and March 2006.

INDEX

Musicians and music educationists in Bombay

Tanras Khan
(Source: Vajahat Hussain Khan)

Balkrishnabuwa Ichalkaranjikar

Nazir Khan Bhendibazaarwale
(Source: Rohit Desai)

Aman Ali Khan Bhendibazaarwale
(Source: Rohit Desai)

Natthan Khan Agrewale
(Source: Rohit Desai)

Alladiya Khan
(Source: Rohit Desai)

Seated from left to right: Azmat Hussain Khan, Alladiya Khan and Natthan Khan
(Source: Vajahat Hussain Khan)

Manji Khan
(Source: Rohit Desai)

Bhurji Khan
(Source: Rohit Desai)

Bhaskarbuwa Bakhale
(Source: Rohit Desai)

Faiyaz Khan
(Source: Vajahat Hussain Khan)

Abdul Karim Khan
(Source: Rohit Desai)

Vilayat Hussain Khan
(Source: Vajahat Hussain Khan)

Khadim Hussain Khan

Ramkrishnabuwa Vaze
(Source: Rohit Desai)

Rajab Ali Khan
(Source: Rohit Desai)

Moujuddin Khan (Source: Rohit Desai)

Mogubai Kurdikar
(Source: Kausalya and Dinker Manjeshwar)

Anjanibai Malpekar
(Source: Rohit Desai)

Kesarbai Kerkar
(Source: Suresh Chandwankar)

Kesarbai Kerkar in performance
accompanied by Yeshwant Kerkar (tabla) and Pandharinath Kale (harmonium)
(Source: Sudhir Nayak)

Shrimatibai Narvekar
(Source: Rohit Desai)

Vishnu Narayan Bhatkhande
(Source: Rohit Desai)

Vishnu Digambar Paluskar
(Source: Rohit Desai)

S.N. Ratanjankar
(Source: Rohit Desai)

Munir Khan
(Source: Gert M. Wegner)

Omkarnath Thakur
(Source: Rohit Desai)

Ahmed Jan Thirakwa
(Source: Arvind Mulgaonkar)

Amir Hussein Khan
(Source: Arvind Mulgaonkar)

Bharatiya Sangeet Kalakar Mandal, 1953

From left to right: Arvind Parikh, Lakshman Kalgutkar, Anant Bellare, Kausalya Manjeshwar, Nalini Mulgaonkar, Sushil Kavalekar, Justice Vyas, B.R. Deodhar, Narayanrao Vyas, Amir Hussain Khan, Alla Rakha, Balkrishnabuwa Kapileshwari, Yashwant Purohit, Firoz Dastoor, Mahadev Indorkar

(Source: Kausalya and Dinker Manjeshwar)

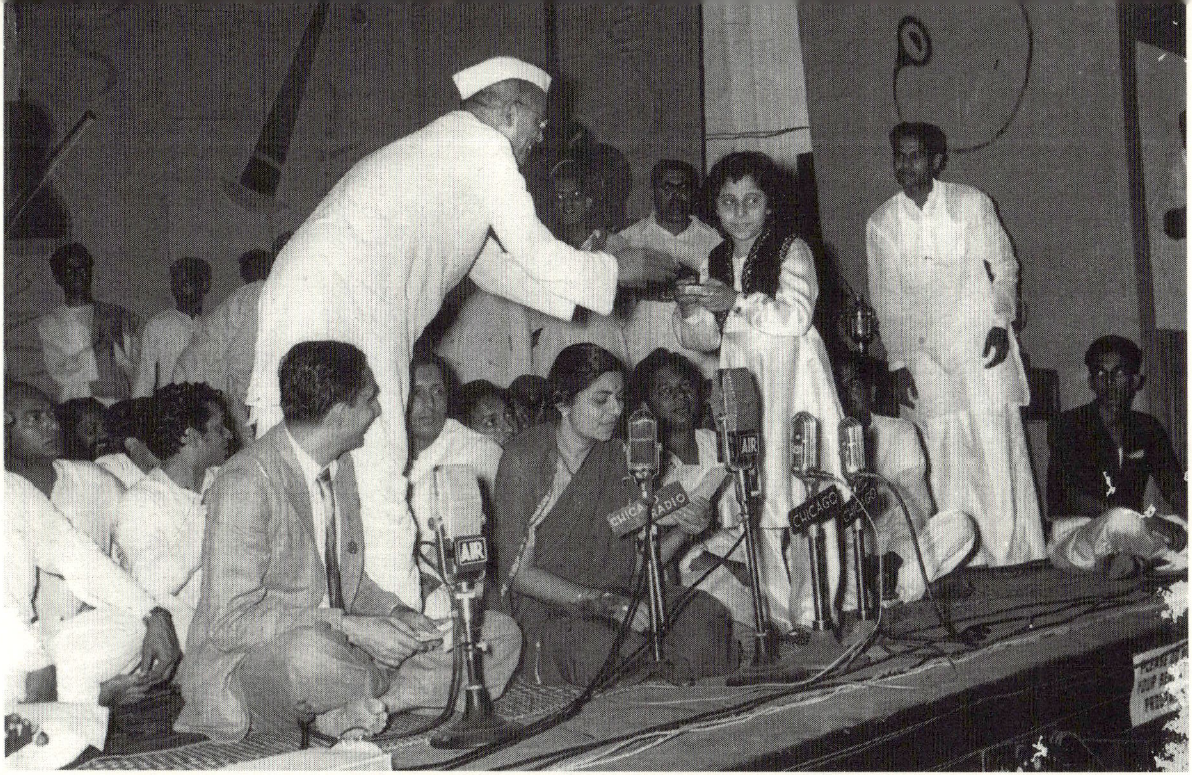

Swami Haridas Sammelan

Seated from left to right: Ali Akbar Khan, Nikhil Ghosh, Ravi Shankar, Kausalya Manjeshwar (addressing the gathering), Ram Narayan. Zarine Sharma nee Daruwala (*Little girl in the picture*)

(Source: Kausalya and Dinker Manjeshwar)

Deodhar's School of Indian Music

(Source: Girish Gogate)

Professor B.R. Deodhar

Centre: Annie Beasant. *To her left*: Bhajekar and B. R. Deodhar (with cap).
Photograph taken on the occasion of Annie Beasant's visit to Deodhar's School of Indian Music sometime between 1925 and 1928.

School of Indian Music Orchestra

Students of the School of Indian Music Orchestra

Students of the School of Indian Music

Students of the School of Indian Music

Venues in Bombay

(Photographs by Aneesh Pradhan)

Laxmi Baug

Jinnah Hall

Blavatsky Lodge

Marwari Vidyalaya

Muzaffarabad Hall

Bombay Sangeet Kalakar Mandal

Kennedy Bridge

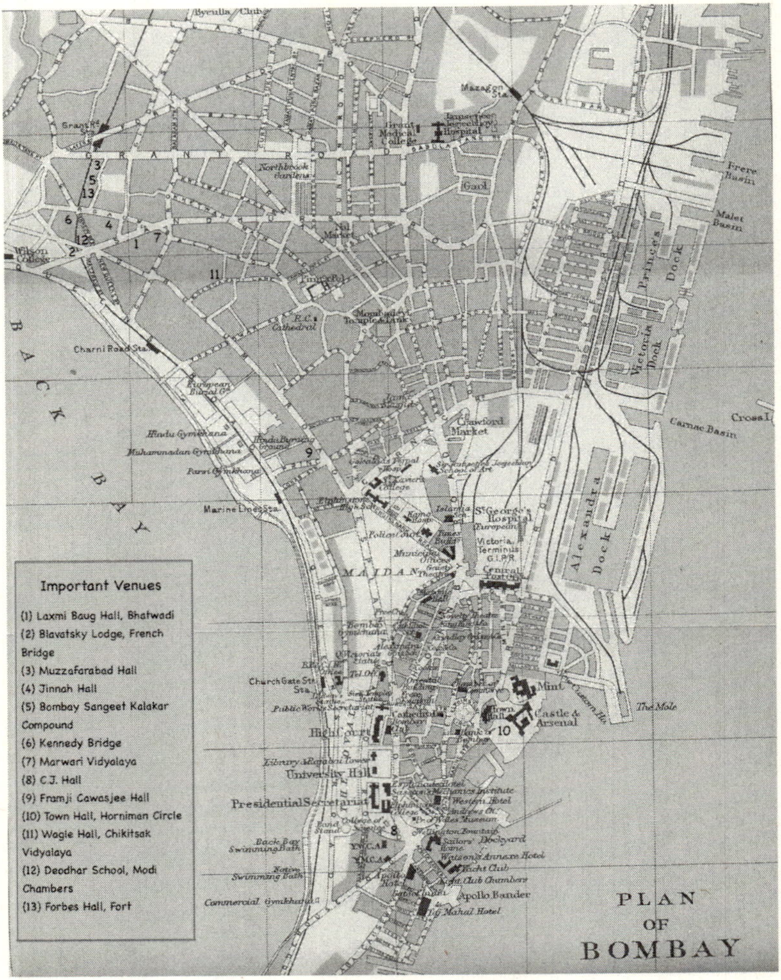

Bombay in 1924